Reason and Inquiry

The Erotetic Theory

Reason and Inquiry

The Erotetic Theory

PHILIPP KORALUS

Great Clarendon Street, Oxford, OX2 6DP,
United Kingdom

Oxford University Press is a department of the University of Oxford.
It furthers the University's objective of excellence in research, scholarship,
and education by publishing worldwide. Oxford is a registered trade mark of
Oxford University Press in the UK and in certain other countries

© Philipp Koralus 2023

The moral rights of the author have been asserted

First Edition published in 2023

Impression: 1

All rights reserved. No part of this publication may be reproduced, stored in
a retrieval system, or transmitted, in any form or by any means, without the
prior permission in writing of Oxford University Press, or as expressly permitted
by law, by licence or under terms agreed with the appropriate reprographics
rights organization. Enquiries concerning reproduction outside the scope of the
above should be sent to the Rights Department, Oxford University Press, at the
address above

You must not circulate this work in any other form
and you must impose this same condition on any acquirer

Published in the United States of America by Oxford University Press
198 Madison Avenue, New York, NY 10016, United States of America

British Library Cataloguing in Publication Data

Data available

Library of Congress Control Number: 2022946083

ISBN 978-0-19-882376-6

DOI: 10.1093/oso/9780198823766.001.0001

Printed and bound in the UK by
Clays Ltd, Elcograf S.p.A.

Links to third party websites are provided by Oxford in good faith and
for information only. Oxford disclaims any responsibility for the materials
contained in any third party website referenced in this work.

Contents

Acknowledgements vii
List of Figures ix

1. Introduction 1
   1.1 Tales of a Superpower 1
   1.2 Failures of Reason 10
   1.3 Computational Theory 15
   1.4 Reason and Ideal Rationality 18
   1.5 Plato's Problem and Mental Logic 25
   1.6 Bayesianism and Aims of Reason 29
   1.7 Mental Models and Competence 33
   1.8 Toward Content-Based Theories of Reason 42
   1.9 The Erotetic Theory 49
   1.10 Aspects of a Content-Based Theory of Reason 56
   1.11 The Way Ahead 59

2. Core Reasoning and Erotetic Equilibrium 61
   2.1 Defining Views 66
   2.2 Updating Questions with Answers 71
   2.3 Negating and Factoring 78
   2.4 Reasoning with Suppositions 83
   2.5 Inquire and Query 86
   2.6 Inference and Erotetic Equilibrium 90
   2.7 Restricted Erotetic Equilibrium 94
   2.8 Norms 99

3. Conditionals and Information Source Selection 103
   3.1 Erotetic Suppositional "If...Then" 106
   3.2 Supposition and Presupposition 109
   3.3 Disequilibrium Implication 112
   3.4 Selection Tasks and Information Seeking 114
   3.5 Order Effects 119
   3.6 "Only" with "If" 121
   3.7 Asking What Is Possible and What Follows 125

4. Predicate Reasoning 128
   with Vincent Wang, Sean Moss, Beau Mount
   4.1 Views of Arbitrary Objects 135
   4.2 Basic Objects and Dependency Relations 137
   4.3 Predicate Views and Aboutness 142
   4.4 Axioms, Absurdity, and Analyticity 147
   4.5 View Interpretation of $\mathcal{L}_{PC}$ 150

4.6 View Algebra, Merge, and Restriction	154
4.7 Universal Product and Existential Sum	162
4.8 Division and Factor	168
4.9 Query and Inquire	170
4.10 Suppositions and Commitment	178
4.11 Inference and Absolute Erotetic Equilibrium	179
4.12 Generics and Restricted Erotetic Equilibrium	182

5. Reasoning with Uncertainty — 188
with Sean Moss

5.1 Equilibrium Answer Potential and Extended Views	200
5.2 Answering with EAP	203
5.3 Generating Graded Uncertainty	206
5.4 Conditionals and Uncertainty	215
5.5 Universal Product	222
5.6 Conjunction Fallacy and Memory Search	225
5.7 Remaining Operations	232
5.8 Bayesian Updating	234
5.9 Erotetic Equilibrium and Probabilistic Coherence	237
5.10 Expert Forecasting and Restricted Erotetic Equilibrium	241

6. Decision and Practical Reasoning — 248
with Sean Moss

6.1 Decision-Making as an Inquiry	259
6.2 Direct Consequence Views	265
6.3 Priorities	267
6.4 Default Decision	272
6.5 Utility Maximization under Erotetic Equilibrium	281
6.6 Affordances and Action-Centered Priorities	285
6.7 The Erotetic Agent with a Human Face	292
6.8 The Sphinx and the Kingdom of Erotetic Agents	295

Appendix A. Formulas and Definitions — 302

A.1 Formula Sheet for Chapter 2	302
A.2 Formula Sheet for Chapter 4	303
A.3 Formula Sheet for Chapter 5	308

Appendix B. Meta-theory for Chapters 4 and 5 — 314

B.1 A Theory of Dependency Relations	314
B.2 The Predicate System Is Well Defined	321
B.3 Tarskian Realization	322
B.4 Soundness under Erotetic Equilibrium	324
B.5 Completeness	326
B.6 Conservativity of Extended Reasoning over Classical	331

References	333
Index	347

Acknowledgements

I would like to give special thanks to my collaborators Vincent Wang, Sean Moss, and Beau Mount. I also thank Thomas Deva for his dedication in seeing the manuscript through the production process.

For helpful comments and discussions I thank Salvador Mascarenhas, Kit Fine, Phil Johnson-Laird, Jenny Zhao, Jack Woods, Sunny Khemlani, Paul Elbourne, Timothy Williamson, Milena Bartholain, Caspar Jacobs, Sam Carter, Matt Parrott, Christian List, Anil Gomes, Ralph Walker, Adrian Moore, Oscar Chang, Joel Hancock, Kieran Marray, Matthew Rimmer, James Kirkpatrick, Chris Barker, Matías Osta Vélez, Ashok Handa, Marc Alfano, David Huffman, Sudhir Anand, Max Hänska, Nancy Abigail Nuñez, Karel Hruda, Jane Friedman, Eric Mandelbaum, Richard Bailey, Susanna Siegel, Andrzej Wisniewski, Christina Dietz, Phil Torr, Rocco Hu, Olivia Ong, Martin Hackl, Mor Segev, Daniel Rothschild, Jens Madsen, Thomas Icard, Hannes Leitgeb, Heidi de Wet, Lucas Kuhlen, JC Smith, David Lobina, Johanne Nedergaard, Chris Timpson, Gavin Lowe, Gideon Rosen, Gaia Scerif, Andrew Elliott, Andrew Dickinson, Justine Pila, Matthew Hewson and Sebastian Pohl. Thanks to Shifu Yan Lei and Liam Nolan for teaching me about reason in motion. All mistakes remain my own.

For encouragement and support at key stages of this project, I thank Kit Fine, Alex Paseau, Ohad Kammar, John Hawthorne, and Bill Fulford.

I also thank the Faculty of Philosophy in the University of Oxford and St. Catherine's College for providing an excellent environment in which to conduct this kind of research. Finally, I thank the trustees of the Laces Trust, and the John Fell Fund for their support of this project.

I dedicate this book to my wife Jenny.

List of Figures

1. A view of the human reasoning capacity — 51
2. Wason card selection task — 104
3. Modified Griggs & Cox selection task — 117
4. The Matryoshka condition — 141

Socrates: ... It appears to me that when the mind is thinking, it is simply carrying on a discussion, asking itself questions and answering them....

(Theaetetus, 189e–190a).

erotetic, *adj.*
Etymology: < Greek ἐρωτητικός, < ἐρωτάειν to question.
Pertaining to questioning; interrogatory.
(Oxford English Dictionary)

1
Introduction

1.1 Tales of a Superpower

The capacity to think and act intelligently is central to most human endeavors. Pushed to its limits, this capacity makes possible modern science, technology, and civilization. Intelligent thought infuses virtually everything we do. We all intuitively understand that if we are smarter, we can solve more problems and make ourselves better off, yielding full pantries, complex societies, and all manner of sophisticated tools and movements no other animal can match. Some philosophers have even suggested that perfect rationality would offer a kind of salvation by making us perfectly moral. More recently, with the prospect of *artificial* intelligence, other clever people have worried that a great enough intelligence would damn humanity to irrelevance or extinction. Reason is like a superpower of legend (perhaps it is the only *real* superpower), and, as in the best legends, it is not always clear at the outset what to expect.

Few objects of study could be more inspiring than a capacity that lies within all of us and that has inspired both transcendental faith and terror. To understand the nature of the capacity to think intelligently seems as worthy a goal as any in science and philosophy. This goal calls for considerable humility. Of course, nobody is likely to have anything like a full picture of intelligence anytime soon. However, precisely because so little is settled, this goal also calls for a certain amount of daring in exploring new foundational ideas. After all, there is little to lose but there may be something to gain. I believe that a truly interdisciplinary team-effort is required for such an endeavor. Investigating a phenomenon that touches so much of human experience requires a broad set of tools. The theory presented in this book is the result of work with collaborators with backgrounds including philosophy, neuroscience, linguistics, computer science, and mathematics, whose contribution is acknowledged in joint authorship of chapters of this book. The present work also heavily draws on cognitive psychology and parts of behavioral economics. We could perhaps simply say that we are drawing on virtually all aspects of cognitive science.

Much work in both artificial intelligence and cognitive science first revolved around the idea that intelligent thought resembles valid deduction in classical logic. More recently, the idea that intelligent thought resembles the updating of probability distributions moved to center stage. Particularly in artificial intelligence, but also more recently in cognitive science, there additionally has been an emphasis on thinking of reason in terms of reasonable behavior, essentially a neo-Humean approach. This book breaks with some of these assumptions, presenting a theory on which classical logic, probability theory, and reasonable behavior are achievements of reason, rather than its foundation. This view should be congenial to those of us who still recall the effort involved in recapitulating some of these achievements in school and who still occasionally struggle with reasonable behavior. At the same time, we will place great emphasis on technical rigor and empirical data.

The theory we will build up through successive chapters in this book flows to a significant extent from three core propositions. The first proposition is that, without any commitment to natural language being essential to reason, the process of raising issues and answering them is more fundamental and a strictly more general foundation for a theory of our capacity to reason than either logic or probability theory. The second proposition is that systematic failures of our capacity to reason, as empirically documented by psychologists and behavioral economists, are *real* and internal to the nature of reason itself (if you are unfamiliar with such failures, you can skip to section 1.2). While historical analogies can often mislead, we might say that the notion that failure is central to reason makes the proposed approach somewhat more neo-Kantian than neo-Humean. The third proposition is that if the internal principles of reason are fully brought to bear, our failures can be overcome. Reason can correct itself: systematically valid inference, probabilistic coherence, and rational choice *can* be secured in principle, and in fact often *are* secured in practice. We can make sense of our failures without making the relationship between our minds and classical rationality a mystery.

The erotetic (*adj.* pertaining to questioning) theory of the capacity to reason presented in this book develops these ideas in great detail. Much in the foregoing must be left vague for now and can only provide a hint of what is to come through the following chapters.

Let us take a step back and begin by looking at reason the way we encounter it as reasoners. We can apply intelligent thought to all subjects, ranging from the cosmic to the mundane, and ranging from questions about facts to questions about what to do. Hilary wonders whether the four specks of light she sees through a telescope are really one star. She concludes that they are, reasoning from her view that the gravity of a distant galaxy can bend light in a way similar to a lens. Elsewhere, Paul is deciding whether to go to the fridge.

He decides to go, because he thinks that someone put lemonade in the fridge and because his priority is to find a refreshing drink. Now, we could imagine a kind of angel whose perception directly compensates for gravitational lensing, and who perceives a fridge as imperatively labeled "open me" whenever the fridge holds contents that satisfy her priorities. In light of what humans can do, such perceptual powers alone would not seem too exciting. We can take our existing thoughts and arrive at new and, when all the work is done, often correct ones, in virtually any domain of inquiry. What we can do goes beyond any special-purpose perceptual abilities we might be granted. We might say that we have the capacity to achieve a "change in view" (Harman, 1986), *without looking*. If you were invited to trade any fantastical super perceptual ability (short of a God's eye for all facts and apt decisions) for your ability to change your view without looking, for the superpower *light of reason* as you might call it, I doubt you would accept. At any rate, I do not know how the story would continue if you were to accept this kind of deal; you would probably not be able to read this book with understanding!

Nature would not be a great dramatist if she created superpowers without flaws. Flaws make a story interesting. Flaws of human reason in the sense I have in mind are distinct from simple constraints on time and memory. We have all encountered puzzles that are too complex for us to solve or even understand in a reasonable amount of time. Yet, the observation that such puzzles exist is primarily indicative of capacity limitations that any physically real information processing system must have, intelligent or not. More interestingly, we are subject to predictable and systematic failures of judgment in cases that seem straightforward and not subject to serious time pressure, while we can handle extremely similar cases without a problem (Johnson-Laird (1983); Tversky and Kahneman (1983); Evans (2002); Byrne (2005), among many others). We will look at some problems of this nature in the next section, and we will consider a large number of them throughout this book. Striking systematic failures of *practical* judgment have drawn particular attention in recent decades, since they bear on economics and public policy (Kahneman (2011); Thaler and Sunstein (2008); Ariely (2009); Mullainathan and Shafir (2013)), and their discovery has yielded more than one Nobel Prize over recent decades.

In large part, this book will be concerned with reconciling a catalog of failures with the fact that human reason remains justly considered a superpower. This reconciliation is both necessary and difficult. As Pinker recently put it, "A list of the ways in which we're stupid can't explain why we're so smart: smart enough to have discovered the laws of nature, transformed the planet, lengthened and enriched our lives, and not least, articulated the rules of rationality that we so often flout" (Pinker (2021)).

There is no shortage of illustrations of reason as a superpower. In science, as in politics, history can sometimes help us see just how much we take for granted as barely remarkable. The inscription on Kant's tombstone in Kaliningrad (Prussian Königsberg, in his day, now part of Russia), famously reads, "Two things fill the heart with ever new and increasing admiration and awe, the more often and steadily the mind attends to them: the starry heavens above me and the moral law within me."[1] Of course, for Kant, "the moral law within" fundamentally is an aspect of rational agency. Less than two hundred years after Kant's death in 1804, an AI system with a rational agent model at its core operated without human supervision to chase a comet, guiding NASA's Deep Space 1 (Muscettola et al., 1998). Some influential models of agents in AI are indeed directly based on work in the philosophy of practical reason (Bratman, 1987; Georgeff and Rao, 1991; Wooldridge, 2000). In Kant's day, the notion that rational reflection upon something in the ball-park of "the moral law within" could help us so concretely grasp "the starry heavens above," would doubtlessly have seemed utterly fantastical. Turning lead into gold and various other traditional concerns of magic and alchemy seem like small beer by comparison. Reason is a superpower so great that, in a sense, even turned on itself it can help reach the stars.

As we shall see, the problem of how to make sense of both the successes and failures of reason is as old as philosophy itself, and even influential contemporary views sometimes still have to grapple with objections already known to the ancients. Yet, what approach we take to making sense of reason bears on what we can consider plausible foundations for a variety of disciplines, including economics and other social sciences, various parts of linguistics and cognitive science, as well as artificial intelligence.

There are significant differences in reasoning performance between individuals, but the systematic failures psychologists and behavioral economists have discovered can hardly be attributed to generally insufficient smarts. Participants in some of the most striking experiments were drawn from students at elite universities, and some experiments have even been replicated with professional statisticians. It is hard to avoid the conclusion that certain quirks of human judgment are present to some extent in everybody. It is

---

[1] The German original reads: "Zwei Dinge erfüllen das Gemüt mit immer neuer und zunehmender Bewunderung und Ehrfurcht, je öfter und anhaltender sich das Nachdenken damit beschäftigt: Der Bestirnte Himmel über mir und das moralische Gesetz in mir."

by now a fairly widespread idea that many systematic mistakes in judgment stem from deeper facts about human reason, whose nature remains poorly understood. What is perhaps not so widespread an idea yet is that these deeper facts may be facts about reason more generally that would remain even if we were to set aside some very specifically human limitations in trying to design a more ideal system.

There are other, arguably better understood areas where a study of failures has proven fruitful even if we are ultimately interested in understanding success with enough generality to inform system design. Consider vision. Unlike shallow capacity limitations like the limits to our ability to see far-away objects, visual illusions teach us something deeper about the nature of vision as an information processing problem and they hold clues about the structure of the visual system. Examples of visual illusions with serious aesthetic merit can be found in the *Structural Constellation* series by Bauhaus artist Joseph Albers. (The reader is invited to use Google here for images—unfortunately, academic books do not include a budget for expensive image rights.) Inspecting Albers's drawings, we can learn that our visual system detects separate cues to depth that are to some extent independent of a holistic evaluation of where things are in space. After all, we know that the page is flat but still perceive apparent depth. On closer examination, the experience of viewing these drawings even brings a suggestion that our visual judgments are not entirely constrained by what could be a possible object in the real world. Many other examples can be found in virtually any psychology textbook. In a certain light, the experience of viewing the drawing corresponds to a failure of visual judgment. At the same time, *our* visual system as yet remains the best general-purpose visual system, even if machines can outperform us on various specific visual discrimination tasks. Studies of the human visual system, including illusions, have in fact informed some of the best machine vision architectures, a line of work that came to prominence with Marr, Poggio, and Brenner (1979) and continues to this day (Nematzadeh et al., 2020).

Drawing a parallel between visual illusions and failures of reason, a study of apparent failures of judgment in humans may yet help us gain a better understanding of the structure of the best general capacity for *successful* judgment; after all, human agents are the only agents with general intelligence we currently have, artificial or otherwise. Perhaps we can even find some elegance in failures of judgment, just as we seem to be able to find elegance in visual illusions. To take up our narrative theme again, the better superpower legends involve flaws. Yet, in the very best superpower legends, an understanding of those flaws in a constructive light ultimately brings the quest to a successful conclusion.

Before we proceed further, we will have to delineate our object of study more clearly. The informal concept of intelligence is hard to pin down and plausibly decomposes into a variety of related capacities. This book takes the view that the most interesting (and challenging) core aspect of intelligence is *reason* (read as a noun): roughly the domain-general human capacity that leads an agent to novel judgments and decisions from both old and new information. The term "domain-general" is key; it separates our notion of reason from other capacities like vision that are also sources of judgment but that are almost exclusively driven by one type of information about one class of facts and whose outputs are generally insulated from other relevant information that is in fact accessible to the agent. For example, if we look at Joseph Albers's drawings, we get a visual judgment of depth that is largely insulated from our background knowledge that the page is flat. This visual judgment is insulated from our all-things-considered judgment provided by reason that the page is flat: we know it is flat but it still "looks like" a three-dimensional constellation. Exceptions to the encapsulation of visual judgment seem marginal at best, and some researchers even hold that they are non-existent once our terms are properly defined (Firestone and Scholl, 2016; Quilty-Dunn, 2020). By contrast, reason gives us the power to make judgments that are manifestly not limited to any particular class of facts; neither in the range of the conclusions we might draw, nor in the range of sources of information we might bring to bear. Domain-general reasoning in this sense includes reasoning from possibly extensive background knowledge, including generalizations about novel kinds of objects provided using language. This is an area in which statistical machine learning tools, which are chiefly responsible for the resurgence of interest in AI in the recent decades, are unlikely to be successful on their own without some level of symbolic representations (Levesque, 2017; Russell and Norvig, 2016). If this holds true for the less constrained project of AI as engineering, it will certainly hold true for models of reason in cognitive science.

A formally significant hallmark of the domain-generality of human reason is the possibility of recursion: in principle, any of our judgments could themselves become inputs to further judgments. This seems to be a prerequisite for humans to be able to be lost in their thoughts along paths that could seemingly lead anywhere, without those thoughts being directly explicable in terms of new external stimulation. We have this domain-general capacity and we would not be intelligent without it. That said, we could certainly still be passable survival-and-reproduction machines without reason in the sense under discussion.

In many specific environments, simple and relatively inflexible planning is most likely superior for survivability and reproductive success, with general reason a mere distraction. Optimal performance on clearly delineated tasks in familiar environments often seems to rely on learning how to think less rather than think more. In almost any given natural environment, it seems like we can find organisms that are unintelligent by our standards but that are nevertheless more narrowly successful than we are in that environment, assuming we are not already benefiting from technology or advance preparation through what we are taught by our elders. I suspect that the most striking advantages of reason emerge once we are in the business of shaping environments and exploring new environments beyond known frontiers, even beyond earth. Shaping environments and exploring novel domains seems to be the business humanity excels at above all other known species, natural or artificial. In this light, perhaps the ability to travel into space is the most distinctive success of the power of reason, and the failure to balance short-term energy needs with a long-term need for a sustainable environment is its most distinctive failure.

Even our physical strengths as a species seem to lie in generality and versatility. For any narrow motor skill of one of our limbs, there seems to be some animal that is faster and stronger. However, no animal comes anywhere close to the variety of physical skills humans can display by stringing together whatever basic skills we have, even if we set aside the use of tools (think of movement in dancing or the martial arts). These kinds of considerations bear on the general outlook we might take in approaching reason and intelligence. For example, in their standard textbook on artificial intelligence, Russell and Norvig (2016), like many others in AI, advertise an approach based on "general principles of rational agents and on components for constructing them," in contrast with, "approaches based on human behaviour or human thought" because, they argue, "human behaviour...is well adapted for one specific environment and is defined by, well, the sum total of all the things that humans do," with the implication that this is too limited in scope. On the contrary, it would appear that since no other known system is as flexible in the problems and environments it can tackle, a clearer look at human reason would in fact very much be in service of the approach Russell and Norvig advocate, especially since, as they point out, perfect rationality in the sense of always doing the right thing is unachievable anyway for any system, artificial or human. We will return to these issues in greater detail in a later section of this chapter. What makes the view developed here slightly contrarian is the suggestion that the structures that account for the limits to human rationality could turn out to be sufficiently general and elegant to be relevant for any realizable intelligent system that is based on reason.

Besides domain-generality, another important aspect of the capacity to reason is that it *leads* agents to novel judgments and decisions. The idea here is that one of the hallmarks of reason is that it provides direction, even if the destinations are constructed out of materials taken from outside of reason. For example, in ordinary cases, if we consider that we could get lemonade from the fridge in light of the priority of finding a refreshing drink, we cannot help but see that we have a (potentially defeasible) reason to open the fridge. Similarly, if we learn that gravity can bend light, and if we already believe that we are most likely seeing one star provided that gravity can bend light, we cannot help going on to entertain that we are looking at one star. Exactly what thought transitions of this nature are direct is an empirical question about human reason, as is the question of what it takes to have something become an input to our reasoning capacity. Certainly, we do not directly transition to all thoughts that are logically entailed or probabilistically supported by what comes before reason (Harman, 1986). Nonetheless, it seems to be a hallmark of reason that unless we try hard to resist, it *gets us somewhere*, sometimes to unexpected places.

Now, what we have carved out so far is not a definition or a theory, much less a formal one. We are still pointing at humans to pin down our object of study. However, it should now be somewhat clearer in what direction we are pointing. If we take reason in this ostensive sense and give a theory of it with adequate formal clarity, we will also have a theory of what reason is as a general property of systems. Successive chapters will rigorously build up a very specific theory of reason: the erotetic theory.

According to the erotetic theory of reason, the core of reason and thus the core of human general intelligence is the capacity to raise issues and answer them in a way that reduces the complexity of our issues as directly as possible. As we shall see, while this process can lead us astray, it is provably constrained to yield a classically correct judgment (by the relevant standards of validity, probabilistic coherence, and decision theory) given a specific condition. This condition is *erotetic equilibrium*: a state in which raising further issues cannot decisively block the judgment.

The core chapters of this book are devoted to explaining in great detail what this means and how it applies to concrete aspects of reasoning and decision-making. In this chapter, we will continue to look at this material from a bird's-eye perspective. The theory holds that the core processes of raising issues and answering them are central to explaining both the successes and the failures of human reason. We speak of "issues" rather than "questions" to avoid any misleading suggestion that reason is based on natural language. Issues, as we conceive them here, are in the realm of representational contents, just like propositions. In fact, we can for now just think of issues as sets of alternative propositions. It is certainly no more mysterious how we could represent such a thing than it is mysterious how we could represent a probability distribution. Indeed, a probability distribution simply is a set of alternative propositions together with a particular kind of function taking that set as its domain. Indeed, we will see in a later chapter that we can think of probability distributions as a certain kind of issue, in our sense.

On the erotetic theory, failures of reason primarily stem from being insufficiently inquisitive for our purposes as we try to answer certain issues. However, systematic success is possible as well. Satisfying formal constraints on "correct" forms of rational inference as may be found in logic, probability, and decision theory requires that our judgments be in erotetic equilibrium. Roughly speaking for now, erotetic equilibrium is a state in which the answers that remain as our judgments are robust to further issues we might raise in the process of arriving at those answers. The erotetic theory allows that we can escape fallacious judgment in any particular case by raising more issues. However, the theory also holds that such flaws are unavoidable as in-principle features of reason because the central aim of answering issues as directly as possible is at odds with in-advance guaranteeing erotetic equilibrium whenever we use reason. Moreover, insisting on absolute erotetic equilibrium in every case is in itself a failure of reason, since it leads us to skepticism and paralysis. We will turn to this issue toward the end of Chapter 2.

Of course, for an intelligent agent, more is required than the narrow capacity to reason. For example, we need memory, perception, motor control, and likely multiple learning capacities that may not all be reducible to the activity of reason in the sense I have in mind. However, I hypothesize that reason is what brings those aspects of the mind together into an integrated whole.

The erotetic theory does not hold that reason tries to "approximate" logic or probability theory and sometimes fails because we do not have enough time and memory. Rather, reason aims at something else entirely, something that under closer examination turns out to be formally more general, namely raising issues and answering them as directly as possible. This question-answer process is more general in the sense that it can provably become equivalent to standard logical and probabilistic inference in special cases, but *only* in special cases. Many robust empirically observed human judgments fall outside of those special cases. These ideas will be built up step by step across subsequent chapters.

There are extremely fruitful approaches in the literature without which it would have been impossible to develop the erotetic theory. The development of the erotetic theory involved drawing on aspects of philosophy, linguistics, mathematics, computer science, cognitive psychology, and behavioral economics, among other areas. As work progressed, it soon became clear that the resulting theory would not neatly fit an established format within any one of these fields. For starters, I am not aware of mathematically clearly specified alternative approaches that cover all of the desiderata for a theory of reason that we will lay out in this chapter. While this does not render more systematic comparison with other approaches useless, it does mean that detailed comparisons would require quite substantial introductions to other views. We will have to leave this largely for elsewhere to save room for what is already an ambitious amount of material for one book. For now, we will have to limit comparisons to the architectural level.

The rest of this chapter will delineate further what is required for a theory of reason in the intended sense. The proof of such a theory being possible will then be in the pudding of the subsequent chapters. In the next section, we will begin to consider what we might learn about the structure of reason from some of its apparent failures.

1.2 Failures of Reason

Some philosophers have come close to suggesting that domain-generality makes anything in the ball-park of reason impossible to study (Fodor, 1983). Once we avoid the standard philosophical move of thinking only about ideal reasoners, we in fact find a wealth of robust and replicable findings about domain-general reasoning. Those findings bear on domain-general reasoning in that they were obtained using generic problem settings that do not presuppose much, if any, domain-specific knowledge. In this section, we will briefly consider some examples that are representative of many more to be discussed in subsequent chapters.

We ultimately want a mathematical theory of the capacity to reason. The best-understood bodies of mathematical theory concerned with systematizing constraints on correct inference and judgment can be found in logic, probability theory, and decision theory. One challenge for a theory of reason is to explain how intelligent creatures like us make systematic mistakes in judgments that should be easy if we imagine ourselves as having anything like logic, probability theory, or decision theory as the foundation of reason. We will briefly consider a few examples. As in the case of visual illusions from the previous section, we will want to look for hints of what such failures might teach us about the structure of reason. Consider the following simple inference problem.

> A computer terminal gives you two pieces of information about a nuclear reactor:
> (1) Either exhaust 1 is jammed and valve 2 is open, or exhaust 4 is jammed and valve 5 is open.
> (2) Exhaust 1 is jammed.
> What if anything follows?

A large majority of participants who tend to give correct answers to many reasoning problems freely make inferences in problems of this kind that would amount to concluding that valve 2 is open (Walsh and Johnson-Laird, 2004; Koralus and Mascarenhas, 2016). However, on reflection, for all we know given the information provided, we could also be in a situation in which exhausts 1 and 4 are jammed and valve 5 is open, but valve 2 remains closed. The conclusion remains unwarranted, even if we interpret "...or..." as "...or...but not both" (we will consider more sophisticated attempts at pragmatic explanation in Chapter 2). It appears that one aspect of human reason is that important relevant alternative situations are simply not considered or dismissed too quickly. Phil Johnson-Laird once argued that fallacious inferences from neglected alternatives might have been behind the operator mistakes contributing to the catastrophic nuclear meltdown at Chernobyl in 1986 (Johnson-Laird, 2008). Other inference problems that are actually more complex from the perspective of a standard deductive logic calculus provide little difficulty. For example, from "some of the children have balloons" and "everyone with a balloon has a party hat," it is straightforward to correctly infer that some children have balloons and party hats (Johnson-Laird, 1983):

Just as there are cases like the above in which we are tempted to think we can draw a conclusion that our information does not warrant, there are other cases in which all necessary information is right in front of us, but the conclusion is elusive for many. *The Guardian* newspaper presented the following puzzle due to Hector Levesque to its readers (Bellos, 2016):

> Jack is looking at Sally, but Sally is looking at George. Jack is married, but George is not. Is a married person looking at an unmarried person?
> (A) Yes
> (B) No
> (C) Cannot be determined.

Of the readers who replied to the column, 77% voted in favor of (B) or (C). However, once we properly ask ourselves what holds in the case in which Sally is married and also what holds in the case in which Sally is unmarried, it becomes clear that (A) is the correct answer. In the problem at the beginning of this section, neglecting to fully consider alternative possibilities yielded an unwarranted conclusion; in this case, neglecting to fully consider alternative possibilities *obscures* a fully warranted conclusion.

Let us consider another example from a very different domain. Many inferences we make are based on information that bears on a question we want to answer, but whose relationship to our conclusions is a matter of probability rather than entailment. Modern science, banking, and insurance would be inconceivable without a solid understanding of such inferences. Yet, a grasp of how to correctly make inferences involving probability emerged relatively late in intellectual history, and only began to spread around the seventeenth century (Hacking, 1975). A proper understanding of how to use probabilities to make inferences from experimental data emerged even later. If we strain ourselves as a species, we are clearly capable in principle of systematically coherent reasoning with probability. At the same time, we are also subject to systematic fallacies of reasoning with probability. Consider the following problem:

> A device has been invented for screening a population for a disease known as psylicrapitis. The device is a very good one, but not perfect. If someone is a sufferer, there is a 90% chance that he will be recorded positively. If he is not a sufferer, there is still a 1% chance that he will be recorded positively. Roughly, 1% of the population has the disease. Mr. Smith has been tested, and the result is positive.
> *What is the chance that he is in fact a sufferer?*

In an early study, Hammerton (1973) found that the average estimate was 85% in participants who were not doctors. The correct estimate is about 50%. While Hammerton initially suggested that the problem might be a lack of medical knowledge, subsequent studies have shown that the same mistake is also made by doctors in problems using realistic numbers on real and familiar diseases (Hoffrage and Gigerenzer, 1998). The problem is that our judgments have a tendency to neglect the information that the vast majority of people do not have the disease. If the vast majority of people do not have the disease, then even for a test with a relatively low rate of false positives, a very large proportion of positive test results of randomly selected people are going to be false positives. The lack of responsiveness to this fact in our judgments is usually called "base-rate neglect," and it also appears in professional judgments, both in doctors, legal professionals, and others (Tversky and Kahneman, 1973). Base-rate neglect can have severe consequences. Some patients are led to believe that they almost certainly have a terminal illness when in fact the probability of them having the illness is still very small, which has, in documented cases, led to tragedies that could have been avoided (Gigerenzer, 2002).

What can we learn about human reason from base-rate neglect? It appears that however we conceptualize uncertainty, the structure of reason is such that it becomes possible to treat a conditional probability of positive-test-given-disease as directly settling the question of whether someone probably has a disease. This is remarkable, since that conditional probability by itself is quite simply the wrong kind of object for that role from the perspective of probability theory, unlike a rounding error or an overly coarse approximation. Anecdotally, from the present author's experience teaching undergraduates at the University of Oxford, many otherwise clever people immediately volunteer a judgment in these kinds of problems before there is even a chance to *mention* any base-rate information for them to neglect. Maybe this should not be too surprising. Systematically correct reasoning with probability seems like it was a hard-won achievement in intellectual history. Even a towering figure like Leibniz, who was enough of a genius to discover differential and integral calculus independently of Newton, made mistakes in probability problems that now seem basic (Hacking, 1975).

When inferences become observable in intentional behavior, they ultimately have become part of a process of making decisions. It would seem most natural to consider reason from the start as encompassing issues of both inference and decision, which are in practice often treated separately in the philosophy, psychology, and behavioral economics literature, with a few notable exceptions (Foley, 1991; Johnson-Laird, 1993). At the very least, we might decide to *report* what we have just inferred, without that last step requiring much additional thought. More paradigmatic cases of decision involve a more complex interaction between what we take to be the facts about choices available to us and what our practical priorities happen to be.

Various studies have shown that humans are also subject to apparent failures in the domain of decision, or practical reasoning (for an overview see Hastie and Dawes (2010); Tversky and Kahneman (1981); Kahneman (2011)). For example, Shafir et al. (1993) presented two groups of participants in an experiment with the following vignette:

Imagine that you serve on the jury of an only-child sole-custody case following a relatively messy divorce. The facts of the case are complicated by ambiguous economic, social, and emotional considerations, and you decide to base your decision entirely on the following few observations.

For half of the participants, this vignette was followed by the question, "to which parent would you award sole custody of the child?" For the other half, it was followed by the question, "which parent would you deny sole custody of the child?" In both cases, the question was accompanied by the following information:

Parent A: average income, average health, average working hours, reasonable rapport with the child, relatively little social life.

Parent B: above-average income, very close relationship with the child, extremely active social life, lots of work-related travel, minor health problems.

Given the "award" question, parent B was the majority choice for being awarded custody, and given the "deny" question, parent B was also the majority choice for being denied custody. However, as the vignette makes clear, denying one parent custody amounts to awarding it to the other, and vice versa. Thus, how the objective choice scenario is framed here changes who, on average, gets custody of the child. Intuitively, we do not want to be the sorts of individuals for whom this kind of framing would make a difference.

Many other framing effects can be found in the literature (Hastie and Dawes, 2010). Some cases of framing effects are of an applied kind of concern in the business of marketing (Barden, 2013). One suspects that various framing effects were in fact intuitively grasped by marketing practitioners before they were experimentally demonstrated. Koralus and Alfano (2017) showed that similar patterns of framing effects also apply to moral judgments about what actions are morally obligatory and impermissible in various scenarios.

To explain this kind of data about decision-making, one approach would be to suggest that humans have an intrinsically irrational way of valuing alternative choices. For example, many data points can be modeled on the hypothesis that we assign more value to losses than to gains relative to a reference point that is not fixed by objective choice situations and that can be manipulated by framing, as in prospect theory (Kahneman and Tversky, 1979; Tversky and Kahneman, 1992). However, just as we should not forget that we do often behave irrationally, we should also not forget that we are often capable of making what seem like nearly optimal choices in systematic ways. Many irrational choice patterns, particularly with regards to economic behavior, seem highly fragile to learning and experience (List, 2003; List, 2004), which makes it less appealing to lay the blame on some fundamental flaw in our mechanism for assigning value to possible choices. As in the case of reasoning, both systematic failures and systematic success require explanation. One possibility is that human reason often approaches decision questions in some important sense at face value, without first bringing into view the implications of the available choices, even in very simple hypothetical worlds. If participants in Shafir's experiment based their decisions on a more complete view of what is implied by the choices, there should be no difference between conditions, since both involve equal amounts of awarding and denying, once we consider what the possible outcomes are. At the same time, it may well turn out that there is no tractable way of guaranteeing in advance that we will always consider our choices in enough detail to avoid irrational choice patterns.

In sum, human reason poses a dual challenge. On the one hand, we have the problem of giving full due to the possibility of systematically correct inference and controlled decision-making, without which much of modernity would become a mystery. On the other hand, we have the problem of making sense of systematic failure. Our superpower has its flaws. A satisfactory theory of reason *as humans have it* must ultimately account for both the systematic successes and the systematic failures. It will not suffice to just look to logic, probability, and decision theory.

1.3 Computational Theory

We will be looking for what David Marr would call a *computational* theory of human reason. According to Marr's (1977; 1982) famous formulation, a result in artificial intelligence or cognitive science "consists of the isolation of a particular information processing problem, the formulation of a computational theory for it, the construction of an algorithm that implements it, and a practical demonstration that the algorithm is successful." A computational theory in Marr's sense specifies the aim of a system, which involves a specification of the mapping that is being computed and an explanation of why it is being computed by the system. Unlike in a result of this nature in pure computer science, the object of our theorizing is initially identified in part by pointing at *us*.

A point emphasized by both Marr (1982) and Chomsky (1995) is that the most explanatorily powerful theory of a cognitive system would be able to explain most of the system directly in terms of the mapping that the system is computing. A textbook example would go as follows. Suppose I am studying a system that dispenses ink on a slip of paper in a certain pattern when certain plastic discs are pressed. If I am told that the system maps prices of goods to the sum of those prices and creates portable representations of those sums (receipts), because it is a cash register, I feel like I have understood the system. By contrast, if I am only provided with a flow chart showing how various patterns of button presses correspond to various patterns of ink marks, then even if the flow chart is reasonably complete with respect to all observed behavior generated by the system, it still seems like I lack an explanation of what is going on in an important sense. Moreover, I gain little in the way of guidance as to how to build a similar system artificially, short of duplicating it at a relatively fine grain of detail. As in other domains of inquiry, a data set, and even a set of empirical generalizations representing that data set compactly, are distinguishable from an explanatory theory. Moreover, having such a theory seems to be connected to our ability to build similar systems.

The erotetic theory of reason holds that, at its core, reason maps issues and putative answers to (hopefully) smaller issues. Specifying the theory properly will involve defining the objects of this mapping and the mapping itself as a function, which we will begin to do in the next chapter. Furthermore, the theory holds that this mapping is computed by the system *because it is a question-answer system*. If the theory is true of humans, this means that we have brain mechanisms that allow us to represent questions and answers and to transform those representations in a way that follows the functions described by the erotetic theory.

As Marr observes, a computational-theory approach to explanation demands a degree of neatness of our objects of study that not all potential objects of study are likely to possess. In consequence, it is a substantive hypothesis that reason is the kind of system that admits of any computational theory, erotetic or otherwise. In Marr's terminology, our hypothesis would be that reason is what he calls a Type 1 theory problem. While a Type 1 theory problem allows an explanation in terms of a computational theory with an intelligible mapping and a clear notion of what the system is aiming at, a Type 2 theory problem does not admit of such an explanation. Various systems only admit of a Type 2 theory: systems whose behavior is entirely due to "the simultaneous action of a considerable number of processes, whose interaction is its own simplest description" (Marr, 1977). For example, even though gene transcription is based on an essentially computational genetic code the functional core of which can be represented by four letters, the subsequent folding of complex proteins downstream from gene transcription seems like it can only be fully captured in a simulation of the molecular components involved, since their "interaction is its own simplest description."

This observation about protein folding still seems to hold some forty years later, even if innovative machine learning models like those by Deep Mind trained on very large data sets can often make very accurate predictions about protein structure (a practical engineering solution can be extremely useful even if it does not always get the right answers or capture the underlying mechanisms). If by intelligence we mean being able to think like you and me in practice in a very broad sense, then it is hard to imagine anything short of a Type 2 theory being adequate to the task and probably such a theory would be too complicated and cluttered to understand with any benefit. It seems to me that the only reasonable question is if those aspects of our thinking that seem to be unconstrained by any particular domain of information might have a common functional core. We might call this functional core "reason," and the erotetic theory then is a theory of reason. The argument that there is such a functional core will not be entirely separable from my arguments in favor of the erotetic theory. Note that taking there to be such a functional core does not have to be at odds with possible big-data or simulation-based models of reason and intelligence but could be used to define the search-space for such models (perhaps reminiscent of how genetic code helps define a search-space for proteins), a point we will briefly return to in section 1.10.

In short, this book will make the case that the erotetic theory can explain, in a unified way:

1. why humans are prone to various misjudgments by default, regardless of whether they involve propositional reasoning, reasoning with quantifiers, probabilities, or decisions, *and* ...
2. ... why we are not irretrievably lost to those misjudgments: they are fragile to questioning.

There are several possible levels of success this book could achieve here. The top level would be that I manage to convince you of the erotetic theory as roughly the right theory of reason. A close second would be that by showing, over the course of successive chapters, that both success and failure of judgment across a wide range of problems can be explained by a relatively compact set of conceptually motivated principles, I convince you that there probably is an intelligible Type 1 theory of reason to be had, which would still be more than what reading Fodor (1983) might lead us to expect. A third might be to at least convince you more loosely that when it comes to mathematical theorizing about reasoning and judgment, it is possible to consider both success and failure data *together* at the level of computational aim in a principled way that does not have to be less systematic than, say, the consideration of linguistic meaning in works like Heim and Kratzer (1998). I will take as a fourth fallback that even if you walk away still preferring a neo-Humean view of reason in terms of reasonable behavior, based on either logic, probability, or expected utility theory, you might do so with a clearer sense for why you like these ingredients, having seen that others are available.

1.4 Reason and Ideal Rationality

We will now consider to what extent we might be able to obtain something like a computational theory of reason directly from standard mathematical notions of rational inference and decision. We will be taking for granted that we are looking for a domain-general theory of reason, which will be important to keep in mind in evaluating the criticisms of various possible approaches.

In formally conceiving of reason, there are at least two different approaches we could take. One approach is to define reason in terms of reasonable behavior. Another approach is to define reason as a capacity and define reasonableness in terms of this capacity. The former approach is broadly speaking due to Hume (1739) and is at the foundation of the dominant mathematical approaches to rationality and intelligence. The latter approach is broadly speaking due to Kant (1781). Unlike the broadly Humean approach, the broadly Kantian approach embraces failures of reason as core to the nature of reason, in the sense that reason can lead itself astray by following its own intrinsic aims. Such ideas have never had much currency in mainstream AI work, though some more speculative remarks by Minsky (1986, 5.2) could be interpreted as an exception.

On a Kantian approach, even if we find that we do not fit external standards of reasonableness too well, our activity could in some sense be the direct result of reason. By contrast, a broadly speaking Humean approach will tend to drive apparent unreasonableness back into reasonableness, back into some form of success, or otherwise account for it as emerging from outside of reason, for example "the passions." As noted at the outset, the erotetic theory presented in this book is in an important sense more Kantian than Humean. Yet, we must begin with an examination of the descendants of the Humean approach, since this is where the best-developed mathematical views can be found.

Many influential authors in behavioral economics (Simon, 1955), philosophy (Cherniak, 1986), and computer science (Russell, 1997) have made it clear that defining anything in the ball-park of reason, rationality, or intelligence as something that could be possessed by real systems is extremely difficult from the standpoint of mathematical ideals. Even if we disregard our desire to make sense of the kinds of data points regarding systematic failures of reason we have already considered, it appears that mathematical notions of ideal rationality hit roadblocks surprisingly quickly. I will briefly trace some familiar observations along these lines, adapted to our specific search for a computational theory of reason.

A starting point familiar in many disciplines would be to define reason as whatever it is that allows an agent to maximize the satisfaction of a global performance measure when confronted with the environment. In other words, reason is the mapping, regardless of how it is undertaken, from a performance measure and an environment to the actions that maximize the measure in that environment. The rational utility maximizers of classical microeconomic theory are agents governed by reason in this sense (Mas-Colell, Whinston, and Green, 1995). However, outside of reduced notions of environment and utility in the context of relatively specific problems, there could be no actual rational agents in this sense, because the notion makes no allowance for capacity limitations like processing time that any physical system, however well designed and rich in resources, must possess.

We could instead say that reason is any set of procedures that, were they executed infinitely fast with no resource constraints on processing, would result in perfectly rational behavior. Russell (1997) calls this notion "calculative rationality." Unfortunately, this notion allows for systems that are entirely unreasonable in practice. For example, a system that will never make any decision within a human lifetime could potentially qualify. The problem of combinatorial explosion seems to ultimately hamper calculative rationality proposals regardless of whether they are based on formal logic or probability and decision theory, unless we abandon domain-generality in favor of a restricted class of decision problems (Levesque, 1988; Russell, 1997). Both Russell (1997) and Harman (1986) conclude that both logical and decision-theoretic approaches to calculative rationality founder on computational intractability if we are interested in anything approaching domain-generality.

Next, we could consider a nearby notion of calculative rationality that includes calculative rationality in *reasoning about* resource-appropriate reasoning to mitigate the combinatorial explosion problem. There are many productive and interesting results about meta-reasoning that would lead us too far afield to discuss here. However, as Russell (1997), Harman (1986), and others have pointed out, meta-reasoning does not fundamentally change the nature of the problem. Russell summarizes the argument as follows:

> [T]he concept of metalevel rationality as a formal framework for resource-bounded agents does not seem to hold water. The reason is that, since metareasoning is expensive, it cannot be carried out optimally. The history of object-level rationality has repeated itself at the metalevel: perfect rationality at the metalevel is unattainable and calculative rationality at the metalevel is useless. Therefore, a time/optimality tradeoff has to be made for metalevel computations.... Within the framework of metalevel rationality, however, there is no way to identify the appropriate tradeoff of time for metalevel decision quality. Any attempt to do so via a metametalevel simply results in a conceptual regress. Furthermore, it is entirely possible that in some environments, the most effective agent design will do no metareasoning at all, but will simply respond to circumstances. (Russell 1997)

Taking stock, from a philosophical perspective, we end up with the conclusion that logic cannot be a theory of reasoning Harman (1986). From an AI perspective, we get that McCarthy (1958) classical AI project of building artificial "common sense" upon the notion of logical consequence fails. Arguably, we get that similar classical views in psychology also fail (Inhelder and Piaget, 1958). As both Harman (1986) and Levesque (2017) point out, shifting from logical entailment to probabilistic support does not fundamentally offer a way out of the problems faced by the calculative rationality approach.

We can of course still design calculatively rational systems that perform in a way that seems intuitively reasonable, but we cannot then rely on the notion of calculative rationality alone to tie down the class of those systems. In other words, calculative rationality can potentially be a guide to building useful systems for certain purposes, but it cannot serve as a theory of reason, since we would need an independent notion of reason to tell us which among the calculatively rational systems are supposed to qualify, seeing that many such systems are patently unreasonable.

In place of calculative rationality, a more promising alternative is bounded optimality (Russell credits this term to Horvitz (1988)). Take a type of machine M like a brain or a computer with a certain kind of specification and let P_M be the set of all programs that can be run on M. A boundedly optimal agent is an agent whose behavior is governed by a program p that is (one of) the best of those in P_M at maximizing a performance measure U when confronted with a set of environments E.

Encouragingly for our purposes, Russell argues that the notion of bounded optimality may be more suitable for "those who wish to emulate human intelligence" (Russell, 1997). We could then try to give the following theory of reason: Relative to a type of system, environment, and a performance measure, reason is any set of procedures that is optimal relative to the performance measure, among those sets of procedures that the system can run in that environment.

The bounded optimality perspective is a major improvement in the sense that it allows us to keep formal notions of ideal rationality relevant in the face of limitations. However, it is not clear that even *bounded* optimality is as useful a guide as it might at first appear, if we are interested in domain-general intelligence of the kind that we can so far only study in humans. Firstly, one might worry about what one might call the *problem of cognitive slack*: If we look at any standard-issue human adult, it is usually hard to imagine that they could not be making themselves better off (i.e. further improve on a relevant performance measure) even by their own lights in at least some small degree if they only thought certain things through slightly more at otherwise no notable cost (i.e. following a slightly better feasible procedure). We may have serious resource constraints, but any normal human arguably has cognitive slack. However, we would not want to say that we ipso facto lack reason or intelligence if we fail to be boundedly *optimal* for this reason. There is a strong intuition that it is perfectly appropriate to say that we can be better or worse at using reason given the resources we have at least to some extent, but this is in tension with trying to *define* reason in terms of optimality given the resources we have.

At first, it might seem that we can sidestep the problems with optimality rather easily by switching from demanding bounded *optimality* to what we might call *bounded satisficing*. This move would be in the spirit of Simon (1956), who made the case that much human economic activity is better explained by the notion that agents seek to achieve results above a certain threshold rather than optimal results. The idea for bounded satisficing would then be to only demand that the agent reaches a certain satisfactory level on a performance measure, instead of full-on optimality. However, we then have to specify a threshold for when a given system has reason according to this revised notion. Charges of arbitrariness in the choice of such a threshold could then be made. However, one might counter that any serious scientific theory requires postulating some constants.

A more serious objection to a notion of reason based on bounded satisficing seems to be what one might call the *problem of shallow success*: what it takes to be merely good at a problem is often so qualitatively different from what it takes to be optimal that being merely good does not hold even remotely the same interest as being optimal. I think this problem should be quite intuitive to anyone who has spent time designing exams, since we constantly have to guard against this problem. One of the challenges of good exam design is to arrange things so that something less than a full score is still indicative of an interesting level of underlying competence. For those of us not in the examination business, we will illustrate this point with a slightly different example. Consider what rate-of-increase in net-worth tells us about someone who owns a house in an unusually up-and-coming neighborhood but who is in a persistent vegetative state. Now consider what a steady but slightly lower rate of increase in net-worth tells us about a highly talented entrepreneur who runs several businesses with significant revenue. If we regard *optimal* net-worth growth rate as a standard for "business reason," the vegetative house-owner case is unlikely to qualify. Being in a vegetative state prevents him from managing some of his house as a rental property for additional income, and it also prevents him from selling up and diversifying, and so on for other opportunities that require some conscious involvement. By contrast, if we take *good* net-worth growth as a standard for "business reason" we might end up finding that the vegetative house-owner dominates, if it turns out that the relevant real estate is among the best investments to be had at the moment.

The shallow-success worry then proceeds as follows in the context of applying a notion of bounded satisficing to general intelligence. A sufficiently modest goal-post on a global performance measure that is flexible enough to accommodate the wide variety of things expected of a general intelligence threatens to be reachable by extreme success in some narrow task combined with complete lack of competence in almost everything else; in short, achievable without possessing anything recognizable as domain-general reason or intelligence. In complex systems, the difference between being in the neighborhood of optimality and being optimal can be a dramatic qualitative difference. The (unfortunately unworkable) standard of optimality has the advantage of not leaving anything out. Once we demand less than optimality, we have to recognize that not all ways of being "good" according to some global performance measure amount to something qualitatively interesting.

Of course, we can find useful thresholds for bounded near-optimality for particular problems that will usually succeed in sorting more interesting systems from less interesting systems, particularly if we can use antecedently understood notions of interestingly intelligent systems to help pick the threshold. However, the point here is that being in the neighborhood of optimality is not in general enough to guarantee a qualitatively interesting type of reason. At the same time, because of cognitive slack, the qualitatively most interesting type of reason does not guarantee optimality. As a result, it would seem unhelpful to *define* reason in terms of bounded optimality or bounded near-optimality. As in the case of calculative rationality, such notions only seem to work if we can at least tacitly appeal to an antecedently understood notion of reason, making them useless as definitions.

There is another problem for using the bounded optimality perspective to get a theory of reason. This problem is rendered invisible if we are focused on relatively tightly delineated settings like games or other relatively specific tasks. The problem is that outside the confines of the laboratory, it is not clear how to decide what the right notion of environment and performance measure should be for a general intelligence. If we leave those parameters empty, the notion of bounded optimality becomes trivial: every system is optimal in any environment according to some criterion of success. There would appear to be entire armies of spiritual instructors devoted to showing people the benefits of taking that perspective on themselves at least occasionally: *you are exactly who you need to be*. However, as Russell (1997) himself points out, what counts as a boundedly optimal procedure is not generally robust to even small variations in the notions of environment and performance measure.

Even if we take a coarse bird's-eye perspective, we plausibly get different results depending on whether we consider (1) the environment in the context of natural selection, (2) the developmental environment of the child, (3) the environment of the adult at present, or some combination thereof.

It is even less clear what would count as a reasonable global performance measure. In the context of specific problems like winning at chess, the answers may be obvious, but in the context of domain-general intelligence, this is far less clear. We could try a familiar notion of preference satisfaction, but that just seems like issuing a promissory note for a performance measure that we would then still need to provide. If the proposal has to work for *all* (coherent) preferences, then we end up demanding bounded optimality with respect to (roughly speaking) *all* performance measures, since (roughly speaking) all such measures are going to be representable in terms of preferences. It is hard to imagine that any real system could be boundedly optimal with respect to all performance measures, so this would significantly undermine the initial appeal of the bounded optimality approach.

Now, someone might suggest that we could simply take a large number of special-purpose heuristic systems that are individually boundedly optimal to obtain a roughly domain-general boundedly optimal system. However, this idea seems to run into what one might call the *fusion problem*: bounded optimality of systems is not a property that is automatically conserved by fusing systems to make them jointly responsible for a broadened environment and performance measure. For example, imagine you have a visual system that is boundedly optimal at detecting dangerous predators in the dark and a visual system that is boundedly optimal at detecting predators in daylight. Assuming that false negatives are always equally bad (you get eaten), given that there are fewer good cues available in darkness, it is likely, all other things being equal, that the best system for predator detection in darkness is going to have a slightly higher false positive rate. Now, the difference between lightness and darkness is a matter of degree. This means that if we are simply fusing the systems, we will likely get some cases of avoidable and unnecessary false positives because our darkness-optimized predator-detector starts getting involved while our daytime detector would still be best. We can of course sensibly find the optimal mixture of these two systems, where we give progressively more decision weight to the system for darkness as light fades. However, notice that we have now done something much more than simply fuse the systems: we have formed a third system with additional structure, which takes two systems and unifies them with an optimal scheduler. But of course, some individually boundedly optimal systems are going to lend themselves better than others to this kind of scheduling management. Moreover, if we are interested in global bounded optimality, we might find that individually less optimal components would in fact yield a better fit with global bounded optimality. We can compare this to a dilemma sometimes encountered in team sports: the best team is often *but not always* formed of the best individual athletes. Being a good team player is its own dimension for optimization and composing a good team might involve considering how one player's weaknesses relates to another player's strengths. This kind of problem should arise wherever we are dealing with subsystems that are not characterized by fully separable input streams, as is the case with domain-general reason, as opposed to, say, systems for detecting sound and light, which are less likely to significantly share their input domains. In sum, local bounded optimality of subsystems does not generally guarantee bounded optimality of the fusion of these subsystems.

In light of these observations, it would appear that if we are seeking a global theory of reason, it will not obviously help to center our work around postulating limited-scope individual psychological heuristics that might be boundedly optimal under local assumptions for narrow problem types. Of course, none of this is obviously a problem if we are primarily interested in solving particular information processing problems for practical purposes.

It seems to me that the bounded optimality perspective is entirely appropriate for a research program that decomposes into many individual projects of generating special-purpose information processing systems to solve relatively tightly delineated problems with clear notions of the environment and the relevant performance measure. Luckily, many special-purpose problems turn out to be reducible to essentially the same fundamental classification process, meaning that very striking cumulative progress is possible in following this program. The practical engineering success of AI in recent years bears witness to this fact. However, it does not at all seem clear how the notion of bounded optimality can help us define domain-general reason or intelligence.

In sum, variants of "ideal rationality" approaches are not of much help in getting us a computational theory of domain-general reason. We will now turn our attention to more psychological approaches, where much interesting work has been done in recent decades on reasoning, judgment, and decision-making. We will now consider to what extent we might be able to find a computational theory of reason in this area. As in the previous section, we will be primarily concerned with broad architectural features.

1.5 Plato's Problem and Mental Logic

Mental logic theories hold that human reasoning is underwritten by a psychologically real natural deduction system similar to quantified predicate logic (Rips, 1994; Braine and O'Brien, 1991). The main sources of empirical predictions are hypotheses about the catalog of inference rules we have internalized. If we take data about mistakes seriously, this would have to involve fallacious rules (Jackendoff, 1988) and hypotheses about the degree of difficulty we have in applying various rules (Rips, 1994). On this take, mental logic does not necessarily reduce to a special version of the calculative rationality notions considered in the previous section.

Mental logic theories like Rips (1994) have the virtue of being quite precisely specified so that there is little ambiguity as to the predictions and commitments of the theory, making it fairly unusual in cognitive psychology. The mental logic literature is concerned with deductive inference, but it is possible to represent decision problems as inference problems as well in principle. We could then say that reason, as humans have it, is the capacity to apply a mental logic derivation system like that proposed by Rips (1994) (plus some fallacious extra rules). A system of this kind is not guaranteed to be boundedly optimal, nor is it guaranteed to be calculatively rational.

One immediate problem is that mental logic theory appears to be entirely couched in terms of verification procedures. In other words, we can take a putative conclusion and ask whether it follows from a set of premises according to the rules of mental logic, but we cannot give it a set of premises and ask what follows. This is not surprising for an approach that takes logic as a starting point. As Harman (1986) points out, logic is not in the business of telling us what to infer from a given set of premises. However, as noted already, and as Philip Johnson-Laird has often pointed out, it seems to be a hallmark of reason that it provides direction; reason allows us to arrive at novel conclusions and not just evaluate them. From an empirical perspective, it is a hallmark of human reason that there are striking regularities in what conclusions people freely propose from a given set of premises. These regularities can be seen in virtually any study that uses a free-form response paradigm for reasoning problems. There seems to be a natural direction reason will take if provided with a certain supply of information.

Another problem emerges once we have included fallacious rules to make sense of fallacies: how do we now explain our ability to *avoid* fallacies? As Johnson-Laird (1983) put it, "a species incapable of valid inference could never have invented logic." One might add that we would be incapable of discovering and maintaining definitions of valid inference if our own thinking was not highly sensitive to the validity of arguments in some fairly systematic fashion. Logical formalism can do no more than help us systematize and generalize what must in the first instance be graspable with our own reasoning faculties.

The problem of explaining how a system that is prone to invalid inference can learn to make valid inferences is a version of what might, in Chomskyan fashion, be called *Plato's problem*. Perhaps surprisingly, Plato's problem is not easy for a mental logic approach to solve. Either we include fallacious inference rules in our mental natural deduction system or we do not. If we do not include fallacious rules, we cannot explain the systematic fallacies we commit. If we do include fallacious rules, the question arises how we could learn from inside the system that we should drop those rules in learning how to reason correctly, rather than some other rules that are not fallacious. Furthermore, supposing that we did learn that some rule was fallacious thereby prompting us to abandon it, the question arises why we would then not become completely fallacy-free reasoners across the board. What is striking about many systematic fallacies in human reasoning is that even experts will often still fall prey to them (Kahneman, 2011). Our experience with fallacious reasoning just does not make it seem plausible that our reasoning capacity is such that we could just identify some contained "defective" bits and learn to conclusively set them aside (say, the way we might learn not rely on a defective clock to tell the time), leaving us with something equivalent to quantified predicate logic (or a probability calculus, or whatever you prefer) as a remainder.

In response to Plato's problem, one move would be to postulate two or more systems, where at least one system is calculatively rational while some of the other systems produce fallacies. On one such view, we have a quick-and dirty System 1 that is liable to make mistakes, and a slower, more deliberate and accurate System 2. Various researchers understand this metaphorical picture in more or less literal ways, ranging from cognitively distinct systems (Wason and Evans, 1974; Sloman, 1996) to mere taxonomical categories instead of theoretical postulates (Kahneman, 2011). Just as much of AI research is tacitly Humean, a large chunk of the relevant cognitive psychology is more or less Platonic at this juncture. If we take the dual systems literally as a postulate to help us with the problem at hand, we are answering Plato's problem in a way that more or less takes a page from his *Republic*, by saying that the rational System 2 can learn to govern the irrational System 1, in the sense of overruling its outputs in the production of a judgment. However, this move appears to beg the question of how learning to reason validly is possible, since we have merely turned the initial question into the question of how we can learn to let our capacity for valid reasoning govern other cognitive systems. We can of course stipulate that the more rational of those systems has "cognitive control" powers that other systems lack, but that seems reminiscent of explaining the efficacy of sleeping pills by attributing "dormitive powers" to them. Something in the ball-park of this worry about what happens if we postulate a distinctive rational part of the psyche was already familiar to the ancients (see Aristotle's *De Anima*, 1.5, 4.11 in response to Plato's *Republic* IV, 442a, cited in Lorenz (2006)).

If it were available, a theory that describes human reason in terms of just one system, both in success and in failure, would be preferable to a multi-systems theory. Such a theory might allow us to explain the dominance of relevant standards of correctness as internal to reason. Moreover, from a scientific perspective, an advantage of an approach that looks for a unified-system explanation is that we can continue to look to breakdowns and illusions as sources of evidence for core principles of the system, rather than as peripheral to core reason. The particular unified-system explanation we pursue in this book, according to which it is taking on board further questions that allows us to avoid fallacies, further has the virtue of opening the door for an account of how arguing with others can improve our reasoning (see Mercier and Sperber (2017)). To the chagrin of philosophers and to the benefit of pundits, not all ways of convincingly going through the motions of arguing are conducive to ending up with warranted conclusions. So how can we explain why arguing is broadly speaking beneficial to reason? On the erotetic theory, we can observe that probing questions, both implicit and explicit, are a hallmark of serious argumentation. Since such questions tend to be beneficial to correct reasoning in increasing our chances at erotetic equilibrium, we have an explanation of why arguing helps improve reasoning. Thus, the erotetic theory suggests an account of the potential benefits of dialog that Socrates might recognize. In fact, toward the end of Chapter 6, we will explore how an erotetic conception of agents could ground a better account of what gains in legitimacy a deliberative conception of democracy might provide.

Note that while we have been talking about specifically human aspects of failures of reason, some of the foregoing concerns arguably also arise in building AI systems in the spirit of bounded optimization, if they incorporate decision procedures that depart from idealized normative correctness. While the particular patterns of departure do not have to track the departures seen in humans, any such system with sufficient complexity and ambition will likewise need to deal with the possibility that some of its heuristic decision procedures will be inadequate for a particular problem that the system is trying to solve. Here too, the issue arises how reason can learn to correct itself, as well as the issue of how different potentially conflicting components of the system govern themselves.

Even from a point of view that takes learning to be perhaps more central than reasoning to get at general intelligence, there may be good reasons to look at fallacies of reasoning. As Valiant (2013) suggests, to get at human-like general intelligence through learning, we may have to take into account a longer evolutionary context in which our learning systems themselves evolved. Now, we might go further and suggest that data on systematic fallacies is more likely to carry information about the structure and mechanisms that resulted from the evolutionary context of learning, since the world at any given point cannot teach you fallacies as a likely prediction. In other words, the data available to one organism cannot teach that Linda is more likely to be a bank teller then a feminist bank teller, since the world is not incoherent, so this kind of judgment has to somehow arise from prior influences on the structure of the system.

1.6 Bayesianism and Aims of Reason

One of the most influential recent approaches in the cognitive science of reasoning is Bayesianism. Like the erotetic theory, "Bayesian models are typically formulated at Marr's (1982) level of "computational theory...," (Griffiths, Kemp, and Tenenbaum, 2008) with the central claim that "... human learning and inference approximately follow the principles of Bayesian probabilistic inference" (Griffiths, Kemp, and Tenenbaum, 2008). Bayesian inference is much more naturally directional than the mental logic approach considered in the previous section, since it centers on taking a prior probability distribution and updating it with new information to obtain a posterior probability distribution.

Bayesians like Tenenbaum and Griffiths hold that "the most promising routes to understanding human intelligence in computational terms will involve... sophisticated statistical inference machinery operating over structured symbolic knowledge representations" (ibid.). In practice, Bayesian modeling efforts focus on taking particular problems and then showing that Bayesian approximation methods can be created that approximate human performance on each those problems.

We might then say that reason is the capacity to represent probability distributions and update them coherently in light of new data. To cover decisions, we could supplement this with either a standard kind of utility maximization view of how representations of facts relate to decisions or with an alternative (not classically rational) theory like Kahneman and Tversky (1979)'s prospect theory.

Since Bayesians take Bayesian updating to be the fundamental computational aim of reason, those problems that do not superficially seem to have a probabilistic format need to be given an analysis on which they are covertly probabilistic. For example, Bayesians have held that problems that would appear as propositional or syllogistic in nature are in fact approached by reasoners as in the realm of reasoning with probabilities (Evans, Handley, and Over, 2003; Oaksford and Chater, 2007; Tenenbaum, Griffiths, and Kemp, 2006; Chater, Tenenbaum, and Yuille, 2006). Given a suitable set of background assumptions and a suitable analysis of the meaning of expressions like "all" and "if," various inferences humans make that are not deductively valid, or apparently fallacious, can be analyzed as probabilistically justified.

Many of the intuitions that motivate Bayesianism are surely correct. For example, it seems highly plausible that reasoners mostly arrive at conclusions by finding partial support for those conclusions that comes in *degrees*. However, an oddity of the Bayesian approach is that it sometimes appears that the more directly something is a textbook Bayesian inference problem, the less the theory fits in any straightforward way. Nothing is more Bayesian than updating a prior probability of a hypothesis in light of new data by using the conditional probability of the data given the hypothesis and conditional probability of the data given the negation of the hypothesis. However, as we saw in section 1.2, if we explicitly give humans all information necessary for a basic Bayesian inference, they will mostly make a hash of it. Humans, even relevant professionals, are famously just as much subject to systematic fallacies in probabilistic reasoning (Tversky and Kahneman, 1983) as they are subject to the apparent logical fallacies that some Bayesians want to explain by appeal to Bayesian updating. Of course, defenders of Bayesianism could say that apparent fallacies are really due to interpretative difficulties with the materials supplied to the participants, due to tacit additional assumptions made by the participants, or due to some other process that makes the participants not quite understand the vignettes the same way as their creators.

In practice, Bayesians tend to propose heuristics for various particular tasks where those heuristics have in common that given certain tacit assumptions made for these particular tasks, the heuristics are Bayesian approximations. Many Bayesians seem completely clear in their proposals that our psychological processes for reasoning are heuristics-based (Oaksford and Chater, 2007; 2009). This would then allow us to say that we have quasi-Bayesian machinery for almost everything except, presumably, for canonical Bayesian inference problems stated explicitly.

Relative to the aims we have so far developed in this chapter, there are worries about how Bayesian heuristics (or, really, any set of heuristics) can explain the general capacity for systematic multi-premise reasoning. One might also wonder if Tenenbaum and Griffiths would want to limit all operations over their "structured symbolic knowledge representations" to Bayesian ones. However, it would arguably not be the end of the world if Bayesianism had to be supplemented by non-Bayesian (i.e. not even approximately Bayesian) procedures. Bayesians would be free to say that the core of intelligent cognition is Bayesian, while the rest is non-core, non-Bayesian periphery. It would be a mistake to reject such a move purely on charges of arbitrariness, since it is often the case that we only really recognize the core of phenomena in light of a theory.

I still think that Bayesianism cannot serve as a computational (Type 1) theory of domain-general capacity to reason in the sense we have been considering. There is no guarantee that a collection of individually approximately Bayesian heuristics for specific problem domains combine to form a domain-general globally approximately Bayesian system for judgment (recall the fusion problem from section 1.4). It seems to me that Bayesianism offers Type 1 computational theories of individual heuristics, but that domain-general reason would have to be relegated to a Type 2 theory, bottoming out in the interaction of those heuristics. I suspect that many Bayesians might happily accept this conclusion ("and so much the worse for your search for a Type 1 theory," they might add).

However, there may be problems in this area even if we give up on a Type 1 theory. As the Bayesian heuristics literature is growing and looking at an increasingly diverse set of problems in cognition, it is not entirely clear if anyone is keeping track if the local assumptions made for individual heuristics to come out as approximately Bayesian are consistent between different postulated heuristics for different problem types that might potentially overlap in their applicability. Moreover, it would seem that the more distinct assumptions we have to make for a range of heuristics to come out as having an approximately Bayesian computational aim, the less insight is provided by analyzing them as Bayesian.

There are other, broader questions about what status we should give approximations in arguing for a particular view of the computational aim of a system. It often seems to go unaddressed that there is what we might call an aim-approximation gap. Sometimes, a system decently approximating one function is still best understood as doing something quite different, for the purposes of explaining the computational aim of the system. For example, a pseudo cash-register designed for stealing from weary customers must very likely also be a good approximation of a cash register, in order to have any success in deceiving people. Yet, we might still reasonably think that "thieving device" is a better explanation of the system than "approximate cash register." Ultimately, the theory presented in this book holds that we can sometimes get the equivalent of Bayesian updating as the result of a system that does not primarily have Bayesian coherence as its aim. We will be in a position to return to this idea in more detail toward the end of Chapter 5.

Clearly, Bayesians are fundamentally correct in suggesting that what our reasoning systems are aiming at has to be rethought relative to the logic-oriented intellectual landscape on which Bayesianism was first proposed in cognitive science, in some ways mirroring the probabilistic turn in AI. However, the particular reorientation proposed by Bayesians is not radical enough. On a Bayesian approach, since we cannot reasonably think of genuine Bayesian updating as what our psychological processes for reasoning are characteristically engaged in, we have to describe humans as reasoning via heuristics that can lead us astray in ways that are accommodated but not explained by the *aim* of following Bayesian updating (and for reasons already discussed, appealing to notions of bounded optimality is unlikely the help fill the gaps if we are interested in the capacity to reason). We could bite this bullet, but not if we wish to find a systematic explanation of both the success and failure of reason, which we have taken as a starting point in this book. In addition, nobody has shown how such heuristics could amount to a characterization of a domain-general and systematic capacity to reason.

The premise of this book is that it is still worth trying to find an account of domain-general reason in terms of its aim and an algorithmic procedure that would accomplish this aim fairly directly. Ideally, you would start with an account that postulates mental representations and operations that are more or less isomorphic to the mapping described as the computational aim. This kind of account is more or less foreclosed to the Bayesian when it comes to inferential reasoning. By contrast, in the case of various aspects of cognition that are close to sensory-motor inputs and outputs, including aspects of perceptual processing and motor-control, Bayesian accounts may turn out to be explanatorily adequate on these terms, in part because it is possible to interpret the relevant neural activity in Bayesian terms fairly directly (Richard and Lippmann, 1991). Whether success in the case of sensory-motor systems is a good reason to think of all brain functions as essentially Bayesian or, even more specifically, engaged in "predictive processing" (Clark, 2015) is far from obvious. For another recent criticism of Bayesianism in the context of aspects of cognition closer to reasoning, see Mandelbaum (2019).

What is clear is that the further up the visual stream one proceeds, the more notions of ideal information gain seem to be clearly illuminating. For example, the retina, regarded as a photon detector, seems to perform surprisingly close to the absolute signal-detection accuracy limit imposed by thermodynamics (Bialek, 2012).

It seems to me that Harman (1986) had it right that Bayesian probability theory is a theory of probabilistic coherence and classical logic is a theory of entailment. Neither are theories of reason, though coherence and entailment are sources of rational constraints. We are capable as humans to come to respect and recognize rational constraints of this sort. Unlike the Bayesians who seek to reduce common sense to probability calculus, we will, in Chapter 5, reduce probability calculus to common sense. What we need to avoid is the assumption that the only way we could come to respect constraints like probabilistic coherence is by having our system aim for these constraints from the get-go.

1.7 Mental Models and Competence

We are in the business of trying to explain reason in terms of functions and algorithms. If we are committed to reason admitting of such an explanation, we are committed to the possibility of machines having reason, insofar as they can compute these functions and algorithms. Some seventy years ago, Turing speculated, "that at the end of the century the use of words and general educated opinion will have altered so much that one will be able to speak of machines thinking without expecting to be contradicted" (Turing, 1950). It would appear that his prediction was at least partially correct as far as loose talk is concerned. What certainly did not turn out to be correct was the idea that this would happen as a result of computers succeeding in his "imitation game." The idea behind this game, now remembered as the "Turing test," was that if we can hold a conversation with a computer while being unable to distinguish whether we are dealing with a computer or a human interlocutor, then no meaningful reason remains to deny that computers can think.

Turing's operational notion of having the capacity to think fit well with the behaviorism that was ascendant in both philosophy and psychology around the period when Turing's paper was published (Hempel, 1949; Sellars, 1953; Quine and Van, 1960; Skinner, 1974). Roughly, behaviorism is the view that that all differences in apparent mental properties are ultimately reducible to differences in the history of observable behavior and external stimulation from the environment. Part of this view is to regard humans as essentially blank slates that acquire complex behavior patterns through some kind of reinforcement learning. Turing's own intuitions seem to be in line with this picture, writing that "presumably the child brain is something like a notebook as one buys it from the stationer's. Rather little mechanism, and lots of blank sheets. (Mechanism and writing are from our point of view almost synonymous.) Our hope is that there is so little mechanism in the child brain that something like it can be easily programmed" (Turing, 1950). The view of human cognitive development Turing speculates about here has been decisively refuted (Chomsky, 1967; Pinker, 2002). The view about how some kind of general AI might be developed through something "easily programmed" has similarly failed so far. Now, what about the idea that computers can think?

Searle (1980) provided a thought experiment that was intended as a general argument against the view that the mind could be explained as a kind of computer. If the argument succeeds, then even success in the Turing test, which remains elusive and no longer inspires much research, fails to suffice:

> Imagine a native English speaker who knows no Chinese locked in a room full of boxes of Chinese symbols (a data base) together with a book of instructions for manipulating the symbols (the program). Imagine that people outside the room send in other Chinese symbols which, unknown to the person in the room, are questions in Chinese (the input). And imagine that by following the instructions in the program the man in the room is able to pass out Chinese symbols which are correct answers to the questions (the output).
> (Searle, 1999)

With the right notion of correctness, the "Chinese room" (CR) will pass the Turing test in Chinese. However, there is a whole family of closely related notions that we would be loathe to attribute to the CR, for example, understanding, knowledge, or thought. Searle argues that "computation is defined purely formally or syntactically, whereas minds have actual mental or semantic contents, and we cannot get from syntactical to the semantic just by having the syntactical operations and nothing else." Block (1981) more modestly concludes that not all internal structures of a system are compatible with having thought or intelligence, regardless of what set of input-output relations are being exhibited. The upshot might seem rather disappointing: even if we pull-off the incredible feat of engineering required to pass the Turing test, there may be in-principle considerations to suggest that the result would not be as interesting as Turing hoped.

The force of the arguments just considered may be part of what explains why interest in human-like general intelligence as a serious research topic in AI has waned (in addition to the fact that, as we saw, general intelligence is difficult to define besides being difficult to mimick). Nevertheless, discussion about whether Searle's thought experiment establishes any in-principle limits to AI or the computational theory of mind continues (Cole, 2014).

We will focus on the narrow claim that the CR does not have understanding. There is a strong intuition that this claim is correct. This is relevant to the project of this book, since it is hard to imagine a full-blown notion of reason that does not go hand in hand with a notion in the ball-park of understanding. The question that remains is what understanding requires, and what exactly the right notion is that is worth caring about. For Searle, presumably nothing short of a human mind/brain with phenomenal consciousness will pass muster. Like many others, I do not think that his thought experiment gives us a good reason to believe that. However, the thought experiment does show that our intuitive notion of understanding imposes constraints that cannot be met by just exhibiting the right response patterns.

One way in which the CR differs from an ordinary person with understanding is that the CR supports very different counterfactuals (Haugeland, 2002; Block, 2002; Chalmers, 1996; Cole, 2004). For example, it is not guaranteed that had the inputs provided to the CR been different, the outputs would have been appropriately different too. After all, nothing guarantees that a book of rules that is fit for one set of inputs will remain fit for a different set of inputs. However, being counterfactually robust to varying inputs seems like a requirement for our attribution of understanding.

Anyone who designs examination papers for humans has a solid grasp of the fact that an exam is supposed to give us evidence of underlying competence driving the answers, where the answers themselves are not what is of primary interest. A good exam is such that good performance on it provides strong evidence that many other questions would have been answered correctly as well, had they been posed, because of underlying competence. Intuitively, we attribute competence concerning a subject matter to an agent if we think they have a reasonably correct view of this subject matter that could inform all sorts of actions that the agent might be able to perform, even if we can only get evidence for this ability by asking some finite set of questions.

Instead of focusing on whole-system input-output equivalence, we might ask more directly what is involved in a knowledge-based agent who has competence. I suggest that what is worth caring about in the notion of understanding for the purposes of reason is *competence*. I think that it is best to focus on competence instead of *understanding*, because I suspect that understanding is what we might call a "phenomenal glow" concept (adapting a phrase from Chalmers (1995)) that relates to competence in much the way in which the value-laden concept of murder relates to intentional killing. In other words, I think that in many people's usage, attributing understanding involves attributing phenomenal experience in addition to attributing competence, just like calling somebody a murderer involves accusing someone of moral wrongdoing in addition to attributing an intentional killing to them. It may well be the case that many kinds of competence relevant to reason in humans go hand in hand with phenomenally conscious experience, but this seems to me to be neither a necessary feature of competence nor a feature that is obviously crucial for reason.

How then should we characterize competence as relevant to reason? Craik (1943) made a seminal suggestion in this area that, unlike his tripartite characterization of a knowledge-based agent (Russell and Norvig, 2016), has not had much impact in AI and has proven challenging to articulate precisely. The idea is that knowledge-based agents have "thought models." The suggestion will be that what it means, in the relevant sense we have been discussing, to have competence with a subject matter is to have an appropriate kind of "thought model." Craik characterizes his thought models as follows:

> My hypothesis then is that thought models, or parallels, reality....
>
> By a model we thus mean any physical or chemical system which has a similar relation-structure to that of the process it imitates. By "relation-structure" I do not mean some obscure non-physical entity which attends the model, but the fact that it is a physical working model which works in the same way as the process it parallels, in the aspects under consideration at any moment. Thus, the model need not resemble the real object pictorially; Kelvin's tide-predictor, which consists of a number of pulleys on levers, does not resemble a tide in appearance, but it works in the same way in certain essential respects.... (Craik, 1943)

The idea that a knowledge-based agent should be using mental models that have a "similar relation-structure" as what is being represented and that work "in the same way in certain essential respects," seems to give us a better purchase on a notion of competence than any black-box notion of whole-system input-output equivalence, since it allows us to recognize from the outset that not all input-output equivalent internal structures are sufficient for competence, since not all of those structures will support the same counterfactuals.

Imagine a variant of the CR that can correctly answer questions about the Great Western Railway network. It seems to me that a kind of iterative Turing test that allows us to look inside the box in service of finding evidence of "similar relation-structure" and of working "in the same way in essential respects", could in fact increase our willingness to attribute a degree of competence to the system. Imagine that after finding that the system correctly answers various queries (but, let's say, not all such queries), you look inside the box and find that the internal rule-book provides instructions about how to move miniature model trains around on a model railway set that corresponds to the layout of the Great Western Railway network and then provides instructions about what characters to output depending on the behavior of the set. If facts about the model railway set and the input and output characters are related in the right way to facts about an actual railway, it seems that our willingness to attribute competence concerning the railway to the system should increase. Moreover, if a detailed analysis reveals that were we to remove certain model railway pieces, the system would produce outputs that would be appropriate if the corresponding pieces of the real railway were removed, our willingness to attribute competence should increase further. On the other hand, if we look inside the box and determine that the system would still produce the same outputs if the model railway set were destroyed, showing that the behavior of the model railway set is not what is allowing the system to produce correct answers, we might be less willing to attribute any kind of competence to the system. What counts is not that the box includes a model railway set that visually reminds us of real railways. What counts is that if this model railway is hooked up to the rest of the system in the right way, it functions as a physical implementation of a partial *view* of the railway, and we are willing to attribute competence to the extent to which we think we can attribute views to the system. It is easy to imagine iteratively following a process of interacting with the system through inputs and outputs, while occasionally looking inside the box to form hypotheses about what falls within the scope of the competence of the system and what does not. The more we get evidence in this way that there is a domain within which the system can treat the subject matter correctly with systematicity, the more it seems apt to attribute a view, and thus some competence, to the system. This goes hand in hand with evidence that the system supports counterfactuals similar to counterfactuals supported by our own competence.

Not all ways of attempting to pin down the notion of a mental model can play the role in grounding a notion of competence just discussed. For example, Minsky (1986) characterizes mental models as follows:

> Jack knows about A means that there is a model M of A inside Jack's head.
>
> Jack considers M to be a good model of A to the extent that he finds M useful for answering questions about A.
>
> Our definition allows a model to be anything that helps a person answer questions... a person's mental model of a car need not itself resemble an actual car in any obvious way.

If "anything that helps a person answer questions" can be a mental model, then arguably the original CR set-up with look-up tables qualifies, and the notion becomes more or less indistinguishable from something like any old encoding scheme. However, it seems clear that Craik had something more substantive in mind when he wrote of mental models having a similar "relation structure" to the thing being modeled.

For the most systematic and fruitful work on mental models, we have to look to cognitive psychology. The more substantive notion of a mental model that Craik gestured at was developed into a theory of reasoning by Johnson-Laird (1983) and his collaborators over several books and a large and growing number of papers, such as Johnson-Laird and Byrne (1991), Johnson-Laird et al. (2018), among many others. According to the mental model theory following Johnson-Laird, reasoning with successive premises involves combining the sets of mental models corresponding to each premise into one. What inferences we are likely to draw depends on what we can gather from the integrated set of mental models yielded by procedures for combining the mental models from individual premises. Mental model theory predicts demonstrated effects of premise order on reasoning, for which there currently seem to be no fully systematic alternative explanations (Girotto et al., 1997) besides the erotetic theory. Mental model theory also predicts certain fallacious inferences so compelling that they have been called "illusory inferences" (Johnson-Laird and Savary, 1999; Walsh and Johnson-Laird, 2004), some of which we considered in the section 1.2 on failures of reason. Mental model theory diagnoses the kind of reasoning mistakes we considered in section 1.2 as due to reasoners thinking they have support for a conclusion because in combining mental models they miss some of the alternative possibilities compatible with the information provided. At the same time, this approach allows us to say that we are not irretrievably lost to these mistakes, since we could in principle construct more complete integrated mental models.

On Johnson-Laird's view, mental models are mental representations that have the same structure as what they represent (Johnson-Laird, 1983), and this is the only amount of structure that makes a difference to reasoning. This is his take on Craik's idea that mental models "parallel" the "relation structure" of what the models are *models of*. It seems to me that the notion of mental models as representations that have the same structure as what they represent is the right approach to help us gain a notion of competence. In my view, we can illustrate this even with a very simple example. Most familiar formal systems for reasoning are nothing like mental models in the sense discussed. For example, in the propositional calculus under the usual semantic interpretation, the formula *P&Q* clearly has more structure than the proposition represented by that formula, namely that P and Q are true. This is witnessed by the fact that *P&Q* and *Q&P* are distinct representations that have the same proposition as their content. Since mental models have to have the same structure as what they represent, a mental model of the proposition that P and Q are true cannot be thought of as a conjunctive formula in the propositional calculus. This is relevant for our discussion of competence because it bears on what counterfactuals seem true of a system. Notice that it would be quite easy to specify a reasoning system with the above ingredients that can tell me that from $P\&Q$ it follows that P without being able to tell me that it follows that Q. For example, I could have an inference procedure for right conjunction elimination but leave out an inference procedure for left conjunction elimination. Thus, for a system for reasoning with conjunctive contents specified in terms of left and right conjunction elimination procedures over a standard logical syntax, it seems true that it could have been that the system can only infer P from $P\&Q$, without being able to infer Q. Because this counterfactual seems true of the imagined system, this system does not seem like a good candidate for a system that understands or has competence with conjunction, following the line of reasoning considered earlier in this section.

Now, suppose instead we have a representation whose structure corresponds to what is being represented. In the case of a conjunctive thought, we might plausibly say that all there is to the content is that all elements of a certain set of propositions are true. To represent that content without imposing structure not pertaining to the content, we could simply take the set (note well: *not* the set-theoretic *formula*) $\{P, Q\}$. Unless I generally have inference procedures that have specific atoms in their application conditions, it is not so clear how to have a setup where I am able to infer P but not Q. Thus, it does not seem true that it could have been that I can only infer P, without being able to infer Q (or, at any rate, we intuitively have to consider more remote possibilities). I claim that this makes the envisaged system a better candidate for an attribution of competence with (or understanding of) conjunction. A mental-model-based picture (in the sense of representations with the same structure of what is being represented) of inferences from conjunction is a better theory of competence with conjunction, because it is better at supporting the kinds of counterfactuals that competence with conjunction should support.

I will now briefly sketch three objections to the picture just presented. Firstly, someone might think that there simply is no fact of the matter which syntactic structure or program the system is following above and beyond facts about what outputs are produced for what inputs. This is more or less Quine's (Quine and Van, 1960) stance on grammar: beyond the distribution of grammatical sentences, there is no fact of the matter which grammar is the "correct" one that is actually in our heads. It is fair to say that most of contemporary linguistic theory is unintelligible if we take this stance, which, since the cognitive revolution, has been concerned with hypotheses about right account of the internalized system of rules that account for a speaker/hearer's linguistic competence (Chomsky, 1972).

A second objection would hold that the structural distinctions we made in the above example concerning conjunction are not available for computational theory, because computational theory must be specified in terms of transformations of linear strings. Turing's notion of computing machines is grounded in the notion of writing ("Mechanism and writing are from our point of view almost synonymous" Turing (1950)). Indeed, a Turing machine is nothing but a mechanism for writing and rewriting symbols on a tape. If we think of computation fundamentally in this way, then it might seem like any computational theory of reasoning would be a form of mental logic in some sense. However, all that is required to ground a notion of computation is that we have a clear notion of formal structure and a clear notion of transformations of that structure. Whether our notion of computation ends up being universal is then just a matter of how rich the structure and primitive transformations are. Nothing prevents us from treating set formation and choice of elements from a set as primitive, even if it might make it messier to present a physical implementation of a machine employing these primitives. As in the reply to the previous objection, we can already find precursors in linguistic theory. According to Chomsky's Minimalist Program (2000a), an operation for set formation (called 'merge') is fundamental to the language faculty, and the structures generated by merge are only linearized for phonological output (N.B. it is not of our concern whether this particular view of the language faculty is correct).

A third objection worth briefly considering goes as follows. A mental model could only support a notion of competence in the sense discussed if the elements of the mental model are themselves grounded in further competence or understanding. This would seem to require that we have mental models of the elements as well. Given that these mental models unpack into further elements and further mental models and so on, competence with anything is impossible without competence concerning (almost) everything. Thus, we cannot have competence in a system that does not almost completely mirror everything a human understands, making a mental models approach useless unless we mirror virtually all of a human mind at once. To put it differently, perhaps we can only attribute competence concerning the Great Western Railway network to a system that can also conclude that something like Agatha Christie's *Murder on the Orient Express* might have taken place in it, etc., etc. In reply, I think it is clear that we already have a common-sense notion of competence at different depths. It simply is not the case that we have further descriptive information available for all concepts that figure in our understanding of the world. After what could be called an "externalist revolution" in philosophy (Putnam (1975); Kripke (1980); Fodor (1998); Soames (2002), and many others), the burden of proof seems to be on those who want to maintain that having access to one concept would *always* require having access to very many others, let alone to definitions in terms of yet further concepts. This is not to say that certain concepts, for example those related to space or color, might not be best understood as being intrinsically tied to a structure involving several other concepts. For example, a concept of "left" without a concept of "right" seems deficient in a crucial way (see, for example, models of such concepts in Gärdenfors (2004)).

Though we do not have to space here to explore ethical issues in detail, one might think that there are all sorts of settings where we have a legitimate moral claim on others to make decisions about us in a way that is based on competence. For example, in hiring decision, I have a legitimate claim on the committee to base their decision on a competent view of my relevant skills. In light of the earlier remarks about what it takes for a system to have competence, it may well be the case that some purely statistical machine-learning-based AI applications in hiring (Dattner et al., 2019) and criminal justice (Hao, 2019) are profoundly immoral, because they do not seem to support an attribution of competence. This suggests that there may be reasons to explore competence-based approaches even if they were technically more challenging and even if they turned out to lend themselves less well to easily developed commercial products. Once we are alert to these distinctions, it may well turn out that the range of problems where a competence-based approach must be demanded is larger than it might seem at first. We ought to resist the temptation to freely redefine such problems simply to suit easily available commercial solutions.

If competence in the sense discussed is particularly worth caring about in many contexts in a way that, in some guise, already has a significant hold on our intuitions, we might look for evidence that people routinely test each other for such competence at least indirectly. Through this lens, we might take a new look at phenomena like anaphora resolution in natural language. Take a statement like, "Bo refused Mo a permit because he opposed the GOP." Depending on the details of how we imagine the background situation, we could resolve the reference for "he" either way. What benefit would the natural use of "he" have in this sort of statement? Perhaps we could appeal to counterfactually robust minimal message length ("Bo" could have been "Beaufort," making "he" obviously shorter). While this approach should not be entirely dismissed, we might observe a more substantial further benefit: requiring the hearer to resolve the anaphora imposes an indirect test on whether the hearer has a certain type of competence concerning what is being discussed. I do not need to have a substantial view of the context we are in or of what scenarios are being discussed to take on board "Bo refused Mo a permit because Bo opposed the GOP." However, I do need such a view to reliably interpret the anaphoric version. After all, I need a view of who has political power and how that might relate to the issuing of permits, and so on. In the form of so-called Winograd Schemas (Winograd (1972); Levesque (2014)), anaphora resolution has often been taken as a kind of mini-Turing test in the AI literature. For a given set of stock sentences, mechanically resolving anaphora like average human informants do is difficult without at least indirectly representing standard world knowledge. The main computational challenge then lies in either encoding standard-issue world knowledge explicitly or in approximating it indirectly via some form of statistical learning. If you will, going in the opposite direction, we might consider that humans are routinely performing such tests on each other because so much of what we want to talk about is in fact not contained in any stable standard-issue knowledge-base that we can presume most adults to have (otherwise, why talk at all?). The normal use of anaphora in conversation allows us to indirectly check whether our view of the world is sufficiently similar to that of our interlocutors as the conversation proceeds. We could call this a "view parity check" theory of the functional role of anaphora.

1.8 Toward Content-Based Theories of Reason

I believe that something reminiscent of mental models is the best approach to what is worth caring about in the notion of understanding (viz. competence) and thus the best approach for a theory of reason. In Koralus and Mascarenhas (2013), we explicitly developed the erotetic theory as a theory of reasoning based on mental models. However, I now believe that these ideas have to be approached from a different perspective to obtain a computational theory of reason that is as general as possible with as much explanatory power as possible. Firstly, I propose that we see the entire core of reason as based on representations that have the same structure as their contents, as far as they make a difference to reason. This would then allow us to talk about reason directly in terms of contents and transitions between those contents: we can just talk about reason in terms of *changes in view*. By contrast, mental model theory was not intended to explain all of what is involved in reasoning in terms of mental models (Philip Johnson-Laird, personal communication) and thus could not ground that kind of reorientation toward content.

It is worth briefly exploring why mental model theory as it stands is not enough to allow us to achieve a reorientation toward a fully content-based theory of reason. There are several longstanding criticisms of mental model theory. For example, in the cognitive psychology tradition, there currently does not exist a clear set of formal definitions for mental model theory that would allow us to calculate predictions for arbitrary reasoning problems with something like the expressive power of quantified predicate logic with relations, which, as Russell and Norvig put it amusingly, is what we need "to represent the most important aspects of the real world, such as action, space, time, thoughts, and shopping" (Russell and Norvig, 2016). Partly in lieu of a set of definitions, there exists a program called mReasoner (Khemlani and Johnson-Laird, 2022), which is continuously being updated and that allows users to get mental model predictions for a wide range of reasoning problems, though not with full generality for predicates and relations.

Another criticism of mental model theory is that it has not been made entirely clear in the literature what the representational contents of the mental models are Braine and O'Brien (1991); Bach (1993); Hodges (1993). While this *is* a problem for the purposes we are pursuing in this book, these criticisms are hardly devastating for mental models as an approach in empirical cognitive psychology. Science tends to proceed ahead of mathematical foundations. Moreover, few bodies of work concerned with human judgment have yielded more systematic and surprising experimental results in the last four decades, ranging from propositional reasoning to reasoning with quantifiers, modals, probabilities, and causes. Indeed, we will encounter many of those results in almost every chapter of this book. The fact that the work of Johnson-Laird and collaborators has received less attention outside of psychology than that of, say, Tversky and Kahneman may largely be due to the fact that the latter transparently took aim at assumptions of mainstream economic theory.

Let us take a closer look at what might be barriers to an account of the contents of mental models. Mental models have to be finite. If mental models have the same structure as their contents, these contents have to be finite as well. However, this makes it unclear how ordinary human reasoning can cope with potentially infinite or even just very large domains. Even simple examples like the content of "all dogs bark" already seem to take us beyond finite models. On closer examination, it looks like the idea that reasoning is based on mental models and that mental models have the structure of their contents was never strictly maintained by mental model theorists. Early approaches in the mental models literature took universal generalizations to give rise to mental models with a certain number of concrete instantiations as exemplars, combined with a "mental footnote" to stand in for the notion that indefinitely more exemplars could be added (Johnson-Laird, 1983). However, it is extremely unclear in what sense a "mental footnote" can bring a finite set of exemplars all the way to the import of "all dogs bark" without being a mental logic formula for "all dogs bark." More recently, the proposal seems to be to treat quantified statements as giving rise to an "intension" that generates mental models of exemplars, but which have to be carried alongside the mental model (Khemlani et al., 2015) and which presumably have to be potentially freshly generated for novel universal conclusions. Neither approach is incoherent, but neither would allow us to say that the core of reason is entirely based on mental models. We will return to some of these issues in Chapter 4.

It now seems to me that if we take it as foundational that the mental representations that make reasoning possible have the same structure as their contents as far as reasoning is concerned, and we are looking for a computational-level theory, we might as well develop a theory of reason entirely in terms of the contents entertained by the reasoner. We can then let the mental representations themselves remain more-or-less anonymous, subject to the constraint that, whatever the representations are, they have to have the same structure as the contents they bear (again, as far as it makes a difference to reasoning), and subject to the constraint that whatever algorithmic operations support the process of reasoning, those operations exactly track the possible content-transitions we specify at the level of computational theory. In a certain light, this would mean while the capacity to reason is grounded in something in the ball-park of Craik and Johnson-Laird's mental models *at the level of representational vehicles and algorithms*, the same capacity is grounded in *views* and *changes in view* (Harman (1986)), when regarded *at the level of computational theory*.

On this view, a reasoner may regard one set of contents in light of another set of contents or entertain those contents under different attitudes, but she will have no access to the form of representational vehicles of those contents. For example, we might entertain the possibility that there is milk in the fridge, and then take a questioning attitude toward the possibility that there is milk in the fridge. On this sort of view, reasoning involves changes in view, but those changes have to be entirely explicable in terms of the relationship between views themselves without reference to some particular logical form or representational vehicle that might be used to represent views.

Of course, any cognitive theory in some sense ultimately explains thought processes in terms of transformations of vehicles of representation (what Fodor (1979) called "methodological solipsism"). The proposal here is not a genuine departure from that idea. At the risk of sounding repetitive, what it means to have a content-based theory of reasoning in the cognitive science context is to have a theory based on the *principle of content-representation correspondence*. According to this principle, the cognitive states computationally underwriting reasoning have the same structure as their representational contents, as far as structure making a difference to reasoning is concerned (i.e. whatever excess structure the cognitive states have is not making a difference to reasoning). If this principle holds, it becomes possible to talk about the process of reasoning directly in terms of transitions between contents without loss (even if, strictly speaking, contents themselves do not have causal powers).

Now, if we are committed to a view on which our cognitive states have the same structure as their contents, our contents have to be finite. After all, there can be no infinitary cognitive states. So far, it has been unclear how to rigorously articulate a content-based theory of ordinary human reasoning for premises that cover potentially infinite or very large domains. We might call this the *cardinality problem* for a content-based theory of reason. In brief, by including arbitrary objects, roughly in Kit Fine's sense, in our account of the representational contents we reason with, our cardinality problem can be solved. Arbitrary objects are non-individual entities, each associated with a range of application, and having only "those properties common to the individual objects in its range" (Fine, 1985b). Fine (1985a) showed that a theory of arbitrary objects is coherent and can provide a semantics for classical logic. Adapting this framework for our purposes, when we think a thought that corresponds to a general statement like "all dogs bark," we are thinking about an arbitrary dog that barks. In other words, the representational content of the cognitive state corresponding to the thought expressed by "all dogs bark" includes an arbitrary dog as a constituent (as well as a property and a relation) just as the thought expressed by "Fido barks" includes a particular dog as a constituent. Neither case includes a potentially infinite set of particular dogs.

Now, thought contents involving arbitrary objects are true of the world in virtue of properties and relations of (potentially infinitely many) particular individuals. However, we do not take those ontologically fundamental truth-makers of our thought contents to be necessarily included in our thought contents. Nor, note well, do we concede that these contents are somehow "not really true" for lack of ontological fundamentality.

The job of defending the metaphysics of arbitrary objects here will be left to Fine. My view is that if the notion is coherent and scientifically useful, it has more than earned its keep. We only briefly observe the following to address concerns that arbitrary objects are overpopulating our ontology: some slippage between the content of our thoughts and the ontologically fundamental truth-makers of those thoughts generally seems to be expected. For example, most of our thoughts about moving objects having a certain speed are intuitively about a monadic property. Of course, physics teaches us that the ontologically fundamental physical truth-makers of those thoughts in fact consist of *relational* properties between objects. It is not too disturbing if intuitively monadic thoughts are ultimately true in virtue of facts based on relations. It seems no more disturbing if thoughts about arbitrary dogs are ultimately true in virtue of facts about particular dogs. Ontological non-fundamentality is no reason to stop ordinarily thinking of speed as if it were a monadic property, and ontological non-fundamentality is no reason to doubt that arbitrary objects can be part of ordinary thought contents. Certainly, there is use for a restricted notion of content that coincides with ontologically fundamental truth-makers, but we do not see a strong case for holding that all scientifically useful notions of content must be of this type (on this point, also see Chomsky (2000b) and Mendelovici (2013)).

So how exactly do we characterize the representational contents involved in reasoning? The erotetic theory takes the following approach. The mental configurations involved in reasoning have sets of alternative states at the core of their representational content.

Since Hamblin (1973), semanticists commonly regard the content of interrogative sentences as *questions*, and in turn analyze questions as amounting to sets of alternatives. Following the inquisitive semantics tradition, as in e.g. Groenendijk (2009) and Mascarenhas (2009), we shall also accept the converse, namely that sets of alternatives themselves are to be treated as questions or "issues" (we will keep using these terms as synonyms). On this approach, we treat all forms of speech that supply sets of alternatives as their meaning as fundamentally raising questions. This means that questions are ubiquitous (Ciardelli et al., 2018). For example, not only can we think of the interrogative sentence "is there a party or not?" as giving us the question $\{p, \neg p\}$, we can also think of the disjunction "either there is a party or not" as giving us the question $\{p, \neg p\}$ (see Kratzer and Shimoyama (2017)). In both cases, we get a set of alternatives including a p state and a not-p state. Since sets of alternatives do not necessarily have to be supplied by linguistic premises, we can also find issues in many other places where we might not have expected them (unlike in "erotetic logic" there is actually little concern for the time being about inferences between interrogative sentences, cf. Wisniewski (1995)). For example, in Chapter 6, we will take the view that a decision problem is fundamentally an issue as well.

Having said something about alternatives, we next have to say something about states. Setting aside some nuances that will only become relevant once we reach Chapter 6, by a state, we shall roughly mean a putative fact obtaining in the world. Here, we could speak of situations instead of states, except that we also admit inconsistent states (Fine (2012); Barwise and Perry (1983); Barwise and Etchemendy (1990)), which is ruled out on some natural uses of "situation" (usages differ). The idealized notion of a maximally specific and consistent state corresponds to the more familiar notion (in semantics at least) of a possible world.

In connection with these states, we will, as the chapters progress, successively include further structure to deal with predicates and uncertainty. We will call a structured representational content unit incorporating all of the above a *view*. We will say that forward reasoning means transitioning from a cognitive configuration representing one view to a cognitive configuration representing another. Since, as noted, all that matters is that the cognitive configurations correspond to the views they represent, we will simply talk about the views and the transitions between them.

Now, we must acknowledge that in many quarters, notably including linguistic semantics, standard approaches take possible worlds themselves as fundamental, rather than states. Instead of taking a Finean perspective that begins with states, we could reconstruct states in terms of possible worlds (see Yablo (2014) and responses in Fine (2020)). It is not necessary to take a strong stance here on whether the framework in this book can be successfully reconstructed in terms of possible worlds. Much can be done with possible worlds and sufficient additional structure. However, such an approach would only seem confusing given our present aims. For example, we wish to be able distinguish states even if they are included in all the same possible worlds. This corresponds to the observation that, in reasoning, thinking a premise is not always the same as thinking a logically equivalent conclusion based on this premise. Similar concerns have motivated situation-semantics (Barwise and Perry (1983); Barwise and Etchemendy (1990)). Since we are pursuing a *content-based* theory of reason, we cannot handle these cases by appealing to different mental sentences with the same contents. Perhaps unsurprisingly, a content-based theory of reason imposes more constraints on a suitable theory of content than a mental logic type theory would. Moreover, we want to distinguish indefinitely many absurd atomic states that could not be included in any possible world, though this will not become apparent until Chapter 4.

One potentially attractive and conciliatory view of the relationship between the present approach and possible-worlds semantics of natural language might be as follows. Possible worlds semantic analyses of natural language should not in the first instance be directly concerned with modeling ordinary and potentially fallacious reasoning data. The proposals in this book could be seen as working toward a *generalization* of more classical approaches to the formal analysis of representational content. From the perspective presented here, standard analyses of natural language statements based on possible-worlds semantics can be seen as concerned with a certain interesting special case. Within the erotetic theory, we can think of those analyses as studying what statements representationally commit us to under *erotetic equilibrium* (which we will define formally in Chapter 1), using intuitive data about *erotetic equilibrium inferences* we can make from those statements. In other words, once we have the material in Chapter 1 on the table, we can recharacterize the traditional project in formal semantics of natural language as *semantics under erotetic equilibrium*, which is simply not concerned with non-equilibrium fallacious inference patterns but is concerned with a stable target rooted in a special case of our what our cognitive apparatus affords in principle under heavy idealization. This is not to say that it will always be obvious whether a given linguistic intuition must be taken to bear on the equilibrium or the non-equilibrium case, or that it will always be obvious whether some class of intuitions can be accounted for in a principled manner without considering non-equilibrium machinery. For example, Chapter 3 argues that we need non-equilibrium machinery to make sense of "if."

Incidentally, in Chapter 6, we will be making parallel claims about how to understand classical microeconomics in the face of modern behavioral economics. Rational choice theory as the foundation of classical microeconomics will be reconstructed as concerned with the special case of decision-making under erotetic equilibrium. Even though behavioral economics has meanwhile found various cases that fall outside this special case, we do not have to conclude that the classical model is wrong in some straightforward sense. Like Newtonian mechanics, we could see classical models of this sort as a kind of low-velocity approximation that essentially remains as a prerequisite for making sense of the more general case.

One of the core tenets of the erotetic theory is that sets of alternative states are treated in reasoning as questions to be answered (i.e. we take a "questiony" attitude toward them) and that further sets of alternative states, incrementally taken on board as premises, are treated as answers to those questions. The default aim of reasoning is to reduce the set of alternative possibilities we envisage, thereby moving from more inquisitive states to less inquisitive states. There are parallels to be drawn here between the erotetic theory's characterization of reasoning as question-answering and the Bayesians' characterization of reasoning as uncertainty reduction (Oaksford and Chater, 2007; Tenenbaum et al., 2006). Both the erotetic theory and Bayesian approaches give a central role to sets of alternatives, though Bayesianism gives an even more central role to a probability measure over such sets of alternatives, while the erotetic theory goes to work on the sets of alternatives directly.

Reasoning operations in the erotetic theory broadly divide into operations that tend to reduce the questionyness of a state of inference and operations that tend to increase the questionyness of a state of inference. This corresponds to increasing and reducing the number of alternative states represented. Again, since we hold that the structure of cognitive states that underwrite our reasoning only matters up to the structure of their representational contents, we regiment our theory directly in terms of transitions between views, rather than in terms of transitions between formulas in some language of thought.

1.9 The Erotetic Theory

We will now add a bit more detail to the sketch of the erotetic theory of reason, as a preview to the more formal detail in subsequent chapters. We presuppose that a creature with the capacity to reason possesses the capacity to represent views and that this creature has such views available through a form of memory. We also assume that such a creature has action systems that can execute on views of what to do.

Definition 1.1 (The erotetic theory of reason).
(*Content-based changes in view*) The capacity to reason is the capacity to change views by applying reasoning operations whose results are solely determined by what is contained in views. This includes views of what is the case and views of what to do.
(*Directed inference lenses*) Applying a reasoning operation involves taking a view, from the perspective of another view, through the lens of the operation, resulting in an updated view.
(*Answerhood*) The primary aim of reason is to answer issues as directly as possible. Every operation that allows us to take on board a view

amounting to an additional premise or commitment D, relative to a prior view G, includes an attempt to treat D as a maximally strong answer to G.

(*Erotetic equilibrium*) The secondary aim of reason is to weakly pursue erotetic equilibrium. An inference to a conclusion is in erotetic equilibrium with if and only if raising further issues before taking something on board as an answer cannot decisively block our operations from reaching the conclusion of this inference.

(*Erotetic disequilibrium*) All failures of *commission* (e.g. making an unwarranted judgment) of our core capacity to reason are based on making inferences outside of erotetic equilibrium. All failures of *omission* (e.g. failing to make a judgment we ought to make) of our core capacity to reason result from taking on board an inappropriate set of issues.

We can then get a definition of an agent in terms of the foregoing.

Definition 1.2 (Erotetic agent). An erotetic agent is an agent whose behavior is controlled by the capacity to reason as described by the erotetic theory.

To get a proper sense of how these notions play out, reading the rest of this book is unfortunately unavoidable. We will nevertheless do our best to unpack these principles at least to some degree for a preliminary overview. We shall briefly consider each of the core principles of the erotetic theory in turn. The commitment to a content-based theory has already been discussed at length. The key idea is that from the perspective of the reasoner (not necessarily phenomenally conscious), our reasoning moves only have access to representational contents (even if the reasoner and everything she does is *made up of* blind computations at a different level of description). Our theory is formally defined in terms of a particular account of what these contents look like and how we transition between them.

Reasoning operations on the erotetic theory are essentially lenses through which we change our views. These operations could be seen as inducing something like the "taking relation" that Boghossian takes to separate inference from merely associational thinking in which there is no sense that our thoughts are directly supported by prior thoughts (Boghossian, 2014; 2018). On the view we develop here, an inference proceeds by the reasoner taking a certain view from a certain vantage point through a certain lens. Our kind of "taking" does not involve a further premise-like belief that one has justification for one's conclusion and is more akin to perception than to submitting a case to a jury. This thin conception of "taking" in inference does not require reflection and leaves open the question of how much inferring is involved in perception proper.

Merely associational thinking would mean simply having a new view pop up without us "seeing" it through the lens of one's other views, so to speak. Note that on the erotetic theory, inferences are not always rationally justifiable (see our failure examples in section 1.2) and that, partly as a result, some forms of thinking that might be deemed merely associational by some are actually characterized as inferences. Note though that while we admit inferences that are not *justifiable* (e.g. illusory inferences), we still hold them to be rationally *evaluable*. Indeed, the theory holds that illusory inferences are undermined by asking the right questions.

Formally, all reasoning operations take the form of update procedures of the form $G[D]^O = G'$, using the notation inspired by (Veltman, 1996) that we already used in Koralus and Mascarenhas (2013). We will generally refer to G in this configuration as the "external argument" of O and we will similarly refer to D as the "internal argument" of O. For example, once we have defined the update operation $\circlearrowright$, it will turn out that $\{ps, q\}[\{p\}]^{\circlearrowright} = \{ps\}$. What this means is that applying the reasoning operation $\circlearrowright$ from the perspective of the view $\{p\}$ to the occurrent view $\{ps, q\}$ yields the new occurrent view $\{ps\}$.

The visual analogy in Figure 2 of a video-game controller with various buttons to fill in for O may be helpful to some readers. In Figure 2, imagine that our view is $\{ps, q\}$ on the display, and that we decide to press $\circlearrowright$ after selecting $\{p\}$ as a perspective. This is merely an architectural preview. How this works in practice will become clear once we develop operations step by step in Chapter 2 and apply them to concrete reasoning problems.

In Figure 1, the buttons on the left of the schematized control pad correspond to moves available to the reasoner that tend to make a view less

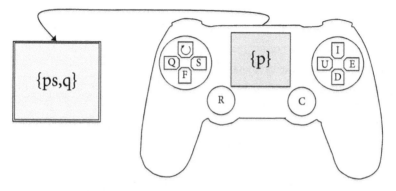

Fig. 1 A view of the human reasoning capacity

inquisitive or "questiony," in the sense that these moves tend to reduce the number of alternative states to consider or tend to reduce the number of atoms in those states. For example, ↻ decomposes into a sequence of operations, one of which treats the internal argument as a maximally strong answer to the question in the external argument. This effectively means that executing $\{ps, q\}[\{p\}]^{↻}$ in part means asking "am I in a p and s situation or in a q situation?" and then taking "you are in a p situation!" as a maximally strong answer, leading us to pare down our set of alternatives to "I'm in a p and s situation!" This is an example of the kind of pattern behind the answerhood principle. This principle holds that insofar as we are not just unpacking the implications of one view, but taking on board multiple views in succession that could be regarded as premises, reason will attempt to process successive views as answers to previous views (cf. Part 1 of the erotetic principle in Koralus and Mascarenhas (2013)).

Other operations will tend to raise issues. The buttons on the right of the schematized control pad correspond to moves that tend to make our view more inquisitive, in the sense of tending to add alternative states, tending to add atoms to states, or tending to add additional views to our set of commitments.

This brings us to the principle of erotetic equilibrium. This principle claims that the secondary aim of reason is to weakly pursue erotetic equilibrium. Firstly, the key idea behind this principle is that there is something special about inferences and views that are robust with respect to the raising of further issues. In the following chapters, we will provide formal notions of erotetic equilibrium that provably guarantee classical soundness (and completeness) up to the usual fragments of expressive power, as well as probabilistic coherence (Chapter 5) and rational choice (Chapter 6). Now, erotetic equilibrium is an external rather than an internal notion. What this means is that erotetic equilirium does not per se require raising further issues; it only requires that if further issues were raised, it would not force us to change our judgment. Since erotetic equilibrium in this sense does not require reflection or actually raising further questions, we could potentially even deem perceptual inferences to be rational according to a standard based on erotetic equilibrium. Now, it is impossible for a finite agent to always directly aim for erotetic equilibrium in a productive fashion, in the sense of always trying to take on board all possible questions to make sure that no such questions could change our judgment. At the same time, there is a sense in which making judgments at all is threatening to be pointless if those judgments just turn out to be an accident of the questions we happen to be entertaining. Here then is a compromise : the capacity to reason weakly pursues erotetic equilibrium in the sense that an signal is required to prompt more questions to be raised. This signal has to come from outside of the narrow capacity to reason, though not necessarily from outside of our cognitive economy. We could also say that reason seeks to maintain a *fragile hope* for erotetic equilibrium. What this means is that we expect and look forward to being in equilibrium with our judgments, but are sensitive to signals that we are not in fact in erotetic equilibrium. If we receive appropriate signals, such as finding that something we thought followed from our information in fact does not obtain or finding that the value of the outcome of our answers to our questions of what to do is too low, we will be on notice to raise some more questions in this kind of scenario in the future. However, once we have raised some more questions, we go back to our fragile hope for equilibrium again. The degree to which our hope is "fragile" (e.g. what signals prompt us to adopt more questions), and to what topics of future inquiry we will add additional questions is a parameter that has to be fixed outside of the capacity to reason narrowly conceived (we will keep our mathematical treatment focused on the narrow capacity to reason). If our degree of fragility of our hope for equilibrium is well calibrated, experience with a certain type of problem and "failing" a few times will (hopefully) ultimately result in us raising a range of questions that ensures reasonably robust equilibrium in practice.

Moving on, the principle of erotetic disequilibrium holds that whenever we commit a fallacy in reasoning, it can ultimately be traced back to a case of having treated something as an answer to an issue without having first asked *more* questions. By "fallacy" we roughly mean the natural kind of mistakes that are usefully regarded as internal to the reasoning process itself. This would be something that can deserve to be called "reasoning badly." Mistakes that consist in making pointless or distracting inferences that are nonetheless warranted by our information are not fallacies in our sense, nor are absurd conclusions drawn from inconsistent premises. Nor are we including cases of external errors like memory glitches or certain forms of distraction. We *are* of course including the cases we highlighted in the introduction, and many cases of a similar nature in the experimental psychology literature. An otherwise perfect erotetic reasoner would only make mistakes under erotetic disequilibrium.

The second part of the erotetic disequilibrium principle creates a tension between the aims of reason described in the answerhood and erotetic equilibrium principles. No general wholesale approach to being in erotetic equilibrium at all times can be adopted by reason to simultaneously satisfy the aim of direct answers and the aim of erotetic equilibrium. For starters, in the general case, raising too many questions yields intractable combinatorial explosion. However, even if we allow ourselves infinite computational resources, we may still get forms of rational paralysis if we unthinkingly demand absolute erotetic equilibrium. Demanding erotetic equilibrium with respect to too broad a set of questions likely condemns us to skepticism and inaction. If we are discussing what will be served for lunch it is no good to ask about Cartesian skeptical scenarios.

To give the theory empirically testable content, we need to provide hypotheses about what sequences of inference steps are made by reasoners in experimental settings and we need hypotheses about how premises presented in linguistic format are interpreted into views in the system. Such particular hypotheses about procedures for reasoning performance are to a significant extent separable from the core principles of the erotetic theory.

As far as linguistic interpretation is concerned, we will sketch interpretation rules in successive chapters with enough detail to make them reasonably systematic, but we will not attempt to rebuild a fully technical account of linguistic semantics in the view-based framework in this book, which will have to be left for future work. We will take it that whatever we propose as views corresponding to forms of language should also have some plausibility on linguistic grounds, particularly if we consider what contents those views would correspond to under erotetic equilibrium.

As for principles of reasoning performance, we will specify various procedures in terms of the operations of our theory. These are guided by a few plausible minimal principles of core reasoning performance, setting aside aspects of performance due to external factors like fatigue, distraction, language processing, the influence of background knowledge, and so on. In broad strokes, these principles mirror similar ideas proposed by Johnson-Laird.

Definition 1.3 (Principles of core reasoning performance).
(*Default strategy*) Systematic patterns in core reasoning performance in particular types of reasoning tasks stem from default reasoning strategies recruiting the reasoning capacity in simple sequences of operations.
(*Creative inquiry*) Differences in core reasoning performance stem from creative use of different inference steps and, in particular, from varying propensities to raise issues.
(*Erotetic complexity*) All other things being equal, the likelihood of an inference step being made is inversely proportional to the degree of inquisitiveness of the result of this step.
(*View-change complexity*) All other things being equal, the likelihood of an inference being made is inversely proportional to the number of changes in view required to make the inference.

We will briefly discuss these principles in turn. The default strategy principle corresponds to the idea that if a certain inference pattern is attractive to naïve reasoners in a given kind of reasoning task, regardless of whether it is a fallacious inference, there should be a reasonably general yet simple default procedure that can generate the observed pattern of inference in this kind of task. We will provide a preliminary default procedure in the next chapter. The creative inquiry principle holds that differences in core reasoning performance are due to reasoners pursuing different inferences with a different choice of sequences of operations. In particular, the chances of getting a difficult problem right will often depend on choosing to raise the right issues at the right point in an inference. One suspects that if the *rationality quotient* (Stanovich et al., 2016; Toplak et al., 2011) holds up as a useful construct, the ability to raise issues strategically will be central to its underlying cognitive mechanisms.

Since, in studying fallacies or repugnant validities, we are interested in non-equilibrium responses, there is an intrinsic source of variability that can shift performance significantly between subjects and between experiments. This, in my view, makes meta-analyses across studies, particularly if they include ones with small numbers of participants studied in different contexts, hard to interpret. In light of that, we will mostly focus on data points that are particularly striking and well replicated and on data points that are directly related to particular theoretical predictions. Future work would benefit from an effort to produce for the study of human-like reasoning and human-like decision-making a database of uniformly obtained and usefully stratified data points similar to what is standardly used in evaluating models of human-like image classification (cf. Fei-Fei Li's ImageNet, Deng et al. (2009)). Even with such a database it would remain important to remember that there can be no full predictive theory of what conclusions someone will draw from a given set of premises, just as there can be no full predictive theory of what people are going to say next in conversation. Reason, like language, must in the first instance be understood as a competence system.

Moving on, the erotetic complexity principle holds that the number of alternative states in the views we need to consider is key in determining how difficult inferences are, which aligns with one of the key commitments of mental model theory in cognitive psychology (Johnson-Laird, 1983; Johnson-Laird and Byrne, 1991). This principle dovetails with our above discussion about why we cannot have general strategy for always guaranteeing erotetic equilibrium: this would require us to make our views include too many alternatives to be manageable. The absence of a practicable and simple general strategy to guarantee erotetic equilibrium arguably explains why we can still study reasoning fallacies in educated individuals.

Finally, the view-change complexity principle holds that inference steps actually occur as cognitive computations and that taking more computational steps is harder. The "all other things being equal" clause is necessary, since there is no reason to assume that different types of premise combinations cannot have effects on performance in other ways. Neither should we assume that the mind cannot find ways to turn a *sequence* of inference steps for a certain problem type into something that behaves like a simple inference step. We take these complexity principles to hold regardless of whether a derivation is generated by a default procedure or by creative reasoning.

Experimental data on reasoning is the result of people using reasoning strategies. We primarily want to give a theory of the ingredients out of which such strategies are built. While we offer concrete proposals for default strategies that capture central tendencies in data, I think that theories of default reasoning are in an important sense secondary to the overall explanatory project. If we are searching for general principles, it seems less important in the first instance to find the best default procedure that can capture the greatest amount of detail, while it seems more important to show that some of the most distinctive observations about apparent irrationality across a wide range of domains can be explained by the same core principles.

1.10 Aspects of a Content-Based Theory of Reason

In light of the foregoing discussion, we might want to take a content-based approach to reason (for other arguments in favor of a content-based approach see Valaris (2017)), rather than a more traditional approach that takes reasoners to be aware of the syntactic structure of their thoughts on top of their contents (Broome, 2013).

In considering the material in the following chapters, it is useful to distinguish three core aspects of a content-based theory of reason.

(1) A theory of views

(2) A theory of the dynamics of reason

(3) A view calculus

A theory of views is required for any theory of reason that is content-based. Such a theory must give an account of what the contents are that serve as the objects of reason. It seems useful to call those contents, however we exactly characterize them, as "views," to signal that they have to be in some sense partial. Different theories of content face different challenges here. For example, a possible-worlds theory of content applied to a content-based theory of reason would face the challenge that sets of possible worlds always already include all the content that follows and do not at all include content that does not follow. However, what follows is often not obvious without reasoning effort and we often take things to follow that do not follow at all. On the other hand, a structured theory of content still faces the challenge of saying what the structure consists in and how thought with large or infinite domains is possible (while remaining a theory of content).

Moving on, a theory of the dynamics of reason is required for any theory of reason that recognizes reason as driving state changes. We need an account of the computational aim of reason that explains why reason would transition from one state to another. A Bayesian theory might say that the computational aim is to update prior probability distributions in light of new evidence. The erotetic theory says that the primary aim of reason is to raise issues and answer them as directly as possible.

Finally, a content-based theory of reason can only be fully articulated if we have a formal theory of views that is accompanied by a view *calculus*. This allows us to precisely articulate our theory of view dynamics, to calculate predictions, and to investigate under what conditions various global properties of the system are secured by reason as we describe it. For example, this book develops a view calculus that formalizes the erotetic theory in a way that allows us to formally derive many of the main data points on failures of reason that we are concerned with, and this view calculus also allows us to prove that under conditions of erotetic equilibrium, the dynamics of reason respect classical constraints on ideal rationality.

Even though the development of all three components is tightly interlinked in the erotetic theory as we will expound it in the following chapters, it is worth pointing out that we could envisage an erotetic theory with a different theory of views (and a correspondingly different view calculus), though with the same core principles; we also could envisage a different view calculus that articulates the erotetic theory in a different way; and finally, we could envisage a variant of the view calculus presented here to articulate an entirely different theory of the dynamics of reason.

Several observations are worth making about the formal dimensions of these components to manage expectations. Firstly, any view calculus required to articulate a conceptually rich theory of view dynamics is going to look relatively complicated, if we are formally expressing this view calculus in a very basic mathematical structure like an algebra or set theory. A correct theory of view dynamics in reasoning has to be at least in the ball-park of tracking substantial aspects of conscious processes in reasoning (N.B. we are in no way committed to all reasoning being conscious). Now, it is a familiar observation in computer programming that higher-level languages are more intuitive, in the sense of being closer to intuitive concepts that we normally think about, but that articulating their components in terms of a more mathematically basic language is correspondingly going to look complex and intricate. In that sense, I believe that any reasonably good theory of view dynamics that has some footing in conscious intuition is going to require a view calculus that, when expressed in a mathematically basic framework, is going to be somewhat complicated on a first look. We will try to mitigate this as far as possible by building up the formal aspect of the theory step by step through successive chapters.

The reasonable way to proceed in the case of programming languages is to build a compiler for the high-level language so that we can proceed to just express ourselves in terms of the high-level language without having to worry about how it might be expressed in more fundamental code. For our purposes, this would mean building a computer simulation of reason as seen by the erotetic theory, to facilitate exploring how the theory applies to various observations. Vincent Wang developed several iterations of calculators for early versions of the erotetic theory that provided crucial help in studying the behavior of various operations.

In fact, the aim of building simulations is not just a way to manage complexity; it is central to the aim of understanding reason and its role in intelligent behavior. There remains the overarching issue whether there can be a Type 1 theory of reason at all. However, even if there is a Type 1 theory of reason, as this book maintains, the kind of problem-solving that we would normally think of as evidence of intelligence may be an emergent effect of the Type 1 components going to work in complex configurations. This means that it may well be the case that only through simulation can we show that we have understood something of the foundations of intelligence in a context beyond simple toy problems.

In Madsen, Bailey, Carella, and Koralus (2020) we used a model of extremely simplified erotetic agents to simulate adaptive behavior of fishery fleets in an agent-based model (ABM) simulation. The individual boats were simply modeled as asking themselves every day where on the map to fish and were given the ability to update their views about the presence of fish at locations on the map through experience. The agents were further given a set of reasonable (though not economically rational) priorities to serve as partial answers to the question of where to fish. Our simulations showed that even very simple agent models of this kind are sufficient to generate complex adaptive behavior that is similar to actual patterns of adaptive behavior observed in real-world fishery fleets, including the response to new constraints like the imposition of marine protection areas or fishing quotas, as well as the emergence of illegal practices in the face of extreme economic pressures. Moreover, for a fleet of such agents in the aggregate, the behavior looks broadly rational even though the underlying principles at the individual-agent level are not constrained to be classically rational in the sense of microeconomic theory. Even for the extremely simplified agent model used in this simulation, it was hard to foresee the behavior before conducting a computational experiment. This should make clear enough that we cannot expect to be able to simply intuit how a more realistic and complex erotetic theory-based model would behave without simulation. Systematic consideration of computational simulation must be left for future work. The theoretical work that we *will* focus on is at any rate a prerequisite.

1.11 The Way Ahead

In sum, the main contribution of the book is a systematic presentation of a theory of reason. In the following chapters, the theory is developed with formal rigor and with close attention to a large number of data points from the experimental literature. Over successive chapters, we will develop the erotetic theory through successive fragments that build on each other vertically, beginning with propositional and quantified reasoning, moving on to reasoning with uncertainty, and decision-making.

Chapter 2 presents a full erotetic theory of reasoning for premises centered on "and," "not," and "or." This chapter in essence presents a modernized version of the theory first presented in (Koralus and Mascarenhas, 2013). The chapter also formally introduces the notion of erotetic equilibrium. This includes both absolute erotetic equilibrium that will guarantee classical soundness, as well as the key notion of restricted erotetic equilibrium that will allow a notion of rational inference that is not classically valid.

Chapter 3 uses the framework from Chapter 2 to make sense of reasoning with "if," including an account of how we reason toward where to look for further information. This will allow us to make sense of the apparent confirmation bias people exhibit in Wason's famous card selection task. In this chapter, we also encounter the idea that some types of statement have important inferential import even though they may turn out to be vacuous. We will also briefly consider reasoning with "might" statements.

Chapter 4 extends the erotetic theory to first-order equivalent predicate reasoning. This chapter is perhaps the technically most challenging chapter of the book and is the result of a collaboration with Vincent Wang, Sean Moss, and Beau Mount. We will encounter a number of surprising inference patterns, including the so-called "Politician's syllogism," the "married people puzzle" from our introduction, among many others. We will also get an account of Sellarsian conceptual inferences. With our notion of restricted erotetic equilibrium from Chapter 2 and our notion of vacuous inferential import from Chapter 3, we will also be able to provide a new account of reasoning with generic statements congenial to arguments about their meaning made by Sarah-Jane Leslie. In an appendix, we show that under absolute erotetic equilibrium, the erotetic theory of predicate reasoning is classically sound and complete.

Chapters 5 and 6, both developed in collaboration with Sean Moss, extend the erotetic theory to reasoning with uncertainty and, finally, decision-making. Chapter 5 shows how the erotetic theory, with a more general notion of answer potential, can make sense of a variety of fallacies of reasoning with probability while also be able to make sense of the possibility of probabilistic coherence and Bayesian updating. The picture of reasoning with uncertainty that the erotetic theory provides also sheds some light on how it is possible for ordinary people to sometimes outperform experts on prediction tasks.

Chapter 6 extends the erotetic theory to practical reasoning in a way that echoes Michael Bratman's Belief-Desire-Intention model, while giving center stage to reasons or priorities. The account helps make sense of a number of framing effects. At the same time, we get that erotetic equilibrium can secure classically rational choice as utility maximization. The account also allows us to see careful consequentialist decision-making and rapid action-centered decision-making on a spectrum. The discussion is rounded out with an account of how the perception of affordances fits into practical reasoning and ends with some perspectives on how an erotetic conception of agents may help justify deliberative conceptions of democracy.

The best way to get a full grasp of the erotetic theory all the way up to agency is by following the sequence of the chapters. Definitions in subsequent chapters build on those in previous chapters, with the exception of Chapter 3, which does not introduce important new definitions. The opening sections of all chapters can be read together as an overview of some of the empirical issues that a general theory of the human capacity to reason must contend with.

2
Core Reasoning and Erotetic Equilibrium

We want to develop a mathematical theory of reason that can make sense both of empirically documented fallacies and of the possibility of systematically correct inference. In this chapter we will begin by developing a fragment of such a theory for the equivalent of sentential reasoning, with the possibility of systematic classical validity as our standard of correctness. Many of the core concepts in this chapter were initially developed in Koralus and Mascarenhas (2013).

We begin with a simple data point, similar to that discussed in the introduction.

> **Example 1.** (*Illusory inference from disjunction*)
> P_1 Either Jane is kneeling by the fire and she is looking at the TV or else Mark is standing at the window and he is peering into the garden.
> P_2 Jane is kneeling by the fire.
> C Jane is looking at the TV.

When presented with the above two premises and asked what if anything follows from them, Walsh and Johnson-Laird (2004) found that around 90% of participants responded that Jane is looking at the TV. However, this seems to be a fallacious inference. After all, we could be in a situation in which Jane is kneeling by the fire but not looking at the TV, while Mark is standing at the window and is peering into the garden. In other words, both premises could be true while the conclusion is false, showing that the conclusion does not follow from the premises.

How can we make sense of this inference? Someone might observe that "or" could be interpreted as communicating "one or the other but not both." As Grice taught us (1975; 1989), in addition to what is semantically expressed by an utterance (what is *said*), there is what is pragmatically inferred from additional assumptions about having a cooperative interlocutor. For example, while what is semantically expressed by "some of the students came to class" more or less boils down to the commitment that the class was not empty, we normally take an utterance of such a sentence to further implicate that *not all* students came to class. There is an ongoing contemporary debate concerning the extent to which such phenomena are proper extra-linguistic inferences and to what extent they are essentially grammatical phenomena (Atlas and Levinson, 1981; Levinson, 2000; Sperber and Wilson, 1986; Chierchia et al., 2012).

Now in the case at hand, the conclusion does not follow from the premises regardless of whether we interpret "or" inclusively or exclusively as "or...but not both," so such an interpretation would not help explain the fallacious inference. Simply consider that all premises on either reading are true in the case in which Jane is kneeling, and not looking, while Mark is standing and peering.

Someone might instead suggest that the first premise could be interpreted along the lines of "either Jane is kneeling by the fire and she is looking at the TV *and nothing else is going on*, or else Mark is standing at the window and he is peering into the garden *and nothing else is going on*." If those who conclude that Jane is looking at the TV are indeed interpreting the first premise in this way, with what would be called an embedded exhaustivity implicature, we have to grant that the conclusion is indeed supported (even if it might still seem presumptuous).

One preliminary way of testing the implicature explanation would be to add expressions that are pragmatically at odds with an "and nothing else" interpretation. One expression that comes to mind is "at least": if I say that I have *at least* two cards in my hand, that clearly does not generate an implicature that I have *at most* two cards. Following the same protocol and procedure of Mascarenhas and Koralus (2017), we presented the following to 124 participants on Amazon Mechanical Turk, a crowdsourcing platform allowing researchers to anonymously recruit for web-based tasks like surveys about reasoning problems:

> **Example 2.** (*Illusory inference with* "at least")
> P_1 There is at least an ace and a queen, or else at least a king and a ten.
> P_2 There is a king.
> Question: *What if anything follows?*
> C There is a ten (and a king). [83% of respondents]

83% of the participants (excluding from analysis three who had given irrelevant responses about things not mentioned in the problem) wrote that there is a ten, or something directly entailing that, without making any (other) mistakes. The same participants gave a similar percentage of correct answers to control problems like the below:

Example 3. (*Correct control inference* disjunctive syllogism)
P$_1$ There is at least an ace and a king or else there is at least a queen and a jack.
P$_2$ There isn't an ace.
Question: *What if anything follows?*
C There is a queen and a jack. [84% of respondents]

84% of the participants correctly made the (so-called *disjunctive syllogism*) inference that if the left side of the disjunction is ruled out, the right side must be true. In sum, the vast majority of participants, who reasoned quite well on control problems, still made the inference even with "at least" included in the premises. This makes it seem doubtful that a pragmatic implicature explanation suffices to make sense of Walsh and Johnson-Laird's illusory inference pattern. In fact, we will see that participants are also happy to make these kinds of inferences with premises of greater complexity where "and nothing else" interpretations of the premises would yield a contradiction rather than the specific conclusions that participants in fact report (the impatient may consult example 15 further below). Furthermore, we will shortly consider order effects in this type of problem that cast doubt on any explanation that would generate the pattern from factors wholly present in the main premise.

In any case, the range of reasoning problems we would like to understand is far broader than the simple "warm up" cases we have so far considered in this chapter, so it seems better to press on with developing a theory of the capacity for reason and to leave for another time the question of what aspects of the deployment of this capacity might be further intelligible as pragmatic inferences about speaker intentions, and so on (particularly since pragmatic theory often tends to *assume* a more-or-less ideal capacity to reason as given in the background).

According to the erotetic theory of reason, the core aim of reason is to take on board issues and answer them as directly as possible with available information. Issues, or questions, are contents. Following Hamblin (1958), we mathematically treat issues as sets of alternatives and, following the inquisitive semanticists (Groenendijk, 2009; Mascarenhas, 2009; Ciardelli et al., 2018), we take sets of alternatives as issues, wherever they arise.

Next, we take the alternatives participating in those sets to be *states*. In this usage, states are similar to situations, except that they include inconsistent states (Fine, 2012). A possible world would then be a maximally specific and consistent state. We could instead take possible worlds as fundamental and construct states from them (see Yablo (2014) and responses in Fine (2020)) but this would unnecessarily complicate things for our purposes. By Chapter 4, we will ultimately distinguish indefinitely many absurd atomic states that would be awkward to model in terms of sets of possible worlds. More immediately, we will also want to distinguish states that are part of all the same possible worlds. This is motivated by the need to distinguish between thinking a premise and thinking logically equivalent conclusions that may be inferred from it. In the context of an account of inferential reasoning, part of our job is to understand how we might succeed and fail in realizing that some conclusion is *entailed* by our premises, that is, *true in all possible worlds in which the premises are true*. If we begin by characterizing the representational content of our thoughts as identical to the set of possible worlds in which they are true, then it will be cumbersome to try to allow for failure. On the plausible view that we think *contents*, if all there is to the content of our thoughts is the set of worlds in which those thoughts are true, then thinking the premise encompasses thinking the conclusion. To the chagrin of everyone from small children to senior mathematicians, the business of thinking usually does not seem quite as straightforward as that. While we do not have to be committed to ruling out an erotetic theory founded on possible worlds with additional structure (also see remarks about possible worlds semantics of natural language in section 1.8), we will set this avenue aside for now.

In the fragment of the erotetic theory that is purely concerned with the equivalent of sentential reasoning, sets of alternative states are what make up a *view*. The mental configurations involved in reasoning have views as their representational contents. The process of reasoning is the process of effecting "changes in view" (Harman, 1986), which, according to the erotetic theory, means transitioning from a mental configuration with one view as its representational content to a mental configuration with another view as its representational content. The erotetic theory is a content-based theory of reason, holding that the structure of mental representations only makes a difference to reasoning insofar as it corresponds to structure in its representational contents. As a result, the erotetic theory is specified directly in terms of contents and transitions between contents (i.e. in the realm of semantics).

According to the erotetic theory, views are incrementally taken on board as issues and answers. The default aim is to reduce the main set of alternative states in the view we have taken on board as a question. In the example we have just considered, the premise "there is an ace and a queen or a king and a ten" is treated by our reasoning capacity as raising the issue of whether we are in an ace-and-queen situation or in a king-and-ten situation. The next premise, "there is a king" is then taken as a maximally strong answer to that question, reducing our question to those alternatives involving kings, leading us to conclude that we are in a king-and-ten situation, since the only alternative with a king in it envisaged by our question also includes a ten. Of course, taking a premise as an answer presupposes having a question, so the illusory inference should be less available if we are provided with the categorical premise before the disjunctive premise. We will shortly see that there is indeed a relevant order effect.

Though the theory holds that further information supplied to reason as premises will always be regarded through the lens of issues and answers, there are of course other moves that reason is capable of. The theory is, in the first instance, a capacity theory in the sense that it describes the moves that an agent can make in reasoning. Our reasoning operations will broadly divide into ones that roughly tend to increase the "questionyness" of our view, and those that roughly tend to reduce it.

While the erotetic theory has it that it is the core aim of our natural reasoning capacity that yields a classically invalid inference in the example we just considered, the theory in fact accounts for both our default tendency to commit fallacies as well as for our ability to reason correctly and recognize our mistakes. We will ultimately see that illusory inferences are blocked if the reasoner takes on board enough further issues, though this is effortful and not automatic and, indeed, requires a willful departure from our primary aim of answering issues as directly as possible.

In the rest of this chapter I will make the erotetic theory precise until we have a fully fledged theory of propositional reasoning. The system maintains the core ideas in Koralus and Mascarenhas (2013), but considerably reworks and simplifies the 2013 formalism, in part by recasting it in terms of set theory. With the help of this recast formalism, we will be able to perspicuously define "good" inferences as inferences in erotetic equilibrium, where the scope of that equilibrium is potentially restricted to some topic of inquiry. Roughly, making an erotetic equilibrium inference with respect to a topic of inquiry means making an inference that would still go through regardless of how many further questions from this topic of inquiry we raise before attempting to treat any information as an answer. The special case of classically valid inference is recast as erotetic equilibrium without restriction. As we will see formally in due course, treating premises as maximally strong answers to our questions can lead us astray, but we are on solid ground if our inferences are in equilibrium with respect to further questions that might be raised as we try to reason to a conclusion.

2.1 Defining Views

A basic view is a set of alternative complex states, where complex states are themselves sets of atomic states. In the first instance, we say that we have states like the state of John Smith sitting at the table, and the state of it raining in Oxford. For the purposes of propositional reasoning, we can treat such states as atomic, that is, not decomposing into smaller entities. Complex states consist of sets of states of this kind. For example, we have a complex state that has as its elements the atomic state of John Smith sitting at the table and the atomic state of it raining in Oxford. We then have basic views as sets of such complex states. For example, we have, {{Smith is sitting at the table }, {it is raining in Oxford}}. We can think of a view as a question of which of its alternatives holds, e.g. "Am I in a situation in which Smith is sitting at the table or in a situation in which it is raining in Oxford?"

The primary structure in which views are couched are sets. We will just briefly consider some truisms about sets as a warmup. Sets are only distinguished by the elements they have and are not to be confused with their (multiple) algebraic representations on the page. For example, $\{a,b,c\}$ is the set that has a, b, c, and nothing else, as its members, and this set is identical to $\{b,c,a\}$. You cannot be "more" than a member of a set, so $\{a,a\} = \{a\}$. Next, $b \in \{a,b,c\}$ means that b is an element of $\{a,b,c\}$. Being an element of a set S is not the same as being an element of a set that is itself an element of S. For example, $\{a\} \in \{\{a\},b\}$, but $a \notin \{\{a\},b\}$ (where $\notin$ means "not an element of").

Views (for the purposes of this chapter) are made up of sets of atomic states, which include states that are the negations of other atomic states. For p an atom, we represent the negation of p with $\bar{p}$, which we also treat as an atom. We use this notation instead of '¬', to emphasize that views only include negation at the level of atoms. We can alternatively regard the set of atoms as the set of atomic verifiers and falsifiers. Unlike in classical model theory in logic, we need to include "negative states," or falsifiers, in our views, because our views do not represent fully specific ways the world might be, which means that we cannot take the absence of a commitment to something being the case (the absence of a verifier) as a commitment to it *not* being the case. This aligns the structure of our views with that of truth-maker semantics (Fine, 2012; van Fraassen, 1969). In the below definition we use the standard convention that the union of S_1 and S_2, written $S_1 \cup S_2$, is the set of all the elements of S_1 and all the elements of S_2. We then take the "big union" of a set S, written $\bigcup S$, to be the union of all the elements of S.

Definition 2.1 (Atoms $\mathcal{A}$). Let $\mathcal{A}$ be the set of atomic verifiers p and their corresponding atomic falsifiers $\bar{p}$.

Moving on, states, as would be articulated by a conjunction, are sets of atoms. Instead of speaking of "states," we could speak of "situations," but we understand them to include impossible states like the state consisting of p and $\bar{p}$. Now, there is no barrier to giving truth-conditions for views in terms of the more familiar possible-worlds framework, though we will not be concerned with that for the purposes of our project. Very briefly, we can understand a world to be a maximal set of atomic states. A *possible* world would then be a maximal set of consistent atomic states. We can then say that a set of states Γ is true at a possible world w if at least one of the states represented by $\gamma_1, \ldots, \gamma_n$ is part of w. We in turn take a state γ to be part of w if all of the verifier atoms in γ are included in w and none of the atoms in w have corresponding falsifier atoms in γ. We could go even further and take atomic truth-makers to be the sets of possible worlds in which the corresponding atomic sentences are true and atomic false-makers as the sets of possible worlds in which the corresponding atomic sentences are false (Fine (2012). We will briefly return to why we want to stick with talk about states rather than possible worlds a bit later in the section. For now, we press on to get our basic definitions on the table.

We will allow that a state can be the empty set, corresponding to no commitments at all, making it a *tabula rasa* state. For convenience, we will notate the empty set as 0 when it occurs as a state. Since its lack of commitments means it can never be false, it can be thought of as corresponding to the *truth* atom in classical logic. We can then define states as follows. The set of all subsets of a set S has all sets that can be formed from elements of S as its members.

Definition 2.2 (States $\mathbb{S}$).
Let $\mathbb{S}$ be the set of finite subsets of $\mathbb{A}$. Write "0" for "{ }" in $\mathbb{S}$.

There is a distinguished subset of primitively absurd states that we will further define.

Definition 2.3 (Primitive absurd states $\mathbb{K}$).
Let $\mathbb{K}_{\subseteq \mathbb{S}}$ contain, $\forall p_{\in \mathcal{A}}$, at least: $\{p, \bar{p}\}$

Primitive absurd states will play a crucial role in reasoning, particularly once we move to more expressive extensions of the theory in later chapters.

Primitive absurdities are the sorts of states that we hold are transparently recognizable as absurd by a reasoner.

As noted, views amount to issues consisting of multiple alternative states. In addition, views envisage alternative states under *suppositions*. So, for example, we could have a view amounting to, "supposing that it is Hilary Term or Trinity Term, am I in a situation in which Smith is sitting at the desk or in a situation in which it is raining in Oxford?" We regiment this in a view by indexing a main set of states ("am I in a situation in which Smith is sitting at the desk or in a situation in which it is raining in Oxford?") to a set of states corresponding to our supposition ("it is Hilary Term or Trinity Term"). The equivalent of a supposition-free issue would then be a view indexed to the set with 0 (i.e. "truth") as its sole element. We can then define views as follows. For two objects S_1, S_2, we use the notation $\langle S_1, S_2 \rangle$ to denote the ordered pair of S_1 and S_2. Using ordered pairs allows us to distinguish the main set of alternatives (the first element of the pair) from the set of alternatives corresponding to the supposition of a views (the second element of the pair).

Definition 2.4 (Views $\mathbb{V}$).
For Γ, Θ finite subsets of $\mathbb{S}$, $\langle \Gamma, \Theta \rangle \in \mathbb{V}$ (abbreviated $\Gamma^\Theta \in \mathbb{V}$). Write $\top$ for $\{0\}^{\{0\}}$ and $\bot$ for $\emptyset^{\{0\}}$.

A view can be "empty," as in $\emptyset^{\{0\}}$ meaning that there are no states at all, as far as the view is concerned, which corresponds to the contradiction (*falsum*) in classical logic. Similarly, a view can make no commitments at all so that it is guaranteed to be true, as in $\{0\}^{\{0\}}$.

In order for a reasoner to have a picture of the world, a single view is not enough. Sets of multiple views make up our overall commitments with regard to what is the case. On the algorithmic level, we think of reasoning as involving transitions between states of inference. States of inference consist of representations corresponding to our cognitively available views about a variety of things we might consider, such as a set of premises, and a view that is the current focus of our thinking. We will call the content of such states of inference *commitments*.

Definition 2.5 (Commitments $\mathbb{C}$).
For $C \subseteq \mathbb{V}, G \in \mathbb{V}, \langle C, G \rangle \in \mathbb{C}$.

We will be adopting some notational simplifications for use in examples. For the fragment of the theory presented in this chapter, the main simplification is that we suppress the curly braces around the atoms of a state and write a state simply as a string of atom letters, without any significance to their order. In addition, we suppress suppositions if they are {0}. Below are a few indicative examples of this notation.

> **Example 4.** (Some views)
> Mary jumps or John crouches.
> Simplified notation: $\{M,J\}$ Official notation: $\{\{M\},\{J\}\}$
>
> Either John dances, Bill dances, or Mary does not smoke.
> Simplified notation: $\{J,B,\bar{M}\}$ Official notation: $\{\{J\},\{B\},\{\bar{M}\}\}$
>
> Supposing there is gym class, Mary jumps and John crouches.
> Simplified notation: $\{MJ\}^{\{G\}}$ Official notation: $\{\{M,J\}\}^{\{\{G\}\}}$

There is no such thing as sentential negation in views. However, we will shortly define a negation operation corresponding to sentential negation that allows us to translate negated (compound) sentences into views.

First, we define a notion of *product* on sets of states. The Product operation "multiplies" the alternatives in the sets of states that serve as its arguments. For example, if I am to envisage the alternative situations *A* and *not A* in light of a further set of alternative situations *B* and *not B*, then I have to envisage four alternatives (*A and B, A and not B, B and not A, not A and not B*). To construct the definition, we will use the standard set-builder notation $\{x : \Phi(x)\}$ to stand for the set of all things *x* that satisfy the condition in Φ.

Definition 2.6 (Product of sets of states).
Let $\Gamma, \Delta \subseteq \mathbb{S}$ be finite sets of states. We define the product or conjunction of Γ and Δ to be

$$\Gamma \otimes \Delta = \{\gamma \cup \delta : \gamma \in \Gamma, \delta \in \Delta\}.$$

Even though we do not have the equivalent of the negation of sentences in views, we do have an operation that takes us from one view to another view that is logically equivalent to its negation. First, we merely consider sets of states. From a logician's perspective, negation for sets of states takes the form of an algorithm pushing negation down to the level of atoms *à la* De Morgan.

Definition 2.7 (Negation on sets of states).
For a finite set of states $\Gamma = \{\gamma_1, \ldots, \gamma_n\}$, we define the *negation* by:

$$\hat{\Gamma} = \{\{\bar{p}\} : p \in \gamma_1\} \otimes \ldots \otimes \{\{\bar{p}\} : p \in \gamma_n\},$$

We now provide an interpretation function from sentences in propositional logic into views, followed by an articulation function that takes us from views to sentences in propositional logic. In defining both, we assume for convenience that the set of atoms in views and in the language of propositional logic are shared.

Definition 2.8 (Interpretation function $\circ : \mathcal{L}_S \mapsto \mathbb{V}$).
For a formula $\varphi \in \mathcal{L}_S$ we define a finite set of states $\varphi^{\circ\circ}$ by recursion on the formula φ. We then have $\varphi^\circ = (\varphi^{\circ\circ})^{\{0\}}$:

$(\varphi \vee \psi)^{\circ\circ} = \varphi^{\circ\circ} \cup \psi^{\circ\circ}$;
$(\varphi \wedge \psi)^{\circ\circ} = \varphi^{\circ\circ} \otimes \psi^{\circ\circ}$;
$(\neg \varphi)^{\circ\circ} = \widehat{\varphi^{\circ\circ}}$;
$\top^{\circ\circ} = \{\{\}\}$;
$\bot^{\circ\circ} = \{\}$;
$A^{\circ\circ} = \{\{A\}\}$ for an atom A.

Note that we are not using views with non-trivial suppositions in this interpretation function, nor are we offering a clause for the conditional. Of course, this makes this interpretation function no less complete from the perspective of sentential logic, since material implication can be paraphrased away without loss. However, "if" is clearly more interesting and subtle and deserves its own chapter, following this one.

We can also provide an "articulation" procedure that allows us to express a view with a sentence in propositional logic.

Definition 2.9 (Articulation $*$ of views as sentences in $\mathcal{L}_S$).
For $A, \bar{A} \in \mathcal{A}$, we define $A^* = A$ and $\bar{A}^* = \neg A$.
Let $\gamma = \{P_1, \ldots, P_n\} \in \mathbb{S}$ be a state. We define $\gamma^* = P_1^* \wedge \ldots \wedge P_n^*$ for $n \neq 0$, and for $n = 0$ define $\gamma^* = \top$. Let $\Gamma = \{\gamma_1, \ldots, \gamma_n\}$ be a finite set of states. We define $(\Gamma^{\{0\}})^* = \gamma_1^* \vee \ldots \vee \gamma_n^*$ for $n \neq 0$, and for $n = 0$ define $(\Gamma^{\{0\}})^* = \bot$.

This articulation procedure requires an arbitrarily chosen ordering on the atoms in a state and on the states in Γ. Since any ordering will give a logically equivalent result, this is not a defect. The lack of a unique result is due to the fact that while languages like English and propositional logic have linearly ordered expressions, views do not. This is not surprising, since views are in the realm of contents, rather than in the realm of syntactic vehicles. There is no reason to assume that thought is completely linearly ordered in the way externalized language is. Indeed, on some views, natural language is a cognitive tool for creating a mapping between unordered thought systems and inherently ordered articulation systems (Chomsky, 1995). Another observation is that the procedure does not translate views with non-trivial suppositions. This does not render the procedure incomplete, since we will see soon that any view with a non-trivial supposition can be directly converted into a view without one.

The articulation and interpretation procedures just given are duals, which can be seen fairly easily be observing how the clauses of the procedures reverse each other. We leave more detailed discussions of proofs for a later chapter once we consider the more powerful interpretation and articulation procedures for views and predicate logic.

2.2 Updating Questions with Answers

In this section, we will define the first batch of operations of the erotetic theory that will allow us to model the basic illusory inference pattern from the start of this chapter.

First, we define an operation that allows us to take the product of views in a way that is similar to the product operation on sets of states we defined for our interpretation procedure, and that roughly has the force of conjunction. The product of Γ^Θ with Δ^Ψ is a "pseudo-Cartesian product" (with sets instead of ordered pairs) of all those states in Γ that contain all the atoms of at least one state in Ψ, with the states in Δ. Meanwhile, Θ stays unchanged. We can think of this as a conjunction of states in Δ with those states in Γ that fit the supposition Ψ.

Definition 2.10 (Product).

$$\Gamma^\Theta \otimes \Delta^\Psi = (\{\gamma_{\in\Gamma} \cup \delta_{\in\Delta} : \exists \psi_{\in\Psi}(\psi \subseteq \gamma)\} \cup \{\gamma_{\in\Gamma} : \neg\exists\psi_{\in\Psi}(\psi \subseteq \gamma)\})^\Theta$$

$$\bigotimes_{i\in P}\Delta_i^{\Psi_i} = \{0\}^{\{0\}} \otimes \Delta_1^{\Psi_1} \otimes \ldots \otimes \Delta_n^{\Psi_n}, \text{ given } \Delta_1^{\Psi_1}\ldots\Delta_n^{\Psi_n}$$

For example, if we apply this operation with $\{pr, p, qs\}^{\{0\}}$ as the left argument and $\{t, u\}^{\{p\}}$ as the right argument, we obtain $\{prt, prupt, pu, qs\}^{\{0\}}$.

Notice that if we are dealing with two views $\Gamma^{\{0\}}$ and $\Delta^{\{0\}}$ that have no non-trivial suppositions, then $\otimes$ becomes commutative. Formally, in those cases, we have $\Gamma^{\{0\}} \otimes \Delta^{\{0\}} = \Delta^{\{0\}} \otimes \Gamma^{\{0\}}$. We also get commutativity if nothing in the supposition Ψ fits Γ and nothing in the supposition Θ fits Δ. This means that in many cases, we can unambiguously abstract sequences of products of views as $\Delta_1^{\Psi_1}\ldots\Delta_n^{\Psi_n}$ as $\bigotimes_{i\in P}\Delta_i^{\Psi_i} = \{0\}^{\{0\}} \otimes \Delta_1^{\Psi_1} \otimes \ldots \otimes \Delta_n^{\Psi_n}$. We will continue to suppress indices in our notation if no non-trivial suppositions are involved.

Example 5. (Applying product)
(i) $\{\gamma, \delta\} \otimes \{\varepsilon, \theta\} = \{\gamma \cup \varepsilon, \gamma \cup \theta, \delta \cup \varepsilon, \delta \cup \theta\}$
(ii) $\{\{p_1, q_1\}, \{r_1, s_1\}\} \otimes \{\{p_2, q_2\}, \{r_2, s_2\}\}$
$= \{\{p_1, q_1, p_2, q_2\}, \{r_1, s_1, p_2, q_2\}, \{p_1, q_1, r_2, s_2\}, \{r_1, s_1, r_2, s_2\}\}$
(iii) $\{\gamma, \delta\} \otimes \emptyset = \emptyset$ since there is nothing in $\emptyset$ with which to form any states.
(iv) $\{\gamma, \delta\} \otimes \{0\} = \{\gamma, \delta\}$
(v) $\{0\} \otimes \{\gamma, \delta\} = \{\gamma, \delta\}$

With the foregoing, we can now provide a sketch of an interpretation rule for conjunctions and atomic statements in English into views. We will generally provide interpretation rules for the key fragments of language driving the premises and conclusions we try to understand in this book. To avoid overburdening an already challenging discussion with extensive discussions of grammar, we eschew any attempt to make those interpretation rules formally systematic. It is enough for our purposes to tie down interpretations into views sufficiently so that we can avoid falling into the trap of using ad hoc interpretations that would lessen our explanatory power with respect to natural language reasoning data. We will adopt the convention that $[\![\varphi]\!]$ stands for the linguistic meaning of φ in terms of views.

Definition 2.11 (Informal interpretation rule for "and").
$[\![\varphi \text{ and } \psi]\!] = [\![\varphi]\!] \otimes [\![\psi]\!]$

Since we are only dealing with sentential reasoning in this chapter, we will help ourselves to directly interpreting simple sentences in terms of "atomic" views.

Example 6.
$[\![\text{There is an ace and there is a king}]\!] = [\![\text{there is an ace}]\!] \otimes [\![\text{there is a king}]\!] = \{\{a\}\} \otimes \{\{k\}\} = \{\{a, k\}\}$.

Next, we need to be able to interpret "or." What is key to the erotetic theory explanation of illusory inferences from premises involving "or" is that disjunctions raise issues that we then attempt to answer with further premises. Several semanticists, in the UMass (Kratzer and Shimoyama, 2002), Amsterdam (Groenendijk, 2009; Ciardelli, 2009), and Paris (Mascarenhas, 2009) traditions have proposed that disjunctions in natural language are *inquisitive*;

that they raise questions. As noted before, questions or issues, as understood here, are in the realm of contents, not to be confused with an interrogative sentences. We take issues to be sets of alternatives states, so we will need to define a "sum" operation to build up such sets.

Moving on, the Sum operation allows us to bring together the alternatives of the main set of alternatives of two views into one set.

Definition 2.12 (Sum).
$$\Gamma^\Theta \oplus \Delta^\Theta = (\Gamma \cup \Delta)^\Theta$$
$$\bigoplus_{i \in P} \Delta_i^\Psi = \emptyset^\Psi \oplus \Delta_1^\Psi \oplus \ldots \oplus \Delta_n^\Psi$$

For example, $\{\{P\}\} \oplus \{\{Q\}\} = \{\{P\}, \{Q\}\}$. Clearly, where defined, $\oplus$ is commutative.

Definition 2.13 (Informal interpretation rule for "or"). Where defined,

$$[\![\varphi \text{ or } \psi]\!] = [\![\varphi]\!] \oplus [\![\psi]\!]$$

Example 7.
$[\![\text{There is an ace or there is a king}]\!] = [\![\text{there is an ace}]\!] \oplus [\![\text{there is a king}]\!] = \{\{a\}\} \cup \{\{k\}\} = \{\{a\}, \{k\}\}$.

Notice that $\oplus$ is only defined for matching suppositions on the views being combined. As a result, the interpretation rule for "or" is undefined for sentences like, "supposing it's raining, I'll take an umbrella or supposing it's not raining, I'll take a hat" (assuming for the sake of argument that "supposing" roughly translates to view suppositions). This seems reasonable, since it often feels unnatural to give such sentences proper logically disjunctive interpretations with "supposing it's raining, I'll take an umbrella" and "supposing it's not raining, I'll take a hat" as genuine disjuncts. Otherwise, the following disjunctive syllogism inference should seem like a natural inference: (P1) Supposing it's raining, I'll take an umbrella or supposing it's windy, I'll take a hat. (P2) It's windy and I'm not taking a hat. Therefore, Supposing it's raining, I'll take an umbrella. However, this does not at all seem like an attractive inference.

We can now turn to the disjunctive illusory inference problems from the start of the chapter. Koralus and Mascarenhas (2016) found that around 92% of 241 participants from the Amazon Mechanical Turk community freely made the illusory inference in the below example (without making further mistakes on the same problem), which we can now annotate with view interpretations. As before, we will use our abbreviated notation for reasoning examples.

Example 8. (*Illusory inference from disjunction*)
P_1 There is an ace and a queen, or else a king and a ten. $\{aq, kt\}$
P_2 There is a king. $\{k\}$
Question: *What if anything follows?*
C There is a ten (and a king). [92% of respondents] $\{t\}$

According to the erotetic theory, the default procedure is to sequentially update a view of issue under investigation with premises as they come in, treating later premises as maximally strong answers to issues raised by earlier premises, where this is possible.

We now define how one view can be treated as a maximally strong answer to another view. We define an Answer procedure in terms of a notion of the extent to which a given alternative state y in an issue is supported by a view Δ^Ψ we are treating as an answer.

First, we define a notion of answer potential. There will be more than one notion of answer potential to be discussed in this book. For now, we will be concerned with a notion of *atomic* answer potential, having to do with the amount of atomic overlap between two views. The overlap between a set S_1 and a set S_2, notated $S_1 \cap S_2$, is the set of all elements that are in both S_1 and S_2. The number of things in a set S, the cardinality of the set, is notated as $|S|$. For example, $|\{a, b\}| = 2$. For Γ a set of states, we let $\mathcal{A}(\Gamma) = \bigcup \Gamma$.

Definition 2.14 (Atomic answer potential). $\Gamma[\Delta]^{AP} = |\mathcal{A}(\Gamma) \cap \mathcal{A}(\Delta)|$

Having a graded notion of answer potential as a central workhorse, we can observe that the erotetic theory shares some of the aspects that make Bayesianism initially plausible, notably the idea that reasoners arrive at conclusions by finding partial support for those conclusions, where that support often comes in *degrees*. We will see in a later chapter that, with further additions in expressive power, answer potential will in fact have a Bayesian special case for a more expressive notion of views that capture probability.

It is possible to conceive of other notions of answer potential. For example, one could try to define notions like "confirmation" potential, "representativeness" potential, or "relevance" potential between views, and use them in the system instead of the above. However, depending on how such alternative notions are defined, they may not conserve the attractive properties of the erotetic theory with regard to data coverage and with regard to explaining the possibility of systematically valid reasoning, which we consider toward the end of this chapter.

We now define the result of treating a view Δ^Ψ as an answer to a view Γ^Θ as the set of those alternatives in Γ whose constituents have maximal answer potential support from Δ. This is most perspicuously expressed formally using what mathematicians call the arguments of the maxima of a function f, notated $\arg\max f$, which are the *arguments* of f that maximize f. For example, if $\{John, Mary, Bill\}$ is my set of friends and $f(x)$ is a function that returns the amount of alcohol consumed by its argument, then $\arg\max_{x\in\{John, Mary, Bill\}} f(x)$ returns those of my friends that drink the most. Using this notation, our Answer operation will then take $\{y : y \in \Gamma\}$ as the domain of arguments and answer potential from Δ for $\{\{p\} : p \in y\}$ as the function to be maximized.

There are several conventions we adopt throughout to keep the definitions of inference operations as simple as possible. Firstly, we define operations as going to work on views even though we will later formally define a state of inference as a pair of a view and a set of commitments. We also stipulate that an operation returns its left argument untouched if it is not otherwise defined for the particular set of arguments.

The core definitions of operations in our theory are of a form that could be paraphrased into English as "the result of the procedure OP applied to a view Γ with the argument X is the view Γ'" as $\Gamma[X]^{OP} = \Gamma'$. This notation is familiar in certain areas of semantics (Veltman, 1996).

Definition 2.15 (Answer).
$$\Gamma^\Theta[\Delta^{\{0\}}]^A = (\arg\max_{y\in\Gamma} \Delta[\{\{p\} : p \in y\}]^{AP})^\Theta$$

Answer-updating a view Γ^Θ with a view $\Delta^{\{0\}}$ leaves those alternatives in Γ that have maximal overlap with everything that is envisaged in any of the alternatives in the answer Δ. This will be our way of formalizing the idea that we treat one view as a maximally strong answer to another view considered as a question. Note that the Answer operation is deliberately only defined for cases in which the supposition of the argument view is $\{0\}$ (i.e. no substantive supposition).

We can now apply Answer-update to the previous example.

> **Example 9.** (*Illusory inference from disjunction*)
> $\Gamma = \{aq, kt\}; \Delta = \{k\}; \Gamma[\Delta]^A = \{kt\}$.
> The state $\{k,t\}$ has a greater number of atoms in common with the atoms that have been mentioned in the answer (i.e. k), compared to the alternative $\{a,q\}$ (nothing in common with anything in the answer), so only $\{k,t\}$ remains after the application of Answer.

As we can see in the example, Answer-update generates the observed illusory inference. A notable feature of explaining the illusory inference as a result of treating the categorical premise as an answer to the inquisitive premise is that it predicts an effect of premise order. After all, you cannot treat something as an answer to an issue without having the issue first, which is reflected in the fact that Answer does *not* treat Γ (the issue) and Δ (the putative answer) symmetrically. If we provide the inquisitive premise *after* the categorical premise that would be serviceable as an answer, the reasoner needs to make an extra step to make sure she updates the second premise with the first rather than the other way round (otherwise no new conclusions are generated).

We put this to the test in Koralus and Mascarenhas (2016) and indeed found a decrease in the uptake of the illusory inference in the reversed order that was statistically significant and that did not apply to control problems of similar complexity. The control problems were such that finding a new conclusion does not depend on treating one premise as an answer to another.

> **Example 10.** (*Reversed premises blocking illusory inferences*)
> $\Gamma = \{k\}; \Delta = \{aq, kt\}; \Gamma[\Delta]^A = \{k\}$.
> With reversed order, Answer does not produce any new conclusions.

Notice this order effect would not be predicted on a view on which we directly interpret a disjunctive statement as pragmatically strengthened in a way that would yield the illusory inference. For example, if we interpreted the premise as "there is an ace and a queen *and nothing else* or a king and a ten *and nothing else*," then the entailment to the conclusion would hold on a strengthened reading regardless of premise order.

We have to consider illusory inference patterns in cases of further complexity, and we will also have to consider how they differ in detail from control problems in which participants have no problems drawing correct inferences. In order to do this, we will first have to cover some more machinery in service of our goal of ending up with a fully fledged theory of propositional reasoning.

The erotetic theory holds that we do not just update a question with a premise to try to directly answer it but that we also try to further develop whatever remains of the question with the new information we take on board from additional premises. We regiment this idea by saying that when we encounter a new premise, we first Answer with it and then "Merge" with it to develop what remains after Answer with the information in the new premise. In definitions to follow, we will frequently chain operations. For example, $G_0[G_1]^{O_1}[G_2]^{O_2}$ denotes the result of applying $[G_1]^{O_1}$ to G_0 and then applying $[G_2]^{O_2}$ to the result.

Definition 2.16 (Update).
$$\Gamma^\Theta[\Delta^\Psi]^\circlearrowleft = \Gamma^\Theta[\Delta^\Psi]^A[\Delta^\Psi]^M$$

To use this definition we now have to define Merge.

Definition 2.17 (Merge).
$$\Gamma^\Theta[\Delta^\Psi]^M = \bigoplus_{\gamma \in \Gamma}\left(\{\gamma\}^\Theta \otimes \Delta^\Psi\right).$$

As the reader can easily verify, for the cases in this chapter, Merge reduces to Product. We will nevertheless write Merge in a slightly different way that will make it easier to understand gradually more complicated versions of this operation in later chapters. The key observation we highlight here is that we can compute a product with the internal argument for each of the states in the external argument separately, and then gather up the results. This way of splitting things up will be helpful once some of those individual steps will involve substitutions, once we get to the equivalent of variable instantiation in Chapter 4.

We will consider some examples of update. Firstly, the reader can easily verify that the example of the illusory inference from disjunction goes through by simply updating the view of the disjunctive premise with the view of the categorical premise.

Example 11.
(i) $\{aq, kt\}[\{k\}]^\circlearrowleft = \{kt\}$
(ii) $\{j, m\}[\{d\}^{\{j\}}]^\circlearrowleft[\{e\}^{\{m\}}]^\circlearrowleft = \{jd, me\}$, which can be glossed as, "Either

> John smokes or Mary smokes. Supposing John smokes, John drinks. Supposing Mary smokes, Mary eats. Therefore, either John smokes and drinks or Mary smokes and drinks."

The studies of illusory inferences discussed in this section used disjunctive syllogism inferences as control problems. Naturally, we next want to show that the erotetic theory also captures the fact the vast majority of participants produced correct conclusions for those problems. To do this, we will have to find a way to deal with contradictory alternatives in views and define an operation corresponding to an inferential step to eliminate them.

2.3 Negating and Factoring

So far, we have only defined negation for sets of states. We now extend this definition to views.

Definition 2.18 (Negation).
$[\Gamma^\Theta]^N = (\Theta^{\{0\}} \otimes (\widehat{\Gamma})^{\{0\}})$

As defined, negation takes the supposition of a view and conjoins it with the negation of the view's main set of alternative states (where we already defined the negation of a set of states earlier). This amounts to taking the negation of "Γ supposing Θ" to be "Θ and not-Γ."

We will directly turn this into an interpretation rule as well.

Definition 2.19 (Informal interpretation rule for "not").

$$[\![\text{not } \varphi]\!] = [\![\varphi]\!]^N$$

Example 12.
(i) It is not the case that P or Q or R

$$[\{\{p\},\{q\},\{r\}\}]^N = \{\bar{p}\bar{q}\bar{r}\}$$

(ii) It is not the case that P and Q and R

$$[\{\{p,q,r\}\}]^N = \{\{\bar{p}\},\{\bar{q}\},\{\bar{r}\}\}$$

(iii) It is not the case that, supposing S, ((P and Q) or R)

$$[\{\{p,q\},\{r\}\}^{\{s\}}]^N = \{s\} \otimes \{\bar{p}\bar{r}, \bar{q}, \bar{r}\} = \{\{s, \bar{p}, \bar{r}\}, \{s, \bar{q}, \bar{r}\}\}$$

Of course, on this definition of negation, it is computationally more costly to compute and represent the negation of a conjunction than the negation of a disjunction, if we want to access all possible alternative scenarios that are compatible with those negations. Experimental evidence supports this asymmetry. Khemlani et al. (2012b) found that participants were much better at reporting what is possible given a denied disjunction than at reporting what is possible given a denied conjunction. On the view of negation just provided, this is to be expected. In the case of a denied disjunction, the view directly corresponds to the set of possible scenarios (there is only one). In the case of conjunction, the view does not make all distinct possibilities explicit (we will consider how to make them explicit in due course).

As is clear from the definitions provided so far, the theory distinguishes no fewer contradictory representational states than there are atomic representations. $\{p\bar{p}\}$, $\{q\bar{q}\}$, etc. are all independent absurd views. Absurd states are not automatically eliminated in the theory. There is in fact some evidence that reasoners do not automatically recognize contradictions (Morris and Hasson, 2010). However, we clearly have the ability to recognize absurd putative possibilities and eliminate them, though doing so does not appear to be free of processing costs.

We will define an operation that allows us to try to remove things from a view, leaving potentially reduced view as a remainder. We want to be able to get what remains of a view once we remove what is absurd. In addition, we want to be able to get what remains of a view once we remove an issue that is in some sense wholly contained in it. The operation we will define for this purpose is Factor. We start with the case in which we are trying to factor out absurdities. We use $S_1 \subseteq S_2$ to mean that all elements of S_1 are also elements of S_2.

Definition 2.20 (Factor part 1).
For $\Delta^\Psi = \bot$,
$$\Gamma^\Theta[\bot]^F = \{\gamma \in \Gamma : \neg \exists \delta_{\in \mathbb{K}}(\delta \subseteq \gamma)\}^\Theta$$

For the case in which we are factoring out $\bot$, we are invoking our definition of primitively absurd states $\mathbb{K}$. For propositional reasoning, the only primitive absurdity derives from the law of excluded middle. Thus, for example, $\{p, q\bar{q}, s\}[\bot]^F = \{p, s\}$.

With this machinery, we can start to work through disjunctive syllogism inferences. Consider the following which yielded 89% correct inferences from 241 participants on Amazon Mechanical Turk.

> **Example 13.** (*Disjunctive syllogism*)
> P_1 There is an ace and a king or a queen and a jack. $\{ak, qj\}$
> P_2 There isn't an ace. $\{\bar{a}\}$
> Question: *What if anything follows?*

The canonical conclusion most reasoners draw is that there is a queen and a jack. We can begin to approach this formally as follows. Starting from a *tabula rasa* view $\Gamma = \{0\}$, we update with view interpretations of the premises in sequence. Thus, we have $\{0\}[[P_1]]^\circ[[P_2]]^\circ$, which gives us $\{0\}[\{ak, qj\}]^\circ[\{\bar{a}\}]^\circ = \{ak, qj\}[\{\bar{a}\}]^\circ$. Now, Answering $\{ak, qj\}$ with $\{\bar{a}\}$ does not eliminate any alternatives, so all that remains is to Merge, yielding $\{ak\bar{a}, qj\bar{a}\}$. We can now apply the Factor operation $[\bot]^F$, yielding $\{qj\bar{a}\}$. In words, we have inferred "there is a queen and a jack but not an ace." This is fine as it goes, but we noticeably take the canonical conclusion to be that there is a queen and a jack. This is not a problem that arises because of the rote nature of disjunctive syllogism; there is a similarly strong tendency toward a reduced conclusion in the unfamiliar illusory inference problems as well. How do we account for these reduced conclusions?

According to the erotetic theory, what yields the "smaller" canonical conclusion in the foregoing example is a reflection of the general aim to reduce the complexity of our issues in search of novel answers. One way to reduce complexity is to find answers that eliminate alternatives. Another way is to eliminate absurdities. A final important way to reduce complexity is to factor out given issues and retain only what remains.

To define an appropriate notion of Factor for this purpose, we first need a notion of view division. The division operation intuitively removes a question Δ that is fully present in a question Γ. We use $\exists x \Phi(x)$ to mean "there exists an x satisfying Φ," $\iota x \Phi(x)$ to mean "the *unique* x satisfying Φ," and we use $\forall x \Phi(x)$ to mean "for all x, x satisfies Φ."

Definition 2.21 (Division).
If $\forall \delta_{\in \Delta} \exists \psi_{\in \Psi} \exists \gamma_{\in \Gamma}(\delta \subseteq \gamma \land \psi \subseteq \gamma)$, then
$\Gamma^\Theta \oslash \Delta^\Psi = \{\gamma \oslash_\Gamma \Delta^\Psi : \gamma \in \Gamma\}^\Theta$, where
$\gamma \oslash_\Gamma \Delta^\Psi = \gamma - \iota\delta(\delta \in \Delta \land \delta \subseteq \gamma \land \exists \psi_{\in \Psi}(\psi \subseteq \gamma))$

This complex definition is best understood by considering examples. We first consider examples with trivial suppositions.

> **Example 14.**
> (Factoring out a categorical fact) $\{pq, pr\} \oslash \{p\} = \{q, r\}$.
> (Factoring out a categorical fact but only targeting alternatives that match a supposition) $\{pqs, prs, pr\} \oslash \{p\}^{\{s\}} = \{qs, rs, pr\}$.
> (Separating orthogonal questions) $\{pr, qs, ps, qr\} \oslash \{p, q\} = \{r, s\}$.
> (No effect without a unique matching alternative in Δ) $\{pr, qs\} \oslash \{p, r\} = \{pr, qs\}$.
> (Factoring with a Δ that only has overlap with some alternatives Γ) $\{pr, qs, t\} \oslash \{p, q\} = \{r, s, t\}$.
> (All alternatives in Δ must be contained in some alternative in Γ) $\{pr, qs\} \oslash \{p, q, t\} = \{pr, qs\}$.
> (Factor may sometimes reduce an alternative to an empty molecule) $\{pr, qs, p\} \oslash \{p, q\} = \{r, s, 0\}$.

We can then use division to define Factor. As in the case of Merge, a simpler formula could be had for the purely propositional case (division suffices), but we instead write the formula in a way that will make the continuity with later chapters easier to recognize and help us build up expressivity modularly.

Definition 2.22 (Factor part 2).
For $\Delta^\Psi \neq \bot$,
$\Gamma^\Theta[\Delta^\Psi]^F = \{(\gamma \oslash_\Gamma \Delta^\Psi) : \gamma \in \Gamma\}^\Theta$

In the propositional case, $\Gamma^\Theta[\Delta^\Psi]^F = \Gamma^\Theta \oslash \Delta^\Psi$, so the foregoing examples carry over.

We will now turn to illusory inferences with greater complexity. An attentive reader might have noticed that the illusory inferences we considered did not really specifically recruit the notion of treating a new premise as a *maximally strong* answer to the issue raised by the previous premise. So far, there was only one plausible alternative in the first premise that could be considered as receiving any support at all from the answer, since no other alternative in the issue had anything in common with the "answer." What if we have multiple alternatives in the issue that share atoms with the answer?

To address this issue, Koralus and Mascarenhas (2016) presented 121 participants on Amazon Mechanical Turk with variations of problems of the following form. We found that 79% of participants made an illusory inference in at least one content variation of problems of this form (all problems used card names as in the above example). For example, in the below case, an illusory inference would be to conclude that there is a two in the hand. By contrast, only 25% made mistakes in at least one disjunctive syllogism problem of matched complexity. In other words, making the incorrect illusory inference in this kind of problem is similarly cognitive accessible as making the correct inference on the disjunctive syllogism problem.

Example 15.
(P1) There is an ace and a jack and a queen, or else there is an eight and a ten and a four, or else there is an ace. $\{ajq, etf, a\}$
(P2) There is an ace and a jack, and there is an eight and a ten. $\{ajet\}$
(P3) There is not a queen. $\{\bar{q}\}$
   What if anything follows?

Updating the view of the first premise with that of the second, Answer will eliminate the *ace* alternative, since both other alternatives share more atoms with the union of everything mentioned in the second premise (the premise we are treating as an answer). We get $\{ajq, etf, a\}[\{ajet\}]^{\circ} = \{ajqet, etfaj\}$. Updating with the second premise, Answer does nothing, but the result of Merge gives us, $\{ajqet, etfaj\}[\{\bar{q}\}]^{\circ} = \{ajqet\bar{q}, etfaj\bar{q}\}$. Now we clearly have an alternative that contains a primitive absurdity. Applying $[\bot]^F$, we get $\{etfaj\bar{q}\}$. Now, if we try to Factor P1, nothing happens, since P1 as an issue is no longer contained in the view at hand. However, we can successfully Factor P2, yielding $\{f\bar{q}\}$ as well as Factor P3, yielding the observed inference $\{f\}$.

Just as it was straightforward to arrive at a *fallacious* conclusion in the illusory inference problem with the erotetic theory, it is straightforward to arrive at a *correct* conclusion in a very similar disjunctive syllogism problem, using the same strategy.

Example 16. (*Triple disjunctive syllogism*)
(P1) There is a ten and an eight and a four, or else there is a jack and a king and queen, or else there is an ace. $\{tef, jkq, a\}$
(P2) There isn't a four. $\{\bar{f}\}$
(P3) There isn't an ace. $\{\bar{a}\}$
Question: *What if anything follows?*

The same machinery even more directly yields a correct inference if we are dealing with two mutually exclusive alternatives, as in this very easy inference:

Example 17.
P1 There is a king in the hand and there is not an ace in the hand, or else there is an ace in the hand and there is not a king in the hand. $\{k\bar{a}, a\bar{k}\}$
P2 There is a king in the hand. $\{k\}$
C There isn't an ace in the hand. $\{\bar{a}\}$

2.4 Reasoning with Suppositions

We will now consider reasoning with suppositions. The first observation is that suppositions can sometimes make difficult-seeming problems easier. Johnson-Laird (2008) called attention to the following problem, which is difficult to solve on a first look.

Example 18.
P_1 The broadcast is on network TV or it is on the radio, or both. $\{n, r, nr\}$
P_2 The broadcast is not on the radio or it is on cable TV, or both. $\{\bar{r}, c, c\bar{r}\}$
What, if anything, follows?

It takes considerable effort to conclude anything of substance from these two premises. However, as Johnson-Laird points out, if we begin with a strategic supposition, in light of which we interpret the premises, then it becomes much easier to find a suitable conclusion. If we suppose that the broadcast is not on network TV, then it becomes much easier to see that we can conclude that either the broadcast is not on network TV but on the radio and on cable, or it is on network TV. To give a systematic account of reasoning with suppositions like this, we must define an operation to take on board a supposition, reason with it, and then reintegrate our conclusions in light of the fact that they emerged from a supposition.

To use a phrase of Will Starr's, for suppositions, we need to formalize logical tourism with a return ticket. Accomplishing this will require being clear both on our origin and our destination. We will define an operation that allows us to update both our main view and its suppositional index with what we are supposing, as well as an operation to undo a supposition and return us to a view with the trivial {0} "truth" supposition.

Definition 2.23 (Suppose).
$$\Gamma^\Theta[\Delta^\Psi]^S = \Gamma^{(\Theta \otimes (\Delta \cup \Psi))}[\Delta^\Psi]^A[\Delta^\Psi]^M$$

Definition 2.24 (Depose).
$$\Gamma^\Theta[\top]^D = \Gamma^{\{0\}} \oplus \widehat{\Theta}^{\{0\}}$$

We will illustrate these definitions by formalizing the example from the beginning of the section, in which it appeared that a reasoning problem could be simplified by clever use of supposition.

Example 19. (*Simplifying reasoning with supposition*) We suppose $\{\bar{n}\}$, Update and Factor, and finally Depose.

$$\{0\}[\{\bar{n}\}]^S = \{\bar{n}\}^{\{\bar{n}\}}$$
$$[\{n, r, nr\}]^\circlearrowright = \{n\bar{n}, r\bar{n}, nr\bar{n}\}^{\{\bar{n}\}}$$
$$[\bot]^F = \{r\bar{n}\}^{\{\bar{n}\}}$$
$$[\{\bar{r}, c, c\bar{r}\}]^\circlearrowright = \{r\bar{n}\bar{r}, r\bar{n}c, r\bar{n}c\bar{r}\}^{\{\bar{n}\}}$$
$$[\bot]^F = \{r\bar{n}c\}^{\{\bar{n}\}}$$
$$[\top]^D = (\{r\bar{n}c\} \cup [\{\bar{n}\}]^N)$$
$$= \{r\bar{n}c, n\}$$

The problem is still intuitively hard and requires repeated application of Factor to avoid explosion of alternatives, but it is appreciably more manageable with a supposition than with a direct reasoning strategy. The direct reasoning strategy beginning with simple update with the two premises would require us to represent nine alternative possibilities before we could start simplifying. Examples like this make it seem that a strong theory of suppositional reasoning has to be a core ingredient of any realistic theory of reason that has sets of alternatives at its foundation. A strategic use of Suppose is a significant cognitive skill that we clearly are able to deploy, and that some reasoners will be more skillful at than others.

Some premises will supply us with suppositional views (interpretation rules for such cases will be discussed in the next chapter). This will give rise to inferences that are primarily driven by the Merge operation expanding our issue on the basis of alternatives in that issue matching suppositions in the view we update with.

Example 20. We are faced with a card game. Who wins this game is determined by what the cards will turn out to be. The following seems like an intuitively straightforward inference.

(P1) Either there is a king in the hand or a queen in the hand. $\{k, q\}$
(P2) On the supposition that there is a king, Mary wins. $\{m\}^{\{k\}}$
(P3) On the supposition that there is a queen, Bill wins. $\{b\}^{\{q\}}$
(C) Either Mary wins or Bill wins. $\{m, b\}$

We get this inference directly using the same sequence of operations as for previous examples, $\{\emptyset\}[P1]^{\circlearrowleft}[P2]^{\circlearrowleft}[P3]^{\circlearrowleft}[P1]^{F}[P2]^{F}[P3]^{F} = \{m, b\}$.

Moving on, one of the more surprising facts in the logic textbook is that we can derive whatever we please from a contradiction (*ex falso quodlibet*), a crucial classically valid inference. This inference is naïvely repugnant and most people begin by doubting that it is a valid inference (Harman, 1986). The erotetic theory can make sense of this phenomenon. After all, the aim of reasoning is to reduce our issue set, moving toward answers. To get the *ex falso* inference, we have to go against that aim. Firstly, a view of a particular absurdity like $\{p\bar{p}\}$ can be made even less inquisitive by Factor, moving us to $\emptyset$. Now, starting from this absurd view we would have to gratuitously move to a more inquisitive state via Suppose and Depose. Moreover, we specifically have to pick what we are Supposing to then derive that very thing, which again seems to be against the aim of reasoning to answer questions.

Example 21. Any view $\Delta^{\{0\}} = [\Delta'^{\{0\}}]^N$ can be derived from the absurd view $\varnothing$.

$$\varnothing^{\{0\}}[\Delta'^{\{0\}}]^S = \varnothing^{\Delta'}$$
$$[\ ]^D = (\varnothing \cup [\Delta']^N)^{\{0\}}$$
$$= ([\Delta']^N)^{\{0\}} = [\Delta'^{\{0\}}]^N = \Delta^{\{0\}}$$

This does not quite amount to canonical *ex falso quodlibet*, since not every Δ has a Δ' such that $\Delta = [\Delta']^N$. However, we will later show that the erotetic theory guarantees that for every view, we can derive one that is at least logically equivalent to it from a contradiction. In other words, we get *ex falso quodlibet* up to classical semantic equivalence, which is all that is required for classical completeness.

2.5 Inquire and Query

We have seen cases in which we are tempted to draw fallacious inferences from simple premises with disjunctions. Of course, there are also examples of simple *valid* inferences involving conjunctions that seem repugnant to naïve intuition. One such repugnant validity we just saw was *ex falso quodlibet*. Repugnant validities are just as much in need of explanation as tempting fallacies, particularly if their repugnance cannot be explained by the intrinsic complexity (or absurdity) of the premises.

Consider the case of disjunction introduction, where "A or B" is inferred from "A." This pattern is very counterintuitive. Braine et al. (1984) found that only 52% of participants judged the conclusion to follow from the premise in such cases.

The erotetic theory holds that the aim of default reasoning is to use successive premises to get from a question representing more alternatives to an issue with fewer alternatives, ideally a singleton set corresponding to a categorical fact that is novel relative to what is in the premises. This process cannot get us from a categorical fact to an issue.

However, the erotetic theory allows that we are able to raise further questions, without those questions being specifically prompted by premises encoding them and without having to make factual assumptions, as we go along with our reasoning process. In particular, it is always legitimate to raise a polar question on any propositional atom without making any assumptions, just as we may always ask whether something is the case.

We regiment this ability to raise questions as follows.

Definition 2.25 (Inquire).
$$\Gamma^\Theta[\Delta^\Psi]^I = \Gamma^\Theta_{RI} \otimes (\Delta \oplus \hat{\Delta})^\Psi)[\bot]^F.$$

We shall say that if we apply $[\Delta^\Psi]^I$ to some view, we are "inquiring on Δ^Ψ." In case Ψ and Θ are $\{0\}$, $\Gamma^\Theta[\Delta^\Psi]^I$ becomes commutative, so for a set of views $\Sigma = \{\Delta_1^{\{0\}}, \ldots, \Delta_n^{\{0\}}\}$ we can unambiguously write $[\Sigma]^I$ for $[\Delta_1^{\{0\}}]^I \ldots [\Delta_n^{\{0\}}]^I$. This will help with certain definitions in the next section.

I suggest that the use of Inquire is effortful because it goes against the main aim of reasoning to answer the questions we already have and because it tends to lead to an explosion of alternatives in our issue. However, Inquire allows us to uncover fully explicit alternative situations compatible with our information. For example, we can use Inquire to make an effort to obtain the full range of alternative states compatible with the negation of a conjunction, which reasoners find very difficult (Khemlani et al., 2012b). To get the full range of alternatives compatible with the negation of the conjunction, we have to use Inquire on each conjunct.

Example 22. It is not the case that A and B and C.

$$[\{abc\}]^N = \{\bar{a}, \bar{b}, \bar{c}\}$$
$$\{\bar{a}, \bar{b}, \bar{c}\}[\{\{\{a\}\}, \{\{b\}\}, \{\{c\}\}\}]^I =$$
$$= \{\bar{a}bc, \bar{a}b\bar{c}, \bar{a}\bar{b}c, \bar{a}\bar{b}\bar{c}, \bar{b}ac, \bar{b}a\bar{c}, \bar{c}ab\}$$

Now, applying the Inquire operation not only allows us to make inferences that we are not naïvely inclined to make on a first look, Inquire also allows us to block fallacious inferences. In fact, we will be able to characterize classical reasoning as reasoning that is in a certain kind of equilibrium with respect to questions that might be raised.

On a first look, one might have thought that we get fallacies from the erotetic theory because our Answer procedure, treating one view as an answer to another, is akin to a fallacious inference rule. However, there is nothing inescapably fallacious about Answer. It does not produce fallacious inferences if we raise enough further issues. Let us consider how applications of Inquire can block illusory inferences from disjunction, taking the example from Walsh and Johnson-Laird (2004) from the beginning of this chapter.

> **Example 23.**
> (P1) Either Jane is kneeling by the fire and she is looking at the TV or else Mark is standing at the window and he is peering into the garden. $\{kl, sp\}$
> (P2) Jane is kneeling by the fire. $\{k\}$
> (C) Jane is looking at the TV. $\{l\}$
>
> $$\{0\}[\{kl, sp\}]^{\circ} = \{kl, sp\}$$
> $$[\{k\}]^{I} = \{kl, spk, sp\bar{k}\}$$
> $$[\{k\}]^{\circ} = \{kl, spk\}$$

After inquiring on whether Jane is kneeling and updating with the premises, we no longer get the fallacious conclusion that Jane is looking at the TV. The Inquire operation allows us to make explicit alternatives that are otherwise left merely tacit. Systematic use of Inquire is costly, in that it multiplies the number of alternative states to consider, but gives us the ability to guarantee valid inference. The diagnosis the erotetic theory offers for tempting fallacies is in line with the mental models tradition. The key is that mistakes stem from neglected alternative possibilities envisaged in our questions. This type of explanation gets some support from experiments suggesting that asking subjects why a conclusion might be incorrect reduces errors (Baron, 1993; Anderson, 1982; Arkes et al., 1988; Hoch, 1985; Koriat et al., 1980). One might take a question as to why a conclusion is incorrect as motivation to inquire on alternatives that one has not fully considered yet.

As just seen, we can make inferences using the operations of the erotetic theory in a way that avoids fallacies. We will in fact see that if we systematically inquire on all atoms mentioned in premises, our inferences using the operations of the erotetic theory are classically sound and complete (Koralus and Mascarenhas, 2013). Building on the 2013 result, we will be able to characterize classical reasoning as reasoning that is in a certain kind of equilibrium with respect to questions that might be raised.

With creative use of Inquire, we can then capture the fact that we are able to make a disjunction introduction inference, even though it requires some creativity that naïve reasoners in a hurry may fail to exhibit.

Example 24.
P1 There is an ace. $\{a\}$
C There is an ace or a queen. $\{a, q\}$

$$\{a\}[\{q\}]^I = \{aq, a\bar{q}\}$$
$$[\{q\}]^F[\{a\}]^F = \{q, a\}$$

While Inquire allows us to take on board new issues, we will also want an operation that allows us to determine whether a *given* conclusion is directly supported by a view. For this, we define a Query operation. We will generally take it that Query is used for tasks in which participants are asked if a given conclusion follows. If Query returns the conclusion, the answer is "yes," otherwise the answer is "no." Of course, Query does not try to see if the conclusion can be derived in any odd way, since that would amount to stuffing an entire inference algorithm into one procedure. Rather, Query tries to see if a given putative conclusion can be directly lifted from our premise, by the equivalent of reducing conjuncts and disjuncts. Deployed in this way, Query has parallels with the notion of tautological entailment (Anderson and Belnap, 1962; van Fraassen, 1969; Yablo, 2014).

If an alternative in the external argument of Query remains that cannot be reduced to an alternative in the internal argument, we get 0 remaining as an alternative in the result, which amounts to getting the judgment that the internal argument of Query "might" hold.

Definition 2.26 (Query).
$\Gamma^{\Theta}[\Delta^{\Psi}]^Q = (\{0 : \neg\exists\delta_{\in\Delta}\exists\gamma_{\in\Gamma}.\Phi(\gamma,\delta)\} \cup \{\delta \in \Delta : \exists\gamma_{\in\Gamma}.\Phi(\gamma,\delta)\})^{\Theta}$,
where $\Phi(\gamma, \delta) \leftrightarrow \exists\psi_{\in\Psi}(\psi \cup \delta \subseteq \gamma)$

The operation is best understood by tracing it through a number of examples.

Example 25.
$\{pq, pr\}[\{p\}]^Q = \{p\}$
$\{pq, pr\}[\{q\}]^Q = \{0, q\}$
$\{pq, pr, s, t\}[\{p, s\}]^Q = \{p, s, 0\}$
$\{pq, pr, s, t\}[\{p, s, t\}]^Q = \{p, s, t\}$
$\{pqs, prs\}[\{p\}^{\{s\}}]^Q = \{p\}$
$\{pqs, prs\}[\{p\}^{\{t\}}]^Q = \{0\}$

In cases in which we might be interested in determining whether a suppositional conclusion Δ^Ψ follows, we will take it that we first suppose Ψ and then Query on Δ^Ψ. This can yield fallacies if we have not used Inquire enough to make the alternative possibilities explicit. The following seems like a tempting fallacy, and closely mirrors an experimentally confirmed example we will discuss in the chapter on conditionals.

> **Example 26.**
> Either John plays and wins, or Mary plays, or Bill plays.
> *Does it follow that supposing John plays, John wins?*
>
> Following the procedure just discussed, we have $\{jw, m, b\}[\{j\}]^S[\{w\}^{\{J\}}]^Q = \{jw\}^{\{J\}}[\{w\}^{\{J\}}]^Q = \{w\}^{\{J\}}$

The key claim of the erotetic theory that emerges is that when we make mistakes in reasoning, be it that we make an inference that is not supported by our premises or be it that we miss an inference that is in fact supported, we are not robust to further questions. If we reason validly, then no amount of questioning can lastingly detract us from our conclusions, and if we take on board sufficient questions, then there is no classically valid inference that we could not make in principle. Our naïve reasoning performance is neither sound nor complete by classical standards, but the reasoning capacity we deploy naïvely in fact contains sound and complete reasoning as a special case that can incrementally be brought to the fore by raising questions. Something like this picture about the mind is as old as philosophy itself. However, the erotetic theory, initially articulated in Koralus and Mascarenhas (2013), makes this idea formally precise in the context of a descriptive theory of our reasoning capacity that takes reasoning successes and failure equally seriously.

2.6 Inference and Erotetic Equilibrium

We will now consider the notion of inference in the erotetic theory more systematically. Firstly, we will pull together the discussion of the previous sections into a default inference procedure, which covers the data points we have considered so far. The erotetic theory allows for a wide range of hypotheses about default reasoning procedures for different kinds of tasks, as well as for the possibility of systematic individual differences in reasoners.

Some default procedures must be hypothesized to make predictions about response tendencies of groups of reasoners, and the simpler and more systematic those hypothesized procedures are the more explanatory power is gained. In fact, this relatively simple procedure will suffice mostly unmodified for the central data points discussed in the next two chapters, all the way through predicate reasoning.

> **(Default inference procedure).**
> For $S = \langle P_1, \ldots, P_n \rangle$ a sequence of views incrementally given as premises,
> (Basic step) Let $G' = \mathsf{T}[P_1]^\circlearrowleft [\mathsf{T}]^D [P_2]^\circlearrowleft \ldots [P_n]^\circlearrowleft [\bot]^F$
> *(Sub-procedure for "what if anything follows?" tasks)*
> (1) Let $G'' = G'[P_1[\mathsf{T}]^D]^F \ldots [P_n]^F$. If $G'' = \bot$ or $G'' = \mathsf{T}$, then go to (2), otherwise go to (4).
> (2) Start again at Basic step, with $P_n, \ldots, P_1$ in place of $P_1, \ldots, P_n$. If we have already done that, go to (3).
> (3) Report "nothing follows."
> (4) Report G''.
> *(Sub-procedure for "does Δ^Ψ follow?" tasks)*
> (1) Let $G'' = G'[\Psi^{\{\circleddash\}}]^S [\Delta^\Psi]^Q$. If $G'' = \Delta^\Psi$, report "Yes." Otherwise go to step 2.
> (2) Start again at Basic step, with $P_n, \ldots, P_1$ in place of $P_1, \ldots, P_n$. If we have already done that, go to (3).
> (3) Report "no."

Recall that, officially, a state of inference corresponds to a pair consisting of a set of commitments, and a view that is the current focus of reason. After having arrived at a novel conclusion with our focused view, we will sometimes want to add it to our stock of commitments. We will include an operation for this purpose.

Definition 2.27 (Commit).
$\langle C, \Gamma^\circleddash \rangle [\mathsf{T}]^C = \langle C \cup \{\Gamma^\circleddash\}, \Gamma^\circleddash \rangle$

In addition, we may wish to reorient our focus toward a different view in our set of commitments. For this, too, we add an operation.

Definition 2.28 (Reorient).
For $\Delta^\Psi \in (C \cup \{\Gamma^\circleddash\})$, $\langle C, \Gamma^\circleddash \rangle [\Delta^\Psi]^R = \langle C, \Delta^\Psi \rangle$

We can now give a general definition of inference in the erotetic theory. The span of reason as described by the erotetic theory is defined by the set of inferences. As we expand the expressive power of the theory through successive chapters, this span will include an increasingly larger share of our actual competence.

Definition 2.29 (Inference).
An inference $\mathcal{J}$ is a finite sequence of inference steps defined as follows, relative to an inference state consisting of a commitment $\langle C, G \rangle \in \mathbb{C}$. If $D \in \mathbb{V}$ and $O \in \{[D]^\circlearrowleft, [D]^S, [D]^Q, [D]^F, [D]^R, [D]^I, [D]^D, [D]^C\}$, then O is an inference step applicable to $\langle C, G \rangle$, whose result is an inference state in $\mathbb{C}$. We write $C \models_{\text{ETR}} E$ if and only if there is an erotetic theory inference $\mathcal{J}$ s.t. $\langle C, \top \rangle \mathcal{J} = \langle C', E \rangle$.

We will now be concerned with developing a notion of equilibrium under questioning, or *erotetic* equilibrium. This will allow us to think more systematically about correct reasoning in the erotetic theory. Erotetic equilibrium will allow us to characterize precisely how we can obtain classically correct reasoning. In addition, erotetic equilibrium restricted to a topic of inquiry will allow us to begin to make sense of cases in which we are entirely as we ought to be as reasoners even though we make classically invalid inferences (a topic we will return to at greater length once we consider probability in Chapter 5).

First we define a notion of erotetic equilibrium for a view Γ with respect to a set of polar questions (i.e. "yes/no" questions). The reason we are interested in polar questions, as produced by applications of Inquire, is that polar questions do not import any new logical commitments. In the propositional reasoning case, polar questions are, if you will, what is informationally neutral. Of course, it would not be surprising if the addition of questions that include additional information makes a difference to the inferences we can make. However, it is quite interesting if the addition of questions that are *not* including any new information makes a difference. We saw in the last section that such questions can indeed make a difference in inference, on the erotetic theory.

Definition 2.30 (Erotetic equilibrium of a view).
G is in erotetic equilibrium with respect to a finite set of views Σ if and only if $\forall D(D \in \Sigma \rightarrow G[D]^I = G)$.

Erotetic equilibrium relative to a set of views means that raising more questions using those views will no longer make a difference; we have reached *equilibrium* with respect to those questions.

Example 27. (i) $\{pq, \bar{p}\bar{q}\}$ is in erotetic equilibrium with respect to $\{p\}$ and $\{q\}$, but not with respect to $\{r\}$.
(ii) $\{pq, \bar{p}\}$ is in erotetic equilibrium with respect to $\{p\}$ but not with respect to $\{q\}$.

It will be useful to be able to refer to all those polar questions that can be raised using atoms involved in a given view.

Definition 2.31 ($\mathbb{V}_A(X)$).
Let $\mathbb{V}_A(X)$ be the set of views $\{G : \mathcal{A}(G) \subseteq \mathcal{A}(X)\}$.

We are interested in a notion of inference from premises to a conclusion that is in erotetic equilibrium. On the erotetic theory, an inference from premises to a conclusion is a kind of inquiry, in which, at various stages, premises are taken as answers to issues. The relevant notion of equilibrium will be as follows: your inference to a conclusion is in erotetic equilibrium if every time you treat some D as an answer to an issue G, as part of your inference, it does not make a decisive difference to your ability to reach the conclusion whether G and D are in erotetic equilibrium with respect to polar issues that can be raised from atoms in D.

Definition 2.32 (Absolute erotetic equilibrium of an inference).
An inference $\mathcal{I}$ with premises C and conclusion D is an absolute erotetic equilibrium inference if and only if there exists an inference $\mathcal{I}'$ with premises C and conclusion D such that whenever we have an instance of $\Gamma^\Theta[\Delta^\Psi]^A$ in an inference step, then either $\mathcal{A}(\Gamma) \cap \mathcal{A}(\Delta) = \emptyset$ or both Γ^Θ and Δ^Ψ are in erotetic equilibrium with respect to $\mathbb{V}_A(\Gamma) \cap \mathbb{V}_A(\Delta)$. In such a case, we write $C \vdash_{\text{CETR}} D$ (with "CETR" standing for "Classicized" ETR). We call $\mathcal{I}'$ a *manifest erotetic equilibrium inference*.

Thus, absolute erotetic equilibrium of an inference roughly means that for any application of the Answer operation, raising certain further issues in advance will not make a decisive difference to the outcome. This means that no matter how many further issues are raised, we can always return to our conclusion if we wish; *the conclusion is in equilibrium with respect to further issues*. What is significant about absolute erotetic equilibrium for propositional reasoning is that erotetic equilibrium guarantees classical soundness while maintaining classical completeness, in terms of our interpretation (i.e. ○) and articulation (i.e. ∗) procedures that relate views to the propositional calculus. Where ⊢ denotes classical derivability in the propositional calculus, we have:

Theorem 2.1 (Soundness). *Let $C \cup \{D\}$ be a set of views. If $C \models_{\text{CETR}} D$, then $C^* \vdash D^*$.*

Theorem 2.2 (Completeness). *Let C be a set of views and let φ be a sentence of $\mathcal{L}_{PC}$. If $C^* \vdash \varphi$, then $C \models_{\text{CETR}} \varphi^\circ$.*

A similar result was shown for an earlier version of this system described in Koralus and Mascarenhas (2013). We will leave the proof of the above claims as a special case of the stronger claim about the more expressive fragment of the erotetic theory that covers predicate reasoning to be discussed in Chapter 4.

In sum, the erotetic theory allows us to characterize classically valid inference as inference under absolute erotetic equilibrium. The picture of human rationality that emerges from this theory is quite Socratic. We can be sure that our conclusions are valid if we could still reason our way to them, regardless of how much hostile questioning we might have to endure. Later chapters will present broaden these results to more expressive fragments of the theory. Of course, demanding *absolute* erotetic equilibrium as a standard for all rational inference is implausible, just as classical logical validity is implausible as a standard for all rational inference.

2.7 Restricted Erotetic Equilibrium

Even if classical logical validity is too demanding a standard for all rational inference, it seems quite plausible that every rationally defensible inference has to be in equilibrium with respect to *some* appropriate set of questions. At least in philosophy, if we come to see that we are wrongheaded with respect to some view in a way that does not hinge on learning new facts, it is usually because someone asks us a probing question that makes us see a gap between our reasons and our judgments. At the same time, it often seems excessive to demand that all alternative possibilities we might ask about have to be ruled out. It is worth exploring the possibility of a correspondence between norms for different types of rational inquiry on one side and notions of *restricted* erotetic equilibrium with respect to various sets of questions on the other. Note that a norm demanding (possibly among other things) erotetic equilibrium with respect to a certain set of questions does not have to include a requirement that the reasoner *takes herself to be in equilibrium*; such norms are best regarded as being external. Otherwise, there is little scope for construing normal unreflective reasoning as basically rational. For familiar reasons of threatening regress, if normal unreflective reasoning cannot be rational, then it is unlikely that we will be able to construe any reasoning as rational, since even prima facie reflective reasoning will have to include unreflective components. Full exploration of these issues has to be left for elsewhere. We shall focus on how one might begin to regiment ideas of this kind within the erotetic theory.

It should be highlighted that the notion of an erotetic equilibrium inference treats all sorts of inferences as equilibrium inferences that do not in fact involve the reasoner asking further questions. For example, suppose we start with $\{pq, \bar{p}\}$ and update with $\{p, pr\}$, which includes in the first instance treating the latter as an answer to the former (followed by Merge). We get $\{pq, pqr\}$. In this case, neither the "issue" view nor the "answer" view was in erotetic equilibrium with respect to questions based on the atoms in the answer. However, the inference is an erotetic equilibrium inference because there exists an alternative inference with the *same premises* and the *same conclusion*, in which we bring the issue and the answer into equilibrium first. In other words, default reasoning will often produce classically sound erotetic equilibrium inferences, even without raising further issues. However, only if we are prepared to bring our views into erotetic equilibrium will the default inference procedure yield valid inferences in all cases.

So far, we have only considered reasoning success insofar as it corresponds to avoiding conclusions that do not logically follow from our premises and obtaining conclusions that do. This is far too narrow a notion of correctness for rational inference. However, the erotetic theory can allow a larger range of "good" inferences for different purposes, even before we add notions of uncertainty to our system in Chapter 5. I suggest that there are various instances in which we are entirely as we ought to be as reasoners, even though we jump to conclusions in ways similar to the illusory inferences discussed earlier.

James (1890, ch. XI) famously noted, "every stir in the wood is for the hunter his game; for the fugitive his pursuers," and "every bonnet in the street is momentarily taken by the lover to enshroud the head of his idol." As outputs of an inferential process (which I think some of these cases are), some of these "takings" are clearly mistakes. However, I suggest that there are cases in which we are rationally entirely as we ought to be when we make these sorts of inferences.

96 CORE REASONING AND EROTETIC EQUILIBRIUM

Suppose we are being actively hunted by a tiger. Next, we see a flash of orange pelt in front of us. We might reason as follows.

Example 28.
P1	Is there a tiger?	$\{t, \bar{t}\}$
P2	Supposing there is a tiger, there is orange fur.	$\{to\}^{\{t\}}$
P3	There is orange fur.	$\{o\}$
C	There is a tiger!	$\{t\}$

Updating with P1, P2, and P3, we get $\{to\}$. After Factoring out what we can, we get $\{t\}$, and thus conclude that there is a tiger. The crucial step in the inference in this example follows the same classically invalid pattern as in the illusory inferences from disjunctions discussed at the beginning of this chapter. However, I would suggest that in this kind of scenario, we can be entirely as we ought to be as reasoners in making this inference. Bayesians might be disposed to agree, but the erotetic theory holds that we can make sense of this without appeals to tacit assumptions about probability.

Someone might respond to these kinds of cases by saying that we are *practically* as we ought to be as agents, since the risk of false negatives far outweighs the risk of false positives in our situation, making it advisable to treat any strong tiger indicators as practically conclusive as far as our choice of action is concerned. However, the standard response continues, we are still not *epistemically* as we ought to be, and the inference is still to be regarded as defective.

I maintain that there is an interesting sense in which we can be entirely as we ought to be as reasoners in the above example, without trying to recast the inference as a practical decision. We could instead take the view that what sorts of inferences are permitted depends on the type of inquiry we are engaged in. Practical issues then may be part of what determines what kind of inquiry we should be conducting, but once we are in a certain kind of inquiry, the appropriateness of an inference *relative to that inquiry* does not need further appeal to practical reasons. Note that this does not mean that we have to think of our tiger inference case as involving the settling of a question of fact with a practical reason, even if practical reasons may be what justifies or rationalizes conducting an inquiry with the "relaxed" standards that make the conclusion possible.

I suggest that in the tiger example, we are conducting an inquiry in which we can permissibly ignore further alternatives involving non-tigers, such as those involving non-tigers with with orange fur, unless forced upon us (regardless of whether the reasoner reflectively considers that). The inference is not in erotetic equilibrium with respect to issues concerning non-tigers, but it does not have to be. The inference is in erotetic equilibrium *restricted* to the set of issues involved in the kind of threat inquiry we are conducting. I suggest that reasoning well only requires our conclusions to be in equilibrium restricted to issues that are part of an appropriate topic of inquiry. A *reasonable person* is in erotetic equilibrium restricted by a certain topic of inquiry in a certain kind of circumstance, and we are as we ought to be as reasoners if our inferences in this kind of circumstance are similarly in erotetic equilibrium restricted by this topic, regardless of whether we are conscious of this as reasoners. Being in this kind of equilibrium neither requires the reasoner to have raised all issues, nor does it requires her to be consciously entertaining the topic. What topic of inquiry might provides a relevant rational standard in particular cases is a separate question, which we briefly consider in the next section.

To regiment the notion erotetic equilibrium restricted by a topic, we will first have to define topics of inquiry.

Definition 2.33 (Topic of inquiry). A topic of inquiry TI is set of states circumscribing what is at issue in an inquiry.

We would like to carve out those alternatives in some issue Γ that fit our topic of inquiry. In our example, "tiger cases" is our topic of inquiry, so we have $TI = \{\{t\}\}$ as our view of what is at issue. To get those alternatives in Γ that are concerned with our topic of inquiry, we take those alternatives in Γ that contain at least one state in TI. In the case at hand, we simply have $\{t\}$. Then, to assess equilibrium of an inquiry restricted by a topic of inquiry TI, the remaining alternatives are what needs to be evaluated for equilibrium with respect to issues that emerge from what we treat as answers.

Definition 2.34 (Restricted erotetic equilibrium of an inference). An inference $\mathcal{J}$ with premises C and conclusion D is an erotetic equilibrium inference restricted by a topic of inquiry TI if and only if there exists an inference $\mathcal{J}'$ with premises C and conclusion D such that whenever we have an instance of $\Gamma^\Theta[\Delta^\Psi]^A$ in an inference step, then either $\mathcal{A}(\Gamma) \cap \mathcal{A}(\Delta) = \emptyset$ or both $\{\gamma \in \Gamma : \exists \varphi_{\in TI}(\varphi \subseteq \gamma)\}^\Theta$ and Δ^Ψ are in erotetic equilibrium with respect to $\mathbb{V}_A(\Gamma) \cap \mathbb{V}_A(\Delta)$.

It is easy to see that erotetic equilibrium of an inference restricted by $TI = \emptyset$ is absolute erotetic equilibrium.

Now, our tiger inference is in restricted erotetic equilibrium with respect to the topic of inquiry {{t}}. Thus, we get that our tiger inference is a fine inference according to a restricted erotetic equilibrium standard, for a topic of inquiry confined to tiger cases (a topic like "tigers, snakes, etc." would work too). To be clear, this kind of restricted erotetic equilibrium does not amount to flatly assuming as a premise that we have tiger cases, nor does it amount to assuming as a premise that all non-tiger cases are false. Instead, it roughly means that in making inferences centered on treating something as an answer, we are not on the hook for first taking on board more issues (or, equivalently, alternative states) centered on states that do not include any state of our topic (in this case, non-tiger states), unless further premises directly force this upon us. Another loose way of putting it would be that our topic of inquiry for assessing restricted erotetic equilibrium tells us which partial questions we do not have to fully expand before fairly treating something as an answer.

In the very simple example we considered, one might worry that restricted erotetic equilibrium trivializes standards of inference completely, and that out topic of inquiry amounts to assuming the conclusion. To see why this worry is misplaced, let us consider a slightly more complex case in which we have two tigers, call them Sherekhan and Dawon. Let us assume that distinguishing these two tigers is quite important. Friendly Dawon is your only hope for ultimate survival. If you find him, you can jump on him and ride far away to safety. By contrast, if you find evil Sherekhan, you can perhaps hide behind a tree and hope he does not detect you. So we have that $TI = \{\{d\}, \{s\}\}$. Now, you hear some rustling in front of you and reason as follows.

Example 29.

P1 Is there Sherekhan or instead Dawon or instead something else?
$\{s\bar{d}, d\bar{s}, x\bar{d}\bar{s}\}$

P2 Supposing it is Sherekhan, then there is orange fur. $\quad\{so\}^{\{s\}}$

P3 There is orange fur. $\quad\{o\}$.

F It's Sherekhan and not Dawon. $\quad\{s\bar{d}\}$

In this case, we are not entirely as we ought to be, even as fearful reasoners in a hurry. The natural response when looking at this line of reasoning is, "what about Dawon's fur?" Even within the constraints of the restricted topic of inquiry, we are not robust with respect to all the relevant questions. We are not in restricted erotetic equilibrium for our topic of inquiry $\{\{d\}, \{s\}\}$. Consider what we have once we update P1 with P2: $\{s\bar{d}o, d\bar{s}, x d\bar{s}\}$. If we now update with P3, we get $\{s\bar{d}o\}$. So we get that Sherekhan is there. However, this is not an erotetic equilibrium inference.

Even the relevantly restricted view before the answer step, $\{s\bar{d}o, d\bar{s}, x d\bar{s}\} - \{x d\bar{s}\}$ is not erotetic equilibrium with respect to $\mathbb{V}_A(P3)$. It would make a difference if we applied $[\{\{o\}\}]^I$, so we are not in equilibrium. By contrast, we would be in restricted equilibrium with respect to our tiger inquiry TI if we had $\{s\bar{d}o, d\bar{s}o, d\bar{s}\bar{o}, x d\bar{s}\}$ and then updated with P3. But now, taking this equilibrium step as a starting point, we no longer get the conclusion that we are in a Sherekhan case. Instead, we get that we are in a Sherekhan case *or* in a Dawon case. I suggest that this would be a fine inference for the purposes of that inquiry. Yet, it would still be a fallacy from the perspective of *absolute* erotetic equilibrium. After all, we are not in equilibrium with respect to questions about whether it might have been something else; a crazed Princeton alumnus in a tiger costume, for example.

It is a relatively subtle question, whether a particular topic of inquiry is such that being in restricted erotetic equilibrium with respect to it guarantees that we have met an interesting rational standard. This may also depend on what further questions we intend to raise within the inquiry we are engaged in, as part of your overall circumstances.

2.8 Norms

I will now consider what rational norms might look like if articulated within the framework of the erotetic theory. The following seems quite plausible.

Definition 2.35 (Equilibrium requirement for rational judgment). If your judgment is not in erotetic equilibrium restricted to a topic of inquiry a reasonable person would take to be called for in your overall circumstances, you are not entirely as you ought to be as a reasoner.

This seems plausible, since it looks like there is something amiss if your judgment had not been made if you had considered a question of the kind that a reasonable person would have taken to be called for. In this framework, we can then characterize those who maintain that no invalid inference could yield a rational conclusion to an inquiry as being committed to the position that the only reasonably acceptable topic of inquiry for commitments about putative facts is unrestricted (i.e. the empty set).

Absolute erotetic equilibrium is a very strong condition. Notably, as we will see over successive chapters of this book, erotetic equilibrium of the right kind can guarantee classical validity, probabilistic coherence, and classically rational choice. At the same time, we will not take the view that rationality for reasoning amounts to classical validity, etc. (also see Harman (1986)). This means that *absolute* erotetic equilibrium cannot be necessary for rationality. If there is an erotetic equilibrium rational norm, it has to be about restricted erotetic equilibrium.

A more controversial principle would be the following.

Definition 2.36 (Equilibrium guarantee for rational judgment). If your judgment is in erotetic equilibrium restricted to a topic of inquiry a reasonable person would take to be called for in your overall circumstances, you are entirely as you ought to be as a reasoner.

If something like this were true, it would most likely require considering questions that go beyond what we can treat mathematically in this book, including questions about what lines of inquiry to pursue and other kinds of meta-reasoning. As usual, a guarantee is harder to defend than a requirement. To the extent that the erotetic theory of reason is plausible as a descriptive claim about human reason, both putative principles of rational inquiry would deserve to be explored further. For now, we limit the discussion of norms to a few preliminary remarks.

To apply the putative norms for erotetic reasoners properly, we would need an account of the topics of inquiry of a reasonable person in a given set of circumstances. Rather than arbitrarily select certain standard issues as required for being reasonable, we could focus on how questions we ask in a given task might evolve with experience.

If a normal person sees that they have failed at a task but also sees that if they had raised a certain kind of question they might not have failed, they will be more likely to raise this kind of question in the future when faced with this kind of task. Something like this seems like it is required by the secondary aim of the capacity to reason, which is to weakly pursue erotetic equilibrium. Of course, fleshing this out would still depend on further hypotheses about how people generalize their task experience, a mathematical treatment of which would take us beyond the scope of this book. Assuming this can be fleshed out, we could take it that an appropriate topic of inquiry for assessing rationality would be derived from what experience suggests must be considered to avoid mistakes. More stringent standards might be based on a more specialized experience set.

Moving on, we now consider how the framework of the erotetic theory might help us make sense of various rational norm constraints that have been proposed elsewhere in the literature (Broome, 2013; MacFarlane, 2004). Our aim will not be to consider all plausible constraints exhaustively but to show that the proposed approach is fruitful in this area. With some reframing from MacFarlane (2004) and Broome (2003), we can tabulate some of these constraints as follows.

> (Priority) How we ought to revise our beliefs should not normally depend on our knowledge of logical entailment.
> (Excessive demands) It is not a rational requirement that we believe all consequences of our beliefs.
> (Logical obtuseness) It is wrong to believe P, Q, but refuse to take a stand on P&Q.
> (Strict consequence) For a significant number of views P, Q, if you believe P but not its logical consequence Q, you are not entirely as you ought to be.
> (Explosion) It is not a rational requirement to infer that I am the Pope from P and not-P.
> (Absurdity) It is wrong to believe that P and to then adopt the belief that not-P.

Taking "belief," for the sake of argument, as simply a view we infer, we can take many of these kinds of constraints as satisfied in virtue of being an erotetic reasoner. For example, the priority constraint falls out of the proposal that reasoning normally just means following the process of question answering and updating a view.

The excessive demands constraint falls out of the fact that we are not required to raise all questions. Many consequences of our views require raising further questions to be able to infer them. Not all such questions are worth raising. There is nothing amiss with raising and answering some questions without also answering others, even if one would logically be in a position to do so.

The logical obtuseness constraint is automatically satisfied as long as we are still in the business of reasoning at all on the erotetic theory. The view you get from taking A and B on board is the same you get from taking A&B on board.

The strict consequence constraint looks different depending on your intuitions about the relevant set of cases. At a minimum, we get a requirement against logical obtuseness. Without a limit to what counts as a strict consequence, the strictness test would clash with the excessive demands constraint.

However, there are certain consequences q that do seem like we rationally ought to accept them, if we accept p. If you ask whether q, and p directly answers your question (just by interpreting p) but you refuse to take q as answered, then you have given up on the reasoning process.

For explosion inferences, you would have to cook up an appropriate question (through inquire or supposition) and answer it with P and not-P. However, nothing seems to rationally require raising such a question (see the discussion earlier in this chapter on *ex falso quodlibet*). Finally, it is wrong to take the view that P and to then adopt the view that not-P. This falls out of the fact that an absurd view is never in erotetic equilibrium.

Other candidate norms are worth considering as well, but this would lead us too far afield for present purposes. The aim here was simply to show that norms of reasoning may well become more intelligible through an erotetic lens. The erotetic theory of the capacity to reason does not have to be committed to the particular details of the approach to norms sketched here. However, I believe that the foregoing shows that the erotetic theory provides a useful framework for articulating rational norms.

3

Conditionals and Information Source Selection

We have already encountered a fairly wide range of interesting reasoning phenomena, even though we have so far limited ourselves to premises that center on "or," "and," and "not." We shall now turn our attention to reasoning with "if." Any serious treatment of reasoning with conditional premises has to have something to say about the first experimental result in the study of reasoning that drew significant attention from the cognitive science community: Wason's card selection task.

Evans et al. (1993) rightly describe Wason's card selection task as "the most intensively researched single problem in the history of the psychology of reasoning." Inspired by the view in the philosophy of science that falsification is the key deductive inference in scientific inquiry (Popper, 1959), Wason (1966) presented participants in an experiment with the following vignette.

> **Example 30.** (Wason card selection task) Each of the below cards has a letter on one side and a number on the other. Which cards do you have to turn over to determine if the following statement is true?
>
> *If a card has an E on one side then it has a four on the other side.*

In a result that has been widely replicated, the vast majority of participants turn over the "E" card and the "4" card. The crucial "5" card that could in fact falsify the conditional is omitted by 90% of respondents (Wason, 1966). An early suggestion was that our information-seeking behavior is subject to a form of confirmation bias in the selection of information sources. The notion of a confirmation bias is a useful taxonomic category, but too close to a mere description of the phenomenon to count as a satisfying explanation. Moreover, a general notion of confirmation bias overgenerates. For example, (Evans, 1972) found that a majority of respondents (60%) produce correct answers if the consequent of the conditional is negated. Try the previous problem again

Fig. 2 Wason card selection task

with the conditional, "if a card has an E on one side then it does not have a four on the other side." Further interesting effects regarding premise content were found by Griggs and Cox (1982), Cheng and Holyoak (1985), and Sperber et al. (1995), among others.

Approaches based on primitive "biases" or "heuristics" are unsatisfying if we take them seriously as *theoretical postulates* rather than mere *empirical generalizations*. There is a tendency to conflate the two. These approaches do not tend to readily generate predictions about what sorts of minimally different problems might generate fewer mistakes and they shed little light on our overall reasoning capacity. Indeed, such approaches raise questions that seem unanswerable without stipulation. For example, since we are clearly able to understand on further reflection why we ought to e.g. select the "5" card, we would need to stipulate something about how a putative heuristic responsible for the wrong selection relates to a general reasoning capacity that can operate over the same domain of inputs. While we might stomach such stipulations, a general strategy of "outsourcing" mistakes to heuristics, instead of attempting to see them as results of bearing on the nature of reason, in fact radically reduces the evidence-base available to shed light on this capacity.

Other areas of cognitive science seem to avoid these types of problems. For example, visual cognitive neuroscience treats visual illusions as part of the evidence-base for general models of our visual system, treating them as edge-cases that can help shed light on the normal cases, where the normal case of visual perception is, loosely speaking, "correct" by the standards of ordinary people. The right approach for the cognitive science of reasoning would seem to be to similarly treat surprising reasoning mistakes as a guide to the nature of our general reasoning capacity

As in previous chapters, we will continue to pursue a general and principled approach. In order to address reasoning and information-seeking with conditional statements, we will first need to provide an account of how "if...then" statements are interpreted into views. Since we are not providing an account of modal reasoning in this book, we shall only consider indicative interpretations of "if...then."

A reasonable starting point is to ask what alternative possibilities are taken to be compatible with "if...then" statements by naïve reasoners. As it turns out, we seem to get all alternative possibilities in the truth-table for material implication. Barrouillet et al. (2008) report that they "have demonstrated in many studies" that if participants are asked to *list cases* in which a conditional is true, the equivalent of the full classical truth-table tends to appear, including cases in which the antecedent is false. In addition, it seems fairly clear that *modus ponens* inferences are among the best examples of very easy inferences. Insofar as we are constructing an account of the interpretation of "if... then" in terms of alternative states, this makes it very appealing to take a set of alternatives that is logically equivalent to material implication. This is not a fashionable view, to say the least. However, we shall see that once we take into account *how* alternative states for "if... then" are generated in interpretation and in the dynamics of reasoning, this view seems to be extremely powerful. Interestingly, when people are asked to report which of a set of given cases make a conditional true, false antecedent cases are omitted (Evans et al. 1993). This observation shows that there is more to the conditional than material implication, and the account we will propose in this chapter will make sense of that.

We will adopt the view that even just interpreting conditionals involves a form of suppositional reasoning. This means that we will in fact construct an erotetic theory version of Ramsey's view of the conditional, who was arguably the first to propose that conditionals are intrinsically connected to suppositional or hypothetical reasoning (Ramsey, 1929).

However, unlike the view we will construct, Ramsey (1929) went from the idea that "if... then" involves a kind of hypothetical or suppositional reasoning directly to the to the idea that "if... then" gives voice to a conditional probability. This view received further articulation in Adams (1975). Chater and Oaksford (1999) developed the suppositional approach in its probabilistic form into a proposal about how we reason with conditionals. There are many other approaches to conditionals in linguistics and philosophy, and the ever-growing literature is a testament to the fact that there is no generally agreed account of how they should be treated. Von Fintel (2011) painfully observes that theory fatigue about conditionals goes back to the ancients, providing the following entertaining quote from Cicero's *Academica*:

> In this very thing, which the dialecticians teach among the elements of their art, how one ought to judge whether an argument be true or false which is connected in this manner, "If it is day, it shines," how great a contest there is; Diodorus has one opinion, Philo another, Chrysippus a third. Need I say more?

Bringing us back to the present, von Fintel adds, "[i]t is unclear whether we are any closer to solving Cicero's Problem." Now, in the presumably most important sense, we have long solved Cicero's *problem of judging arguments*, since we have transparently understood regimented notions of "if" into which we can paraphrase any conditionals we care to use in serious inquiry.

We should not trust to find our problems already solved in linguistic theory, because reasoning falls almost entirely into a blindspot of mainstream linguistic semantics, which is primarily concerned with idealized interpretations of logically omniscient speaker-listeners. As noted in Chapter 1, from the perspective of the erotetic theory, we would say that mainstream semantics is concerned with properties of linguistic interpretation that are invariant under erotetic equilibrium. The importance of studying these properties is not to be dismissed. However, if what makes "if...then" particularly interesting is its connection to reasoning and argumentation, we would be well advised to broaden our perspective to the more general case outside of erotetic equilibrium.

3.1 Erotetic Suppositional "If...Then"

We take a view of "if...then" that is a variant of the view in Koralus and Mascarenhas (2013). This view also has similarities with dynamic analyses of the meaning of the indicative conditional proposed by others like Starr (2014) and Mackie (1973), and Carter (2021).

The linguistic meaning of "if A then C" encodes a sequence of instructions. The gist of these instructions simply is this: suppose the antecedent and update with the consequent, presupposing that the antecedent is an acceptable supposition.

Definition 3.1 (Informal interpretation rule for indicative "if A, then C"). Where $[\![A]\!]$ is an acceptable supposition relative to the current state of inference.

$$[\![if A, C]\!] = \mathsf{T}[\![A]\!]^S \otimes ([\![C]\!][\mathsf{T}]^D)$$

For example, this interpretation rule will give us $\{pq\}^{\{p\}}$ for "if p then q," assuming that $\{p\}$ is an acceptable supposition relative to our current state of inference. We will shortly consider the notion of acceptable supposition in detail.

An interesting feature of the present account is that it can provide a plausible link between "if" as occurring in conditional statements and in content clauses of interrogatives (see Harman (1979); Haiman (1978); Starr (2014)).

Example 31. If Jack danced, the music must have been good. John asked if Jack danced.

The second example above raises a polar question with the alternatives $\{d, \bar{d}\}$ following standard approaches to the semantics of questions. We can obtain a question-interpretation for "if" from our interpretation rule for "if... then" by simply leaving the "then"-clause as an "empty" T view and then Deposing.

Since our main order of business is reasoning, we will first want to look at some simple inferences that do not hinge on this notion.

On the present analysis, we can straightforwardly capture that *modus ponens* inferences are among the easiest one can make (Braine and Rumain, 1983). As before, we generate our example inferences using the default reasoning procedure, but only list those operations that succeed in transforming their external argument.

Example 32. (Modus ponens)
P1 If P then Q. $\{pq\}^{\{p\}}$
P2 P. $\{p\}$
C Q. $\{q\}$

$T[P1[T]^D]^\circ[P2]^\circ[P2]^F = \{pq, \bar{p}\}[P2]^\circ[P2]^F = \{pq\}[P2]^F = \{q\}.$

P1 P. $\{p\}$
P2 If P then Q. $\{pq\}^{\{p\}}$
C Q. $\{q\}$

$T[P1]^\circ[P2]^\circ[P1]^F = \{p\}[P2]^\circ[P1]^F = \{pq\}[P1]^F = \{q\}.$

We next consider what is perhaps the best-known tempting but fallacious inference of all, *affirming the consequent*, which is notoriously tempting in ordinary inference.

Example 33. (*Affirming the consequent*)
P1 If the card is red then the number is even. $\{re\}^{\{r\}}$
P2 The number is even. $\{e\}$
Fall. The card is red. $\{r\}$

$T[P1[T]^D]^\circ[P2]^\circ[P2]^F = \{re, \bar{r}\}[P2]^\circ[P2]^F = \{re\}[P2]^F = \{r\}.$

Note that the above is not an erotetic equilibrium inference. We only get the fallacious conclusion because, in reasoning forward from a given set of premises, we do not by default inquire about cases in which we have an even number but no red card, before we treat "the number is even" as an answer to "are we in a red and even situation or in a not-even situation?" Under erotetic equilibrium, the fallacy is of course blocked. If we raise enough further issues, a conditional premise gives us the set of alternative possibilities envisaged in a truth-table for material implication. Via Deposing the supposition and an application of Inquire, we get the classical truth-table alternatives for material implication as follows: $\{pq, \bar{p}\}[\{q\}]^I = \{pq, \bar{p}q, \bar{p}\bar{q}\}$. This means that access to all the classical alternatives is possible, but requires a little non-default effort. The ability to raise these questions is how the erotetic theory explains the empirically documented (Barrouillet et al., 2008) ability of reasoners to list all possibilities compatible with a conditional, if asked to do so.

A satisfactory account of the conditional should also explain when we are prepared to accept a conditional conclusion as following from a set of premises. To do this, we can essentially take Ramsey's famous quote at face value: "[I]f two people are arguing 'if A will C' and are both in doubt as to A, they are adding A hypothetically to their stock of knowledge and arguing on that basis about C" (Ramsey, 1929). In erotetic theory terms, we evaluate if a conditional follows by supposing the antecedent (using the Suppose operation), and asking whether we get both the antecedent and the consequent (using the Query operation). If this yields a view of the conditional, we conclude that the conditional follows. In fact, our default reasoning procedure for assessing whether a given conclusion follows will already generate this strategy for a conditional putative conclusion.

There are various accounts in the literature that are in some sense building on Ramsey's view. However, as far as we can tell, none of them are naturally able to make sense of cases like the below in which people seem to find it tempting to endorse a fallacious conditional conclusion.

> **Example 34.** Koralus and Mascarenhas (2013) reported that 20 out of 20 participants recruited on Amazon Mechanical Turk answered "yes" to be below.
> (*Illusory conditional inference*).
> P1 There is a jack and a king or there is a queen and an ace.
>   Does the following conclusion follow from the premise?
> C If there is a jack, then there is a king.
> None of the participants answered "yes" in the below control problem.
> P1 There is a jack or there is a queen or an ace.
>   Does the following conclusion follow from the premise?
> C If there is a jack, then there is a queen.

Applying our erotetic theory version of Ramsey's strategy to the question of whether it follows that $\{jk\}^{\{J\}}$, we get $\{jk, qa\}[\{jk\}]^S[\{jk\}^{\{J\}}]^Q = \{jk\}^{\{J\}}$, hence the answer is (fallaciously), "yes." The answer to the control problem, following the same strategy, is a straightforward "no."

Before moving on to more examples of fallacies, including those in selection tasks, we will return to the nuts and bolts of our account of the linguistic meaning of "if...then." We had it that the antecedent had to be an *acceptable supposition* relative to the current state of inference. We will now examine this notion more closely.

3.2 Supposition and Presupposition

What does it take to make a supposition acceptable? An important aspect of the proposed view is that the indicative interpretation of "if A, then C" is *indicative* because the Suppose operation that this interpretation draws upon is itself best understood as indicative. The point of the Suppose operation is to allow us to reason forward from our state of inference by hypothetically taking on board additional commitments. Being able to reason forward with additional hypothetical commitments is very different from being able to reason counterfactually about what might have been the case had such-and-such been different. The former kind of hypothetical reasoning boils down to "borrowing" an additional premise and keeping in mind that one must eventually return what is owed in some sense. By contrast, counterfactual hypothetical reasoning amounts to building a view of a new world out of select pieces from a view of the actual world. Without selective rebuilding, we just immediately get an absurd view and we might as well not bother asking what might hold on such a view. Thus, making a *counterfactual* supposition is a computationally intricate exercise that is quite different from indicative, or if you will, *ordinary* suppositional reasoning. Now, not all non-indicative conditionals are counterfactual in the sense of inviting us to take on board a supposition as false by uttering the conditional. For example, we might say "if the butler had done it, there would be blood on the kitchen knife" (Stalnaker, 1975) and then proceed to argue for the conclusion that he butler did not do it because there is no blood. However, it is also reasonably clear that the line of reasoning we are beginning with this supposition is not an ordinary case of reasoning forward from our current state of inference by hypothetically adding further commitments. In other words, non-indicative, *subjunctive* conditionals, whether counterfactual in their antecedent or not, seem to differ from indicative conditionals in the kind of suppositional reasoning they trigger.

Against this background, it may be natural to take "if A, then C" to be ambiguous or sense-general in the following sense: we get an indicative interpretation if the "indicative" Suppose operation is called, and we get a subjunctive or counterfactual interpretation if we instead call a subjunctive suppose operation, which can be indicated by a counterfactual or subjunctive antecedent, or by contextual means. We will not give an account of subjunctive supposition here, but we see no barrier to constructing such an account within the erotetic theory. Of course, ordinary people also reason with subjunctive conditionals, with further interesting empirical data to consider (Byrne, 2005).

If we see the Suppose operation as our tool for indicative suppositional reasoning, it is natural to imagine that there are certain principles that govern how we deploy this operation in a sensible manner. For example, the following seems like a reasonable principle for reasoners to have on board:

Definition 3.2 (Weak epistemically possible supposition principle). An indicative supposition is unacceptable if it is transparently ruled out by the current state of inference. *Inter alia*, if Γ^Θ and Δ^Ψ are such that $\forall \delta_{\in \Delta}. \forall \gamma_{\in \Gamma}. \exists \eta (\eta \subseteq \delta \cup \gamma \wedge \eta \in \mathbb{K})$ then the putative supposition Δ^Ψ is transparently ruled out by a current state of inference $\langle C, \Gamma^\Theta \rangle$.

The point of this principle is to carve out putative suppositions that are obviously inappropriate for indicative (non-counterfactual) suppositions. Together with our interpretation rule for "if...then," the weak epistemic possibility principle allows us to capture the fact that "material antecedent" inferences are blocked. These inferences have been widely discussed as intuitively wrong, in philosophy, linguistics, and psychology (Stalnaker, 1975; von Fintel, 1999; Gillies, 2009; Starr, 2014; Oaksford and Chater, 2007).

> **Example 35.** Bob didn't dance. *Therefore, if Bob danced then Zuckerberg was President.

After updating with the first statement in the above example, every alternative in our current state of inference contains $\bar{d}$. Relative to this state of inference, supposing d violates our weak epistemic possibility principle, and thus the presupposition for "if...then" fails. Faced with this sentence, we can either let the interpretation crash with presupposition failure, or we have to quarantine it in a different set of commitments, separate from the view we build for "Bob didn't dance." Either way, we will not get this pattern as an inference from a premise to a conclusion.

It is important to emphasize that the erotetic theory account is quite different from what a defective truth-table view of the conditional, on which the conditional simply has nothing to say about false-antecedent cases. From the perspective of empirical reasoning data, a problem of the defective truth-table view is that, as noted already, if participants are asked to list cases in which a conditional is true, the full classical truth-table including cases in which the antecedent is false tends to appear (Barrouillet et al., 2008). In other words, reasoners ultimately are able to produce all the possibilities envisaged by material implication. This is hard to explain if we take "if...then" to correspond to a truth-table for material implication with missing values for false antecedent cases. On the erotetic theory account, we can make sense of the fact that the full list of classical alternatives is inherent in "if p then q," even if those alternatives are not directly conveyed.

The key is that starting with a conditional and reasoning forward to what alternatives are possible does not involve trying to compute Suppose relative to a view at which the thing to be supposed is false. By contrast, if participants are given various scenarios and are asked to evaluate for each one of them whether the conditional is true at it, false-antecedent cases are routinely omitted (Evans et al., 1993). This is to be expected, because relative to a *given* false antecedent case, "if...then" will tend to engender presupposition failure. The erotetic account can thus handle both apparently classical and non-classical aspects of indicative "if...then" in a principled manner.

3.3 Disequilibrium Implication

Moving on, another well-known problematic inference is antecedent strengthening.

> **Example 36.** If the match was struck, it lit. *Therefore, if the match was struck and was wet, it lit.

The strengthened conclusion easily follows on the present account, yet the inference seems wrong. However, we might reasonably take it that conditionals of this kind are only offered in the indicative (if they really indicative at all) in the setting of an inquiry that is constrained to certain range of topics (see the end of Chapter 2). This view would be supported to the extent that the witness in the following dialogue seems reasonable.

> **Example 37.** (*Expert witness*) In my expert opinion, if the match was struck, it lit. (*Counsel*) So you are committed to saying that if the match was submerged in water and struck it lit? (*Expert witness*) Correct. The match was a special waterproof kind. (*Counsel*) So you are committed to saying that if the match was being held in stasis by a quantum anomaly and struck, it lit? (*Expert witness*) No, but these science-fiction cases are outside what is being addressed here.

We might say that the evaluation of whether an utterance is true here only needs to be in equilibrium relative to a set of questions limited to the kinds of cases that are reasonably addressed in the inquiry at hand. In the imagined court case, the inquiry is broad enough so that we are on the hook for having considered that the event under investigation might have taken place under wet conditions, while we are not on the hook for having considered magic or extremely unusual phenomena. In an ordinary conversation in which a matchbox conditional is uttered, we might not even be on hook for considering a wet environment. If somebody then suddenly broadens the scope of what is being discussed, we might retreat from our statements.

Note that this kind of proposal is not a version of the view on which matchbox conditionals covertly amount to "if the match was struck and conditions were suitably normal, then it lit." The conditional itself has to encode nothing else, but whether somebody might want to make a relevant conditional claim may depend on the topic of an inquiry to which such a claim is submitted. Somebody making such a claim may not wish to be held to it outside of this inquiry. We do not have to take for granted that a reasoner can only rationally have one commitment structure (in the sense of $\mathbb{C}$ defined in Chapter 2).

Finally, one may still doubt that "matchbox" conditionals are ordinarily interpreted as standard indicative conditionals, particularly if they are *not* in the past tense. Many conditionals of this sort clearly seem to convey claims about causal relationships, for example. But then, as noted, this would take them outside the class of interpretations we propose to model here. It suffices for my purposes to point out that the erotetic theory is modular enough to make it possible to construct an extension for a relevant account.

There is in fact another possible account of how we interpret various ordinary "if...then" statements that we can construct with the machinery we already have. I will call this conditional *disequilibrium implication* (as opposed to *material* implication).

Definition 3.3 (Informal interpretation rule for disequilibrium "if A, then C"). Where $[\![A]\!]$ is an acceptable supposition relative to the current state of inference.

$$[\![if A, C]\!] = \mathsf{T}[[\![A]\!]]^{S}[[\![C]\!]]^{M} \oplus \{0\}^{[[\![A]\!]]}$$

On this analysis, we could interpret "if the match is struck, it lights up" as giving us the view $\{sl, 0\}^{\{s\}}$. What is distinctive about this analysis is that it supports the inference "if the match is struck, it lights up," "the match is struck." Therefore, "the match lights up," but only if we do not first put into question whether the match will light up before we treat "the match is struck" as an answer. In other words, we only get any substantive inferences out of this conditional if we are not making erotetic equilibrium inferences. Of course, it is easy to see that this conditional is truth-conditionally vacuous. However, on the erotetic theory this is no barrier to useful inferential powers! Moreover, against the background of the relationship between rational inference and relative erotetic equilibrium disucssed in Chapter 2, this is no barrier to rationally defensible inferential powers either.

A remaining issue that is not often discussed is where the sorts of beliefs that we might articulate using matchbox conditionals come from. This is something we will return to once we are in a position to analyze predicate reasoning in the next chapter.

Having motivated the basic erotetic theory account of "if...then" we will now continue with selection tasks.

3.4 Selection Tasks and Information Seeking

The upshot of our story about the Wason card task will be that selection tasks provide no special reason for thinking that our strategies for information seeking are particularly distinctive relative to general reasoning procedures. Neither does it seem like reasoners fundamentally fail to appreciate the importance of falsifiers. There is not even anything to limit the observed patterns to statements with "if...then." The proposed approach will ultimately blame mistakes on the fact that detecting contradictions is not generally a trivial matter in human cognition.

A genuinely explanatory account of the patterns found in the card selection task would specify what kind of procedure is invoked by selection tasks more generally. The more complex that procedure is relative to a more general account of reasoning and the more specific the procedure is to specific experimental settings with cards, the less explanatory power we gain. The more the procedure seems like a general approach to problem-solving, the more explanatory powerful the account.

Our proposal will attempt to take at least a few steps in the direction of a general account, building on the machinery we have incrementally motivated in Chapter 2.

Definition 3.4 (Default procedure for information source selection). Relative to an inference state $\langle C, G \rangle$, consider an information source S associated with a view D_S for further investigation if the default reasoning procedure yields a novel conclusion E for G and D_S as sequential premises. If there is a trade-off between considering two sources S_1 and S_2 with respective novel conclusions Γ^Θ and Δ^Ψ, consider S_1 before S_2 if and only if $|\Gamma| < |\Delta|$.

The idea behind this procedure is that we tend to seek information from sources that have a chance of in some way addressing the issue we have under investigation, instead of being orthogonal or redundant relative to this issue. Moreover, if we cannot seek out all sources simultaneously, we start with those that most directly tend toward resolving our issue toward the fewest alternatives.

Let us return to the card selection task from the beginning of this chapter. Applying the default selection procedure to each card as its own reasoning problem means computing $\{e4, \bar{e}\}[Card]^{\circlearrowleft} \ldots [\bot]^F[\{e4, \bar{e}\}]^F[Card]^F$ for each card and turning the card over if the result amounts to a substantive conclusion (i.e. a result other than "nothing follows" in the default procedure). This procedure directly yields the cards that are turned over by most participants (we are numbering cards from the left of the display). In the derivation below, we start after the first default reasoning step, $\{e4\}^{\{e\}}[\top]^D$.

(Card #1) $\{e4, \bar{e}\}[\{e\}]^{\circlearrowleft} \ldots [\bot]^F[\{e4, \bar{e}\}]^F[\{e\}]^F = \{4\}$
(Card #2) $\{e4, \bar{e}\}[\{c\}]^{\circlearrowleft} \ldots [\bot]^F[\{e4, \bar{e}\}]^F[\{c\}]^F = \top$
(Card #3) $\{e4, \bar{e}\}[\{4\}]^{\circlearrowleft} \ldots [\bot]^F[\{e4, \bar{e}\}]^F[\{4\}]^F = \{e\}$
(Card #4) $\{e4, \bar{e}\}[\{5\}]^{\circlearrowleft} \ldots [\bot]^F[\{e4, \bar{e}\}]^F[\{5\}]^F = \top$

A hypothesis implicit in the derivation for the "5" card (Card #4) is that $\{4, 5\}$ is not a primitively absurd state, so that $\{e, 4, 5\}$ is not automatically eliminated by $[\bot]^F$. The idea is that we would have to either infer from our background information that having 5 in a state commits you to not having 4 in that state, or else bring to mind for each card *what is not listed on it* before updating with the information from each card. Clearly, human reasoners can do all of this in principle. However, the task results suggest that it is not intuitively automatic, particularly if we are in the business of computing results for several cards in a row. The lack of automatism is plausible: If I see a card with a letter on it, I do not ipso facto, without further motivated reasoning, see it as *not* having various other letters on it. There are, as it were, embarrassingly many letters *not* on any given card. Similarly, if I have quantified premises that entail that I cannot have various combinations of things at the same time, it still takes a motivated reasoning step to conclude, for some given pair of such things, that I cannot have them at the same time.

We now consider Evans's version of the task that yields better performance from reasoners. The layout of cards remains the same as before.

Example 38. (Card selection task with negated consequent) Each of the below cards has a letter on one side and a number on the other. Which cards do you have to turn over to determine if the following statement is true?

If a card has an E on one side then it does not have a four on the other side.

Evans (1972) found that 60% correct answers are produced if the consequent of the conditional is negated. Our source selection procedure captures that the majority arrive at the correct answer in this case.

(Card #1) $\{e\bar{4}, \bar{e}\}[\{e\}]^{\circ} \ldots [\bot]^F [\{e\bar{4}, \bar{e}\}]^F [\{e\}]^F = \{\bar{4}\}$
(Card #2) $\{e\bar{4}, \bar{e}\}[\{c\}]^{\circ} \ldots [\bot]^F [\{e\bar{4}, \bar{e}\}]^F [\{c\}]^F = \top$
(Card #3) $\{e\bar{4}, \bar{e}\}[\{4\}]^{\circ} \ldots [\bot]^F [\{e\bar{4}, \bar{e}\}]^F [\{4\}]^F = \{\bar{e}\}$
(Card #4) $\{e\bar{4}, \bar{e}\}[\{5\}]^{\circ} \ldots [\bot]^F [\{e\bar{4}, \bar{e}\}]^F [\{5\}]^F = \top$

Unlike in Wason's original version of the task, our "false consequent" case now obviously generates a primitive absurdity. In the case of the "4" card (Card #3), the state $\{e, \bar{4}, 4\}$ is eliminated by absurdity Factor without any further ado, making the correct answer easy to see by just following the default reasoning procedure.

Even though it already became clear with Evans's 1972 version of the selection task that abstract materials are no barrier to good performance, a literature emerged arguing that the difficulty of the original task had to do with its abstract nature. The idea was that humans are wired to reason about concrete topics that are familiar and that better performance would be yielded by "realistic" materials involving deontic rule conditionals or scenarios involving the detection of cheaters (e.g. Griggs and Cox (1982); Cheng and Holyoak (1985); Cosmides (1989)). Sperber et al. (1995) have suggested that it took researchers in cognitive psychology a while to realize that deontic conditionals are logically different from ordinary conditionals as found in the Wason and Evans studies, and that we had better focus on the ordinary cases if we want to understand the mechanisms behind the original selection task. While it would be hard to disagree on the point of logic, it actually seems that some of what made the deontic rule versions of the selection task interesting survives in non-deontic paraphrases. In the original version, Griggs and Cox (1982) asked participants to choose who needs to be checked in order to see if somebody is violating the rule "if a person is drinking beer, then the person must be over 19 years of age," and they found that virtually all participants made the correct selection. It seems to me that the intuitive benefit of this kind of scenario does not depend on using a deontic conditional (I will leave it to the reader to conduct a relevant experiment). The below modified version (see Figure 3) with an indicative conditional still is intuitively much more obvious than the original Wason task.

SELECTION TASKS AND INFORMATION SEEKING

Fig. 3 Modified Griggs & Cox selection task

> **Example 39.** You were a police officer on patrol, who entered a bar. You saw four people in the crowd, about whom you immediately noticed the facts indicated on the diagram. Select the people you checked in order to determine if the following statement was true:
>
> If a person was drinking beer, then that person was over 19.

We can explain the fact that the "Underage Drinking" selection task is much easier than Wason's original task as follows. We let $>_{19}$ stand for "age is greater than 19," 26 for "age is 26," and 16 for "age is 16." The results for the first three people are completely straighforward (we are only listing the steps after the Depose step in the default procedure).

(Beer person) $\{>_{19} b, \bar{b}\}[\{b\}]^{\circ} \ldots [\bot]^F[\{>_{19} b, \bar{b}\}]^F[\{b\}]^F = \{>_{19}\}$
(Coke person) $\{>_{19} b, \bar{b}\}[\{c\}]^{\circ} \ldots [\bot]^F[\{>_{19} b, \bar{b}\}]^F[\{c\}]^F = \top$
(26-year-old) $\{>_{19} b, \bar{b}\}[\{26\}]^{\circ} \ldots [\bot]^F[\{>_{19} b, \bar{b}\}]^F[\{26\}]^F = \top$

For the case of the 16-year-old, we need to consider the materials in the vignette more carefully. One avenue amounts to the auxiliary hypothesis that $\{>_{19} 16\}$ is a primitive absurdity. This amounts to saying that we can transparently see without further substantive inference that it is absurd to think that someone's age can be both 16 and greater than 19. With this hypothesis, we would then get:

(16-year-old) $\{>_{19} b, \bar{b}\}[\{16\}]^{\circ} \ldots [\bot]^F[\{>_{19} b, \bar{b}\}]^F[\{16\}]^F = \{\bar{b}\}$

There is some plausibility to this picture. The idea that being both 16 and older than 19 is a primitive absurdity, while *it is not* a primitive absurdity to have, say, both "5" and "4" written on the side of a card does not seem completely arbitrary. After all, we can easily imagine cards with multiple inscriptions. However, it is worth exploring an alternative account that does not involve a strong commitment about numerical reasoning here.

Let us return to the broader context of the reasoning task. We have argued elsewhere that consciously controlled tasks are guided by implicit questions (Koralus, 2014a). These kinds of questions can plausibly become part of the views we reason with. In this case, we argue for the presence of an extra question on the basis of what is *at issue* in the imagined task for the police officer. If you imagine being a police officer on patrol in a bar deciding whom to investigate, it is very plausible to take yourself to have on board the issue "who around here is underage?" This is much more appropriate for guidance than a question about who is drinking, given that you are entering a bar where *most* people will presumably be drinking. A beat-cop who focuses on likely *drinkers* in a bar will never make Sergeant. In addition, you might think that you are not really interested in people's age as such; you are merely interested in whether they are underage. In other words, you "see" the ages on people's IDs as either "underage" or "not underage." The idea is that reasoners in our task filter what they see through the background question "is the person underage or not?", and that they reframe the conditional along similar lines. This would directly yield the observed selection pattern.

$$\text{(Beer person)} \ \{\bar{u}b, \bar{b}\}[\{b\}]^{\circlearrowright} \ldots [\perp]^F [\{\bar{u}b, \bar{b}\}]^F [\{b\}]^F = \{\bar{u}\}$$
$$\text{(Coke person)} \ \{\bar{u}b, \bar{b}\}[\{c\}]^{\circlearrowright} \ldots [\perp]^F [\{\bar{u}b, \bar{b}\}]^F [\{c\}]^F = \top$$
$$\text{(Not-underage person)} \ \{\bar{u}b, \bar{b}\}[\{\bar{u}\}]^{\circlearrowright} \ldots [\perp]^F [\{\bar{u}b, \bar{b}\}]^F [\{\bar{u}\}]^F = \top$$
$$\text{(Underage person)} \ \{\bar{u}b, \bar{b}\}[\{u\}]^{\circlearrowright} \ldots [\perp]^F [\{\bar{u}b, \bar{b}\}]^F [\{u\}]^F = \{\bar{b}\}$$

In sum, unlike domain-specific approaches, the erotetic theory predicts that the central problem is contradiction detection and that performance improvements are possible in any content domain. Particularly in problem contexts that are rich with background information, further questions can become salient enough to have a direct effect on what cards are easily identified as potential falsifiers. For further plausible examples of this type of process at work, the reader could consider the novel card selection cases presented in Sperber et al. (1995). In those cases in which correct answers are above 50% it seems quite plausible that the scenarios steer us in the direction of background questions that would aid performance from the perspective of the framework just presented.

3.5 Order Effects

As in the case of disjunction, there are interesting order effects in reasoning with conditionals.

> **Example 40.** (Order effect for Modus Tollens but not Modus Ponens) Girotto et al. (1997) provided ninety-two Italian high-school students with a background story describing a pack of cards that has one geometrical shape (O, △, □) on one side (Top / Bottom) and another geometrical shape from the same set on the other side. They were then given two statements about the cards and asked to respond what if anything can be concluded about the card. The presentation of the premises is simplified slightly for the sake of clarity. Background information provided that shapes on the bottom of the card are mutually exclusive. We will now consider *modus tollens* with respect to order effects.
>
> P1 If there is a circle on the top of the card, then there is a square on the bottom. $\{O_T \square_B\}\{O_T\}$
> P2 There is a triangle on the bottom. $\{\triangle_B\}$
> *What, if anything, can we conclude about the top of the card?*
>
> Only 35% of participants made a correct inference in this problem. Approximately 69% of participants correctly made a correct modus tollens inference if the order of the premises was reversed. The effect of premise order was significant. By contrast, there was no significant order effect for modus ponens, with approximately 88% correct answers.
>
> P1 If there is a circle on the top of the card, then there is a square at the bottom. $\{O_T \square_B\}\{O_T\}$
> P2 There is a circle on the Top. $\{O_T\}$
> *What, if anything, can we conclude about the top of the card?*

We first consider the two premise orders for the modus tollens inference. Background information provided that shapes on the bottom of the card are mutually exclusive. So we might reasonably take

$$\{\square_B \bar{\triangle}_B \bar{O}_B, \bar{\square}_B \triangle_B \bar{O}_B, \bar{\square}_B \bar{\triangle}_B O_B\}$$

120 CONDITIONALS AND INFORMATION SOURCE SELECTION

as already included in the view that we are updating with our displayed premises. In fact, we need this additional information to be fully recruited in reasoning to make the two premises interact at all. Without this information, following the default reasoning procedure with the premises in either order will not produce a new conclusion. The fact that the displayed premises themselves are not sufficient to support a modus tollens inference may account for the fact that even in the "easier" order of presentation, only 69% of participants made a correct inference.

If we assume that we already have the background information in our view before we begin updating according to the default reasoning procedure, we get

$$\{\Box_B \bar{\triangle}_B \bar{O}_B, \bar{\Box}_B \triangle_B \bar{O}_B, \bar{\Box}_B \bar{\triangle}_B O_B\}[\{O_T \Box_B\}^{\{O_T\}}[T]^D]^{\circ}[\{\triangle_B\}]^{\circ}[\bot]^F$$

This reduces to the following, which yields no new conclusion.

$$\{\Box_B \bar{\triangle}_B \bar{O}_B\}[\{O_T \Box_B, \bar{O}_T\}]^M [\{\triangle_B\}]^{\circ}[\bot]^F =$$
$$\{\Box_B \bar{\triangle}_B \bar{O}_B O_T, \Box_B \bar{\triangle}_B \bar{O}_B \bar{O}_T\}[\{\triangle_B\}]^{\circ}[\bot]^F = \bot$$

If, on the other hand, we reverse the displayed premises, we have two possible outcomes. One outcome is generated as follows. If the reasoner follows the default procedure exactly as we have specified it so far, then the conditional premise contributes nothing, since nothing in the result of updating the background view with the categorical premise satisfies the supposition. This leaves us with the conclusion that there is no square and no circle on the bottom of the card, but nothing to conclude about the top. Another possible outcome is that the reasoner Deposes the conditional premise, slightly diverging from the default procedure we have sketched, so that it can have an impact on the inference. In this case, we get,

$$\{\Box_B \bar{\triangle}_B \bar{O}_B, \bar{\Box}_B \triangle_B \bar{O}_B, \bar{\Box}_B \bar{\triangle}_B O_B\}[\{\triangle_B\}]^{\circ}[\{O_T \Box_B\}^{\{O_T\}}[T]^D]^{\circ}[\bot]^F$$
$$= \{\bar{\Box}_B \triangle_B \bar{O}_B\}[\{O_T \Box_B, \bar{O}_T\}]^{\circ}[\bot]^F = \{\bar{\Box}_B \triangle_B \bar{O}_B \bar{O}_T\}$$

The question posed in the prompt only asks us to report what we can conclude about the top of the card, which would limit us to $\{\bar{O}_T\}$, a correct modus tollens inference.

We already considered the inference steps in a plain modus ponens inference for both premise orders at the beginning of this chapter, so we will not repeat them here. Including the background information does not make an interesting difference.

3.6 "Only" with "If"

In Philosophers' English, "if P then Q" and "P only if Q" are equivalent. However, utterances of these two types of statement are intuitively quite different with respect to what alternative scenarios they bring into view. "P only if Q" is intuitively similar to "if not Q, then not P," making what happens in cases in which we do not have Q more salient than they would be in the standard indicative conditional.

It would be preferable to have a compositional account of "only...if" in terms of the meaning of "if" and the meaning of "only." However, as before, we will try to sidestep grammatical issues as much as possible. Keeping in mind the paraphrases just discussed, we will consider the following analysis within the erotetic theory.

Definition 3.5 (Informal interpretation rule for indicative "P only if Q").

$$[\![\varphi \text{ only if } \psi]\!] = \top[[\![\psi]\!]^N]^S \otimes [\![\varphi]\!]^N$$

For example, "p only if q" gives us $q \{\bar{q}\bar{p}\}^{\{q\}}$. We can now use this analysis to consider some data points.

Example 41. Evans and Newstead (1977) found that modus tollens inferences are easier for "P only if Q" than for "if P then Q."

P1 P only if Q.	$\{\bar{q}\bar{p}\}^{\{q\}}$
P2 Not Q.	$\{\bar{q}\}$
C Not P.	$\{\bar{p}\}$.

With the "only if" conditional, modus tollens is indeed predicted to be extremely easy. Simple Update suffices to support a successful query for the conclusion. As discussed earlier, the same inference with the ordinary conditional additionally requires eliminating an absurd alternative.

Example 42. Girotto et al. (1997) found no order effect for their modus tollens problem discussed in the previous section if the conditional was rephrased as an "only if" conditional. As in the previous example from

Girotto et al. (1997), background information provided that shapes on the bottom of the card are mutually exclusive.

> P1 There is a circle at the top of the card only if there is a square at the bottom. $\{\bar{O}_T \bar{\square}_B\}^{\{\square_B\}}$
>
> P2 There is not a square at the bottom. $\{\bar{\square}_B\}$
>
> What, if anything, can we conclude about the top of the card?
>
> C There is not a circle at the top. $\{\bar{O}_T\}$

It is easy to see that with "only if," Girotto et al.'s modus tollens inference basically turns into a modus ponens inference. We already saw that this kind of inference is straightforward in both premise orders.

Having considered "if...then" as well as "only...if" we might next consider "if and only if." As it turns out, we can plausibly construct the interpretation of "if and only if," provided we revise our interpretation for "and" to include a depose step.

Definition 3.6 (Revised informal interpretation rule for "and").

$$[\![\varphi \text{ and } \psi]\!] = [\![\varphi]\!][\top]^D \otimes [\![\psi]\!]$$

Definition 3.7 (Informal interpretation rule for "if only if").

$$[\![\varphi \text{ if and only if } \psi]\!] = [\![if\ \psi\ then\ \varphi]\!][\top]^D \otimes [\![\varphi\ only\ if\ \psi]\!] =$$
$$= \top[[\![\psi]\!]]^S[[\![\varphi]\!]]^{\circlearrowleft}[\top]^D \otimes (\top[[\![\![\psi]\!]]^N]^S[[\![\![\varphi]\!]]^N]^{\circlearrowleft})$$

For "p if and only if q," we straightforwardly get, $\{qp, \bar{q}\} \otimes \{\bar{q}\bar{p}\}^{\{\bar{q}\}} = \{qp, \bar{q}\bar{p}\}$, which seems like the right result.

> **Example 43.** (Biconditional facilitation) Johnson-Laird et al. (1992) found that modus tollens is easier with a biconditional than with a conditional premise.

Clearly, both modus ponens and modus tollens are trivial with the above analysis of the biconditional.

Moving on, some interesting data points regarding reasoning with biconditionals involve tasks in which participants are asked whether certain

"ONLY" WITH "IF" 123

statements are consistent (Johnson-Laird et al., 2004). We will take the view that the question of whether a set of statements is consistent is taken as the question of whether there is a view other than $\bot$ that can be obtained by updating with all the statements.

> **Example 44.** (*Illusory consistency judgments*). 97% of responses correctly identified the following statements as consistent (Johnson-Laird et al., 2004).
>
> *Easy consistency case*
> P1 The chair is saleable if and only if it is elegant.
> P2 The chair is elegant if and only if it is stable.
> P3 The chair is saleable or it is stable, or both.
>
> By contrast, only 61% judged the set of statements below to be consistent.
>
> *Hard consistency case*
> P1 The chair is unsaleable if and only if it is inelegant.
> P2 The chair is inelegant if and only if it is unstable.
> P3 The chair is saleable or it is stable, or both.

The easy case is straightforward with our default reasoning procedure, which for this case boils down just two updates. We get,

$$\{se, \bar{se}\}[\{et, \bar{et}\}]^{\circlearrowleft}[\{s, t, st\}]^{\circlearrowleft} = \{set, se\bar{et}, \bar{se}et, \bar{se}\bar{et}\}[\{s, t, st\}]^{\circlearrowleft} =$$
$$\{set\}[\{s, t, st\}]^{M} = \{set\}.$$

The hard case is more subtle. Both direct linguistic intuition and psycholinguistic evidence suggest that antonymy and negation are not semantically equivalent. Depending on context, "not unstable" does not necessarily mean the same thing as "stable," and "not unsaleable" does not necessarily mean the same thing as "saleable." Stability and saleability, as well as instability, etc., bear a scalar interpretation, and there is no linguistic guarantee that e.g. *not* falling into the contextually specified range of "saleable" means falling into the contextually specified range of "unsaleable." As Paradis and Willners (2006) put it, "scalar adjectives do not bisect a domain in an 'either-or' fashion." As a consequence of these linguistic considerations, we have to consider the possibility that some reasoners will e.g. consider "saleable" to be distinct from "Not(unsaleable)" and so on. If our reasoners *do* treat the antonymy in this problem as equivalent to negation, the inference ends up being relatively simple as before, which should explain why 39% of participants did get the correct answer. However, for those reasoners who do not treat the antonymy in this problem as equivalent to negation before updating with the premises, the default reasoning procedure would generate twelve alternative states if we follow it by the letter. By the erotetic complexity principle, it is unlikely that this inference would be completed.

We will next consider what is perhaps the second-most famous fallacy of conditional reasoning, behind affirming the consequent: Denying the antecedent (DA). Our analysis of "only if" will play a crucial role.

It has long been observed that people are liable in some contexts to infer "Not Q" from "If P then Q" and "not P." Many have taken this as an instance of reasoners interpreting premises with a pragmatic exclusivity implicature (Grice, 1989; Johnson-Laird and Byrne, 1991; Koralus and Mascarenhas, 2013).

A generic exclusivity implicature account is not completely satisfying. A putative exclusivity implicature on "if...then" would generate both AC and DA inferences in the same way by turning the conditional into a de facto biconditional. However, this leaves us unable to explain why AC inferences are made more readily than DA inferences (St. B. T. Evans et al. (1995), and why AC inferences are made more quickly than DA inferences, when they are made (Barrouillet et al., 2000).

The simple default reasoning procedure we used so far generates AC but it does not generate DA without either adding new steps to our default reasoning procedure or appealing to some pragmatic interpretative process to modify the interpretation of the conditional premise.

It may turn out that we can make do with considerations that stick close to grammatical considerations. There are linguistic means of marking, roughly, what is especially important in an utterance, which is generally referred to as the 'focus' of an utterance. Pitch accent is a standard way of marking focus in English. The precise contribution of focus marking remains under debate in linguistic theory. However, there are forms of so-called identificational focus that are regarded as behaving "as if a silent 'only' were present" (Stevens, 2017), which even has a syntactic expression in languages like Hungarian (Kiss, 1998).

We could then consider the following possibility: "if p then q," can be given a focused interpretation "IF p then q" that can be paraphrased as "Only if p, q" or "if not p, then not q." For the purposes of reasoning, this would then send us back to the interpretation rule for "q only if p," which yields $\{\bar{p}\bar{q}\}^{\{p\}}$. We then get a DA inference straightforwardly via the default reasoning procedure. In other words, "IF P, then q," and "not P," yield "not Q."

$$\{\bar{p}\bar{q}\}^{\{\bar{p}\}}[T]^D[\{\bar{p}\}]^\circ[\{\bar{p}\}]^F = \{\bar{q}\}$$

Thus, by appeal to identificational focus, we can in fact successfully generate AD inferences through a process that is more complex than the process that generates AC inferences. This added complexity could explain why AD inferences are less frequent than AC inferences, and why AD inferences are slower.

3.7 Asking What Is Possible and What Follows

Having considered some cases of valid but potentially unobvious inferences, I will consider some cases of inviting fallacious inferences resulting from the combination of conditionals and disjunction. One such class of fallacies is yielded by questions about what is possible given some statements.

We will first need an interpretation rule for statements like "it is possible that P" or "it might be that P." We will treat these expressions interchangeably for our purposes. Our focus is on conditionals rather than on a full account of epistemic modality, so we will adopt the following as preliminary view that suffices for the tasks we will consider.

Definition 3.8 (Informal interpretation rule for possibility talk).
$[\![\text{It is possible that } \varphi]\!] = [\![\varphi]\!][T]^D \oplus \{0\}$

For example, "it is possible that John came to the party or Mary came to the party" would amount to $\{j,m\} \oplus \{0\} = \{j,m,0\}$. Clearly, this is the least complex view that makes it so that there is at least one alternative in which φ holds, but without committing us to φ holding. For example, we get "John came. It is possible that Sally came. Therefore, either John came or John and Sally came." A more surprising inference that this account generates is the following.

> **Example 45.** (Conjunction of possibility to possibility of conjunction) Ragni and Johnson-Laird (2018) found that 92% of participants endorsed the following inference.
>
> It is possible that Steven is in Madrid and it is possible that Emma is in Berlin.
> Therefore, it is possible that Steven is in Madrid and that Emma is in Berlin.
> Does the premise imply that the conclusion is true?

The premise gives us $\{M,0\} \otimes \{B,0\} = \{MB, M, B, 0\}$. If we then apply the default reasoning procedure for deciding whether the suggested conclusion follows, we get $\{MB, M, B, 0\}[\{MB, 0\}]^Q = \{MB, 0\}$, which means the answer is "yes." This is surprising, since normative approaches to modal expressions like "possible" would normally not validate this kind of inference.

With this preliminary interpretation rule in place, we can then treat reasoning tasks that involve asking the reasoner whether something is possible along the same lines on which we treat the task of determining whether some given conclusion follows, using the Query operation. We can now turn to a reasoning task that goes from a conditional premise to the question of whether something is possible.

Example 46. (*Impossibility fallacy*). Conditionals together with disjunctions can yield fallacious inferences about what is possible (Johnson-Laird, 2008).

P1 If Pat is here then Viv is here. $\qquad\qquad \{pv\}^{\{p\}}$
P2 Mo is here or else Pat is here, but not both. $\qquad \{m\bar{p}, p\bar{m}\}$
Is it possible for both Viv and Mo to be here?
Fallacy No

We will apply the default reasoning procedure to this problem with the assumption that the question is whether it follows that it is possible for both Viv and Mo to be here. We then get

$$\{pv\}^{\{p\}}[\top]^D[\{m\bar{p}, p\bar{m}\}]^{\circlearrowright}[\bot]^F[\{vm, 0\}]^Q =$$
$$\{pv\bar{m}, \bar{p}m\}[\{vm, 0\}]^Q = \{0\},$$

hence the answer according to the default reasoning procedure is "no." It is worth briefly considering that our procedure would have yielded a different result had out view actually envisaged alternative states that have $\{vm\}$ as a subset. If we had, say, a view $\{vmr, vms, t\}$ and applied $[\{vm, 0\}]^Q$, we would get, $\{vm, 0\}$ so the answer would be "yes."

In sum, using the basic machinery developed in the previous chapter has allowed us to construct a fairly powerful account of reasoning with "if... then." We were able to explain a wide range of interesting reasoning phenomena, including fallacies as well as correct and intuitively simple inferences. Moreover, the account makes sense of the lasting appeal of two seminal ideas that have often yielded conflicting theories: the idea that "if...then" in some fundamental sense boils down to material implication, and the idea that "if...then" involves hypothetical reasoning. The erotetic theory allows us to keep both of these ideas.

4
Predicate Reasoning

Philipp Koralus, Vincent Wang, Sean Moss, Beau Mount

In this chapter, we present an extension of the erotetic theory to reasoning with predicates and relations. In Russell and Norvig's words, this is what we can use "to represent the most important aspects of the real world, such as action, space, time, thoughts, and shopping" (Russell and Norvig, 2010).

Our definitions of views and of various operations will have to be expanded to deal with this new expressive power, but the extension is conservative in several ways. Firstly, the new operations maintain the same behavior for problems that do not involve substantive inferences over the equivalent of quantifiers. Moreover, we will find that the default inference procedure can stay the same unmodified from Chapter 2, even if the operations invoked by this procedure will have to become slightly more complex. The spirit of the operations stays the same. Finally, we maintain the result that we get classical soundness and completeness under erotetic equilibrium.

This chapter will be technically challenging in ways that are unavoidable. To make sure we have adequate motivation to persevere, it will be worth having a look at a range of examples before diving into formal definitions. We begin with what would appear to be the weakest kind of statement that occurs in predicate reasoning: indefinite statements like "somebody smokes." We might ask how statements of this kind fit into the erotetic framework. Luckily, just as there are independent linguistic arguments for analyzing "or" statements as raising questions, parallel arguments have in fact been made for analyzing "some" statements as raising questions, so that "somebody smokes" can be seen as raising the issue of *who smokes* (Kratzer and Shimoyama (2002); Ciardelli (2009); Mascarenhas (2009)). If we are already used to thinking of a disjunction like "either John smokes or Mary smokes" as raising the question of whether John smokes or Mary smokes, the connection between questions and "some" is not particularly surprising. From a logical point of view, it is natural to think of "someone smokes" as the potentially infinite disjunction "either John smokes, or Mary smokes, or..., or n smokes." If we already think of such a disjunction as raising the question of whether John smokes, Mary smokes, or..., or *n* smokes, it is not a big step to think of this as asking, *for which individual i is it the case that i smokes?*

As Mascarenhas and Koralus (2017) point out, given an analysis of a "some" statement as raising a question akin to what would be raised by a corresponding (potentially infinitary) disjunction, the propositional version of the erotetic theory would directly make predictions about illusory inferences from premises using "some" that parallel the illusory inferences from disjunctive premises that we used to motivate the erotetic theory in the introductory chapter. If we are prone to fallaciously reason from "A and B or C" and "A" to "B," the parallel analysis of "some" would yield the prediction that there should be a tendency to fallaciously infer "x As and Bs" from "some A Bs" and "x Bs."

In the abstract, we might not expect a fallacy here. However, something close to it has long entered internet lore as the "Politician's syllogism," reputedly first identified in an episode of the BBC sitcom *Yes, Prime Minister*. In the "BBC form," this syllogism goes as follows: "We must do something. This is something. Therefore, we must do this." The economist Paul Krugman in fact accuses conservatives of roughly making an inference of this sort in a 2012 *New York Times* opinion piece (Krugman (2012)). Conservative commentators have lodged similar accusations elsewhere. A *Spectator* article praised a discussion about Brexit, because it had involved "no deployment of the logical fallacy so common in this debate ('Some nasty fascists don't like the EU, ergo if you don't like the EU you must be a...')" (Tylecote (2019)). Clearly, the temptingness of this kind of inference diminishes if the content of the predicates readily invokes common sense background knowledge, which seems to be what both Tylecote and Krugman are recruiting for rhetorical effect (recall similar kinds of content effects concerning the card selection task discussed in Chapter 3).

What if we test for this kind of fallacy using unfamiliar content? Mascarenhas and Koralus (2017) found empirical support for an illusory inference from indefinites. 39% of 977 participants recruited on Amazon Mechanical Turk fallaciously answered "yes" in the following problem.

Example 47. *Indefinite illusory inference*
  P1 Some thermotogum stains gram-negative
  P2 Maritima is a thermotogum.
     Does it follow that Maritima stains gram-negative?

130 PREDICATE REASONING

This fallacy occurred at a statistically significantly higher frequency than mistakes in invalid control problems. Only 11% of participants made mistakes in the below invalid control problem.

> **Example 48.**
> P1 Some dictyoglomus is thermophobic.
> P2 Turgidum is not a dictyoglomus.
> *Does it follow that Turgidum is thermophobic?*

In both of these cases, the conclusion is logically independent of the premise, yet in the first case, we get a significant rate of endorsement of an inference, while we do not get a comparable endorsement in the second case.

If the fallacy from "some" is indeed the result of the question-answering process hypothesized by the erotetic theory, we expect the fallacy to be mitigated if the order of premises is reversed, as discussed in Chapter 2. After all, it is harder to treat something as an answer if we have not yet taken on board a question. Mascarenhas and Koralus (2017) indeed found that reversing the order significantly reduced fallacious responses to the target problems, while control problems were unaffected. In addition, unpublished data from the same set of studies suggests that the pattern generalizes as one would expect on the disjunction analogy.

In a similar kind of "existential instantiation" problem, 60% of participants fallaciously answered "yes" (unpublished data using methods of Mascarenhas and Koralus (2017)).

> **Example 49.**
> P1 Either there is an ace in Mary's hand and some other player has a king, or else there is a queen in John's hand and some other player has a jack.
> P2 Sally has a king.
> *Does it follow that Mary has an ace?*

For the moment, let us continue to think of "some" as expanding into a question that is based on infinitary disjunctions. Then, the first premise is tantamount to "am I in a situation (A) in which Mary has an ace or Bill has an ace or John has an ace or somebody else has an ace, or in a situation (B) in which Mike has a king?" Here, (A) has more answerhood support from the second premise than does (B). One of the tasks for this chapter will be to update our formalism to capture this.

As with propositional reasoning, we not only have tempting fallacies but also have cases of simple valid inferences that are not obvious to many people on a first look. Recall Hector Levesque's problem (Bellos (2016); Stanovich (2015)) discussed in Chapter 1.

> **Example 50.** *The married people puzzle*
> Jack is looking at Sally, but Sally is looking at George. Jack is married, but George is not. Is a married person looking at an unmarried person?
> (A) Yes
> (B) No
> (C) Cannot be determined

As we already noted in Chapter 1, the vast majority of respondents, both in a newspaper survey by the *Guardian* and in controlled experiments, voted in favor of (B) or (C). However, the correct answer is (A), which becomes more obvious once we consider step by step what holds if Sally is married and what holds if Sally is unmarried, as Stanovich (2015) and others have pointed out. Corresponding to that insight, the core diagnosis of the erotetic theory here will be that we simply have not taken on board the issue of whether Sally is married or unmarried before making a Query on whether the existential conclusion follows.

The source of the reasoning failures we have discussed is not that people are generally incompetent in making inferences with quantifiers. Many valid inferences with quantifiers are easy. For example, only 7% made mistakes in the below quantified modus ponens problem (Mascarenhas and Koralus (2017)), which probably still overestimates the incidence of genuine mistakes in this kind of problem.

> **Example 51.** *Quantified modus ponens*
> P1 Every archaeon has a nucleus.
> P2 Halobacterium is an archaeon.
> Does it follow that Halobacterium has a nucleus?

However, reasoning from premises involving "all" is not exempt from fallacies. It has long been known that naïve reasoners are prone to committing the quantified version of affirming the consequent, which is sometimes called the "conversion fallacy" (Chapman and Chapman (1959)):

Example 52. *Conversion fallacy*
P1 All Fs G
P2 John Gs
F John Fs

In fact, this kind of fallacy does not even require a premise about a particular individual. Newstead and Griggs (1983) reported that a considerable proportion of participants made the following inference:

Example 53. *Universal reversal*
P All A are B.
F All B are A.

This result does not seem too surprising. Anecdotally, it seems to me that many people who are in the business of teaching basic logic to undergraduates will have encountered live instances of people offering such inferences in discussion.

Universal generalizations using terms like "all" and "every" are perhaps the most important form of generalization in the context of science, philosophy, and and other serious forms of inquiry. However, it has often been observed that generalizations that are articulated with generic statements like "chickens lay eggs" and "sharks attack bathers" might play a more central role for ordinary efforts at making sense of the world. However familiar such generalizations are, their inference behavior presents serious puzzles. Particularly in the case of dangerous properties, generics require few, or even just a single confirming instance to be accepted (Cimpian et al. (2010)). At the same time, generic beliefs stably coexist with belief in counterinstances. Even a large number of disconfirming instances is not reliably enough to undermine a generic belief of this kind or to support an opposite generic belief (Leslie (2017)). Yet, Leslie, Khemlani, and Glucksberg (Leslie et al. (2011)) found that a majority of participants (65%) who accepted a generalization about a striking property were also willing to accept its application to an arbitrary individual.

> **Example 54.** *Generic inference to particulars*
> P1 Sharks attack bathers.
> P2 Whitey is a shark.
> C Whitey attacks bathers.

Depending on the set-up, some researchers found participants were willing to infer up to 100% of prevalence based on a generic statement (Abelson (1966), cited in Leslie (2017)). It is surely puzzling that one of our core cognitive tools for generalizations allows us to infer so much based on so little input, and with such robustness to apparent counterevidence. A successful account of predicate reasoning should have something to say about how such inferences are possible. Moreover, there is a serious question what kind of generic inferences should be theorized as normatively correct (Leslie (2017)). As it will turn out, our notion of restricted erotetic equilibrium will have some application to this problem.

Moving on, now that we are considering reasoning with predicates, we will also encounter old questions about how to make sense of inferences that seem conceptually direct single premise inferences, even though they would require multiple premises (some of them potential axioms) from a purely logical point of view. Consider the following example along the lines of Sellars (1953).

> **Example 55.** *Direct conceptual inference*
> (P1) Montreal is north of New York.
> (C) New York is south of Montreal.

Intuitively, this inference is direct in the sense that it does not seem to involve bringing to mind a separate premise about the relationship between north and south. On the erotetic theory, we will be able to say that simply to raise the question of whether New York is south of Montreal in light of the fact that Montreal is north of New York is enough to obtain the conclusion.

Finally, if our approach to predicate reasoning is going to have any interesting generality, it needs to be able to make sense of how multiple quantified premises interact, and it needs to be able to explain how we can reason with the equivalent of quantifiers that depend on each other. The latter lies at the core of the difficulty of constructing any first-order equivalent reasoning system, and is part of the reason it took humanity roughly two thousand years of research to get from Aristotelian syllogisms to modern logic, as it emerged from the work of Frege, Russell and Whitehead, and Gödel. While these types of problems may be less superficially exciting to the student of the human mind (rather than the foundations of mathematics) than some of the examples we have considered so far, they are in fact at the core of what is required for a truly general account of reason.

In the context of dependencies and multiple quantified premises, it is interesting to observe that various correct inferences that would involve relatively complex derivations in standard predicate logic calculus are intuitively obvious. This should lead us to suspect that the way the human mind represents and processes dependencies is not quite congruent with the way we manage them in predicate logic calculus. The below certainly seems like an inference that one can immediately follow.

> **Example 56.**
> P1 Every professor teaches some student.
> P2 Every student reads some book.
> C Every professor teaches some student who reads some book.

The erotetic theory will capture the simplicity of this inference by allowing the reasoner to automatically "instantiate" one arbitrary object with another, based on what is at issue in the premises. Other inferences with multiple quantified premises that are very similar to each other can nonetheless yield very different performance. Khemlani and Johnson-Laird (2012) report that about 90% of respondents produce a valid conclusion for the following two premises.

> **Example 57.**
> (P1) All B are A.
> (P2) Some C are B.
> *Does it follow that some C are A?*

By contrast, Khemlani and Johnson-Laird (2012) report that only about 12% of respondents produce a valid conclusion from the below two premises, where most fallaciously respond that some C are A.

Example 58.
(P1) Some B are A
(P2) All C are B
Does it follow that some C are A?

Our diagnosis of these differences will be that the way premises can determine the dynamics of what amounts to the equivalent of instantiating variables is such that even small details in those premises can influence whether an inference becomes obscure or nearly automatic.

The above survey of examples should suffice to bring into view some of the types of phenomena we want to be able cover with the new machinery we will develop in this chapter.

The next step will be to extend the notion of views to allow us to represent premises involving "some" and "all."

4.1 Views of Arbitrary Objects

As noted in Chapter 1, we are committed to the view that the mental representations that underlie our reasoning machinery have the structure of their representational contents, which allows us to theorize about reason directly in terms of contents. We now face a seemingly impossible set of constraints. On the one hand, our views must be finite, since it is otherwise impossible for mental representations to mirror their structure. On the other hand, we must represent contents that are naturally thought of as amounting to infinitary disjunctions and conjunctions, which do not have finite classical models. Even if we assume that the domain of individuals covered by a statement like "all dogs bark" is not really infinite but only covers, say, all dogs we imagine exist in the Northern Hemisphere (with apologies to our antipodean friends), we would make things finite but arguably still too large to handle given the commitment to a correspondence between the structure of content and the structure of mental representations that can plausibly be implemented in a human head. In Chapter 1, we called this the *Cardinality Problem* for a content-based theory of reason.

It is at first hard to see how we could maintain the idea that our mental representations have the structure of what they represent. For example, standard quantified predicate logic is mismatched for our purposes. Firstly, its formulas are finite even when their content is infinite. Secondly, formulas in quantified predicate logic make distinctions that are not reflected in their content. For example, $\exists x \exists y (Px \wedge Qy)$, $\exists y \exists x (Px \wedge Qy)$ have the same classical content (they are truth-conditionally equivalent), but are distinct formulas. This is unacceptable if we want to maintain the idea that the representations we reason with have the structure of what they represent.

In cognitive psychology, mental model theory is also initially based on the idea that the mental representations underlying reasoning have the structure of what they represent. However, on closer examination it is not clear that extant articulations of mental model theory can truly help us solve our predicament. Early versions of the theory opted for modeling quantified statements through a finite set of exemplars alongside so-called "mental model footnotes" (Johnson-Laird (1983)). However, it is not clear in what sense "footnotes" are in the realm of contents, nor is there a clearly specified set of operations over them that would allow us to cover predicate reasoning in any generality. More recent versions of the theory opt for so-called "intensional representations" alongside exemplars in reasoning (Khemlani et al. (2015)). However, it is similarly unclear in what sense the structures proposed are contents, rather than a hybrid of exemplars and mental logic. Moreover, there is a lack of a clearly defined set of operations that provably covers predicate reasoning in general.

We could respond by interpreting the principle that mental model structure corresponds to the structure of what is represented loosely enough so that things like mental model footnotes or implicit intensional representations satisfy the principle. In this case, it becomes somewhat unclear on what grounds standard formulas in quantified predicate logic fail to count as contents. We are at risk of losing any clear sense of what makes mental models different from any other theory that invokes mental representations with some structure, including mental logic. The other horn of the dilemma would be to treat mental model footnotes or intensional representations as not being fully paid-up members of the mental model club, merely occurring alongside mental models to provide assistance where needed. In that case, it looks like we are abandoning the idea that we reason via mental models in favor of the less principled view that we reason with mental models with some kind of mental logic of footnotes or "intensional representations" on the side.

What will ultimately allow us to solve the Cardinality Problem for a content-based theory of reason is the notion of arbitrary objects. We can have finite mental models that represent arbitrary objects and their properties and that fully maintain the correspondence between content and structure. This move may come as a shock to those who have been brought up in a philosophical tradition that takes the absurdity of such a notion as an arbitrary object as given. Arbitrary objects are non-individual entities, each associated with a range of application, and having only "those properties common to the individual objects in its range" (Fine (1985a): 5). Fine (1985b; 1985a) showed that a theory of arbitrary objects is coherent and can provide a semantics for classical logic. Adapting this framework for our purposes, when we think a thought that corresponds to a general statement like "all dogs bark," we are thinking about an arbitrary dog that barks. In other words, the representational content of the cognitive state corresponding to the thought expressed by "all dogs bark" includes an *arbitrary dog* as a constituent (as well as a property and a relation) just as the thought expressed by "Fido barks" includes a particular dog as a constituent. Neither case includes a potentially infinite set of particular dogs; nor does either case consist of a potentially infinite set of possible worlds.

Now, thought contents involving arbitrary objects are true of the world in virtue of properties and relations of (potentially infinitely many) particular individuals. However, we do not take those ontologically fundamental truthmakers of our thought contents to be necessarily included in our thought contents, just as we do not see a problem with saying that, in ordinary thought, we represent speed as a monadic property, while speed is a relational property in the eyes of physics (see discussion in section 1.8). Nor, note well, do we concede that these contents are somehow "not really true" for lack of ontological fundamentality.

We will now use the foregoing to extend our notion of views.

4.2 Basic Objects and Dependency Relations

Fine summarizes the idea of arbitrary objects as involving three notions, which we will consider in stages. The first of these is:

> the notion of an arbitrary object itself. It is supposed that, in addition to individuals of a given kind, there are arbitrary or generic objects of that kind: in addition to individual numbers, arbitrary numbers; in addition to individual men, arbitrary men.   (Fine (1985a, 22))

We let **A** stand for the set of arbitrary objects. In addition, we need individual objects, including individuals like John and Mary, etc. We will ultimately want to allow ourselves a fair amount of expressive power for further applications, so we will also want to include functions in our system. It will then in fact be easiest to think of individual objects like John and Mary as constant functions in zero arguments, which is a standard simplifying move in many formal systems. We will assume throughout that there exists at least one such individual. We then let F stand for the set of functions of various arities (i.e. numbers of arguments), including arity zero for individual objects.

Next, we will need to consider predicates. Recall from Chapter 2 that at the level of propositional atoms, we have both atoms and their negations, or verifier atoms as well as falsifier atoms. As we will now form atoms from predicates (applied to objects composed from A and F), we will correspondingly include both predicates and their falsifier counterparts. We will let $P^\top$ stand for the set of ordinary predicates like "drinks," "walks," etc., and we will let $P^\perp$ stand for the set of their falsifier counterparts "not-drinks," "not-walks," etc. Predicates from $P^\top$ and $P^\perp$ that are fully saturated with arguments (e.g. if a predicate takes two arguments it is in fact supplied with two arguments, and so on) correspond to atoms and their atomic negations, which are normally called literals in the predicate calculus. We include = as the identity predicate in $P^\top$ and ≠ in $P^\perp$. Finally, we will include ? as a distinguished kind of arbitrary object (not included in A to simplify housekeeping) involved in the formation of issues, more about which shortly. These ingredients form the basic objects out of which we will build views for predicate reasoning. Formally, we characterize these basic objects as follows.

Definition 4.1 (Basic objects).

Let $A, F, \{?\}, P^\top, P^\perp$ be pairwise disjoint countable sets.

(F arity) $\alpha : F \to \mathbb{N}$. Write $f \in F$ as f^k when $\alpha(f) = k$.

(Constants) $\exists w_{\in F}\ \alpha(w) = 0$.

(P polarity) Let $N : P^\top \to P^\perp$ be a bijection. Write $\bar{P}$ for $N(P_{\in P^\top})$.

Let $P = P^\top \cup P^\perp$.

(P arity) $\alpha' : P \to \mathbb{N}$. Write P as P^k for $\alpha'(P) = k$. $\alpha'(P) = \alpha'(\bar{P})$.

(Identity) $=^2\ \in P$.

We now use these basic objects to define terms. Terms are what can serve as arguments for predicates. For example, if *John* is a constant function (recall that we treat ordinary individuals as constant functions), then ⟨*John*⟩ is a term. For functions in more arguments, we need all of those arguments to be supplied in order for us to have a term.

Definition 4.2 (Terms T).
$A \subseteq T$. If $f^0 \in F$, then $\langle f^0 \rangle \in T$. If $f^k \in F \wedge \{t_1 \ldots t_k\} \subseteq T$, then $\langle f^k, \langle t_1 \ldots t_k \rangle \rangle \in T$.

When no confusion arises, will generally eschew the technically necessary official notation for terms in favor of simple letters. For example, we will normally write j instead of $\langle j \rangle$ and fxy instead of $\langle f, \langle x, y \rangle \rangle$. With the notions of terms and predicates, we can then define our revised notion of view atoms $\mathcal{A}$.

Definition 4.3 (Atoms $\mathcal{A}$).
If $P^k \in P$ and $\vec{t} = \langle t_1 \ldots t_k \rangle$ for $t_i \in T$, then $\langle P^k, \vec{t} \rangle \in \mathcal{A}$ (abbrv. $P\vec{t}$). $|\vec{t}| = \{t_1 \ldots t_k\}$.

As in the propositional case in Chapter 2, we define states $\mathbb{S}$ in terms of atoms. Below, we use $\mathcal{P}(S)$ as the standard notation for the set of all finite subsets of a set S.

Definition 4.4 (States $\mathbb{S}$).
$\mathbb{S} = \mathcal{P}(\mathcal{A})$. Abbreviate '{ }' as '0'.

We now have to bring the equivalent of "someone smokes," "everyone loves somebody," etc. into the system. Arbitrary objects are used to give a semantics for both existential and universal quantification. To make sense of this, we need the second key notion involved in an arbitrary object: dependency.

When we reason about a claim of the form $\forall x \exists y\, Rxy$, we can think of this as reasoning with a relation between two arbitrary objects $Ra_1 a_2$. Here, the arbitrary object a_2 differs from a_1 in an important way: a_1 is an independent arbitrary object, but a_2 is a dependent arbitrary object. To take account of these distinctions, we need to incorporate dependency relations into views. The syntax of classical predicate logic naturally limits what dependencies can be expressed to those that are sensible. Since we do not have access to this tool in views, we need to specify more directly what amounts to a well-formed set of dependencies.

Fine himself provides constraints on sets of dependencies between arbitrary objects. Our set of constraints is slightly different from Fine's and is driven by the need for dependency relations to work well under the various reasoning operations we will go on to define. A further departure from Fine's approach is that we admit potentially infinitely many arbitrary objects that have the same properties but are nonetheless distinct. While there are ways around

140 PREDICATE REASONING

that proliferation, some of which are discussed by Fine, we feel that they would unnecessarily complicate our system. Since we already take the position that arbitrary objects are not part of fundamental ontology, we are happy to weightlessly take them on board *en masse* as long as they are helpful for our purposes.

Let us start again with the observation that some arbitrary objects depend on others. Letting $\langle x, y \rangle$ stand for "x depends on y," we form a set D of all such dependencies among distinct arbitrary objects that are involved in a view. Now, we want to distinguish arbitrary objects that do not depend on any arbitrary objects from those that do have dependencies. We thus form two sets U, for arbitrary objects that are independent, and E for arbitrary objects that have dependencies. We will say that elements of E at least *depend on themselves* in addition to whatever dependencies they might have in D.

The choice of letters U and E is not accidental. As we will have it, U arbitrary objects will be articulated using universal quantifiers if we want to express the content of view including such objects in the language of the predicate calculus. By contrast, E arbitrary objects will be articulated using existential quantifiers if we want to express the content of a view including them in the language of the predicate calculus. When there is no risk of confusion, we will sometimes refer to E arbitrary objects simply as "existentials" and U arbitrary objects as "universals." Our set D of dependencies among *distinct* arbitrary objects (i.e. excluding self-dependency) then forms a bipartite graph (i.e. a graph between two types of objects), where dependencies have to go from an element of E to an element of U but not the other way round. To consider a basic example, the arbitrary objects in a view that corresponds to an interpretation of "everybody loves somebody" will have $U = \{a_1\}, E = \{a_2\}$, and $D = \{\langle a_2, a_1 \rangle\}$, where a_1 corresponds to "everybody" and does not depend on anything, while a_2 corresponds to "somebody" and depends on both itself and on a_1.

We want to construct an erotetic theory of predicate reasoning that is equivalent to classical predicate logic under erotetic equilibrium. This means that we need to restrict the dependency relations in our views in a way that guarantees that we can meaningfully translate between views and sentences in the predicate calculus. The main condition we impose on dependency relations in views that will secure this goal is what we call the Matryoshka condition. This condition is best illustrated visually.

In Figure 4, we adopt the convention that independent arbitrary objects are notated x_i, while dependent arbitrary objects are notated a_i. We let all dependent arbitrary objects inside an enclosed area be dependent on the

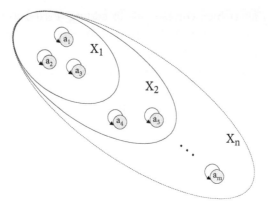

Fig. 4 The Matryoshka condition

independent arbitrary objects enclosed with them. Figure 4 thus depicts the matryoshka condition: a well-formed dependency relation must allow a unique and consistent representation of dependencies on independent arbitrary objects $x_1, \ldots, x_n$ in terms of progressively strictly larger areas of dependence. So while our notion of dependency does not induce a strict linear order of arbitrary objects, it does strictly divide them into what we might call "Matryoshka"-levels.

We now express the foregoing formally as a set of conditions on the set of well-formed dependency relations $\mathcal{R}_\Gamma$ relative to a set of states Γ. We will help ourselves to the notation $A(X)$ to pick out all arbitrary objects involved in X, regardless of whether X is a view, a set of states, a term, or another construct.

Definition 4.5 (Dependency relations $\mathcal{R}$).
Let $\Gamma \in \mathcal{P}(\mathbb{S})$. Let $U, E \subseteq A(\Gamma)$ and $D \subseteq E \times U = \{\langle e, u \rangle : e \in E \wedge u \in U\}$.
Define $\langle U, E, D \rangle \in \mathcal{R}_\Gamma$ iff
(Bipartite) $U \cap E = \emptyset \wedge D \subseteq E \times U$, and
(Matryoshka) For all $u, u' \in U$ $\{e \in E : \langle e, u \rangle \in D\} \subseteq \{e \in E : \langle e, u' \rangle \in D\}$
or $\{e \in E : \langle e, u' \rangle \in D\} \subseteq \{e \in E : \langle e, u \rangle \in D\}$.
For $R \in \mathcal{R}$ write $R = \langle U_R, E_R, D_R \rangle$. For $\langle \emptyset, \emptyset, \emptyset \rangle$ write $0_\mathcal{R}$.

For example, $\langle \{u_1, u_2\}, \{e_1, e_2, e_3\}, \{\langle e_1, u_1 \rangle, \langle e_1, u_2 \rangle, \langle e_2, u_2 \rangle, \langle e_3, u_1 \rangle\} \rangle$ is not a well-formed dependency relation. In order to satisfy the Matryoshka condition, we would also need to add either $\langle e_3, u_2 \rangle$ or $\langle e_2, u_1 \rangle$ among the dependencies, or we would need to remove either $\langle e_3, u_1 \rangle$ or $\langle e_2, u_2 \rangle$. We can compare this to the fact that in a sentence of the predicate calculus with all quantifiers in front (a so-called prenex-normal form sentence) we can have, say,

$\forall u_2 \exists e_2 \forall u_1 \exists e_3 \exists e_1$ (which corresponds to adding $\langle e_3, u_2 \rangle$ to the dependencies) or $\exists e_3 \forall u_2 \exists e_2 \forall u_1 \exists e_1$ (which corresponds to removing the dependency $\langle e_3, u_1 \rangle$). We can think of the Matryoshka condition as enforcing the possibility of articulating a dependence relation in terms of a sequence of quantifiers in a prenex-normal sentence, which is a necessary constraint for a classical first-order equivalent system. At the same time, it is important to note that our dependence relations are not just a way of writing a sequence of quantifiers; such a sequence of quantifiers has more structure than our dependence relations. For example, $\exists e_1 \exists e_2 \forall u_1 \forall u_2$, $\exists e_2 \exists e_1 \forall u_1 \forall u_2$, $\exists e_1 \exists e_2 \forall u_2 \forall u_1$, etc. are all distinct quantifier orders, but they all correspond to the same dependence structure $\langle \{u_1, u_2\}, \{e_1, e_2\}, \emptyset \rangle$. For now, these observations are only intended to help make it easier to grasp the conditions we impose on dependence relations. We will completely formally clarify how to relate our views to sentences in the predicate calculus in a later section. Note that we could adopt a different set of constraints on dependencies. Depending on our choices, we could then develop a version of the system that admits the equivalent of branching quantification. It is unclear whether ordinary reasoning performance requires this descriptive power (Gierasimczuk and Szymanik (2009)). We will not take a stance here and set the issue aside. Finally, the third and last notion involved in an arbitrary object that Fine mentions is that of a value assignment.

> Arbitrary objects receive values. An arbitrary number takes as its values all individual numbers, an arbitrary man all individual men. Moreover, what value one arbitrary object receives may constrain the values that other arbitrary objects receive. The value assignments tell us what values the arbitrary objects can simultaneously receive. (Fine (1985a, 22))

In our system, the terms and predicates in which an arbitrary object occurs in the context of a full view amount to our constraints on our value assignment. We will next turn to defining views.

4.3 Predicate Views and Aboutness

Our ingredients for views for predicate reasoning include sets of states, as in the case of propositional reasoning, but where those states now recognize the further distinctions we developed in the last section. In addition, views include dependency relations as we defined them.

Before we can define views, we need one more ingredient. The way views with arbitrary objects interact in the context of reasoning is determined by the *issue structure* of these views. We will stipulate that issue structure guides operations that perform the equivalent of universal instantiation and so on. For the purposes of articulating a view in the language of the predicate calculus, issue structure makes no difference. In other words, we admit that the contents we reason with include aspects of "aboutness" or "focus" beyond the truth-conditions of sentences in predicate calculus (similar claims about perceptual representation were made in Koralus (2014)). The notion of issue structure will enable successive premises to determine their own ways in which the equivalent of instantiation inferences get made in default reasoning. We will largely confine ourselves to providing a minimal "placeholder" account of issue structure that does the work we need it to do. A more developed theory of issue structure would require a deeper look at notions like "topic" and "comment" in natural language, and similar phenomena in perceptual attention. We will leave this for future work.

An issue structure I in a view consists of pairs of a term and what we shall call an issue predicate. For example, if L is the love relation, and j is the term for John and m is the term for Mary, we hold that $\langle m, L?j \rangle$ is articulated as "Mary falls under the issue of who loves John." We already know what to make of a term like m. To properly define the second element of issue structures, we first need to define notions of open terms and open atoms. In a nutshell, an open term is either ? or a functional term that involves exactly one occurrence of ?. An open atom then is like a regular atom with predicate saturated with an appropriate number of arguments, except that exactly one of those arguments is an open term.

Definition 4.6 (Open terms T_1 and atoms $\mathcal{A}_1$).
$? \in T_1$ and $\langle f^k, \langle t_1, \ldots, t_k \rangle \rangle \in T_1$ whenever $f^k \in F$ and for some $1 \leq i \leq k$, $t_i \in T_1$ and $t_j \in T$ for $j \neq i$. $\langle P^k, \langle t_1, \ldots, t_k \rangle \rangle \in \mathcal{A}_1$, whenever $P^k \in P$ and for some $1 \leq i \leq k$, $t_j \in T$ for all $j \neq i$ and $t_i \in T_1$.

We use open atoms to define issue structures. An issue structure $\mathbb{I}_\Gamma$ for a set of states Γ is a (potentially empty) set of pairs of a term and an open atom, such that if the ? in the open atom is replaced by the term then the result is among the atoms of Γ. We will help ourselves to the notation $\mathcal{A}(X)$ to pick out all atoms involved in X, regardless of whether X is a set of atoms, a state, etc.

Definition 4.7 (Issue structures $\mathbb{I}$).
$I \in \mathbb{I}_\Gamma$ iff I consists of pairs $\langle t, x \rangle$, s.t. $x \in \mathcal{A}_1$ and $x[t/?] \in \mathcal{A}(\Gamma)$.

For example, $\{\langle m, L?j \rangle\}$ is a candidate for membership in $\mathbb{I}_\Gamma$, just in case Lmj is in fact in the atoms of Γ. Issue structures guide reasoning by allowing us to establish that different views that do not involve the same terms are nonetheless in a relevant sense about the same thing in a way that will guide forward reasoning. Among other things, this will account for the fact that "All dogs bark. Fido is a dog. Therefore Fido barks" is a default inference that does not require creative selection of variables for instantiation with creative selection of individuals to instantiate them with. Here it suffices that the two premises are in a relevant sense about the same thing, viz. things that bark. We regiment "being about the same thing" in a notion of issue matches.

Definition 4.8 (Issue matches M_{IJ}).
For $I, J \in \mathbb{I}_\Gamma$, define,

$$M_{IJ} = \{\langle t_1, t_2 \rangle : \exists x (\langle t_1, x \rangle \in I \wedge (\langle t_2, x \rangle \in J \vee \langle t_2, \bar{x} \rangle \in J))\}$$

where, for $x = \langle P^k, \langle t_1, \ldots, t_k \rangle \rangle$, $\bar{x} = \langle \bar{P}^k, \langle t_1, \ldots, t_k \rangle \rangle$.

For example, if we have $I = \{\langle m, L?j \rangle\}$ and $J = \{\langle s, L?j \rangle\}$, then we have $M_{IJ} = \{\langle m, s \rangle\}$. With all ingredients in place, we can finally define views for predicate reasoning. Views are quadruples of a main set of states Γ, a supposition set of states Θ, a dependency relation R, and an issue structure I.

Definition 4.9 (Views $\mathbb{V}$).
For Γ, Θ finite subsets of $\mathbb{S}$, $R \in \mathcal{R}_{\Gamma \cup \Theta}$, $I \in \mathbb{I}_{\Gamma \cup \Theta}$,
$\langle \Gamma, \Theta, R, I \rangle \in \mathbb{V}$ (abbreviated $\Gamma_{RI}^{\Theta} \in \mathbb{V}$).
Write $\top$ for $\{0\}_{0, \mathcal{R} \emptyset}^{\{0\}}$ and $\bot$ for $\emptyset_{0, \mathcal{R} \emptyset}^{\{0\}}$.

As in Chapter 2, the way we envisage reasoning, an inference state consists of a set of views corresponding to our occurrently available commitments, such as a set of premises, and a view that is the current focus of our thinking.

Definition 4.10 (Commitments $\mathbb{C}$).
For $C \subseteq \mathbb{V}, G \in \mathbb{V}, \langle C, G \rangle \in \mathbb{C}$.

While the official definitions of views we just provided are crucial to keep our theory straight, we will adopt certain conventions for further notational simplification in worked examples of reasoning problems. Consider the following view that could serve as an interpretation of "under the supposition that John calls, every student drinks something tasty."

$$\langle \{\{Sa_1, Da_1a_2, Ta_2\}, \{\bar{S}a_1\}\}, \{\{Cj\}\}, \langle \{a_1\}, \{a_2\}, \langle a_2, a_1 \rangle\}\rangle, \{\langle a_1, S? \rangle\}\rangle$$

We will simplify this to $\{S\hat{x}DxaTa, \bar{S}x\}_{a\to x}^{\{Cj\}}$, based on the following conventions:

Notational conventions
(1) We use $x, y, z, \ldots$ as letters for independent arbitrary objects (i.e. ones that would be articulated with a universally quantified variable in predicate calculus); $a, b, c, \ldots$ as letters for arbitrary objects that are *at least* self-dependent (i.e. ones that would be articulated with an existentially quantified variable in predicate calculus); and $j, k, l, \ldots$ as letters for non-arbitrary objects (e.g. individuals like John and Mary). For readability, we will further contrast letters for arbitrary objects by typesetting them in boldface, whenever they occur in example derivations involving full views.
(2) instead of explicitly providing a issue structure I, if I is non-empty we use "⌣" above a term or sub-term that is connected to the atom in which it occurs as an issue, and we suppress any empty I altogether from our notation.
(3) As in Chapter 2, we suppress the curly braces around the atoms of a state, simply writing their elements as a string of atoms, with no significance to the order in which they are written.
(4) Instead of explicitly stating a dependency relation R, when R is non-empty, we indicate what is dependent on what using the $\to$ symbol, except for self-dependencies, which are implicitly marked by our lettering convention in (1). When R is empty, we suppress it altogether from our notation. As in Chapter 2, we also suppress suppositions of the form $\{0\}$.

With these simplifications, we consider a few indicative examples.

Example 59.
Either John dances or Mary does not smoke. $\{Dj, \bar{S}m\}$
Some student jumps. $\{SaJa\}$
All smokers drink.
$\{SxDx\}^{\{Sx\}}$
Everybody loves somebody (i.e. at least one person).
$\{LxaPxPa\}_{a\to x}^{\{Px\}}$
Everybody loves somebody (i.e. someone in particular).
$\{LxaPxPa\}^{\{Px\}}$

Corresponding toy interpretation rules for "all" and "some" would be as follows.

Definition 4.11 (Informal interpretation rule for "all" and "some").
We assume that $[\![\varphi]\!]$ and $[\![\psi]\!]$ are lambda abstracted functions like $\lambda i.Dog(i)$, and that x is a fresh universal arbitrary object that has not yet been used.

$$[\![All\ \varphi\ \psi]\!] = ([\![\varphi]\!](x) \otimes [\![\psi]\!](x))^{[\![\varphi]\!](x)}$$
$$[\![Some\ \varphi\ \psi]\!] = [\![\varphi]\!](a) \otimes [\![\psi]\!](a)$$

As in Chapter 2, we will take it that in default reasoning, if a suppositional view is taken on board as a first premise by a reasoner, it is converted into an equivalent non-suppositional view by $[\ ]^D$ before further reasoning steps are taken, so that the alternative states implicit in the supposition can become available as targets for the answer process. This would give us $\{SxDx, \bar{S}x\}$, $\{LxaPxPa, \bar{P}x\}_{a\to x}$, and $\{LxaPxPa, \bar{P}x\}$, for the relevant above examples. We will take both the suppositional and non-suppositional equivalents to be acceptable view interpretations of universal statements.

Finally, we need to say something about how issue structures are assigned to the views that originate from natural language premise statements, for the purposes of default reasoning. We do not propose to give a proper theory of information structure in natural language in this paper, which would lead us too far afield. We instead will work with the following simplified approach.

Definition 4.12 (Informal focus interpretation rule).

(1) In a sentence involving quantifiers, we will normally take the restrictor of the main quantifier to generate corresponding issues.
(2) In an unquantified sentence, we will normally take there to be an issue corresponding to the subject of the main noun-phrase.
(3) If the two views corresponding to two adjacent premise statements would neither yield shared atoms nor any issue matches, then the issue sets for both views are changed to include issues centered on the first predicate that occurs on both premise statements.

Example 60.
"Everybody loves somebody" will normally have personhood as an issue for the arbitrary object corresponding to "every" (i.e. $\{LxaPxPa\}^{\{P\hat{x}\}}$).

"Mary jumps" corresponds to $\{Jm̂\}$.

"All Fs G" and "John Gs," gives us $\{FxGx̂, F̄x\}$ and $\{Gĵ\}$, since the predicate G is the first that occurs in both premise statements.

These interpretative heuristics are used in our treatment of default reasoning. For non-default "creative" reasoning, there is no constraint on the issue structure, and reasoners can change it at will via the updated version of Reorient we defined further below.

4.4 Axioms, Absurdity, and Analyticity

There is one more ingredient to our views that is not strictly speaking required for the main definition but that crucially defines the behavior of our views in reasoning: primitive absurd states. In the fragment for propositional reasoning developed in Chapter 2, it was enough to include the equivalent of the law of excluded middle to delineate the set of primitive absurdities. For predicate reasoning with identity, this will no longer suffice.

At a minimum, we need to further include the following: (1) any state that contains an atom telling us that an object is not identical to itself, (2) any state that contains atoms telling us that t_1 is identical to t_2 and that a certain predicate holds of t_1 (or of a functional term that has t_1 in it) but that the same predicate does not hold of t_2 (or of a functional term identical to the previous except that it has t_2 in it).

We thus update our notion of primitive absurd states as follows.

Definition 4.13 (Primitive absurd states $\mathbb{K}$).
Let $\mathbb{K}_{\subseteq S}$ contain, $\forall t, t'_{\in T} \forall p_{\in A} \forall x_{\in A_1}$, at least:
(LNC) $\{p, p̄\}$,
(Aristotle) $\{\neq tt\}$,
(Leibniz) $\{=tt', x[t/?], x̄[t'/?]\}$.

For example, $\mathbb{K}$ includes $\{Lmj, L̄mj\}$, $\{\neq jj\}$, and $\{= ks, Lmk, L̄ms\}$.

It should be noted that the first step for expanding the erotetic theory without adding new special operations simply involves adding more absurdity clauses covering new non-logical special predicates. The key is that we can add first-order axioms by reframing them in terms of what they rule out. In this way, we could add arithmetic and various set theories over antecedently given sets. We would add the equivalent of axioms for addition, set membership, intersection, union, etc. via absurdity clauses. For example such axioms, though not translated into absurdity clauses of course, can be found in Russell and Norvig (2010). It should be fairly obvious how to transfer some of those standard approaches to the framework of the erotetic theory.

By including a version of set theory, we could also potentially model reasoning with "generalized quantifiers" like *most* and *more than half* without introducing new reasoning operations. There is empirical evidence to suggest that the meaning of those expressions is more fine-grained than what can be captured by sets regarded purely extensionally (Hackl (2009)). With the present approach, it may become more straightforward to account for those more fine-grained distinctions at the level of view content. This will have to be left for future investigation. By adding further absurdity clauses, we could similarly include reasoning about space by including the equivalent of axioms for relevant spaces, again reframed in terms of what those axioms rule out.

Note that disjunctive absurdities are unnecessary for the avenue of expansion just discussed since, by one of de Morgan's laws, we can replace the negation of a disjunction by a separate primitive absurdity for each disjunct. Thus, any universal sentence can be encoded as a set of absurdities, using the fact that every quantifier-free formula is logically equivalent to one that is the negation of a conjunctive normal form (such a formula is transformed into a disjunctive normal form by pushing the negation down to the atoms). However, we cannot directly encode an existential statement with absurdities. We foresee that, for any such notions that are sufficiently basic to warrant inclusion in $\mathbb{K}$, it will be appropriate to use some Skolemized form (see e.g. Hodges et al. (1997)) of that proposition. For instance, we might say "the empty set has no elements" instead of "there is a set with no elements."

In sum, there is no in-principle barrier to including any first-order axiomatizable subjects in the erotetic theory via primitive absurdities. In the appendix, we prove the following (restated here informally):

Theorem 4.1 (Duality for primitive absurdity).
  (i) *Any first order theory $\mathbb{T}$ formulated in terms of universal axioms in prenex conjunctive normal form can be converted into a valid choice for the set $\mathbb{K}$ of primitive absurdities.*
  (ii) *Any set $\mathbb{K}$ of primitive contradictions can be translated into a set of first-order axioms.*

Note that adding to the scope of the erotetic theory via $\mathbb{K}$ would be quite different from adding axioms as commitments in $\mathbb{C}$, with respect to the effect on reasoning. If we add an axiom as a commitment, reasoners would have to make a choice to take it on board as a premise in making particular inferences about the subject matter the axiom. This would potentially make various direct-seeming inferences seem too easy to miss. By contrast, if an axiom enters the system via $\mathbb{K}$, we are simply postulating that it is absurd to entertain an alternative state in which the commitments of the axiom do not hold. This means that simply raising a question is enough to obtain a conclusion constrained by the axiom. One upshot of this approach is that different (in the choice of absurdities) but logically equivalent ways of axiomatizing the same subject matter will impact what inferences are easily available and what inferences are less available.

Via the choice of whether to cover an inference through absurdity clauses or through commitments, the erotetic theory makes a distinction between (1) inferences that, from the perspective of the reasoner, we obtain directly from the nature of the concepts involved (i.e. entertaining certain things involving those concepts is just absurd) and (2) inferences that hold in virtue of further premise-like facts about those concepts (even if those facts are ultimately derivable as theorems). Given the way primitive absurdities relate to questions in our definitions, we could call this an erotetic analytic-synthetic distinction.

With the foregoing observations, we can provide a model of cases of what seem like direct conceptual inferences. Consider the Sellars (1953) example 55, in which it seemed like we can directly infer that New York is south of Montreal from the single premise that Montreal is north of New York. It should be relatively clear how we can model this inference as erotetic-analytic in a way that does not invoke more than one premise. If we include $\{N(t,t'), \bar{S}(t',t)\}$ as a primitive absurdity, our system supports the above as a single-premise inference in virtue of the concepts of north and south. All we need to do is raise the question of whether New York is south of Montreal, against the background of a view that has it that Montreal is north of New York. Recall from Chapter 2 that our Inquire operation rules out absurd alternatives in $\mathbb{K}$. Thus, raising the question of whether New York is south of Montreal directly gives us our conclusion, without considering any further premises. The inference is erotetic-analytic because it directly arises from merely asking whether the conclusion holds. By contrast, an erotetic-synthetic judgment would require further reasoning steps involving further premises, even if the content of those steps might ultimately derive from steps that are individually erotetic analytic. There is a potential upshot here that might amuse a Kantian, even if it may not be of much consequence. Consider: some erotetic analytic judgments are obtainable a priori in the sense that they can be obtained in a premise-free way using sound inference steps. Now, nothing guarantees that everything that can be inferred erotetic-synthetically in the system entirely from prior commitments obtained as a priori conclusions can be itself be concluded as erotetic-analytic. In other words even if we never take on board any substantive premises, we might have to "separately" reason our way to various intermediate conclusions that we "save" as commitments, before we can integrate those commitments as premises in reasoning to obtain a certain further conclusion. This means that there will be some conclusions that are both erotetic-synthetic, as well as a priori.

Moving on, some readers will be anxious to get a more precise handle on how the views for predicate reasoning relate to sentences in the predicate calculus, particularly since we heavily relied on this relationship in this section. We will next provide rules to allow us to assign view interpretations to sentences in the language of the predicate calculus and to articulate views as sentences in the language of the predicate calculus.

4.5 View Interpretation of $\mathcal{L}_{PC}$

In this section we update our procedures relating views to classical logic. First, we introduce a procedure that allows us to assign view interpretations to sentences in the language of predicate calculus, for which we introduce the symbol ∘. Formally, we define ∘ as a mapping $\circ : \text{Sent}(\mathcal{L}_{PC}) \to \mathbb{M}$. This procedure allows us to interpret premises in the format of sentences of $\mathcal{L}_{PC}$ into our system for reasoning with views. We then introduce a procedure that allows us to articulate a given view as a sentence in the language of the predicate calculus, for which we introduce the symbol ∗. We define ∗ as a mapping $\ast : \mathbb{M} \to \text{Sent}(\mathcal{L}_{PC})$. In Theorem 4.2 we show that these procedures are inverse to each other up to logical equivalence. The procedures in this section subsume the procedures in Chapter 2.

Let $\mathcal{L}_{PC}$ be a first-order language whose logical terms include A as countably many variables $Vars$ and the symbols $\vee, \wedge, \neg, \top, \bot, \forall, \exists$. The signature of $\mathcal{L}_{PC}$ comprises (i) as function symbols of arity k all $f^k \in F$; (ii) as a predicate symbols of arity k every $P^k \in F^\top$. Consequently, we allow ourselves to assume that the set of literals of $\mathcal{L}_{PC}$ is identical to the set of view atoms. Moreover, the logical constant $\top$ corresponds to the empty state 0 and $\bot$ corresponds to the empty set of states ∅. Formation rules are standard, and we use Fmla, Sent, and so on with the obvious meanings. $\mathbb{V}$ denotes the set of views we have defined. We allow ourselves the notation $Vars(x)$ to denote the set of variables that occur within x, whether x be a sentence or a formula.

We first consider the interpretation of a quantifier-free formula $\varphi \in \mathcal{L}_{PC}$ in terms of a finite sets of states $\varphi^\circ \in \mathcal{P}(\mathbb{S})$. First, recall from Chapter 2 the definitions of a product of sets of states and the negation of a set of states.

Definition 4.14 (Product of sets of states).
Let $\Gamma, \Delta \subseteq \mathbb{S}$ be finite sets of states. We define the *conjunction* of Γ and Δ to be

$$\Gamma \otimes \Delta = \{\gamma \cup \delta : \gamma \in \Gamma, \delta \in \Delta\}$$

Definition 4.15 (Negation of sets of states).
For a finite set of states $\Gamma = \{\gamma_1, \ldots, \gamma_n\}$, we define the *negation* by

$$\widehat{\Gamma} = \{\{\bar{p}\} : p \in \gamma_1\} \otimes \ldots \otimes \{\{\bar{p}\} : p \in \gamma_n\}$$

We add to the specification of negation above that $\bar{p}$ for an atom p is defined by,

(i) $\bar{p} = \bar{P}^k t_1 \ldots t_k$ for $p = P^k t_1 \ldots t_k$ and $P^k \in \mathbf{P}^\top$
(ii) $\bar{p} = P^k t_1 \ldots t_k$ for $p = \bar{P}^k t_1 \ldots t_k$ and $P^k \in \mathbf{P}^\top$

We then have:

Definition 4.16 (Interpretation of quantifier-free formulas).
For a quantifier-free formula $\varphi \in \mathcal{L}_{PC}$ we define a finite set of states $\varphi^{\circ\circ} \in \mathcal{P}(\mathbb{S})$ by recursion on the formula φ:

(i) $(\varphi \vee \psi)^{\circ\circ} = \varphi^{\circ\circ} \cup \psi^{\circ\circ}$
(ii) $(\varphi \wedge \psi)^{\circ\circ} = \varphi^{\circ\circ} \otimes \psi^{\circ\circ}$
(iii) $(\neg \varphi)^{\circ\circ} = \widehat{\varphi^{\circ\circ}}$
(iv) $\top^{\circ\circ} = \{\{\}\}$
(v) $\bot^{\circ\circ} = \{\}$
(vi) $A^{\circ\circ} = \{\{A\}\}$ for an atomic formula $A = P^k t_1 \ldots t_k$ for $P^k \in \mathbf{P}^\top$

For simplicity of exposition, we only demonstrate how to interpret sentences of $\mathcal{L}_{PC}$ that are in prenex normal form.

Definition 4.17 (Prenex normal form).

A formula $\varphi \in \mathsf{Fmla}(\mathcal{L}_{PC})$ is in *prenex normal form (PNF)* if it is written as a string of quantifiers followed by a quantifier-free formula. The string of quantifiers is called the *prefix* and the remainder is called the *matrix* of φ. We additionally insist that every quantified variable appears somewhere in the matrix.

Observe that every formula φ is equivalent to a formula in prenex normal form. It is easy to see that such a formula can be found by a sequence of the following operations.

Definition 4.18 (Basic prenexization operations).

Let $\varphi, \psi \in \mathcal{L}_{PC}$ be formulas. The following pairs of formulas are logically equivalent.

(i) $Qx.\varphi$ and φ, if x is not free in φ and $Q \in \{\forall, \exists\}$
(ii) $(Qx.\varphi) \square \psi$ and $Qx.(\varphi \square \psi)$, if x is not free in ψ and $Q \in \{\forall, \exists\}$, $\square \in \{\vee, \wedge\}$
(iii) $\varphi \square (Qx.\psi)$ and $Qx.(\varphi \square \psi)$, if x is not free in φ and $Q \in \{\forall, \exists\}$, $\square \in \{\vee, \wedge\}$
(iv) $\neg(\forall x.\varphi)$ and $\exists x.\neg\varphi$
(v) $\neg(\exists x.\varphi)$ and $\forall x.\neg\varphi$
(vi) φ and φ', where φ' is obtained by capture-avoiding renaming of the bound variables of φ

We can then bring a given formula φ into prenex normal form by iteratively applying the first listed operation that is applicable to a subformula of φ.

Definition 4.19 (Quantifier operations).

Let $R = \langle U_R, E_R, D_R \rangle$ be a dependency relation. Then for $a \in A$, $a \notin A(R)$, we define

(i) $\forall^a R = \langle U_R \cup \{a\}, E_R, D_R \cup \{\langle e, a \rangle : e \in E_R\}\rangle$.
(ii) $\exists^a R = \langle U_R, E_R \cup \{a\}, D_R \rangle$.

Definition 4.20 (∘-interpretation $\mathsf{Sent}(\mathcal{L}_{PC}) \to \mathbb{M}$).

The interpretation ∘ is obtained by restriction from an interpretation defined on arbitrary formulas $\varphi \in \mathcal{L}_{PC}$, where φ must additionally be in prenex normal form. Given $\varphi = Q_1 x_1 \ldots Q_n x_n.\psi$ where ψ is quantifier-free and every x_i occurs in ψ, we define $\varphi^\circ = \Gamma_{R\varnothing}^{\{0\}}$ where

$$\Gamma = \psi^{\circ\circ}$$
$$R = Q_1^{x_1} \ldots Q_n^{x_n} \langle \emptyset, \emptyset, \emptyset \rangle.$$

For $\{\varphi_1, \ldots, \varphi_n\} \subseteq \text{Sent}(\mathcal{L}_{PC})$, $\{\varphi_1, \ldots, \varphi_n\}^{\circ} = \{\varphi_1^{\circ}, \ldots, \varphi_n^{\circ}\}$.

This completes the interpretation procedure. We now turn our attention to the articulation procedure ∗, from views to sentences of $\mathcal{L}_{PC}$. We begin by considering a mapping from states and sets of states into quantifier-free formulas. Notice that the construction rules for sets of view states amount to gathering the exact verifiers and falsifiers of formulas in disjunctive normal form, just as in Koralus and Mascarenhas (2013).

Definition 4.21 (Articulation of states as formulas).
Let $A \in \mathcal{A}$ be an atom. We define A^* to be the quantifier-free formula $A^* = P^k t_1 \ldots t_k$ if $A = P^k t_1 \ldots t_k$ for $P \in \mathbf{P}^{\top}$, and we define $A^* = \neg P^k t_1 \ldots t_k$ if $A = \bar{P}^k t_1 \ldots t_k$ for $P \in \mathbf{P}^{\top}$.
Let $\gamma = \{A_1, \ldots, A_n\} \in \mathbb{S}$ be a state. We define $\gamma^* = A_1 \wedge \ldots \wedge A_n$ for $n \neq 0$, and for $n = 0$ define $\gamma^* = \top$. Let $\Gamma = \{\gamma_1, \ldots, \gamma_n\}$ be a finite set of states. We define $\Gamma^* = \gamma_1^* \vee \ldots \vee \gamma_n^*$ for $n \neq 0$, and for $n = 0$ define $\Gamma^* = \bot$.

As in Chapter 2, we remark that this definition requires us to pick an ordering of the atoms in a state and of the states in a finite set of states, though all such orderings will give a logically equivalent result.

Let R be a dependency relation. Then precisely one of the following is true:

(i) $E_R \cup U_R = \emptyset$;
(ii) there is an $e \in E_R$ such that $\forall u \in U_R.\langle e, u \rangle \notin D_R$;
(iii) there is a $u \in U_R$ such that $\forall e \in E_R.\langle e, u \rangle \in D_R$.

This follows from the Matryoshka condition on dependency relations.

Definition 4.22 (Articulation of $\mathcal{R}$ into quantifier strings).
Let R be a dependency relation. We define R^* by recursion as follows.
(i) If $E_R \cup U_R = \emptyset$, then R^* is the empty string.
(ii) If there is an $e \in E_R$ such that $\forall u \in U_R.\langle e, u \rangle \notin D_R$, then R^* begins $\exists e$ and continues as $\langle U_R, E_R - \{e\}, D_R \rangle^*$.
(iii) If there is a $u \in U_R$ such that $\forall e \in E_R.\langle e, u \rangle \in D_R$, then R^* begins $\forall u$ and continues as $\langle U_R - \{u\}, E_R, \{\langle e', u' \rangle \in D_R : u' \neq u\} \rangle^*$.

Observe that this definition actually depends on which e or u we choose when there is more than one. However, it will easily be seen that the order does not matter, owing to the logical equivalences $(\forall u \forall u'.\varphi) \leftrightarrow (\forall u' \forall u.\varphi)$ and $(\exists e \exists e'.\varphi) \leftrightarrow (\exists e' \exists e.\varphi)$. Alternatively, we may rely on the fact that A is countable to fix a definite order.

Definition 4.23 (∗-articulation $\mathbb{M} \to \mathsf{Sent}(\mathcal{L}_{PC})$)**.**
Let $G = \Gamma_{RI}^{\Theta}$ be a view. Then G^* is defined to be the sentence in prenex normal form with quantifier string R^* and matrix $(\Gamma \cup \widehat{\Theta})^*$. For $\{G_1, \ldots, G_n\} \subseteq \mathbb{V}$, $\{G_1, \ldots, G_n\}^* = \{G_1^*, \ldots, G_n^*\}$

We conclude with a result linking these two procedures together.

Theorem 4.2 (Duality).
$\mathcal{L}$-*Duality:* For all $\varphi \in \mathsf{Sent}(\mathcal{L}_{PC})$ (in PNF), $\varphi \dashv\vdash (\varphi^\circ)^*$.
$\mathbb{M}$-*Duality:* For all views of the form $\Gamma_{R\varnothing}^{\{0\}}$, $\Gamma_{R\varnothing}^{\{0\}} = ((\Gamma_{R\varnothing}^{\{0\}})^*)^\circ$.

The proof can be found in the appendix. With our articulation and interpretation procedures in place, we move on to our updated reasoning procedures.

4.6 View Algebra, Merge, and Restriction

We will now specify the updated reasoning operations, building on the notational conventions from Chapter 2. One of the main changes will be (1) the addition of two entirely new operations to specifically deal with the fact that arbitrary objects can be instantiated with other objects, and (2) modifications to each of the existing operations to deal with the fact that views now have dependency relations and issue structures.

As before, while the operations we will define officially operate on an inference state $\langle C, G \rangle$, we will normally specify operations as directly going to work on a view G, unless we are considering an operation that alters C in other ways. Moreover, we stipulate that for any operation O, $\Gamma_{RI}^{\Theta}[\Delta_{SJ}^{\Psi}]^O = \Gamma_{RI}^{\Theta}$ unless otherwise defined. In other words, operations that are undefined for the inputs provided return their external (left) argument unmodified.

We will first need to define a kind of basic algebra of dependency relations. A first useful operation is the restriction of a dependency relation, which allows us to eliminate all those elements of a dependency relation that involve arbitrary objects that do not occur in a given set X of arbitrary objects.

Definition 4.24 ($\mathcal{R}$ Restriction).
$[R]_X = \langle U_R \cap X, E_R \cap X, D_R \cap ((E_R \cap X) \times (U_R \cap X)) \rangle$.
$[R]_\Gamma = [R]_{\mathcal{A}(\Gamma)}$.
Given $\langle \Gamma, \Theta, R, I \rangle$, we allow ourselves to write $\langle \Gamma, \Theta, [R], I \rangle$ for $\langle \Gamma, \Theta, [R]_{\Gamma \cup \Theta}, I \rangle$.

Among other things, the restriction operation will allow us to recover a well-formed view after all occurrences of some arbitrary object have been deleted from the atoms of a view, which can happen as a result of various operations. For similar reasons, we will also need a restriction operations on issues.

Definition 4.25 ($\mathbb{I}$ Restriction).
Within a quadruple $\langle \Gamma, \Theta, R, [I] \rangle$, let

$$[I] = \{\langle t, x \rangle : \langle t, x \rangle \in I \wedge x[t/?] \in \mathcal{A}(\Gamma \cup \Theta)\}$$

Next, we will need to be able to combine dependency relations. There are various ways in which one could define the fusion of two dependency relations that arises when we wish to combine two views as in a conjunction. The main constraints are that our way of combining dependency relations should ultimately respect soundness (and support completeness as part of the system as a whole) and that it should support inference behavior that seems empirically appropriate for our purposes. We opt for a particular avenue that will work well with our overall theoretical goals. Fusing dependency relations will involve a recursive definition in terms of a simpler operation $\bowtie$ that we will call chaining of dependency relations. Chaining of two dependency relations $R \bowtie S$ is similar to taking a block of quantifiers corresponding to R (see the articulation procedure in the previous section) and sticking it to the left of a block of quantifiers corresponding to S (with the caveats already discussed about the differences between quantifier blocks and our dependency relations). More specifically, for R, S two dependency relations, $R \bowtie S$ gathers up all the universal and existential arbitrary objects as well as all the dependencies in R and S. It then adds further dependencies of all existentials in S on all universals in R. It would not be a good idea to have chaining of dependency relation as our main way of combining dependency relations. After all, chaining generates many unwanted dependencies. For example, if we are forming the equivalent of a conjunction of two views that can be articulated as $\forall x P x$ and $\exists y P y$, there is no reason y should become dependent on x.

To avoid adding too many unwanted dependencies, we will define a slightly different notion of the *fusion* of two dependency structures R and S, notated $R \bowtie S$, recursively in terms of chaining. The recursion steps are as follows. We first find E_0, the set of all existentials in R and S that do not depend on any universals. We then find U_0, the union of (1) the set of those universals u in R such that every existential in R not in E_0 depends on u and (2) the set of those universals u in S such that every existential in S not in E_0 depends on u. We then chain $\langle U_0, E_0, \emptyset \rangle$ with the fusion of $[R]_{E_0 \cup U_0}$ and $[S]_{E_0 \cup U_0}$. In other words, we chain with the fusion of the remainder after E_0 and U_0 have been restricted out of R and S. Computing the fusion of this remainder will in turn lead us to find a new E_0' and U_0' and so on, until the last remaining fusion step is $\langle \emptyset, \emptyset, \emptyset \rangle \bowtie \langle \emptyset, \emptyset, \emptyset \rangle$, the result of which is $\langle \emptyset, \emptyset, \emptyset \rangle$. Formally,

Definition 4.26 ($\mathcal{R}$ Algebra).
Let $R \bowtie S = \langle U_R \cup U_S, E_R \cup E_S, D_R \cup D_S \cup E_S \times U_R \rangle$ and let $0_\mathcal{R} \bowtie 0_\mathcal{R} = 0_\mathcal{R}$.
Let

$$R \bowtie S = \langle U_0, E_0, \emptyset \rangle \bowtie ([R]_{A(R)-(E_0 \cup U_0)} \bowtie [S]_{A(S)-(E_0 \cup U_0)})$$

where $E_0 = \{e_{\in E_R \cup E_S} : \forall u. \langle e, u \rangle \notin D_R \cup D_S\}$ and
$U_0 = \{u_{\in U_R \cup U_S} : \forall e \notin E_0. \langle e, u \rangle \notin (E_R \times U_R - D_R) \cup (E_S \times U_S - D_S)\}$.

At this point we remark that this definition is something of a trade-off between generality and simplicity. A more broadly applicable version of $\bowtie$ is given as Definition B.5 in the appendix. The two definitions agree wherever the former is well-defined, but the latter is more complicated to compute with. All examples in this book fall within the scope of Definition 4.26, so we leave investigation of the merits of Definition B.5 to future work.

Almost any type of inference with quantified premise statements will force us to compute the fusion of dependence relations. We will now go through some examples in detail. Cases in which we have a premise with only universals and a premise with only existentials will involve fusions as follows $\langle \{x\}, \emptyset, \emptyset \rangle \bowtie \langle \emptyset, \{a\}, \emptyset \rangle = \langle \{x\}, \{a\}, \emptyset \rangle \bowtie (0_\mathcal{R} \bowtie 0_\mathcal{R}) = \langle \{x\}, \{a\}, \emptyset \rangle \bowtie 0_\mathcal{R} = \langle \{x\}, \{a\}, \emptyset \rangle$. A more intricate example is the following.

$$\langle \{x,y\}, \{a\}, \{\langle a, x \rangle\} \rangle \bowtie \langle \{z\}, \{b\}, \emptyset \rangle$$
$$= \langle \{x,z\}, \{b\}, \emptyset \rangle \bowtie (\langle \{y\}, \{a\}, \emptyset \rangle \bowtie 0_\mathcal{R})$$
$$= \langle \{x,z\}, \{b\}, \emptyset \rangle \bowtie (\langle \{y\}, \{a\}, \emptyset \rangle \bowtie (0_\mathcal{R} \bowtie 0_\mathcal{R}))$$

$$= \langle\{x,z\},\{b\},\emptyset\rangle \bowtie (\langle\{y\},\{a\},\emptyset\rangle \bowtie 0_{\mathcal{R}})$$
$$= \langle\{x,z\},\{b\},\emptyset\rangle \bowtie \langle\{y\},\{a\},\emptyset\rangle$$
$$= \langle\{x,y,z\},\{a,b\},\{\langle a,x\rangle,\langle a,z\rangle\}\rangle$$

Finally, certain inferences involve fusing two dependency relations with overlapping arbitrary objects. This can happen as a result of certain substitutions that our reasoning operations can perform, which we will see later. Our actual "use cases" for empirically motivated cases will be considerably simpler than the example below.

$$\langle\{v,w,x\},\{a,b\},\{\langle a,v\rangle\}\cup(\{b\}\times\{v,w,x\})\rangle$$
$$\bowtie \langle\{w,y\},\{c,d,e\},\{\langle c,w\rangle\}\cup(\{d\}\times\{w,y\})\rangle$$
$$= \langle\{v,w\},\{e\},\emptyset\rangle \bowtie (\langle\{x\},\{a,b\},\{\langle b,x\rangle\}\rangle \bowtie \langle\{y\},\{c,d\},\{\langle d,y\rangle\}\rangle)$$
$$= \langle\{v,w\},\{e\},\emptyset\rangle \bowtie (\langle\{x,y\},\{a,c\},\emptyset\rangle \bowtie (\langle\emptyset,\{b\},\emptyset\rangle \bowtie \langle\emptyset,\{d\},\emptyset\rangle))$$
$$= \langle\{v,w\},\{e\},\emptyset\rangle \bowtie (\langle\{x,y\},\{a,c\},\emptyset\rangle \bowtie (\langle\emptyset,\{b,d\},\emptyset\rangle \bowtie (0_{\mathcal{R}} \bowtie 0_{\mathcal{R}})))$$
$$= \langle\{v,w\},\{e\},\emptyset\rangle \bowtie (\langle\{x,y\},\{a,c\},\emptyset\rangle \bowtie (\langle\emptyset,\{b,d\},\emptyset\rangle \bowtie 0_{\mathcal{R}}))$$
$$= \langle\{v,w\},\{e\},\emptyset\rangle \bowtie (\langle\{x,y\},\{a,c\},\emptyset\rangle \bowtie \langle\emptyset,\{b,d\},\emptyset\rangle)$$
$$= \langle\{v,w\},\{e\},\emptyset\rangle \bowtie \langle\{x,y\},\{a,b,c,d\},\{\langle b,x\rangle,\langle b,y\rangle,\langle d,x\rangle,\langle d,y\rangle\}\rangle$$
$$= \langle\{v,w,x,y\},\{a,b,c,d,e\},(\{a,b,c,d\}\times\{v,w\})\cup(\{b,d\}\times\{x,y\})\rangle$$

We now have all ingredients in place to update our formal definition of Product. Note that the complicated-looking case for $\Gamma_{RI}^{\Theta} \otimes^T \Delta_{SJ}^{\Psi}$ is only necessary because we will have operations that are defined in terms of multiple products in sequence. For the Product of just two views, what happens to the dependency relations just reduces to fusion of the kind just discussed. Notice that what happens to the states themselves (setting aside dependencies and issue structure) has stayed the same relative to Chapter 2.

Definition 4.27 (Product).

$$\Gamma^{\Theta} \otimes \Delta^{\Psi} = (\{\gamma_{\in\Gamma} \cup \delta_{\in\Delta} : \exists \psi_{\in\Psi}(\psi \subseteq \gamma)\} \cup \{\gamma_{\in\Gamma} : \neg\exists\psi_{\in\Psi}(\psi \subseteq \gamma)\})^{\Theta}$$
$$(\Gamma \otimes \Delta)^{\{0\}} = \Gamma^{\{0\}} \otimes \Delta^{\{0\}}$$
$$\bigotimes_{i\in P} \Delta_i^{\Psi_i} = \{0\}^{\{0\}} \otimes \Delta_1^{\Psi_1} \otimes \ldots \otimes \Delta_n^{\Psi_n}$$
$$\Gamma_{RI}^{\Theta} \otimes^T \Delta_{SJ}^{\Psi} = (\Gamma^{\Theta} \otimes \Delta^{\Psi})_{[(T\bowtie R)\bowtie(T\bowtie S)][I\cup J]}$$
$$\Gamma_{RI}^{\Theta} \otimes \Delta_{SJ}^{\Psi} = \Gamma_{RI}^{\Theta} \otimes^{0_{\mathcal{R}}} \Delta_{SJ}^{\Psi}$$
$$\bigotimes_{i\in P}^{T} \Delta_{iS_iJ_i}^{\Psi_i} = \top \otimes^T \Delta_{1S_1J_1}^{\Psi_1} \otimes^T \ldots \otimes^T \Delta_{nS_nJ_n}^{\Psi_n}$$

158   PREDICATE REASONING

Similar to what we had before in Chapter 2, $\{0\}_{\varnothing\varnothing}^{\{0\}}$ behaves as an identity element for Product, which we identify with "truth," and $\{\}_{\varnothing\varnothing}^{\{0\}}$ behaves as an absorbing element, which we identify with 'false'. We will consider a complex example with dependencies.

$$\{\{\underbrace{Qbx, Qxw, Qwv, Rw}_{\gamma_1}\}, \{\underbrace{\widetilde{Sav}}_{\gamma_2}\}\}\underbrace{{}_{a \to v, b \to \{v,w,x\}}^{\{\{\overbrace{Pw}^{\theta}\}\}}}_{R}$$
$$\otimes \ \{\{\underbrace{Scw}_{\delta_1}\}, \{\underbrace{Tdey, Ue}_{\delta_2}\}\}\underbrace{{}_{c \to w, d \to \{w,y\}}^{\{\{\overbrace{Rw}^{\psi}\}\}}}_{S}$$

$$= \{\gamma_1, \gamma_2\}_{R\varnothing}^{\{\theta\}} \otimes^{0_{\mathcal{R}}} \{\delta_1, \delta_2\}_{S\varnothing}^{\{\psi\}}$$

$$= (\{\gamma_1, \gamma_2\}^{\{\theta\}} \otimes \{\delta_1, \delta_2\}^{\{\psi\}})_{[0_{\mathcal{R}}\bowtie R]\bowtie[0_{\mathcal{R}}\bowtie S]}$$

Since $\{Rw\} =: \psi \subset \gamma_1$, and $Rw \notin \gamma_2$:

$$= (\{\gamma_1 \cup \delta_1, \gamma_1 \cup \delta_2\} \cup \{\gamma_2\})_{[0_{\mathcal{R}}\bowtie R]\bowtie[0_{\mathcal{R}}\bowtie S]}^{\{Pw\}}$$

$$= \{\{Qbx, Qxw, Qwv, Rw, Scw\},$$

$$\{Qbx, Qxw, Qwv, Rw, Tdey, Ue\}, \{Sav\}\}_R^{\{\{Pw\}\}}$$

where $R = \{a,b,c,d\} \to \{v,w\}, \{b,d\} \to \{x,y\}$.

We similarly update our Sum operation.

Definition 4.28 (Sum).
$$\Gamma_{RI}^{\Theta} \oplus^T \Delta_{SJ}^{\Theta} = (\Gamma \cup \Delta)_{[(T\bowtie R)\bowtie(T\bowtie S)][I\cup J]}^{\Theta}$$
$$\Gamma_{RI}^{\Theta} \oplus \Delta_{SJ}^{\Theta} = \Gamma_{RI}^{\Theta} \oplus^{0_{\mathcal{R}}} \Delta_{SJ}^{\Theta}$$
$$\bigoplus_{i \in P}^T \Delta_{S_i J_i}^{\Psi_i} = \varnothing_{0_{\mathcal{R}}\varnothing}^{\Psi} \oplus^T \Delta_{1 S_1 J_1}^{\Psi} \oplus^T \ldots \oplus^T \Delta_{n S_n J_n}^{\Psi}$$

We will again consider an example with substantial dependencies.

$$\{\{\underbrace{Qbx, Qxw, Qwv, Rw}_{\gamma_1}\}, \{\underbrace{\widetilde{Sav}}_{\gamma_2}\}\}\underbrace{{}_{a \to v, b \to \{v,w,x\}}^{\{\{Mw\}\}}}_{R}$$
$$\oplus \ \{\{\underbrace{Scw}_{\delta_1}\}, \{\underbrace{Tdey, Ue}_{\delta_2}\}\}\underbrace{{}_{c \to w, d \to \{w,y\}}^{\{\{Mw\}\}}}_{S}$$

$$= \{\gamma_1, \gamma_2, \delta_1, \delta_2\}_{[0_{\mathcal{R}}\bowtie R]\bowtie[0_{\mathcal{R}}\bowtie S]}^{\{\{Mw\}\}}$$

$$= \{\{Qbx, Qxw, Qwv, Rw\},$$

$$\{Sav\}, \{Scw\}, \{Tdey, Ue\}\}_{\{a,b,c,d\} \to \{v,w\}, \{b,d\} \to \{x,y\}}^{\{\{Mw\}\}}$$

Moving on, our notion of answerhood potential stays unchanged from Chapter 2.

Definition 4.29 ($\mathcal{A}$ Answer potential).
$$\Gamma[\Delta]^{AP} = |\mathcal{A}(\Gamma) \cap \mathcal{A}(\Delta)|$$

Answer in essence stays unchanged as well, except that we need to restrict R and I in case relevant states get eliminated. As before, Answer only does anything if the internal argument has a $\{0\}$ supposition.

Definition 4.30 (Answer).
$$\Gamma_{RI}^{\Theta}[\Delta_{SJ}^{\{0\}}]^A = (\underset{\gamma \in \Gamma}{\arg\max}\ \Delta[\{\{p\} : p \in \gamma\}]^{AP})_{[R][I]}^{\Theta}$$

We next bring our definition of negation up to date to deal with dependency relations. The aspects of negation having to do with states and atoms essentially stay the same. To get the equivalent of negating the "quantificational" aspects of a view, we "flip" its dependency relation.

Definition 4.31 (Negation).
$[\Gamma_{RI}^{\Theta}]^N = (\Theta^{\{0\}} \otimes ([\Gamma]^N)^{\{0\}})_{[R]^N[I]^N}$
$[\Gamma]^N = \bigotimes_{\gamma \in \Gamma} \hat{\gamma}^{\{0\}}$
$\hat{\gamma} = \{\{\bar{p}\} : p_{\in \gamma}\}$
$\bar{p} = \bar{F}\vec{\tau}$ if $p = F\vec{\tau}$; $\bar{p} = F\vec{\tau}$ if $p = \bar{F}\vec{\tau}$
$[R]^N = \langle E_R, U_R, \{\langle a,b \rangle \in U_R \times E_R : \langle b,a \rangle \notin D_R\}\rangle$
$[I]^N = I \cup \{\langle t, \bar{x}\rangle : \langle t, x \rangle \in I\}$

For example, if we apply Negation to

$$\{PxLxa, \bar{P}x\}_{\langle\{x\},\{a\},\{\langle a,x\rangle\}\rangle\ \varnothing}^{\{Rt\}}$$

(e.g. "supposing Tom rules, everybody loves somebody"), we get

$$\{\bar{P}xPxRt, \bar{L}xaPxRt\}_{\langle\{a\},\{x\},\varnothing\rangle\ \varnothing}^{\{0\}}.$$

We will shortly define operations to get rid of alternatives containing primitive absurdities, after which we would obtain $\{\bar{L}axPaRt\}$. In other words, we would get a view that we can gloss as "Tom rules and some person does not love anybody."

Moving on, operations that perform the equivalent of instantiation of variables will require us to be able to substitute arbitrary objects with terms (which may or may not themselves be arbitrary objects). The necessary substitution operation will additionally require us to be able to replace certain arbitrary objects with fresh ones that do not occur anywhere else in an inference step. This need arises because we need to avoid the equivalent of illegitimate variable capture in forming the equivalent of conjunctions and disjunctions as a result of multiple instantiations. For example, from $\forall x \exists y(x \text{ loves } y)$ we want to be able to infer $\exists y \exists z(\text{John loves } y \text{ \& Mary loves } z)$, but not $\exists y$ (John loves y & Mary loves y). Since this substitution process can introduce new arbitrary objects, it will also have to update our dependency relation in a way that ensures we get a well-formed view as a result. The details of this definition are quite intricate, since they were written in a way that facilitates the proofs showing that our operations are well-defined and sound and complete under erotetic equilibrium. Our main purpose in this book is to present the theory in a way that makes it possible for a reader to explore what it says about the capacity to reason, and much of this formal detail would be an unnecessary distraction. Moreover, the core tenets of the erotetic theory at any rate leave some design choice in how exactly we manage novelization and the resulting update of our dependency relations. For our purposes, then, we will leave for the appendix to show that there exists a fully formal definition of substitution that supports its uses below, which we will capture here more informally. We use the standard notation $X[b/a]$ to denote the result of replacing all occurrences of a in X by b.

Definition 4.32 (Substitution (informal)).

For $A(\Gamma) \cap A(\Theta) = \emptyset$,
$\text{Sub}^T_{\langle t,a \rangle}(\Gamma_I^\Theta) = \Gamma_{T'I'}^{\prime\Theta}$, where

- (Γ') Recall that arbitrary objects in a view can be grouped into "Matryoshka"-levels, as in Figure 4. Then, Γ' is $\Gamma[t/a]$ where additionally any arbitrary object at a lower level as well as any existential arbitrary object at the same level (which can only happen when $a \in E_T$) as a is replaced by a novel one that has not yet appeared in the computation of the conclusion of the step.
- (T') T' is T chained (using the $\bowtie$ operation) with a copy of T in which the same novelization replacements as in Γ' have occurred and that is restricted to only the novelized arbitrary objects.

(I') I' is a copy of I in which all the all the same novelization replacements as in Γ' have occurred and in which all occurrences of a are replaced by t.

Note that substitution is an operation that is used as a component of reasoning operations rather than being a reasoning operation itself. Thus, it should not be alarming that the argument of substitution is less than a full view.

We will briefly observe that, given the way we interpret T' in the informal definition above, we get that all new existential arbitrary objects generated as the result of novelization will depend on all new copies of what they initially depended on. A definition generating fewer dependencies would be possible in principle, but it would break certain symmetries required for the definitions in which we use substitution below. It would also be possible in principle to abandon first-order equivalence, which would allow us to introduce even fewer dependencies.

The first operation recruiting substitution for the equivalent of instantiation of universals will be our updated version of Merge. At the level of atoms, Merge will behave in the same way as in Chapter 2. In addition, Merge will now attempt to "instantiate" arbitrary objects in Δ_{SJ}^{Ψ} that are issue matched with terms in Γ_{RI}^{Θ} before performing the Product operation. For example, this operation will allow us to make an inference from "every person eats some sugary thing" and "supposing a thing is sugary then that thing is hated by someone" to "every person eats some sugary thing that is hated by someone." The arguments of Merge will have to meet a precondition. Either no arbitrary objects are shared between the internal and the external argument or, alternatively, the dependency relation of the internal argument could be obtained by restricting the dependency relation of the external argument. This helps us avoid the equivalent of unsound name collision. Next, we have to determine the appropriate subset of issue matches to guide potential instantiations in the internal argument. We will find sets of issue matches with the internal argument separately for each $y \in \Gamma$. In particular, we will find, for each y, those issue matches $\langle t, u \rangle$ involving a universal u in the internal argument, where some state ψ in the supposition of the internal argument would be contained in y if we were to substitute all occurrences of u with t, but where ψ would otherwise not be contained in y. With that restricted set of issue matches, Merge can then try a purely "atomic" product of each y with the internal argument, as well as a product with the internal argument post appropriate substitutions.

Definition 4.33 (Merge).

For either $A(R) \cap A(S) = \emptyset$ or $[R]_{\Delta \cup \Psi} = S$,
$$\Gamma_{RI}^{\Theta}[\Delta_{SJ}^{\Psi}]^{M} = \bigoplus_{\gamma \in \Gamma}^{R \bowtie S} \left(\{\gamma\}_{RI}^{\Theta} \otimes^{R \bowtie S} \Delta_{SJ}^{\Psi} \otimes^{R \bowtie S} \bigotimes_{\langle t,u \rangle \in M'_{IJ}(\gamma)}^{R \bowtie S} \text{Sub}_{\langle t,u \rangle}^{R \bowtie S} (\Delta_{J}^{\{0\}}) \right),$$
where $M'_{IJ}(\gamma) = \{\langle t, u \rangle \in M_{IJ} : u \in U_S \land \exists_{\psi \in \Psi}(\psi[t/u] \subseteq \gamma \land \psi \not\subseteq \gamma)\}$

Formally, our example then proceeds as follows.
$\{PxExaS\hat{a}, \bar{P}x\}_{a \to x}[\{Hby\}_{b \to y}^{\{S\hat{y}\}}]^M = \{PxExaS\hat{a}Hca, \bar{P}x\}_{a,c \to x}$. To take another example, let us consider an inference from "either John smokes or Mary smokes" and "supposing a person smokes then that person loves somebody" to "Either John smokes and loves somebody or Mary smokes and loves somebody."

$\{S\hat{j}, S\hat{m}\}[\{Lxa\}_{a \to x}^{\{S\hat{x}\}}]^M = \{S\hat{j}Ljb, S\hat{m}Lmc\}$. Note that this example illustrates the need for novelization in substitution, to avoid the invalid and entirely unintuitive inference that has John and Mary love the same person.

We can now already begin to consider a substantive example from the introductory section. Though we have not formally defined the updated version of $\circlearrowright$, we can consider an example in which it simple reduces to M. As we introduce more operations, we will incrementally push forward the derivations of our key examples from the introduction, until we have enough operations to complete all of the derivations. This means that the derivations in the text are broken up into different parts (e.g. "part 1," "part 2," etc.), where subsequent parts are to be read as continuing from the steps in the previous parts, and where the original problem statement in English is to be taken from the correspondingly numbered example in the introduction.

Consider the inference to the conclusion that every professor teaches a student who reads some book.

(Example 56 derivation, part 1)
$\{\bar{P}x, Px\, S\hat{a}Txa\}_{a \to \{x\}}[\{SyBbRyb\}_{b \to y}^{\{S\hat{y}\}}]^{\circlearrowright}$ ($\circlearrowright$ reduces to M)

$= \{\bar{P}x, PxS\hat{a}Txa\}_{a \to \{x\}}[\{SyBbRyb\}_{b \to y}^{\{S\hat{y}\}}]^M$
(Merge has a match $\langle a, y \rangle$ for the state $PxS\hat{a}Txa$)
$= \{\bar{P}x, PxS\hat{a}TxaBcRac\}_{a,c \to x}$.

We will return to the remaining steps in the derivation for this example once we have introduced the necessary operations.

4.7 Universal Product and Existential Sum

The key idea behind our revised update operation is that updating an initial view Γ_{RI}^{Θ} with a premise Δ_{SJ}^{Ψ} from our commitment set C decomposes into first trying to make the initial view relevant through operations akin to universal and existential instantiation (where issue matches between I and J determine what gets instantiated) and then, as in Chapter 2, treating Δ_{SJ}^{Ψ} as a putative answer to the question raised by Γ_{RI}^{Θ}, followed by Merging with the argument view to import information from the new premise. One technical point is that we demand that the arbitrary objects in the internal argument of update ($D = \Delta_{SJ}^{\Psi}$) are novelized. This is to avoid the possibility of separate commitments that potentially involve the same arbitrary objects behaving in reasoning as if we absurdly had quantifiers that scope over multiple sentences.

Definition 4.34 (Update).

For $D \in C$, but with all arbitrary objects novelized,
$\langle C, \Gamma_{RI}^{\Theta} \rangle [D]^{\circlearrowleft} = \langle C, \Gamma_{RI}^{\Theta}[D]^{U}[D]^{E}[D]^{A}[D]^{M} \rangle$

We have already defined M and A. It remains to define U and E. U and E are reasoning operations that perform the role of universal instantiation and existential instantiation. We begin with the former. The reasoner does not have to deliberately pick what is to be targeted by the operation. Targets will be automatically selected by issue matches between I in Γ_{RI}^{Θ} and J in the argument view $\Delta_{SJ}^{\{0\}}$ supplied to the operation. However, note that if the argument view carries a supposition other than $\{0\}$, Universal product returns Γ_{RI}^{Θ} unmodified. This ensures that we never have both Universal Product and Merge attempt substitutions in the same Update step.

On the propositional level, we can gloss Universal product as follows. Fundamentally, Universal product performs potentially multiple simultaneous universal instantiation steps, subject to certain constraints. Let us say we have a view Γ_{RI}^{Θ} as the external argument to U. Universal product will take the conjunction of copies of Γ, one for each way of instantiating universals in Γ with terms that are an appropriate match with the internal argument of U. It will then bring that conjunction back under the supposition Θ, fuse potentially new dependencies that arise or eliminate dependencies as appropriate. In order for this to produce the results we want, we have certain constraints on the foregoing. The first constraint is that none of the arbitrary objects featuring in Γ may also feature in Θ. Otherwise, we risk unsound "partial instantiations" as the operation does not perform substitutions in Θ. The second constraint is that either (1) no arbitrary objects are shared between the internal and the external argument, or, alternatively, (2) all arbitrary objects in the internal argument are also in the external argument. This avoids the potential for the equivalent of variable clash, but it still allows us to do the equivalent of instantiating a formula with its own variables. Finally, in determining relevant issue matches between the internal and external argument for the purposes of guiding instantiation of universals in Γ, we only consider universals that are not in Θ, and the operation is only defined if there exists at least one match. The operation additionally is only defined if the supposition of the internal argument is $\{0\}$. A desired consequence of these latter constraints is that in the context of Update, only one of U and M will perform instantiations.

Definition 4.35 (Universal product).
For $A(\Gamma) \cap A(\Theta) = \emptyset$ and either $A(R) \cap A(S) = \emptyset$ or $[R]_\Delta = S$,
$$\Gamma_{RI}^{\Theta}[\Delta_{SJ}^{\{0\}}]^U = \{0\}_{RI}^{\Theta} \otimes^{R \bowtie S} \bigotimes_{\langle u,t \rangle \in M'_{IJ}}^{R \bowtie S} \mathrm{Sub}_{\langle t,u \rangle}^{R \bowtie S}(\Gamma_I^{\{0\}}), \text{ where}$$
$M'_{IJ} = \{\langle u,t \rangle : \langle u,t \rangle \in M_{IJ} \land u \in U_R - A(\Theta)\} \neq \emptyset$

For example, $\{P\hat{x}Exa, \bar{P}x\}_{a \to x}[\{P\hat{j}\}]^U = \{P\hat{j}Eja, \bar{P}j\}$. Unlike standard universal instantiation in the predicate calculus, U allows the reasoner to directly "instantiate" arbitrary objects with other arbitrary objects, so the operation in the example would have yielded the same result if j had been an arbitrary object rather than a non-arbitrary term.

As we saw in Chapter 2, default reasoning in the first instance proceeds by sequentially updating with premises in the order in which they are presented. Depending on what the input premises are, Update can quickly reduce to just a small subset of its constituent operations. U, E, and A notably "pass through" their external arguments unmodified if their internal argument carries a supposition other than $\{0\}$, and neither U or E do anything if there are no relevant issue matches.

We can now consider the conversion fallacy, in which "John Fs" is inferred from "All Fs G" and "John Gs."

(Example 52 derivation, part 1)
$\{\bar{F}x, Fx\,G\hat{x}\}[\{G\hat{j}\}]^{\circlearrowleft}$
(Update decomposes into a sequence of operations)
$= \{\bar{F}x, Fx\,G\hat{x}\}[\{G\hat{j}\}]^U[\{G\hat{j}\}]^E[\{G\hat{j}\}]^A[\{G\hat{j}\}]^M$
($\langle x, j \rangle$ is a match for U. E does nothing)
$= \{\bar{F}j, Fj\,G\hat{j}\}[\{G\hat{j}\}]^A[\{G\hat{j}\}]^M$ (Answer eliminates an alternative)
$= \{Fj\,G\hat{j}\}[\{G\hat{j}\}]^M$ (Merge adds nothing new)
$= \{Fj\,G\hat{j}\}$.

We can contrast the foregoing with quantified modus ponens, which is valid. Notice that the derivation is in fact very similar.

(**Example 51 derivation, part 1**)
$\{\bar{A}x, A\hat{x}\ Nx\}[\{A\hat{h}\}]^{\circ}$
$= \{\bar{A}x\ A\hat{x}\ Nx\}[\{A\hat{h}\}]^{U}[\{A\hat{h}\}]^{E}[\{A\hat{h}\}]^{A}[\{A\hat{h}\}]^{M}$
(U has $\langle x, h \rangle$ as a match.)
$= \{\bar{A}h, A\hat{h}\ Nh\}[\{A\hat{h}\}]^{A}[\{A\hat{h}\}]^{M}$ \hfill (A eliminates an alternative)
$= \{Ah\ N\hat{h}\}[\{A\hat{h}\}]^{M}$ \hfill (Merge has no new atoms to add)
$= \{A\hat{h}\ Nh\}$

We allow the issue structure guiding "instantiations" of arbitrary objects to be changed at will by the reasoner, using an updated version of the reorientation operation we saw in Chapter 2. In addition to allowing us to change the focus of our inquiry, this operation will now also allow us to change the subject of our reasoning by replacing the view under consideration by any currently in C and by substituting in any issue structure. As a result, the reasoner is free to use U as creatively as she might use universal instantiation in the predicate calculus.

Definition 4.36 (Reorient).
For $\Delta^{\Psi}_{SJ} \in (C \cup \{\Gamma^{\Theta}_{RI}\})$ and $J' \in \mathbb{I}_{\Delta \cup \Psi}$,
$\langle C, \Gamma^{\Theta}_{RI} \rangle [\Delta^{\Psi}_{SJ'}]^{R} = \langle C, \Delta^{\Psi}_{SJ'} \rangle$

We now move on to an operation that seems absurd on a first look, for it is tantamount to *existential* instantiation. Existential sum roughly speaking creates a copy of the external argument for each appropriate issue match, performs a substitution of the relevant existential based on this match, and then adds the copy post-substitution to the result as a disjunct. The original external argument remains as one of the final set of disjuncts, which helps guarantee that the result is sound just as disjunction introduction is sound. This is only the rough picture. There are a few more intricate details to consider. Existential sum looks for issue matches between existentials in the external argument and terms in the internal argument. More specifically, we are only looking at issue matches $\langle e, t \rangle$ in which e is an existential (one that does not depend on any universal) in the external argument that is not also in the internal argument. We are setting aside existentials that are also in the internal argument since we want to avoid the possibility of chained substitutions where e is only in the external argument because U put it there in the context of Update. In addition, we demand that e does not depend on a universal and that e does not feature in the supposition of the external argument. Among other things, this restriction avoids invalid inferences that are neither tempting nor expected on a question-based approach to reasoning. For example, relative to John, "Everybody loves somebody" (on a ∀∃ reading) does not directly raise the question of whether everybody loves John; it can only directly raise the question of whom John loves. This means that the following is not predicted to be a tempting fallacy (on the ∀∃ reading):

> **Example 61.**
> P1. All dogs bite some man. $\quad\{DxBxaMâ, \bar{D}x\}$
> P2. John is a man. $\quad\{M\hat{j}\}$
> Claim: It is not at all tempting to conclude the following:
> All dogs bite John. $\quad\{DxBxj, \bar{D}x\}$

To avoid the equivalent of variable clash and other difficulties, we demand that the arbitrary objects of Γ and Θ in the external argument are disjoint sets, and we demand that the arbitrary objects of the internal and external arguments are disjoint sets or that the dependency relation of the internal argument can be obtained from that of the external argument by restriction. This leaves open the possibility of instantiating an existential with other arbitrary objects that also occur in the external argument.

We now turn to the details of the additional disjuncts including "instantiations" of our issue matched existentials. We do not want to copy Γ wholesale for each "instantiation." Firstly, in constructing a "copy" of Γ for instantiation we only include any y in Γ that in fact involves the e that is the target of substitution. Next, we further include, for each such y another set of states based on y. This set of states is as follows. Each of the elements of this set of states itself consists of the union of those atoms of y that do not involve e, together with states not yet subsumed in y that arise from yes/no issues generated from the atoms that support the issue match involving e. The upshot of this construction is that, for example, if we have "Some Ts A" and use Existential sum with "Tm" as the internal argument, we get "Either some Ts A, or Tm and Am, or not Tm." Here, the state corresponding "Tm and Am" is simply one of those y that involve a relevant e. The state corresponding to "not Tm" is a further state that rises from what is at issue in the external argument.

Definition 4.37 (Existential sum).
Let the following conditions be met:

(1) $A(\Gamma) \cap A(\Theta) = \emptyset$ and either $A(R) \cap A(S) = \emptyset$ or $[R]_\Delta = S$.

(2) $M'_{IJ} = \{\langle e,t\rangle : \langle e,t\rangle \in M_{IJ} \wedge e \in E_R - A(\Theta \cup \Delta)$
$\wedge \neg \exists x (\langle e,x\rangle \in D_R)\} \neq \emptyset$.

Then,

$$\Gamma^\Theta_{RI}[\Delta^{\{0\}}_{SJ}]^E = \Gamma^\Theta_{RI} \oplus^{R \bowtie S} \bigoplus_{\langle e,t\rangle \in M'_{IJ}}^{R \bowtie S}$$
$$\text{Sub}^{R \bowtie S}_{\langle t,e\rangle} ((\bigcup_{y \in \{y \in \Gamma : e \in A(y)\}} (\{y\} \cup \{\{x_{\in y} : e \notin A(x)\} \cup \delta :$$
$$\delta \in \bigotimes_{x \in B(y,I,e)} \{\{x\},\{\bar{x}\}\} \wedge \delta \not\subseteq y\}))_I^\Theta),$$

where for $e \in E_R$ and $y \in \Gamma$, let $B(y,I,e) = \{x[e/?] \in y : \langle e,x\rangle \in I\}$.

We can now consider some examples that hinge on the behavior of Existential sum.

(Example 47 derivation, part 1)
$\{T\hat{a}\ Sa\}[\{T\hat{m}\}]^\circlearrowright$ (U does nothing)
$= \{T\hat{a}\ Sa\}[\{T\hat{m}\}]^E[\{T\hat{m}\}]^A[\{T\hat{m}\}]^M$ (E has a match $\langle m, a\rangle$)
$= \{T\hat{a}\ Sa, T\hat{m}\ Sm, \bar{T}m\}[\{T\hat{m}\}]^A[\{T\hat{m}\}]^M$ (Answer eliminates an
$= \{T\hat{m}\ Sm\}$ alternative, M has nothing to add)

Note that the same derivation does not go through if we update with the premises in reverse order, which corresponds to the data discussed in the introduction.

(Example 48 derivation, part 1)
$\{D\hat{a}\ Ta\}[\{\bar{D}\hat{t}\}]^\circlearrowright$
$= \{D\hat{a}\ Ta\}[\{\bar{D}\hat{t}\}]^U[\{\bar{D}\hat{t}\}]^E[\{\bar{D}\hat{t}\}]^A[\{\bar{D}\hat{t}\}]^M$ (Nothing for U)
$= \{D\hat{a}\ Ta\}[\{\bar{D}\hat{t}\}]^E[\{\bar{D}\hat{t}\}]^A[\{\bar{D}\hat{t}\}]^M$ (E has a match)
$= \{D\hat{a}\ Ta\ ,\ Dt\ Tt, \bar{D}t\}[\{\bar{D}\hat{t}\}]^A[\{\bar{D}\hat{t}\}]^M$ (Answer favors one alternative)
$= \{\bar{D}t\}[\{\bar{D}\hat{t}\}]^M$
$= \{\bar{D}\hat{t}\}$

(Example 49 derivation, part 1)
$\{AaHmaK\hat{b}Hcb, QdHjdJeHfe\}[\{K\hat{g}Hsg\}]^\circlearrowright$ (Nothing for U)
$= \{AaHmaK\hat{b}Hcb, QdHjdJeHfe\}$
         $[\{K\hat{g}Hsg\}]^E[\{K\hat{g}Hsg\}]^A[\{K\hat{g}Hsg\}]^M$ (E has a match)
$= \{AaHmaK\hat{b}Hcb, QdHjdJeHfe, AaHmaK\hat{g}Hcg, AaHma\bar{K}\hat{g}\}$
         $[\{K\hat{g}Hsg\}]^A[\{K\hat{g}Hsg\}]^M$

$= \{AaHmaK\hat{g}Hcg\}[\{K\hat{g}Hsg\}]^M$
$= \{AaHmaK\hat{g}HcgHsg\}$

We now have everything we need for our new version of Update. The next operation invoked by the default reasoning procedure that we need to consider is Factor.

4.8 Division and Factor

Next, we update our definition of Division. As in Chapter 2, Division allows us to separate one issue out of another. The same motivation already discussed in Chapter 2 applies, so we will not repeat it here. The only change is that we invoke the restriction operation on R and I in case the relevant material gets eliminated.

Definition 4.38 (Division).
If $\forall \delta_{\in \Delta} \exists \psi_{\in \Psi} \exists \gamma_{\in \Gamma} (\delta \subseteq \gamma \land \psi \subseteq \gamma)$, then
$\Gamma_{RI}^{\Theta} \oslash \Delta_{SJ}^{\Psi} = \{\gamma \oslash_\Gamma \Delta^\Psi : \gamma \in \Gamma\}_{[R][I]}^{\Theta}$
$\gamma \oslash_\Gamma \Delta^\Psi = \gamma - \iota\delta(\delta \in \Delta \land \delta \subseteq \gamma \land \exists \psi_{\in \Psi}(\psi \subseteq \gamma))$

Since there is no significant additional role played by arbitrary objects in Division, we will move on to updating our definition of Factor, which involves more interesting novel cases.

For the case in which we are factoring out contradictions, we have largely the same definition from Chapter 2, except that we now have an expanded class of primitively absurd states to draw on. In addition, we need restriction operations on R and I in case anything relevant gets eliminated. For the case in which we are factoring out a substantive view, things get slightly more subtle. The main idea is that we are not only interested in factoring out static atoms as in Chapter 2, but that we additionally try to factor out particular facts via universals that cover them. In other words, we try to instantiate universals in Δ_{SJ}^{Ψ} based on issue matches with Γ_{RI}^{Θ} and then attempt to factor out the result of those instantiations. Formally,

Definition 4.39 (Factor).
For $\Delta_{SJ}^{\Psi} \neq \bot$,
$\Gamma_{RI}^{\Theta}[\Delta_{SJ}^{\Psi}]^F = \{\gamma[\Delta^\Psi]^F : \gamma \in \Gamma\}_{[R][I]}^{\Theta}$ where
$\gamma[\Delta^\Psi]^F = (\gamma \oslash_\Gamma \Delta^\Psi) \cap \bigcap \{\gamma \oslash_\Gamma (\Delta^\Psi[t/a]) : \langle t, a \rangle \in M_{IJ} \land a \in U_S\}$, and

where we let $\gamma' \cap \bigcap \emptyset = \gamma'$.

For $\Delta_{SJ}^{\Psi} = \bot$,

$$\Gamma_{RI}^{\Theta}[\bot]^F = \{\gamma \in \Gamma : \neg\exists \delta \in \mathbb{K}. \delta \subseteq \gamma\}_{[R][I]}^{\Theta}.$$

Our expanded definition of primitively absurd states now allows us to make more inferences with Factor. For example, $\{\{Sa, = ab, Sb\}, \{Sa, = ab, \bar{S}b\}\}[\bot]^F = \{\{Sa, = ab, Sb\}\}$. Similar examples can easily be constructed targeting the other primitively absurd states.

As noted, Factor now also allows us to factor generalizations out of specifics. For example, if we have $\{F\hat{j}G\hat{j}\}$, we could decide to factor out $\{Gx\}^{\{F\hat{x}\}}$, leaving us with $\{F\hat{j}\}$. If representing additional facts in an occurrent view comes at a psychological cost, as one suspects it does, it may be a useful for an intelligent reasoner to be able to "compress" as many particular facts in light of known general facts as possible, when the particular facts do not directly bear on a question under consideration.

To take another example in which generalizations are eliminated, if we carry through the Factor stage of our inference process for the somewhat uninformative example "Every professor teaches some student," "Every student reads some book," and treat this as a search for a novel conclusion using Factor, we get what we might gloss as "either some student reads a book, or something else is the case." We shall consider this example again later.

(Example 56 derivation, part 2)
$= \{\bar{P}x, PxS\hat{a}TxaBcRac\}_{a,c \to x}$

$$[\bot]^F[\{\bar{P}x, Px\, S\hat{a}Txa\}_{a \to x}]^F[\{SyBbRyb\}_{b \to y}^{\{S\hat{y}\}}]^F$$

$= \{0, BcRac\}$

Our main aim in this book is to define procedures for default reasoning performance, as well as show that an adequate set of such procedures can in fact also explain the possibility of reliably correct reasoning. However, the machinery here could be used to explore other potential applications that go beyond default reasoning. For example, we might observe that given a view G of many facts about particular individuals and their properties, some "universal claim" view D conceivably will, under Factor, achieve a greater reduction of the complexity of G than other such views will. In that case, one might decide that in a certain sense, D has greater value for an erotetic reasoner than alternative universal-claim views. This kind of valuation in complexity reduction under Factor may bear an interesting relationship to the question of what kind of universal-claim view would be more satisfying for the reasoner

170   PREDICATE REASONING

to adopt as a type of theory of the facts about particular individuals being considered.

4.9 Query and Inquire

Our updated version of Query will maintain its role from Chapter 2, but it will now also allow us to perform the equivalent of existential generalization. This will be key to allowing us to make sense of the "married people puzzle" from the introduction. Different features of arguments will give rise to varying degrees of intricacy in how the result of Query is determined, with the main source of complexity stemming from dependencies. We will go through the possible cases step by step before pulling everything together into a formal definition of Query.

The first question we need to ask is whether the internal argument of Query involves any arbitrary objects. If it does not, Query behaves just like in Chapter 2, and the result is determined at the level of atoms as before. If the internal argument does involve arbitrary objects, Query is only defined if those among them that are universal arbitrary objects are already in the external argument. For example, this means that we can use Query to conclude that it follows from "all mathematicians like chalk and blackboards" that "all mathematicians like blackboards," but only if we recruit the same arbitrary objects in the internal argument of Query that we find in the external argument.

If all existential arbitrary objects in the internal argument are also in the external argument, Query again behaves like in Chapter 2, with the result determined at the level of atoms. If some existential arbitrary objects in the internal argument are not in the external argument, but they are not implicated in any topic matches, then, again, the result will be determined at the level of atoms as in Chapter 2.

The remaining and more intricate cases arise when the internal argument involves some existential arbitrary objects that are not already in the external argument, and where those existential arbitrary objects are topic matched with terms in the external argument. This is the case that gives rise to the equivalent of potentially multiple simultaneous existential generalizations.

As in Chapter 2, Query centers on a test $\Phi(\gamma, \delta)$, applied to all combinations of states γ from the body of the external argument and states δ from the body of the internal argument. Going beyond the purely propositional case, Φ will now ask whether, based on issue matches in M'_{IJ}, there is a possible sequence of substitutions of existential arbitrary objects in the internal argument that can make it so that δ, post-substitution *or after no substitutions*, is contained in γ. In addition, as in Chapter 2, for an application of the Φ test to come out true we demand a ψ from the supposition of the internal argument of Query to also be in γ (which is trivially satisfied if the supposition of the internal argument is $\{0\}$). So, for example, if we have $\gamma = \{Ljm\}$ and $\delta = \{Lab\}$, where we imagine that $\langle j, \mathbf{a}\rangle$ and $\langle m, \mathbf{b}\rangle$ are in M'_{IJ} and that $\Psi = \{0\}$, then clearly $\Phi(\gamma, \delta)$ is true, since $\{Lab\}[j/a][m/b] = \{Ljm\}$. Query then takes the set consisting of 0 in place of those elements of Γ for which no element of Δ yields a positive $\Phi(\gamma, \delta)$ together with those elements of Δ for which some element of Γ yields a positive $\Phi(\gamma, \delta)$.

The dependency relations of the internal and external arguments are combined in a way that ensures the result is classically valid. The minimum requirement for soundness is that the result of Query includes all of the dependencies from the external argument that apply to any arbitrary objects from the external argument that remain in the result of Query. In addition, we will fuse those dependencies with potentially additional ones for the novel existential arbitrary objects that an application of Query might introduce.

The additional dependencies are built-up incrementally as follows, giving a gloss to the sets D_1 through D_6 in the formal definition of Query below. Note that the formal definition below is easier to apply than it might seem on a first look, since most use cases will transparently not involve all the potential steps we will now incrementally consider (for example, by not involving multiple substitutions or by not involving substitution of any complex terms). Firstly, we include the dependencies from the internal argument involving those existentials of the internal argument that are not already in R. Secondly, we include extra dependencies for cases in which multiple terms from the external argument are substituted with the same existential from the internal argument. Such existentials will become dependent on all universals in U_R. This proliferation of dependencies is to avoid spurious "identities." For example, if we have it that "every teacher teaches John or Mary," we do not want to be able to conclude that "there is some student such that every teacher teaches this student." Formally, if we have $\{T(x, j)C(x)S(\hat{j}), T(x, m)C(x)S(\hat{m}), \bar{C}x\}$ and we Query with $\{T(x, a)C(x)S(\hat{a}), \bar{C}(x)\}$, we should never get $\{T(x, a)C(x)S(\hat{a}), \bar{C}(x)\}$. However, with the same inputs to Query, we *do* want to get $\{T(x, a)C(x)S(\hat{a}), \bar{C}(x)\}_{a \to x}$. In this latter case, the novel existential a has been made dependent upon x. Thirdly, for all u that are involved in a term for which an e_m from the internal argument will be substituted, we add $\langle e_m, u\rangle$.

172   PREDICATE REASONING

Fourthly, if there is a term t for which an e_m from the internal argument will be substituted and where t involves an existential e that depends on a universal u, then we add $\langle e_m, u \rangle$. Fifthly, we have to consider possible further dependencies arising from how universals in a complex term to be substituted relate to other universals in the Matryoshka levels of R. To express this as a formula, we first need to define Matryoshka level orderings.

Definition 4.40 (Matryoshka level ordering).
  For existentials, we have $e \lesssim_R e'$ iff $\forall \langle e', u \rangle \in D_R (\langle e, u \rangle \in D_R)$. For both existentials and universals, let the relation $\triangleleft_R$ be the transitive closure of the relation made up by the ordered pairs in $D_R \cup (E_R \times U_R - D_R)^{op}$, where op reverses the order of pairs in a set of pairs.

We then say (see formula for D_5 below) that we add $\langle e_m, u \rangle$ for all those cases in which u is higher in the Matryoska level ordering than the universals on which dependencies were introduced in steps three and four above. Finally, and sixthly, we preserve the dependency order of existentials in S, adding more dependencies as necessary.

Pulling the foregoing together, we get:

Definition 4.41 (Query).
For $U_S \subseteq U_R$ and $M'_{IJ} = \{\langle t, e \rangle \in M_{IJ} : e \in E_S \setminus E_R\}$, we define
$\Gamma^\Theta_{RI}[\Delta^\Psi_{SJ}]^Q =$

$$(\{0 : \neg \exists \delta_{\in \Delta} \exists \gamma . \Phi(\gamma, \delta)\} \cup \{\delta \in \Delta : \exists \gamma_{\in \Gamma} . \Phi(\gamma, \delta)\})^\Theta_{[R \bowtie \langle U_R, E_S \setminus E_R, D_{S'} \rangle][I \cup J]}$$

where $\Phi(\gamma, \delta) \leftrightarrow \exists \psi_{\in \Psi} \exists n_{\geq 0} \exists \langle t_1, e_1 \rangle, \ldots, \langle t_n, e_n \rangle_{\in M'_{IJ}} \forall i, j$

$$(\psi \cup \delta[t_1/e_1, \ldots, t_n/e_n] \subseteq \gamma \wedge e_i = e_j \rightarrow i = j);$$

and $D_{S'} = D_1 \cup D_2 \cup D_3 \cup D_4 \cup D_5 \cup D_6$ is constructed by taking: original dependencies from the internal argument

$$D_1 = [D_S]_{A/E_R},$$

extra dependencies for multiple terms substituted with same e

$$D_2 = \{\langle e_m, u \rangle : \exists m \exists m' \in M'_{IJ}(e_m = e_{m'} \wedge t_m \neq t_{m'}) \wedge u \in U_R\},$$

dependencies resulting from complex terms being substituted

$$D_3 = \{\langle e_m, u\rangle : \langle t_m, e_m\rangle \in M'_{IJ} \wedge u \in U_R(t_m)\},$$
$$D_4 = \{\langle e_m, u\rangle : \langle t_m, e_m\rangle \in M'_{IJ} \wedge e \in E_R(t_m) \wedge \langle e, u\rangle \in R\},$$
$$D_5 = \{\langle e_m, u\rangle : \langle t_m, e_m\rangle \in M'_{IJ} \wedge u \in U_R \wedge \forall u'_{\in U_R(D_3 \cup D_4)}(u' \triangleleft_R u)\},$$

additional dependencies necessary to preserve the dependency order of existentials in S

$$D_6 = \{\langle e, u\rangle : e, e' \in E_S - E_R \wedge e \lesssim_S e' \wedge$$
$$(\forall m, m' \in M'_{IJ}(e_m = e' \wedge e_{m'} = e') \to t_m = t_{m'}) \wedge$$
$$\langle e', u\rangle \in D_1 \cup D_2 \cup D_3 \cup D_4 \cup D_5\}.$$

We will choose some cases to help illustrate how Query deals with dependencies. For example, from "everybody teaches either John or Mary, both of whom are students," it clearly follows very intuitively that "everybody teaches some student." Let us consider

$\{TxjS\hat{j}S\hat{m}, TxmS\hat{j}S\hat{m}\}[\{Txa S\hat{a}\}_{a\to x}]^Q$. We have $E_S \backslash E_R = \{a\}$ and the precondition on R and S is met. We also have $M_{IJ} = \{\langle j, a\rangle, \langle m, a\rangle\}$. Since $A(j) = A(m) = \emptyset$ and $a \in E_S \backslash E_R$, $M'_{IJ} = M_{IJ}$. Now, a has two distinct matches in M'_{IJ}, but since $\langle a, x\rangle \in D_S$, the precondition on M'_{IJ} is satisfied. Write $\gamma_j = TxjSjSm$, $\gamma_m = TxmSjSm$, $\delta = TxaSa$. Then $\Phi(\gamma_j, \delta)$ is true since $\delta[j/a] \subseteq \gamma_j$, and $\Phi(\gamma_m, \delta)$ is true since $\delta[m/a] \subseteq \gamma_m$. Also $[R \bowtie \langle U_R, E_S \backslash E_R, D_{S'}\rangle] = S$, hence the result of Query is $\{TxaS\hat{a}\}_{a\to x}$.

Now in contrast to the example just considered, from "everybody teaches either John or Mary, both of whom are students," it *does not* follow that "there is a student whom everybody teaches." In this case, we have

$$\{TxjS\hat{j}S\hat{m}, TxmS\hat{j}S\hat{m}\}[\{TxaS\hat{a}\}]^Q.$$

This works out the same as above except for our calculation of

$$\langle U_R, E_S \backslash E_R, D_{S'}\rangle.$$

But $a \in E_\infty$ since it matches both j and m, and $j \neq m$ (that is not to say that in some given model we could not have $\{\{j = m\}\}$ a valid view, but that j and m are distinct terms). Hence $\langle U_R, E_S \backslash E_R, D_{S'}\rangle = \langle \{x\}, \{a\}, \{\langle a, x\rangle\}\rangle$. Hence the

174   PREDICATE REASONING

output is the same as for the previous example, $\{TxaS\hat{a}\}_{a\to x}$. Note that this is a weaker conclusion than the internal argument of the Query, since a here depends on x. Applying Query with these arguments is thus tantamount to asking "Is there a student whom everybody teaches?" and getting the answer "I (only) believe that everybody teaches some student."

Note that it is a precondition on Query that the universal arbitrary objects in the internal argument have to be drawn from the set of universal arbitrary objects in the external argument. This means that we have to choose our internal arguments carefully. Insofar as we are getting our internal argument from a natural language expression, we have to assume that we are taking universal generalizations to be anaphoric on whatever view we are proposing to Query (existential generalizations do not have this constraint).

(Example 56 derivation, part 3 (cont. from part 1))
$= \{\bar{P}x, PxS\hat{a}TxaBcRac\}_{a,c\to x}[\bot]^F[\{\bar{P}x, PxS\hat{d}TxdBeRde\}_{d,e\to x}]^Q$
$= \{\bar{P}x, PxS\hat{d}TxdBeRde\}_{d,e\to x}$ (so the answer is "yes")

(Example 57 derivation)
$\{BxAx, \bar{B}\hat{x}\}[\{CaB\hat{a}\}]^{\circ}[\bot]^F[\{CbAb\}]^Q =$
$\{BxAx, \bar{B}\hat{x}\}[\{CaB\hat{a}\}]^U[\{CaB\hat{a}\}]^A[\{CaB\hat{a}\}]^M[\bot]^F[\{CbAb\}]^Q$
$= \{BaAa, \bar{B}\hat{a}\}[\{CaB\hat{a}\}]^A[\bot]^F[\{CaB\hat{a}\}]^M[\{CbAb\}]^Q$
$= \{BaAa\}[\{CaB\hat{a}\}]^M[\bot]^F[\{CbAb\}]^Q$
$= \{B\hat{a}AaCa\}[\{CbAb\}]^Q = \{CbAb\}$

Moving on, for example 58, the default reasoning procedure only produces the relevant fallacy if it proceeds to the stage of reversing the premises. This fits with the observation that the valid conclusion to example 57 (needing no premise reversal) is more attractive than the fallacious conclusion in 58, even though both are drawn frequently.

(Example 58 derivation)
$\{B\hat{a}Aa\}[\ ]^D[\{CxB\hat{x}\}^{\{Cx\}}]^{\circ}[\bot]^F[\{CbAb\}]^Q$
$= \{B\hat{a}Aa\}[\{CbAb\}]^Q$
$= \{0\}$ (hence the procedure tries again with reversed premises)
$\{CxB\hat{x}\}^{\{Cx\}}[\ ]^D[\{B\hat{a}Aa\}]^{\circ}[\bot]^F[\{CbAb\}]^Q$
$= \{CaB\hat{a}, \bar{C}a\}[\{B\hat{a}Aa\}]^A[\{B\hat{a}Aa\}]^M[\bot]^F[\{CbAb\}]^Q$
$= \{CaB\hat{a}Aa\}[\{CbAb\}]^Q$ (Hence the answer is "yes")

(**Example 53 derivation**)
$\{AxBx\}^{\{Ax\}}[\ ]^D[\{Bx\}^{\{0\}}]^S[\{BxAx\}^{\{Bx\}}]^Q = \{BxAx\}^{\{Bx\}}$

There is another aspect of Query in the context of reasoning with "some" that is worth considering. Recall from the discussion in Chapter 2 that disjunction introduction, i.e. the inference from "P and Q" to "P and Q or R," is intuitively repugnant. We explained this by observing that this inference would go against the grain of the main aim of reasoning, which is to answer questions rather than gratuitously raise them. The disjunction introduction inference would require gratuitously raising a question. Now, someone might consider an alternative explanation on which disjunction introduction is repugnant because it involves weakening our premise, thereby throwing away information. The question arises if we can find a case in which an inference is still throwing away information but nonetheless not increasing our question load. On the erotetic theory, such a case should be much more acceptable as an inference. It would appear that the erotetic explanation provides an intuitively better fit. An inference from "John smokes and Mary smokes" to "somebody smokes" is intuitively considerably *more* attractive than the disjunction introduction inference. This is to be expected, because unlike in the case of disjunction introduction, a logically weakening "existential generalization" can make our mental model less inquisitive in the framework of the erotetic theory. However, existential generalization throws away information just as disjunction introduction does, so appeal to information loss misses the intuitive asymmetry.

We can now also finally have a formal look at the married people puzzle.

(**Example 50 derivation part 1**)
$\{LjsLsg\}[\{M\hat{j}\bar{M}\hat{g}\}]^{\circ}[\perp]^F[\{LabM\hat{a}\bar{M}\hat{b}\}]^Q$
$= \{LjsLsgM\hat{j}\bar{M}\hat{g}\}[\{LabM\hat{a}\bar{M}\hat{b}\}]^Q$
($M\hat{a}, \bar{M}\hat{b}$ in the internal argument make $\langle j, a \rangle$ and $\langle g, b \rangle$ matches, but Ljg is not supported in the external argument) $= \{LjsLsgM\hat{j}\bar{M}\hat{g}\}$ (So the answer to the query is "no")

The default reasoning procedure captures the fact that reasoners tend to think that it does not follow from the premises that a married person is looking at an unmarried person.

Though we will not require it for the particular empirical data points considered in this chapter, we now also define a "companion" operation to

176   PREDICATE REASONING

Query we shall call Wh-Query. Wh-Query allows us to make queries on view as to *who, what,* or *which* thing has various properties. In the below, we rely on the same definition of M'_{IJ} and Φ that we used for Query above.

Definition 4.42 (Wh-Query). Provided that $U_S \subseteq U_R$,

$$\Gamma^{\Theta}_{RI}[\Delta^{\Psi}_{SJ}]^W = \left(\{0 : \exists \gamma \in \Gamma. \neg \exists \delta_{\in \Delta}.\Phi(\gamma,\delta)\} \cup \{\delta \in \Delta : \exists \gamma_{\in \Gamma}.\Psi(\gamma,\xi)\}\right)^{\Theta}_{[R][I]},$$

where $\Psi(\gamma,\xi)$ iff

$$\exists \psi_{\in \Psi} \exists n_{\geq 0} \exists \langle t_1, e_1 \rangle, \ldots, \langle t_n, e_n \rangle_{\in M'_{IJ}} \exists \delta_{\in \Delta}.$$
$$(\xi \cup \psi \subseteq \gamma \wedge \xi = \delta[t_1/e_1, \ldots, t_n/e_n]$$
$$\wedge \forall i, j.(e_i = e_j \to i = j)).$$

Example 62.

$$\{S\hat{\jmath}DmTn, S\hat{m}Lnm, \overline{S\hat{n}Db}\}[\{S\hat{a}\}]^W = \{S\hat{\jmath}, S\hat{m}, 0\}.$$

Following the approach to "might" in Chapter 3, we might gloss this as "John or Mary might sing."

Example 63.

$$\{S\hat{\jmath}D\hat{n}, Tj\overline{D}\hat{\jmath}D\hat{n}\}[\{D\hat{a}\}]^W = \{D\hat{n}\}$$

Following Slovic, we suggested that by keeping in mind the question of whether Sally is married, we are more likely to come to the correct conclusion in the married people puzzle. We will now update our procedure for Inquire to make use of this intuition. There are two types of cases to consider based on the internal argument. The easy case (which we label the (I) case) arises when the arbitrary objects in the internal argument are included among the arbitrary objects of the external argument. In this case, the definition of Inquire is virtually the same as in the propositional case from 2, except for a minor detail concerning the issue structure.

The more involved case (which we label the (O) case) arises when there is no overlap between the arbitrary objects of the internal and external arguments, and when, additionally, no arbitrary objects are shared between the supposition of the internal argument and its main body. In this case, we create a copy of the body of the internal argument in which all arbitrary objects have been uniformly replaced by novel ones, and "flip" the relevant part of the dependency structure as part of the process of obtaining the "P or not-P" polar question that will get combined with the external argument via Product.

Definition 4.43 (Inquire).
(O) If $A(\Gamma \cup \Theta) \cap A(\Delta \cup \Psi) = \emptyset \wedge A(\Delta) \cap A(\Psi) = \emptyset$, then
$$\Gamma_{RI}^{\Theta}[\Delta_{SJ}^{\Psi}]^I = \Gamma_{RI}^{\Theta} \otimes \left(\Delta_{SJ}^{\Psi} \oplus (\{0\}_{[S][J]}^{\Psi} \otimes Nov([\Delta^{\{0\}}]_{[[S]^N][J]^N}^N))\right)[\bot]^F,$$
where $Nov()$ uniformly replaces all arbitrary objects in its scope by novel ones.
(I) If $A(\Delta \cup \Psi) \subseteq A(\Gamma \cup \Theta)$, then
$$\Gamma_{RI}^{\Theta}[\Delta_{SJ}^{\Psi}]^I = \Gamma_{RI}^{\Theta} \otimes (\Delta_{0_{\mathcal{R}}J}^{\Psi} \oplus ([\Delta]_{0_{\mathcal{R}}[J]^N}^N)^{\Psi})[\bot]^F.$$

With the Inquire operation, we can now also perform identity inferences, since the notion of primitively absurd states recruited by the inquire operations has the axioms for identity *built in*. This allows us to, for example, infer "John smokes" from "Someone smokes and that someone is John." $\{\{Sa, = aj\}\}[\{Sj\}]^I = \{\{Sa, = aj, Sj\}, \{Sa, = aj, \bar{S}j\}\}[\bot]^F = \{\{Sa, = aj, Sj\}\}$. Here we note that the state $\{Sa, = aj, \bar{S}j\}$ is a primitively absurd state, as already discussed, and thus gets eliminated. We can then get our conclusion by factoring out the premise. $\{\{Sa, = aj, Sj\}\}[\{\{Sa, = aj\}\}]^F = \{Sj\}$.

With the inquire operation, we can have another look at the married people puzzle from the introduction. If we inquire about whether Sally is married, and change our issue structure appropriately, we can get the correct conclusion.

(Example 50 derivation part 2)

Update with premises and inquire about Sally.

$$G_1 = \{LjsLsg\}[\{Mj\bar{M}g\}]^{\circlearrowleft}\{LjsLsgMj\bar{M}g\}[\{Ms\}]^I$$
$$= \{LjsLsgMj\bar{M}gMs, LjsLsgMj\bar{M}g\bar{M}s\}$$

Change issue.

$$G_2 = G_1[\{LjsLsgMj\bar{M}\hat{g}M\hat{s}, LjsLsgM\hat{j}\bar{M}g\bar{M}\hat{s}\}]^R$$
$$= \{LjsLsgMj\bar{M}\hat{g}M\hat{s}, LjsLsgM\hat{j}\bar{M}g\bar{M}\hat{s}\}$$

178 PREDICATE REASONING

Query.

$$G_3 = G_2[\{LabM\hat{a}\bar{M}\hat{b}\}]^Q$$
$$= \{LabM\hat{a}\bar{M}\hat{b}\}$$

So the answer is "yes."

We will next turn to suppositional reasoning.

4.10 Suppositions and Commitment

Similar to the updated version of Inquire, our updated Suppose operation will distinguish two different kinds of argument cases. The simple case (we call it the (I) case) arises when the internal argument has no substantive supposition, all its arbitrary objects are also in the external argument, and its dependencies are a subset of those in the external argument. In this case, the updated version of Suppose essentially behaves as in the propositional case from Chapter 2, except that we include U and E steps as we would in our new version of Update. The definition of Depose similarly at its core stays the same from the propositional case.

The more involved new case to consider concerns Supposition in the case in which no arbitrary objects are shared between the internal and the external argument. In the first instance, as before, Suppose will treat the internal argument similar to the way we would update with a new premise. However, as before, what gets treated to this pseudo-update will need to be tracking that we are merely supposing something. To do that, we will have to determine the supposition the resulting view is to have, alongside the relevant aspects of the dependency and issue structures arising from that. The way we determine the supposition of the resulting view is similar to the propositional case, except that we will also novelize whatever arbitrary objects will enter the supposition from the internal argument, to avoid the equivalent of variable clash.

Definition 4.44 (Suppose).

(O) If $A(\Gamma \cup \Theta) \cap A(\Delta \cup \Psi) = \emptyset$, then
$$\Gamma_{RI}^{\Theta}[\Delta_{SJ}^{\Psi}]^S = \Gamma_{[R \bowtie R'][I \cup I']}^{\Theta'}[\Delta_{SJ}^{\Psi}]^U[\Delta_{SJ}^{\Psi}]^E[\Delta_{SJ}^{\Psi}]^A[\Delta_{SJ}^{\Psi}]^M, \text{ where}$$
$$\Theta'^{\{0\}}_{R'I'} = \Theta^{\{0\}}_{RI} \otimes Nov(\Delta_{[S]NJ}^{\Psi}[\ ]^D),$$

where $Nov()$ uniformly replaces all arbitrary objects in its scope by novel ones.

(I) If $A(\Delta) \subseteq A(\Gamma \cup \Theta)$ and $[R]_\Delta = S$,
then $\Gamma_{RI}^{\Theta}[\Delta_{SJ}^{\{0\}}]^S = \Gamma_{RI}^{\Theta \otimes \Delta}[\Delta_{SJ}^{\{0\}}]^U[\Delta_{SJ}^{\{0\}}]^E[\Delta_{SJ}^{\{0\}}]^A[\Delta_{SJ}^{\{0\}}]^M$

Definition 4.45 (Depose).
$\Gamma_{RI}^{\Theta}[T]^D = \langle \Gamma^{\{0\}} \oplus ([\Theta]^N)^{\{0\}}, R, [[I]^N \cup I] \rangle$.

Finally, we update our operation for turning the view we have currently inferred into a commitment. As noted, we stipulate that all inferences proceed relative to a commitment set.

Definition 4.46 (Commit).
$\langle C, \Gamma_{RI}^{\Theta} \rangle [T]^C = \langle C \cup \{\Gamma_{RI}^{\Theta}\}, \Gamma_{RI}^{\Theta} \rangle$

This completes our update of our reasoning operations for predicate reasoning.

4.11 Inference and Absolute Erotetic Equilibrium

With updated versions of our operations in place, it is time to update our official definition of an inference in the erotetic theory. The structure of the definition stays the same, but we have to update our list of operations. In addition, we will take a view E to be ETR-derivable even if we can only get E', where E' is identical to E except for the arbitrary objects it contains. This is motivated by the novelization steps involved in several of our operations. Of course, this "weakening" does not make a difference with respect to truth-conditions.

Definition 4.47 (Inference). An inference $\mathcal{J}$ is a finite sequence of inference steps defined as follows, relative to an inference state consisting of a commitment $\langle C, G \rangle \in \mathbb{C}$. If $E \in \mathbb{V}$ and
$$O \in \{[D]^\circlearrowright, [D]^S, [D]^Q, [D]^F, [D]^R, [D]^I, [D]^P, [D]^E, [D]^U, [D]^C\},$$ then O is an inference step applicable to $\langle C, G \rangle$, whose result is an inference state in $\mathbb{C}$. We write $C \vdash_{ETR} E$ if and only if there is an erotetic theory inference $\mathcal{J}$ s.t. $\langle C, T \rangle \mathcal{J} = \langle C', E' \rangle$, where E' is identical to E up to uniform replacement of A objects.

Next, we can observe that the default reasoning procedure stays virtually unchanged from Chapter 2. The only differences are due to having to specify that the arbitrary objects in argument views have to be novelized at their point of introduction via Update.

(Default reasoning procedure).
For $S = \langle P_1, \ldots, P_n \rangle$ a sequence of views incrementally given as premises, all satisfying the novelty constraint of $\circlearrowright$ at their initial point of introduction,
(Basic step) Let $G' = \top[P_1]^\circlearrowright[\top]^D[P_2]^\circlearrowright \ldots [P_n]^\circlearrowright[\bot]^F$
(Sub-procedure for "what if anything follows?" tasks)
(1) Let $G'' = G'[P_1[\top]^D]^F \ldots [P_n]^F$. If $G'' = \bot$ or $G'' = \top$, then go to (2), otherwise go to (4).
(2) Start again at Basic step, with $P_n, \ldots, P_1$ in place of $P_1, \ldots, P_n$. If we have already done that, go to (3).
(3) Report "nothing follows."
(4) Report G''.
(Sub-procedure for "does Δ_{RI}^Ψ follow?" tasks)
(1) Let $G'' = G'[\Psi_{[R][I]}^{\{0\}}]^S[\Delta_{RI}^\Psi]^Q$. If $G'' = \Delta_{RI}^\Psi$, report "Yes." Otherwise go to step 2.
(2) Start again at Basic step, with $P_n, \ldots, P_1$ in place of $P_1, \ldots, P_n$. If we have already done that, go to (3).
(3) Report G'' or report "no."

Our notion of the erotetic equilibrium of a view stays the same.

Definition 4.48 (Erotetic equilibrium of a view). G is in erotetic equilibrium with respect to a finite set of views Σ if and only if $\forall D(D \in \Sigma \to G[D]^I = G)$.

Definition 4.49 ($\mathbb{V}_A(X)$). Let $\mathbb{V}_A(X)$ be the set of views $\{G : \mathcal{A}(G) \subseteq \mathcal{A}(X)\}$.

The notion of absolute erotetic equilibrium of an inference stays essentially the same as well, except that we again have to observe that we treat conclusions as identical up to uniform replacement of arbitrary objects.

Definition 4.50 (Absolute erotetic equilibrium of an inference). An inference $\mathcal{J}$ with premises C and conclusion D is an absolute erotetic equilibrium inference if and only if there exists an inference $\mathcal{J}'$ with premises C and conclusion D' (identical to D up to uniform replacement of $\mathbf{A}$ objects) such that whenever we have an instance of $\Gamma_{RI}^{\Theta}[\Delta_{SJ}^{\Psi}]^A$ in an inference step, then either $\mathcal{A}(\Gamma) \cap \mathcal{A}(\Delta) = \emptyset$ or both Γ_{RI}^{Θ} and Δ_{SJ}^{Ψ} are in erotetic equilibrium with respect to $\mathbb{V}_A(\Gamma) \cap \mathbb{V}_A(\Delta)$. In such a case, we write $C \models_{\text{CETR}} D$. We call $\mathcal{J}'$ a *manifest erotetic equilibrium inference*.

As for the propositional case, absolute erotetic equilibrium guarantees classical soundness while maintaining classical completeness, in terms of our interpretation (i.e. ∘) and articulation (i.e. ∗) procedures that relate views to the predicate calculus. Where ⊢ denotes classical derivability in predicate calculus, we have:

Theorem 4.3 (Classical soundness and completeness under erotetic equilibrium).
   (Soundness) Let $C \cup \{D\}$ be a set of views. If $C \models_{\text{CETR}} D$, then $C^* \vdash D^*$.
   (Completeness) Let C be a set of views and let φ be a sentence of $\mathcal{L}_{PC}$. If $C^* \vdash \varphi$, then $C \models_{\text{CETR}} \varphi^\circ$.

The proof can be found in the appendix.

We have now provided a full erotetic theory of first-order equivalent reasoning. It is worth briefly remarking on the scope of the theory and the research program it implicates. It is a well-known fact that all of physical science, outside particularly speculative reaches where theoretical physics meets the philosophy of mathematics, and most of an undergraduate mathematics curriculum is expressible *in some way* in a first-order reasoning system. This means that we can in principle extend the present theory to arbitrary subject matters without adding new primitive inference rules.

As in the propositional case, we have made sense of a wide range of data points about the failure of reasoning, with new cases specific to predicate reasoning introduced at the beginning of this chapter. In addition, the soundness and completeness theorems under erotetic equilibrium again show that the erotetic theory can make sense of the possibility of success as well. Again, if the reasoner raises enough issues in the process of reasoning before treating something hastily as an answer, fallacies can be avoided.

In the final section of this chapter, we will consider some ways in which the notion of restricted (rather than absolute) erotetic equilibrium is relevant to cases of predicate reasoning.

4.12 Generics and Restricted Erotetic Equilibrium

Most generalizations that we need for the purposes of science are expressible using the equivalent of "all" and "some." This might suggest that from the point of view of trying to make sense of the core of reason in a way that can explain the greatest successes of reason, not much more is required.

However, the type of generalizations that seem among the most frequently used in ordinary thinking are articulated by generic statements like "chickens lay eggs" or "sharks attack bathers." It is far from clear how these expressions relate to the more precisely delineated generalizations we can express with "all" and other expressions whose import is transparently understood. One might be tempted to take that as a reason to repudiate generics wholesale. However, we will ultimately suggest that this would be unjustified.

One significant fact about generics is that the minimum evidence-base required to lead people to draw generic conclusions is very slim indeed, in a way that is strongly influenced by the subject matter of the generalization. In the case of striking properties, particularly in the case of strikingly *dangerous* properties, generics require few, or even just a single confirming instance to be accepted (Leslie (2017); Cimpian et al. (2010)). For example, even in the knowledge that the vast majority of sharks are harmless, many people would still accept the generic "sharks attack bathers." Such generic beliefs stably coexist with belief in counterinstances. Even a very large number of counterinstances is not reliably enough to undermine a generic belief of this kind or to support an opposite generic belief. Leslie has made the case that generics do not robustly rule out any state of affairs or make a commitment to specific probabilities of various outcomes (Leslie (2007); Leslie (2008)).

The readiness with which some generic beliefs are formed would not be of special concern if the inferences we draw from generics were as weak as the conditions that suffice to give rise to generic beliefs. However, it appears that the inferential powers of generics in ordinary reasoning are in some cases comparable to that of universals. Cimpian, Brandone, and Gelan (Cimpian et al. (2010)) found that many participants were willing to accept a generic statement on the basis of weak information, but were also willing to draw much stronger conclusions from an accepted generic statement. For example, many participants were willing to accept a generic like "lorches have dangerous feathers" on the basis of information like "10% (or 30%, or 50%) of lorches have feathers that can cause massive bleeding." At the same time, participants who were told "lorches have dangerous feathers" gave estimates as high as 100%

for the prevalence of dangerous feathers in lorches. Some psychologists have concluded that generics behave in inference as if "always" had been appended to them (Abelson (1966) cited in Leslie (2017)).

There is evidence that generic beliefs directly drive inferences to particulars in a way that is strikingly independent of closely related background beliefs. For example, most people would endorse "ducks lay eggs" but not "ducks are female." However, when given the information that "Quacky is a duck" significantly more informants agreed to the statement "Quacky lays eggs" than to the statement "Quacky is female" (Khemlani et al. (2009); Khemlani et al. (2012a)). This is puzzling, since, surely, the set of egg-laying ducks is a proper subset of the set of female ducks.

Particularly striking-property generics like "sharks attack bathers" pose interesting challenges, both for the project of making sense of how we in fact tend to reason, and for the project of making sense of how we ought to reason. We need to give an account of how an inference from a generic to a particular instance is possible. We also need an account of what kind of generic inferences should be theorized as normatively correct (Leslie (2017)). From the rarefied perspective of scientific discourse, we might decide to consign generics to the scrapheap of muddled thinking and simply insist on more precise language. However it would be difficult to give up generics in ordinary reasoning.

To make sense of reasoning with generics, particularly if correct reasoning is among the things we wish to characterize, we need an account of the content of generics. It is difficult to specify the content of generic statements, since standard accounts of content are couched in terms of what is ruled out or made more or less probable, while, as noted, generics exhibit limited sensitivity to these factors.

Leslie treats generic statements disquotationally as giving voice to a variable-binding "Gen" operator that cannot be reduced to standard quantifiers. One difficulty with this approach for our purposes is that a new operator would also require us to introduce new inference rules to make sense of the fact that people make non-trivial inferences with generics. Such additions would in turn make it difficult say when it is permissible to use generics in rational thinking for something other than generic conclusions.

The erotetic theory provides new avenues for making sense of generic inferences. For reasons already discussed earlier in this chapter, there is considerable formal flexibility in how we might model various expression types in the erotetic theory, and generics are no exception. We will explore a minimal account based on the following claims:

184 PREDICATE REASONING

(1) No particular set of counterinstances conclusively contradicts a striking-property generic.
(2) Inferences from generics to particulars are not based on dedicated rules of inference.
(3) Inferences from generics to particulars are a bad choice for official scientific discourse.
(4) It is often reasonable to make an inference from generics to particulars.

With the erotetic theory, we get (1) by simply treating generics as logically vacuous. We get (2) by relying on arbitrary objects. We can then make sense of (3) and (4) by considering again what we have said about the role of restricted and absolute erotetic equillibrium in Chapters 2 and 3.

First, we provide a toy interpretation rule for generic statements. Generics may not have explicit grammatical markers forcing a generic interpretation of an expression, so the interpretation considered here may not be forced by grammar alone.

Definition 4.51 (Informal interpretation rule for bare-plural generics).
$[\![$ Sharks attack bathers $]\!] = \{SxAx, 0\}^{\{Sx\}}$

On this analysis, no particular set of counterinstances can conclusively contradict a generic, because the generic is compatible with everything, in virtue of having 0 as an alternative state. At first, this seems like a strange analysis, because it appears not to license any inferences at all. However, this is only the case if we are looking for entailments. In the issue-and-answer-based erotetic theory, this analysis of generics still allows them to have inferential powers.

We will have another look at inferences with generics. Leslie, Khemlani, and Glucksberg (Leslie et al. (2011)) found that a majority of participants (65%) who accepted a striking-property generalization were willing to accept its application to an arbitrary individual. We get a generic to particulars inference as follows, with the default reasoning procedure:

(Example 54 derivation)
$\{S\hat{x}Ax, 0\}^{\{Sx\}} [\ ]^D [\{S\hat{w}\}]^{\circ} = \{S\hat{w}Aw, 0, \bar{S}w\}[\{S\hat{w}\}]^{A,M} = \{S\hat{w}Aw\}$
After Factor, we end up with $\{Aw\}$.

This takes care of claim (2) above. The analysis captures that insofar as we are going to be playing the game of making inferences from these kinds of generics at all, these inferences seem to be about as intuitively easy as quantified modus ponens.

The remaining question is whether we can give an adequate account of claims (3) and (4), namely that it is often rationally permissible to make an inference from a (strictly speaking vacuous) generic to a particular, while it still seems inappropriate to use them in official scientific discourse.

First, we will update our definition of restricted erotetic equilibrium from Chapter 2 to bring it in line with our updated notion of inference.

Definition 4.52 (Restricted erotetic equilibrium of an inference). An inference $\mathcal{J}$ with premises C and conclusion D is an erotetic equilibrium inference restricted to a topic of inquiry TI, if and only if there exists an inference $\mathcal{J}'$ with premises C and conclusion D' (identical to D up to uniform replacement of A objects) such that whenever we have an instance of $\Gamma_{RI}^{\Theta}[\Delta_{SJ}^{\Psi}]^A$ in an inference step, then either $\mathcal{A}(\Gamma) \cap \mathcal{A}(\Delta) = \emptyset$ or both $\{\gamma \in \Gamma : \exists \varphi \in TI (\varphi \subseteq \gamma)\}_{[R][I]}^{\Theta}$ and Δ_{SJ}^{Ψ} are in erotetic equilibrium with respect to $\mathbb{V}_A(\Gamma) \cap \mathbb{V}_A(\Delta)$.

As before, the notions of erotetic equilibrium as we define them are *external* notions, in the sense that when we ask about the existence of an inference $\mathcal{J}'$, we are not asking about an alternative inference the reasoner has in fact made.

In case our topic of inquiry is unrestricted, generic inferences to particulars do not go through as erotetic equilibrium inferences, since the generics are vacuous, while absolute erotetic equilibrium guarantees soundness. This seems adequate enough to yield claim (3). After all, we expect official scientific discourse to be such that we can make *valid* inferences from our generalizations to particulars.

We now still need to explain how generic inferences to particulars could be rationally permissible. One approach would be to hold that the meaning of generics is not vacuous at all but includes reference to some standard of normal cases. One might then think that it is permissible to make generic inferences to particulars as long as one is justified in thinking that one is dealing with relevantly normal cases. We find it doubtful that we represent standards of normalcy for our generics, so we will take a different view.

Recall the equilibrium guarantee hypothesis for rational inquiry (definition 2.36) that was briefly explored in Chapter 2:

> If your judgment is in erotetic equilibrium restricted to a topic of inquiry a reasonable person would take to be called for in your overall circumstances, you are entirely as you ought to be as a reasoner.

186 PREDICATE REASONING

As noted in Chapter 2, an extended investigation of this principle would take us beyond the scope of this book. However, we shall assume this principle or something similar is true for now. We could then make sense of rationally acceptable uses of generics as follows.

Imagine you are in an inquiry restricted to those things that are dangerous, which would not be too far from a variant of our tiger case from Chapter 2. To make this vivid, imagine we are in a nightmarish amusement park in which some things are dangerous and some things are not. Further imagine that we are constantly asked to name reasons for our choices. We are fast going down a water slide approaching a junction. If we lean heavily to the left, we will go down a tube into pool N. If we lean heavily to the right, we will go down a tube into pool S (if we do not lean either way, we will get cut in half by the sharp edge of the junction). Suppose we know that there is a shark in pool N, and some unidentified fish in pool S. It seems to me that we are entirely as we ought to be if we choose pool S in this case, offering the reason that *there is something in pool N that is dangerous*.

On a restricted erotetic equilibrium account, we could capture the reasonableness of the inference from the shark generic to the conclusion that there is something dangerous in the tank by taking the topic of inquiry to be things that are dangerous. Formally, $TI = \{\{Dt_1\}, \{Dt_2\}, \{Dt_3\}, \ldots\}$, where we include $\{Dt_i\}$ for all terms t_i that come up in discourse. The "size" of the topic does not matter for now, since the definition of restricted erotetic equilibrium states an external condition on rational inference rather than a reasoning procedure someone follows.

We then proceed as follows.

(Generic derivation in restricted erotetic equilibrium)
$TI = \{\{Dx\}, \{Da\}\}$
$\{S\hat{x}Dx, 0\}^{\{Sx\}}[\ ]^D[\{S\hat{a}\}]^\circlearrowleft = \{S\hat{a}Da\}$.

To see what follows in restricted erotetic equilibrium, we first apply U and restrict with TI as an intermediate step, before preparing to apply $[\{S\hat{a}\}]^{A,M}$. The restriction yields $\{S\hat{a}Da\}$. We now see about whether $\{S\hat{a}Da\}$ and $\{S\hat{a}\}$ are in erotetic equilibrium with respect to $\mathbb{V}_A(\{S\hat{a}Da\}) \cap \mathbb{V}_A(\{S\hat{a}\})$. They clearly are. Hence, we can proceed with $\{S\hat{a}Da\}[\{S\hat{a}\}]^{A,M} = \{S\hat{a}Da\}$. Clearly, we can get from this to $\{Da\}$, namely the conclusion that there is something dangerous. This means that it is a restricted erotetic equilibrium conclusion that there is something dangerous, with respect to TI. Of course, not all topics of inquiry will make the foregoing into a restricted erotetic equilibrium conclusion.

A virtue of this analysis is that besides giving an account of how generic inferences to particulars can be rationally acceptable, it also gives us the means to articulate why generics can seem unfair, even to sharks. The fact that we maintain generics in "mature" discourse, unlike expletives, may be an indication that we habitually engage in restricted forms of inquiry. However, it is one thing to have as your topic of inquiry things that are dangerous when you are in the strange world our nightmarish amusement park, it is a very different thing if you are deciding on ecological policy and possible shark culls. It seems that we are often entitled to ignore "the other end" of an issue for our purposes. But in doing that we create, if you will, "externalities of reason," just as a factory might generate pollution. We are not always entitled to do that. There may be some generics, such as group stereotype generalizations, that are such that there simply is no context in which a reasonable person could legitimately have the kind of restricted topic of inquiry that would allow those generics to play any justifiable inferential role. For properties the attribution of which might have adverse consequences to the person to whom the properties are attributed, we might owe everyone serious consideration of both the possibility of bearing and *not bearing* those properties. This may well mean that it is not rationally permissible to treat various group stereotype generics as anything other than vacuous, more or less reducing them to expletives.

Moving on, it seems to us that with the present account of generics, we can shed new light on the problem of matchbox conditionals from Chapter 3. Since the discussion of statements like "if the match is struck, it will light" normally takes place in relatively narrow discussions about the meaning of "if... then," we tend to pay more attention to what we might conclude from such a statement, rather than to where the belief expressed by such a statement might come from. The account of generics above suggests the following view: When we believe a statement like "if *this match* is struck, it will light," we characteristically do so in virtue of believing a striking-property generic like "struck matches light," and believing that "*this* is a match." But of course, on the present account, the generic is $\{SxMxLx, 0\}^{\{SxMx\}}$, and what we called the disequilibrium conditional in Chapter 3 is simply $\{StMtLt, 0\}^{\{StMt\}}$, obtainable via U from this generic. Just like generics, many conditionals seem to only seem to generate non-trivial conclusions only relative to a certain restricted topic of inquiry.

This brings us to the end of the chapter. In the next chapter, we will further build on the system to allow us to directly take account of graded uncertainty in reasoning.

5
Reasoning with Uncertainty

Philipp Koralus, Sean Moss

Humans are able to reason not just about what is or is not the case but also about what is uncertain to be the case. This kind of reasoning emerges under various guises. For example, we draw conclusions about what sorts of bets are better than others, about relative risks, about the likelihood of various alternative possible outcomes, and about the propensity of some mechanism to give rise to various events.

As in previous chapters, we are interested in making sense of systematic failures of reasoning as well as of our ability to approach classical success criteria. This chapter presents an extension of the erotetic theory to carry this out.

Success in reasoning with uncertainty is most clearly understood in cases in which it involves bringing events that are uncertain to occur under a proportional measure. The probability calculus provides a systematic statement of what it takes to be coherent in the application of such a measure of uncertainty. Dutch-book arguments and other considerations provide reasons for considering lack of coherence as a significant kind of failure (Ramsey (1926); Hájek (2005)). Empirical science and many of the organizational foundations of modern life like banking and insurance could not be run without such reasoning, and could not be run fairly and efficiently without fairly systematic coherence.

However, there also seem to be systematic examples of failure of reasoning with probability. From the perspective of the broader aim of trying to make sense of our general reasoning capacity, some of the most interesting failures arise in the context of asking people to provide probability estimates in light of incrementally acquired information. Before considering concrete examples of such failures, we will briefly bring into view the constraints on what would count as success. The judgments of a coherent probabilistic reasoner must conform to Bayes's Rule, which encapsulates how to rationally respond to evidence that supports a hypothesis of interest even when we cannot deductively establish the hypothesis based on this evidence. First, we need

Reason and Inquiry: The Erotetic Theory. Philipp Koralus, Oxford University Press. © Philipp Koralus 2023.
DOI: 10.1093/oso/9780198823766.003.0005

to be able to represent how an event A probabilistically relates to an event B through a notion of the probability of A *conditional* on B, which is defined as follows:

Definition 5.1 (Conditional probability). $P(A|B) = \dfrac{P(A\&B)}{P(B)}$.

With the notion of conditional probability, we can model a rational process for figuring out the probability of a hypothesis in light of (1) the evidence, (2) the prior probability of the hypothesis, (3) the conditional probability of the evidence given the hypothesis, and (4) the conditional probability of the evidence given the complement (or negation) of the hypothesis. A coherent "Bayesian" posterior probability (i.e. the probability of the hypothesis after the evidence has been observed) must then satisfy the following rule:

Definition 5.2 (Bayes's Rule). For a hypothesis H and evidence E,

$$P_{Posterior}(H) = \frac{P(E|H) \times P_{Prior}(H)}{P(E|H) \times P_{Prior}(H) + P(E|\neg H) \times P_{Prior}(\neg H)}$$

Bayes's Rule is fairly intuitive if we think about it in terms of a proportion of cases. The posterior probability can be interpreted as the proportion of those cases in which the evidence and the hypothesis hold to the sum of all the cases in which evidence holds (in some of which the hypothesis holds and in some of which it does not hold). As we obtain evidence, we want to know, given that the total "heap of probability" has been reshuffled to cover only those cases in which the evidence holds, what proportion of that reshuffled heap now falls on cases in which the hypothesis holds.

If the mind were primarily Bayesian, we would naturally expect problems that provide us with information about prior probabilities of a hypothesis followed by further evidence to be relatively straightforward. However, this seems far from being the case. A classic example of failures of judgment in this domain comes from Hammerton (1973).

> **Example 64.** (Invented disease base-rate neglect)
> A device has been invented for screening a population for a disease known as psylicrapitis. The device is a very good one, but not perfect. If someone is a sufferer, there is a 90% chance that he will be recorded positively. If he is not a sufferer, there is still a 1% chance that he will be recorded positively.

> Roughly, 1% of the population has the disease. Mr. Smith has been tested, and the result is positive.
>
> What is the chance that he is in fact a sufferer?

Hammerton (1973) found that the average estimate was 85% (the correct estimate is about 50%) in participants who were not doctors. The problem seems to be that naïve default reasoning does not take base rates into account in problems like this and focuses solely on properties of the test instead. At the same time, the fact that neglecting base rates is a serious mistake is in fact completely intuitive after a moment's reflection; if the vast majority of people tested do not have the disease, then most people who score positive on even a very accurate and specific test (though a realistically fallible one) will be false positive cases. Many subsequent studies over the past decades have shown that the same mistake is made in various contexts, including by doctors with problems using realistic numbers on real and familiar diseases, as well as by legal and other professionals (Hoffrage and Gigerenzer (1998); Tversky and Kahneman (1973); Gigerenzer (2002)). For example, Hoffrage and Gigerenzer (1998) presented the following vignette to twenty-four doctors, half of whom responded that the probability was close to 50%, or higher. With 50% being the most popular answer. Participating doctors were reminded the hemoccult test is used for early detection of colorectal cancer.

> **Example 65.** (Base-rate neglect with doctors and realistic disease) Imagine you conduct a screening using the hemocult test in a certain region. For symptom-free people over 50 years old who participate in screening using the hemocult test, the following information is available for this region:
>
> The probability that one of these people has colorectal cancer is 0.3%. If a person has colorectal cancer, the probability is 50% that he will have a positive hemoccult test. If a person does not have a colorectal cancer, the probability is 3% that he will still have a positive hemoccult test. Imagine a person (over age 50, no symptoms) who has a positive hemoccult test in your screening. What is the probability that this person actually has colorectal cancer?

Interestingly, certain presentations of these kinds of "test problems" in terms of frequencies elicit much better performance. All physicians tested by

Gigerenzer and colleagues came up with correct or near-correct answer of around 50% (Gigerenzer (2002), p. 214) in the problem below.

> **Example 66.** (Frequency version of invented disease problem)
> Think of 100 people.
> 1. One has the disease psylicrapitis, and he is likely to test positive.
> 2. Of those 99 who do not have the disease, 1 will also test positive.
> How many of those who test positive do have the disease? out of ?

On some views (Gigerenzer and Hoffrage (1995); Cosmides and Tooby (1996)) the reason participants do well on this problem but poorly on the previous problem is that we are hard-wired to deal with frequencies, but not with Bayesian subjective probability. Obviously, the frequency problem here differs in other notable ways from the previous problem. For example, much less mental arithmetic is required to arrive at a correct answer. As Johnson-Laird et al. (1999) point out, it is unrealistic to expect the difficulty of numerical calculations to have no impact. Urbach and Howson (1993) acerbically suggest that the relevant studies support the "conclusion that their respondents are competent at whole number arithmetic." Gigerenzer's version of the disease inference problem, much of the arithmetic is already done for the participants, and there is not much required in terms of independent insight into how given data relate to the hypothesis of disease. Moreover, other classical examples of base-rate neglect were obtained in a quasi-frequentist setting (Tversky and Kahneman (1973)).

Overall, it would seem that the core of the problem leading to the observed mistakes is that intuitive reasoning simply does not demand information about base rates in order to obtain a substantive conclusion. Notably, press articles sometimes present information as suggestive of a substantive conclusion when no such conclusions can be derived without knowledge of base rates. For example, Hastie and Dawes (2010) provide the following quote from the business press.

> **Example 67.** (Inviting inferences in absence of base rate) "[R]esults of a recent survey of seventy-four chief executive officers indicate that there may be a link between childhood pet ownership and future career success. Fully 94% of the CEOs, all of them employed within Fortune 500 companies, had possessed a dog, a cat, or both, as youngsters." (From an article in *Management Focus* cited in Hastie and Dawes (2010, p. 112).)

The inference about a link between pet ownership and career success we are invited to make here is superficially tempting, until we bring to mind that it may well be the case that more than 94% of children of backgrounds like those of the CEOs had pets and that the dependency is actually negative. To make the problem obvious, Hastie and Dawes invite us to consider the statement with "brushing teeth" in place of "pet ownership."

Some time in late 2016, one of the authors of this chapter was alerted to a similar kind of mistake in an article in *The Sun*. The transportation authority for London had just refused to renew Uber's license to operate in the city. An often-discussed issue was whether Uber cars are unusually dangerous.

> **Example 68.** (Uber conditional probabilities)
>
> "[Uber drivers] were suspects in 32 cases reported by female passengers in the capital across 12 months. The tap-and-ride app, which now operates in 20 UK cities, claims to be the 'safest ride on the road.'"
>
> The article went on to mention that the service was banned in New Delhi after a passenger was raped. Returning to numerical data, the article noted:
>
> "Meanwhile, the Met in London dealt with 154 allegations involving taxi drivers, including minicabs, private chauffeurs and even rickshaw riders. Of those, 32 involved Uber drivers—the equivalent of one alleged attack every 11 days."
>
> (www.thesun.co.uk/archives/news/1205432/uber-drivers-accused-of-32-rapes-and-sex-attacks-on-london-passengers-in-last-year-alone, accessed Nov. 8, 2017.)

It does not seem unfair to suggest that the article invites the inference that Uber is dangerous and that the company's claim to be the "safest ride on the road" is mistaken. Whatever the facts about the safety of Uber may be, the data cited does not support this conclusion. Focusing on London and treating allegations as crimes, we could at best support the estimate that P(an Uber driver is driving | a taxi related crime) = 32/154 = 21%. However, if we want to know whether Uber is dangerous, we need to know P(a taxi related crime | an Uber driver is driving). Unfortunately, the article does not provide information to make the relevant inferences. Whether we should conclude that Uber is especially dangerous as a transportation option or even especially safe, in light of the numbers provided by *The Sun*, can only be determined if we consider what proportion of private hire vehicles in London are operated via Uber.

In sum, the article does not include figures that would allow us to support the conclusion it seems to invite readers to draw. The interesting observation for our purposes is that the writers of the article are probably *not* unreasonable in expecting that their readers will take the article to support the angle that Uber is dangerous anyway, just as the authors of the *Management Focus* article are not unreasonable in expecting that their readers will treat their observations about pet-owning future CEOs as interestingly informative.

Answering questions with conditional probabilities that by themselves could not rationally settle those questions has been observed to be a standard pitfall in legal cases. There seems to be a temptation to say yes to the following sort of question, even in the case of scientific researchers (Eddy (1982); Gigerenzer and Hoffrage (1995); Johnson-Laird et al. (1999)).

> **Example 69.** (Evidence fallacy)
> The suspect's DNA matches the crime sample.
> If the suspect is not guilty, then the probability of such a DNA match is 1 in a million.
> *Is the suspect likely to be guilty?*

There is a strong intuition that we can answer "yes" in the above case. However, we have to remind ourselves that the information provided gives us P(DNA-Match | Not Guilty) while we are interested in P(Guilty | DNA-Match). If there is one real perpetrator who will always test positive among one million people who are tested for a DNA match, then the chances are closer to 50%.

In their sum, these results are hard to ignore. As Hastie and Dawes (2010, p. 169) observe:

> a convincing argument that the judgment errors we have identified are truly irrational is that experimental participants shown their own responses and told the rule that they have violated often conclude, "I made a mistake," or even "Boy, that was stupid, I'm embarrassed." Kahneman and Tversky (1982; 1996), who first identified many of the errors we discussed, label these judgment errors illusions, because they are behavioral habits that we know are mistakes when we think carefully about them, but they still persist when we do not exercise deliberate self-control to counteract our intuitive tendencies very much like the many familiar, but still irresistible optical illusions.

We are subject to systematic fallacies and, yet, we are also capable of systematically coherent reasoning with probability. Laplace's famous dictum, "the theory of probabilities is at bottom only common sense reduced to calculus" (de Laplace (1902)/(1814)) has an intuitive grain of truth, even in the face of widespread fallacies. In fact, if there were no grain of truth to this, it would be a mystery how the kind of reaction to fallacies that Hastie and Dawes describe is possible.

We will ultimately have to explain these kinds of incoherent judgments as well as our ability to make such judgments coherently. There is reason to think that in many cases our ability to make accurate forecasts about uncertain events is held back just as much by flaws of reasoning as by lack of information. Tetlock and Gardner's work (2015) has identified "superforecasters" that in some cases outperform even subject experts with access to classified information in forecasting political events. What sets systematically better forecasters apart seems to be largely a more systematic approach to integrating uncertain information rather than more detailed factual knowledge. These observations make it seem like a better understanding of how we reason with uncertainty is amply worth having. As in previous chapters, we again find ourselves confronted with having to explain both systematic success and systematic failure, without a clear sense in the existing literature of what can bring the two together in one theory.

A relatively strange aspect of the literature on failures in reasoning with probability or frequency information is that it is largely separate from broader discussions of reasoning including the kinds of phenomena discussed in previous chapters. However, Johnson-Laird et al. (1999) point out that we can make very similar inferences with categorical statements. It seems that "yes" is a superficially tempting answer in the below problem, which would not be surprising in light of the fact that affirming the consequent is a tempting fallacy, as discussed in Chapter 3.

Example 70. (Categorical diagnosis inference)
(P1) Pat has either the disease or a benign condition.
(P2) If she has the disease, then she will have a certain symptom.
(P3) In fact, she has the symptom.
So, does she have the disease?

It seems arbitrary to treat this kind of inference as completely separate in origin from the cases at the beginning of this section. We will take the approach of seeking an account of failures of reasoning with probabilities that is continuous with our more general account of reasoning that we have developed in previous chapters. On the erotetic theory account we will develop in this chapter, we can make sense of base-rate neglect in much the same way in which the previous chapters allow us to make sense of the categorical diagnosis inference above: reason allows us to take treat premises as answers in cases where this is neither licensed by probability nor by valid entailment. In the rest of the sections in this chapter, we present the extension of the erotetic theory that will allow us to articulate this formally.

In light of the theories developed in the previous chapters, we would suspect that how we reason with probabilities would have something to do with how we represent alternative possibilities. Shimojo and Ichikawa (1989) presented an early view on which reasoning with probability is driven by representations of alternatives. However, it was not envisaged that those representations may be partial or incomplete. Johnson-Laird et al. (1999) presented a view on which reasoning with probability is driven by partial representations of alternatives. The account we will develop in this chapter is similar in taking it that reasoning with uncertainty is based on partial views. More specifically, we will show that it is possible to understand the cases of success and failure in reasoning with uncertainty to be fundamentally of the same kind as the cases of success and failure we considered in previous chapters.

Proponents of the mental model theory approach have argued that when reasoners try to assess the probability of a proposition but only have information about alternative possibilities available, they will assume that those alternatives are equally probable (Johnson-Laird and Savary (1996); Johnson-Laird et al. (1999)). This can be a respectable Bayesian assumption. However, the alternatives are those in the reasoner's mental model, which are not guaranteed to correspond to a full partition of all possible outcomes, thereby failing to guarantee an unbiased Bayesian judgment based on uniform priors. We will take a similar approach within the erotetic theory. However, we will in fact also be able to make sense of probabilistic coherence under erotetic equilibrium.

Since we are looking for an integrated account of reasoning, it will be relevant to consider cases in which we seem to be able to draw probabilistic conclusions from non-probabilistic premises. Johnson-Laird et al. (1999) presented participants with several problems involving a non-probabilistic premise statement followed by a question about probability. In the below problem, the mean response was 53%.

> **Example 71.** (Probability judgment from propositional premise)
> There is a box in which there is a yellow card or a brown card, but not both.
> *Given the preceding assertion, according to you, what is the probability of the following situation?*
> In the box there is a yellow card and there is not a brown card.

If we imagine that reasoners assume that all possible states are equally likely, this would be a reasonable estimate. We are either in a state in which we have a yellow card and no brown card, or in a state in which we have a brown card but no yellow card, so if each state is equally likely, we get to an answer of 50%. In this case, the alternative states in the issue the premise gives rise to correspond to the full set of alternative possible outcomes, which means that an unbiased "Bayesian" estimate and an estimate based on the alternative states in a view come to the same thing. However, Johnson-Laird et al. (1999) found that in similar problems in which the alternative states in the issue generated by the premise does not correspond to a full partition of possible states, judgments are no longer unbiased.

> **Example 72.** (Illusory probability inference from partial information)
> There is a box in which there is at least a red marble or else there is a green marble and there is a blue marble, but not all three marbles.
> *What is the probability of the following situation:*
> There is a red marble and a blue marble in the box?
> (18 of 25 participants were within +5% of the answer 0)

If we assumed an unbiased inference that takes all possibilities compatible with the statement to be equally likely, then there is a 25% probability of having a red marble and a blue marble. Johnson-Laird et al. (1999) found that problems in which participants are asked to provide probabilities from partial information show a similar pattern. It is intuitively tempting to conclude that the answer is 0.2, even though a moment's reflection suggests that that is unlikely to be correct.

> **Example 73.** (Illusory inference from disjunction with partial probabilities) You have a hand of several cards with only limited information about it.
>
> There is an ace and a queen or a king and a jack or a ten.
> The probability that there is an ace and a queen is 0.6.
> The probability that there is a king and a jack is 0.2.
>
> What is the probability that there is a ten?

What we have so far considered in this chapter is just the tip of the iceberg of a variety of fallacies of probabilistic reasoning, which have been the bread and butter of the empirical study of judgment and decision-making for decades. There is one other class of mistakes in probabilistic reasoning that particularly deserves to be highlighted given our purposes. It appears that naïve reasoners sometimes judge the probability of a conjunction to be higher than the probability of its individual conjuncts, which is of course probabilistically incoherent. The reason this is worth highlighting is that this phenomenon is not entirely surprising if reasoning is based on narrowing down issues in light of the answer potential provided by further information. After all, a complex state can easily receive more answer potential support than a simpler state composed of some of the constituents of the complex state.

A classic example of conjunction incoherence comes from Tversky and Kahneman (1983), who gave 103 doctors vignettes like the following.

> **Example 74.** (Conjunction incoherence in individual medical judgment) A 55-year-old woman had pulmonary embolism documented angiographically 10 days after a cholecystectomy. Please rank order the following in terms of the probability that they will be among the conditions experienced by the patient (use 1 for the most likely and 6 for the least likely). Naturally, the patient could experience more than one of these conditions.
>
> Dyspnea and hemiparesis [A & B]
> Calf pain
> Pleuritic chest pain
> Syncope and tachycardia
> Hemiparesis [B]
> Hemoptysis.

Apparent violations of the conjunction rule, ranking "dyspnea and hemiparesis" over "hemiparesis," ranged from 73% to 100% of responses. As has often been pointed out, these rankings are not incoherent if "hemiparesis" is interpreted as "hemiparesis and *no* dyspnea." At least two observations make this interpretation unlikely to completely explain the effect. Firstly, each vignette was presented to different participants with either both the conjunction and the single conjunct present, or with only one of them. The average ranking of the alternatives across participants was not significantly affected by whether both the conjunction and the single conjunct were presented to the same doctor. This rules out that the effect is explained by an exclusivity interpretation (recall discussion at the beginning of Chapter 2) that is specifically triggered by the juxtaposition of the conjunction with a single conjunct. What if participants generally interpret all of the alternative symptoms in this kind of list exclusively, regardless of whether conjunctions or single conjuncts are present? To control for this possibility, participants were asked a follow-up question:

In assessing the probability that the patient described has a particular symptom X, did you assume that (check one):

☐ X is the only symptom experienced by the patient.
☐ X is among the symptoms experienced by the patient.

60 of 62 checked the second box, making it implausible that participants generally interpreted the alternatives exclusively.

Perhaps the most famous experiment showing evidence of a conjunction fallacy is the so-called "Linda Problem." Tversky and Kahneman (1983) presented the following vignette to participants in an experiment.

> **Example 75.** (The Linda Problem) *Linda is thirty-one years old, single, outspoken, and very bright. She majored in philosophy. As a student, she was deeply concerned with issues of discrimination and social justice and she also participated in anti-nuclear demonstrations. Please rank order by probability (highest to lowest) the following:* [some choices removed for brevity]
>
> Linda is active in the feminist movement.
> Linda is a psychiatric social worker.
> Linda is a bank teller.
> Linda is an insurance salesperson.
> Linda is a bank teller and is active in the feminist moment.

Tversky and Kahneman found that 86% of undergraduates judged that it is more likely that Linda is a bank teller and active in the feminist movement than that Linda is a bank teller. The conjunction was also ranked higher in a between-subjects version of the experiment where only one of the two crucial options was available to each participant.

Sablé-Meyer and Mascarenhas (2020) have drawn a useful parallel between the conjunction fallacy in probabilistic reasoning and the kind of illusory inferences from disjunctions that we have discussed in Chapter 2.

Firstly, they show that participants make illusory inferences from disjunction even when the connection between the disjuncts and the second premise is indirect. For example, more than half of participants answered "yes" in the following problem (Sablé-Meyer and Mascarenhas (2020)).

> **Example 76.** (Guns and guitars)
> (P1) The gun fired and the guitar was out of tune, or else someone was in the attic.
> (P2) The trigger was pulled.
> *Does it follow that the guitar was out of tune?*

Interestingly, the rate at which inferences of this form were endorsed was significantly predicted by the strength of the causal link (as rated in a separate rating task) between the second premise and the targeted conjunct in the first premise.

As Sable-Meyer and Mascarenhas point out, this pattern can be used to explain the "Linda Problem" conjunction fallacy. We effectively have the disjunction "Either Linda is a bank teller and a feminist or Linda is a bank teller." We then get as de facto premises that "Linda is a left-wing activist" and "Linda is a bright humanities graduate." There certainly is a plausible intuition that being a female left-wing activist has a causal connection with being a feminist and there also is an intuition that being a bright humanities graduate has some causal connection with being a bank teller (perhaps at least in the 1980s). Clearly, the conjunction gets more support if we analyze this problem as analogous to Sablé-Meyer and Mascarenhas (2020). This again suggests that some of the most well-known puzzling aspects of human reasoning with uncertainty might admit of a fairly elegant erotetic explanation.

With some of the main quirks of reasoning with uncertainty brought in to view, we now turn to increasing the expressive power the erotetic theory to deal with graded uncertainty.

5.1 Equilibrium Answer Potential and Extended Views

We take reasoning with uncertainty to be grounded in what we will call *equilibrium answer potential*. To develop this notion, let us first take a step back and return to propositional reasoning. Suppose we wish to answer the question $\{p, \bar{p}\}$. In light of this question, $\{p\}$ would be as strong as it gets as an answer. Now, we saw that there are other ways of obtaining an answer, often yielding fallacies in the case of deductive reasoning. For example, $\{p, q\}$ also serves as an answer to $\{p, \bar{p}\}$. Versions of this pattern ultimately explained a host of propositional reasoning fallacies. The problem here is that the q alternative is merely tacit with respect to p and $\bar{p}$. $\{p, q\}$ cannot actually answer $\{p, \bar{p}\}$ in erotetic equilibrium. As soon as we inquire on $\{p\}$, we get $\{p, qp, q\bar{p}\}$, which does not resolve $\{p, \bar{p}\}$ anymore, because we have brought the possibility that p is still not the case into the open. In fact, erotetic equilibrium ensures that we only get to resolve a question in favor of an answer if those answers are validly entailed. In that sense, setting aside a restriction to the topic of inquiry as discussed under the rubric of restricted erotetic equilibrium in previous chapters, any difference in what we called atomic answer potential, short of entailment, is an illusion and will disappear if we raise enough questions.

Now, we wish to have the expressive power to represent some alternative states as having a *greater claim* to contribute an answer to a question implicating p in some of its possible answers than $\bar{p}$, even for absolute erotetic equilibrium inferences. In other words, we want to be able to say that some alternatives have a greater *equilibrium* answer potential support than others even after we have inquired about all possibilities, but without those alternatives being entailed. In a sense, we are taking the view that graded uncertainty is not a fundamental notion for reason. Instead, the nearby fundamental notion is equilibrium answer potential: greater or lesser claim to answer, without entailment but even under absolute erotetic equilibrium. In many cases, equilibrium answer potential mimics probability, but not always. In the next chapter we will see even more clearly that this is not merely a terminological difference, since we will also use equilibrium answer potential to make sense of priorities in decision-making.

Recall that what counts in answering is based on how much overlap there is between atoms in an answer and atoms in competing alternatives in the question we update with this answer. Return to our official set-theoretic notation for states and views that we normally abbreviate. We cannot just write $\{\{p, p\}, \{\bar{p}\}\}$ to signify that we represent p as being twice as "strong" an answer as $\bar{p}$, since $\{\{p, p\}, \{\bar{p}\}\}$ is just identical to $\{\{p\}, \{\bar{p}\}\}$. We need to find a way to allow that we can have a *number* of situations that we are not further distinguishing by what holds in them. Intuitively, if there are twice as many heads situations as tails situations, "heads!" is a better answer than "tails!" to "heads or tails?" We will follow this intuition, though without any commitment to frequentism about probability. We will ultimately represent graded uncertainty through views having varying degrees of equilibrium answer potential. There may be any number of reasons why we assign greater equilibrium answer potential to one alternative rather than another, including but not limited to frequencies of situations, their imaginability, perceived propensities, or even degree of support from some authority. In the following, I will keep talking as if we were interpreting equilibrium answer potential as a count of frequencies of certain contingencies, because that makes it easier to articulate certain things in English. This move is a mere convenience.

To regiment views with equilibrium answer potential, we will define a notion of weighted states. In the first instance, we want to be able to countenance things like the view that there are, say, two p states for every $\bar{p}$ state. However, we also want to continue to be able to entertain an alternative state without committing ourselves to this state having a determinate proportional equilibrium answer potential relative to other states. This corresponds to the intuition that I can believe that "p or q" without having any particular belief which is more likely or how many more cases of the p kind there are than there are cases of the q kind. Thus, we will allow the weight of a state to be empty, which will be distinct from saying that the weight of a state is zero. For non-empty weights, we want to also allow potentially complex terms as weights, including arbitrary objects and functions. I might have the belief that the chance of something happening has a functional relationship to further facts. For example, I might believe that the chance of a certain atom decaying in the next minute is a function of its atomic number (how exactly equilibrium answer potential relates to familiar notions of chance will be discussed in more detail in a later section). We will now augment our definition of views to capture the foregoing.

First, recall from the previous chapter that we postulate that the capacity to reason is a capacity to manipulate a view. What we shall now refer to as a "classical" view consists of a main set of alternative states, a set of states constituting a supposition, a dependency relation over arbitrary objects participating in the states, and an issue structure. We will now construct the notion of an extended view, which adds an assignment of weights to each state in the main set of alternative states in a classical view. Afterwards, we will update our definitions of inference procedures to deal with extended views.

Extended views are a conservative extension over classical views, in the sense that we can always take an extended view, "forget" the weights, and see it as a classical view. An extended view might also directly assign the empty weight to each state; such a view will behave essentially like a classical view even under the updated inference procedures we will go on to define.

In the general case, the weights assigned to a state in an extended sentential view will each be a "bag" or "multiset" of terms, meaning it is an unordered list, possibly with repetitions. This means that each state in an extended view can be multiply weighted, to give us maximum flexibility.

The updated reasoning operations we will define in due course will be conservative as well, in that the inclusion of classical views into extended views commutes with all reasoning operations; and the projection of extended views onto classical views commutes with almost all reasoning operations; the exceptions being operations that are invoked to answer questions (i.e. Answer via Update and Suppose, Query, Which); (see §B.6).

First, we shall revise our definition of terms and augment our collection of basic objects from Chapter 4 with the concept of *weights*.

Definition 5.3 (Weights).
(Weights) The set $\mathbb{W}$ of weights consists of all finite multisets of terms. Given a finite sequence of terms $t_1, \ldots, t_n$, we denote the underlying multiset of that sequence (the set of members in the sequence weighted by their number of occurrences) by $\langle\!\langle t_1, \ldots, t_n \rangle\!\rangle$.

Various of our revised reasoning operations that we will go on to define will have to perform arithmetic with weights, and to support this we need the following enrichment to the set of terms in Chapter 4. We will leave the details of weight arithmetic aside until we turn to operations that require it.

Definition 5.4 (Additional terms).
(Real numbers) Every real number $\alpha \in \mathbb{R}$ is a constant term.
(Multiplication) $\overline{\times}$ is a function symbol of arity 2.
(Summation) σ is function symbol, but rather than taking as an argument a list of terms of fixed size, it takes an arbitrary finite multiset of terms. Thus, whenever $t_1, \ldots, t_n$ is a sequence of terms, $\sigma\langle\!\langle t_1, \ldots, t_n \rangle\!\rangle$ is a term.

Definition 5.5 (Extended set of states). Γ_f is an *extended set of states* if and only if Γ is a finite set $\Gamma \subseteq \mathbb{S}$ of states and f is an assignment $f : \Gamma \to \mathbb{W}$.

Definition 5.6 (Extended views $\bar{V}$). An *extended view* Γ^{Θ}_{fRI} is a view Γ^{Θ}_{RI} such that Γ_f is an extended set of states and such that $\forall y \in \Gamma.A(f(y)) \subseteq A(R)$. We use the convention that $f(y) = \langle\!\langle\rangle\!\rangle$ for $y \notin \Gamma$ (but we do not rule out $f(y) = \langle\!\langle\rangle\!\rangle$ for some $y \in \Gamma$).

We will adopt several simplifying notational conventions for writing up examples, in addition to the conventions adopted in previous chapters. Where there is no potential for confusion,

(1) Γ_f may be written as $\{f(y_1).y, \ldots, f(y_n).y_n\}$, where $\Gamma = \{y_1, \ldots, y_n\}$.
(2) $\{\langle\!\langle t_1 \rangle\!\rangle.y_1, \langle\!\langle t_2 \rangle\!\rangle.y_2\}$ may be written as $\{t_1.y_1, t_2.y_2\}$.
(3) Suppressing empty weights, $\{\langle\!\langle\rangle\!\rangle.y_1, \langle\!\langle t_2 \rangle\!\rangle.y_2\}$ may be written as $\{y_1, t_2.y_2\}$.
(4) Collecting up multiple instances of a term in a weight, $\{\langle\!\langle t_1, t_1 \rangle\!\rangle.y_1, \langle\!\langle t_2 \rangle\!\rangle.y_2\}$ may be written as $\{\langle\!\langle 2.t_1 \rangle\!\rangle.y_1, \langle\!\langle t_2 \rangle\!\rangle.y_2\}$ or $\{2.t_1.y_1, t_2.y_2\}$.
(5) When no ambiguity arises, in the context of example derivations, we will write $\{\langle\!\langle t_1, 5, 2.h(x) \rangle\!\rangle.y_1, \langle\!\langle t_2 \rangle\!\rangle.y_2\}$ as $\{(t_1 + 5 + 2.h(x)).y_1, t_2.y_2\}$, with no significance to the order of the summands.

Our notion of commitments is updated as expected.

Definition 5.7 (Extended commitments $\overline{C}$). For $C \subseteq \overline{V}, G \in \overline{V}, \langle C, G \rangle \in \overline{C}$.

5.2 Answering with EAP

Suppose we must answer the question of whether there will be lunch given information about whether there has been a catering truck in evidence. Loosely speaking, we might have 20 cases of lunch preceded by the appearance of a truck, 5 frustrating cases of no lunch preceded by a truck, 40 cases of lunch without a truck, and 100 uneventful cases with no lunch and no truck. This can be regimented as the view $\{20.TL, 5.T\bar{L}, 40.\bar{T}L, 100.\bar{T}\bar{L}\}$. We can treat this as akin to the question, "am I in one of 20 cases with lunch and truck, one of 5 cases of truck and no lunch, one of 40 cases of lunch without truck, or in one of 100 cases of no lunch and no truck?" Suppose now that we learn that there is indeed a truck. We treat $\{T\}$ as an answer. We will want this to yield $\{20.TL, 5.T\bar{L}\}$. So will there be lunch? If we treat the foregoing as an answer to the issue as to whether there will be lunch, we will want to conclude that there will indeed be lunch. Note that we are not yet making any claims about how this figure relates to a coherent probability measure.

To regiment the foregoing kind of inference, we will now have to update our notion of answer potential between views.

Definition 5.8 ($\mathbb{E}$ Answer potential).

$$\Delta_g[\Gamma]^{\mathbb{E}P} = \sigma\Big(\langle\!\langle \sigma(g(\delta)) \mid \delta \in Y \rangle\!\rangle\Big),$$

where $Y = \{\delta \in \Delta \mid \exists \gamma \in \Gamma . \gamma \subseteq \delta\}$.

For example,

$$\{30.p, 70.q\}[\{p\}]^{\mathbb{E}P} = \sigma\langle\!\langle \sigma\langle\!\langle 30 \rangle\!\rangle \rangle\!\rangle.$$

Now, $\sigma\langle\!\langle \sigma\langle\!\langle 30 \rangle\!\rangle \rangle\!\rangle$ is in the first instance a complex term. We will want that term to be reducible via the arithmetic of weights down to 30. Similarly, $\{30.p, 70.pq, 20.\bar{q}\}[\{p\}]^{\mathbb{E}P} = \sigma\langle\!\langle \sigma\langle\!\langle 30 \rangle\!\rangle, \sigma\langle\!\langle 70 \rangle\!\rangle \rangle\!\rangle$, which we will want to be reducible to 100. Ultimately, we think that such reductions require real reasoning steps on the part of the reasoner. There is no special reason to think that arithmetic comes for free in reasoning about uncertainty-related concepts, and there is also little reason to think that the ability to perform this kind of reasoning is strongly independent from the general capacity to do arithmetic. We suggest this kind of reasoning is possible within the erotetic theory system with suitable absurdity clauses as de facto axioms for arithmetic (also see remarks in Chapter 4). For now, we will make the simplifying assumption that the relevant solutions are simply given, particularly when they are required for the computation of a reasoning operation. Dealing with the arithmetic of weights in a fully explicit way in this context would require branching reasoning procedures, with some inference operations generating new reasoning problems that have to be resolved before the main line of inference may proceed. While we see no barrier to building such extensions, we will set them aside for the purposes of this chapter, and adopt as a simplifying idealization that arithmetic problems as given rise to by our inference procedures are fully resolved in the background.

If there are no alternatives in Δ that contain γ, then $\Delta_g[\{\gamma\}]^{\mathbb{E}P}$ yields 0, since by our assumption $\sigma(\langle\!\langle\rangle\!\rangle)$ is reduced to 0. For the same reason, $\{p, q\}[\{p\}]^{\mathbb{E}P} = 0$.

We can then define a notion of Answer that recruits equilibrium answer potential rather than atomic answer potential. To do this, we will need a bit more machinery. We will define a tool we call "pipe notation" to help us build extended views out of other materials.

Definition 5.9 (Pipe to extended view). Given an extended set of states Γ_f, and given Θ, R, I, such that $A(\Gamma \cup \Theta) \subseteq A(R)$ we define $\Gamma_f|_{RI}^{\Theta}$ to be the extended View $\langle \Gamma, g, \Theta, S, J \rangle$ where:

(1) $S = [R]_{\Gamma \cup \Theta}$,
(2) For $y \in \Gamma$, $g(y) = \langle\!\langle t \in f(y) : A(t) \subseteq A(S) \rangle\!\rangle$.
(3) $J = [I]_{\Gamma \cup \Theta}$.

Definition 5.10 (𝔼 Answer).

$$\Gamma_{fRI}^{\Theta}[\Delta_{gSJ}^{\{0\}}]^{\mathbb{E}A} = \left(\arg\max_{y \in \Gamma} \Delta_g[\{\{p\} : p \in y\}]^{\mathbb{E}P} \right)\bigg|_{f}^{\Theta}{}_{RI}$$

𝔼 Answer is fundamentally a decision procedure. A natural use of a view like $\Delta = \{20.l, 5.\bar{l}\}$ is to help settle the question $\Gamma = \{l, \bar{l}\}$, if we decide to treat Δ as an answer to Γ. On the basis of what criterion we should determine whether such a Δ should be used as an answer to such a Γ ultimately corresponds to the familiar problem of thresholds in decision theory. We could, for example, take the view that we should only treat a Δ as an answer to $\{l, \bar{l}\}$ if Δ supports one alternative a lot more than it supports another. For example, if we wanted to require quite a bit of differential support in order to accept an answer, we could demand only to treat Δ as an answer if we have it that either

$$\frac{\Delta[\{l\}]^{\mathbb{E}P}}{\Delta[\{l\}]^{\mathbb{E}P} + \Delta[\{\bar{l}\}]^{\mathbb{E}P}} \geq 0.9$$

or

$$\frac{\Delta[\{\bar{l}\}]^{\mathbb{E}P}}{\Delta[\{l\}]^{\mathbb{E}P} + \Delta[\{\bar{l}\}]^{\mathbb{E}P}} \geq 0.9.$$

Such choosiness is not hardwired into the system.

As in the case of "atomic" answer potential before, we have it that a less specific view with 𝔼P can answer the issue raised by a more specific view. For example, $\{pq, rs\}[\{90.p, 10.\bar{p}\}]^{\mathbb{E}A} = \{pq\}$. As in the case of our previous notion of Answer, we look for those alternatives that have maximum answer potential support, but this time not in terms of maximum atomic overlap, so we also get $\{akj, sct, a\}[\{5.ak, 1.s\}]^{\mathbb{E}A} = \{akj, a\}$.

Now, for views without relevant equilibrium answer potential, we will want our new definition of Answer to reduce to the old definition of Answer. To combine these notions in the right way, we will rename our old purely propositional version of Answer "*Atomic* Answer" and define our new official definition of Answer as $\mathbb{E}$ Answer followed by *Atomic* Answer.

Definition 5.11 (Atomic answer potential).

$$\Delta[\Gamma]^{AP} = |\mathcal{A}(\Gamma) \cap \mathcal{A}(\Delta)|$$

Definition 5.12 ($\mathcal{A}$ Answer).

$$\Gamma^{\Theta}_{fRI}[\Delta^{\{0\}}_{gSJ}]^{\mathcal{A}A} = (\underset{\gamma \in \Gamma}{\arg\max}\, \Delta[\{\{p\} : p \in \gamma\}]^{AP})_f \Big|^{\Theta}_{RI}$$

Definition 5.13 (Answer). $\Gamma^{\Theta}_{fRI}[\Delta^{\{0\}}_{gSJ}]^{A} = \Gamma^{\Theta}_{fRI}[\Delta^{\{0\}}_{gSJ}]^{\mathbb{E}A}[\Delta^{\{0\}}_{gSJ}]^{\mathcal{A}A}$.

In words, what this notion of Answer does is first reduce Γ to those elements that have maximum equilibrium answer potential from Δ and then reduce the result further, leaving only those of the remaining elements that have maximum atomic answer potential. As before, Answer is capable of generating fallacious inferences similar to the propositional illusory inferences considered earlier. In some cases, both differences in $\mathbb{E}P$ and differences in $\mathcal{A}P$ make a difference to the result. For example, $\{akj, sct, a\}[\{5.ak, 1.s\}]^A = \{akj, a\}[\{5.ak, 1.s\}]^{\mathcal{A}A} = \{akj\}$. It is easy to see that our new definition of Answer strictly generalizes the definition in the previous chapters, in the sense that our new Answer reduces to the previous definition for cases in which $\mathbb{E}P$ does not differ between alternative states in the body of the external argument of Answer.

5.3 Generating Graded Uncertainty

Ultimately, we argue that our naïve judgments of probability are grounded in judgments about equilibrium answer potential. First, consider the simplest possible ways in which $\mathbb{E}P$ counts can get into views. As we saw in the introduction to this chapter, reasoners are very much prepared to draw conclusions about probabilities on the basis of purely propositional premises.

Proponents of the mental model theory approach have argued that when reasoners try to assess the probability of a proposition but only have information about alternative possibilities available, they will assume that those alternatives are equally probable (Johnson-Laird and Savary (1996); Johnson-

Laird et al. (1999)). This can sometimes be a respectable Bayesian assumption. However, the alternatives are those in the reasoner's mental model, which are not guaranteed to correspond to a full partition of all possible outcomes, thereby failing to guarantee an unbiased Bayesian judgment based on uniform priors.

We adopt the same perspective for our framework, which translates to the idea that reasoners generally assume that alternative states in a view are equiprobable. For an erotetic equilibrium view that in fact *will* correspond to a partition of over all possible states of the world with respect to a given set of atoms, this assumption amounts to assuming that all elements of the partition are equally probable. This is a first glimpse of the fact that we will again be able to secure classical normative standards under erotetic equilibrium, in this case, Bayesianism with even prior probabilities under erotetic equilibrium.

We will model the step of making an assumption about equally probable alternatives as something obtained through reasoning rather than by hard-wired commitment. This is crucial to be able to accommodate the intuition that we are sometimes rationally able to refuse to make such assumptions, even if there is a strong drive to make them if we otherwise would not be able to find any kind of new conclusion from the pieces of information we have. First, we need the reasoner to take a view on how probabilities are to be scaled. In the context of a reasoning problem provided in an experimental setup, this is normally contextually fixed as either from 0 to 1 or to 100. Let us call the largest value of our probability scale P_{max}. We can then take a problem scenario as providing the constraint that our view will have to satisfy $\Gamma_f[\{0\}]^{EP} = P_{max}$. In other words, the probability of truth is P_{max}. We can then model the assumption that each alternative is equally likely as the application of a certain kind of question to a view with empty weights (e.g. an essentially classical view). We can enrich a view Γ_{fRI}^{Θ} carrying empty weights with the assumption that all alternatives are equally probable by applying

$$\Gamma_{fRI}^{\Theta}[\langle\!\langle x \rangle\!\rangle.0]^I, \text{ for } x = \frac{P_{max}}{|\Gamma|}.$$

As it turns out, Inquire remains logically neutral, but not informationally neutral once we consider equilibrium answer potential. To simplify discussion, we will assume in the next few sections that P_{max} is always 100, unless stipulated otherwise.

To proceed, we now have to define Inquire and its constituent operations for views with $\mathbb{E}P$s. We will also need to update our Wh operation to allow us to ask about probabilities in light of a given view. To do all of this, we will first need Sum, Product, and Negation.

Definition 5.14 (Sum). For Γ_f, Δ_g weighted sets of states,
$$\Gamma_f + \Delta_g = (\Gamma \cup \Delta)_h, \text{ where } h(\gamma) = f(\gamma) + g(\gamma).$$
We then have,

$$\Gamma_{fRI}^{\Theta} \oplus^T \Delta_{gSJ}^{\Theta} = (\Gamma_f + \Delta_g)|_{(T \bowtie R) \bowtie (T \bowtie S), I \cup J}^{\Theta}.$$

The foregoing definition relies on sums of weights. As multisets, weights support a commutative, associative, unital addition: the sum of multisets, which we specify below.

> **Example 77.**
> - $\langle\!\langle t \rangle\!\rangle + \langle\!\langle t \rangle\!\rangle = \langle\!\langle t, t \rangle\!\rangle = \langle\!\langle 2.t \rangle\!\rangle$
> - $\langle\!\langle 1.z, 6.x \rangle\!\rangle + \langle\!\langle 3.z, 8.y \rangle\!\rangle = \langle\!\langle 4.z, 6.x, 8.y \rangle\!\rangle$
> - $\langle\!\langle m.t \rangle\!\rangle + \langle\!\langle n.t \rangle\!\rangle = \langle\!\langle (m+n).t \rangle\!\rangle$
> - $w + \langle\!\langle \rangle\!\rangle = w = \langle\!\langle \rangle\!\rangle + w$ ($\langle\!\langle \rangle\!\rangle$ is a zero element)
> - $w_1 + w_2 = w_2 + w_1$ (commutativity)
> - $(w_1 + w_2) + w_3 = w_1 + (w_2 + w_3)$ (associativity)

We next turn to Product. We postpone our new definitions of multiple repeated products until we need them.

Definition 5.15 (Product).
$$\Gamma_f \otimes \Delta_g^{\Psi} = P + \sum_{\gamma \in \Gamma \backslash P} \sum_{\delta \in \Delta} \{(f(\gamma) \times g(\delta)).(\gamma \cup \delta)\}$$

where $P = \{f(\gamma).\gamma \in \Gamma \mid \neg \exists \psi \in \Psi . \psi \subseteq \gamma\}$ and $\times$ is the product of weights. As a special case, $\Gamma_f \otimes \Delta_g = \Gamma_f \otimes \Delta_g^{\{\emptyset\}}$. $\Gamma_{fRI}^{\Theta} \otimes^T \Delta_{gSJ}^{\Psi} = (\Gamma_f \otimes \Delta_g^{\Psi})|_{[(T \bowtie R) \bowtie (T \bowtie S)][I \cup J]}^{\Theta}$.

This definition relies on products of weights, which are characterized as follows. Given weights $w, v \in \mathbb{W}$, the *product* $w \times v$ is given by

$$w \times \langle\!\langle\rangle\!\rangle = w$$
$$\langle\!\langle\rangle\!\rangle \times v = v$$

in the case that either w or v is empty, and when $w = \langle\!\langle s_1, \ldots, s_m \rangle\!\rangle$ and $v = \langle\!\langle t_1, \ldots t_n \rangle\!\rangle$ with $m, n \geq 1$ we have

$$w \times v = \langle\!\langle (s_i \overline{\times} t_j) : 1 \leq i \leq m, 1 \leq j \leq n \rangle\!\rangle.$$

Example 78.

- $\langle\!\langle 2.s \rangle\!\rangle \times \langle\!\langle t, 3.u \rangle\!\rangle = \langle\!\langle 2.(s \overline{\times} t), 6.(s \overline{\times} u) \rangle\!\rangle$ (quasi-bilinearity).
- $\langle\!\langle x, 2.t \rangle\!\rangle \times \langle\!\langle \rangle\!\rangle = \langle\!\langle x, 2.t \rangle\!\rangle$ (failure of bilinearity, but $\langle\!\langle \rangle\!\rangle$ is a neutral element).
- $\langle\!\langle s \rangle\!\rangle \times \langle\!\langle t \rangle\!\rangle = \langle\!\langle (s \overline{\times} t) \rangle\!\rangle \neq \langle\!\langle (t \overline{\times} s) \rangle\!\rangle = \langle\!\langle t \rangle\!\rangle \times \langle\!\langle s \rangle\!\rangle$ (failure of commutativity)
- $(\langle\!\langle 3.x \rangle\!\rangle \times \langle\!\langle 4.y \rangle\!\rangle) \times \langle\!\langle 2.z \rangle\!\rangle = \langle\!\langle 12.(x \overline{\times} y) \rangle\!\rangle \times \langle\!\langle 2.z \rangle\!\rangle$
$$= \langle\!\langle 24.((x \overline{\times} y) \overline{\times} z) \rangle\!\rangle$$
$$\neq \langle\!\langle 24.(x \overline{\times} (y \overline{\times} z)) \rangle\!\rangle$$
$$= \langle\!\langle 3.x \rangle\!\rangle \times \langle\!\langle 8.(y \overline{\times} z) \rangle\!\rangle$$
$$= (\langle\!\langle 3.x \rangle\!\rangle \times (\langle\!\langle 4.y \rangle\!\rangle \times \langle\!\langle 2.z \rangle\!\rangle)$$

(failure of associativity).

We now turn to some examples of Product. For views that are based on multiple situations, the results are straighforward. For example, $\{2.p, 3.q\} \otimes \{4.r, 1.s\} = \{8.pr, 12.qr, 2.ps, 3.qs\}$. For cases in which one of the argument views has empty weights, we simply inherit the multipliers from the other argument. For example, $\{2.p, 3.q\} \otimes \{r, s\} = \{2.pr, 3.qr, 2.ps, 3.qs\}$. Finally, if there are only empty weights in either argument, the result is as it would be with our definition in Chapter 4. For example, $\{p, q\} \otimes \{r, s\} = \{pr, qr, ps, qs\}$.

We next revise Negation. For the purposes of this chapter, we will simplify things and not allow interpretations of "not" to take wide scope over "native" probability talk. What this means is that Loglish like "it is not the case that the probability of Q is 50%" can only be interpreted by means of a probability predicate rather than directly through the EAP functions we have defined. It will conveniently turn out that the only use of Neg applied to views with EAP functions will be in the context of Question. However, it will turn out that in those cases, the negated views will cancel out, so Neg will not have the occasion

210 REASONING WITH UNCERTAINTY

to do new things with EAP functions. This means that our previous definition of Neg stays almost the same for our purposes.

Definition 5.16 (Negation). $[\Gamma^\Theta_{fRI}]^N = (\Theta \otimes [\Gamma]^N)\big|^{\{0\}}_{[R]^N[I]^N}$ (N.B. f is not used on the RHS).

Finally, we will need to be able to eliminate primitively absurd states as before.

Definition 5.17 (Factor (contradictions)). For $\Delta^\Psi = \{\}^{\{0\}}$,

$$\Gamma^\Theta_{fRI}[\bot]^F = \{\gamma \in \Gamma : \neg \exists \kappa \in \mathbb{K}. \kappa \subseteq \gamma\}_f\Big|^\Theta_{RI}.$$

With the above ingredients, we are now in a position to define our updated version of Inquire.

Definition 5.18 (Inquire).

(O) If $A(\gamma \cup \Theta) \cap A(\Delta \cup \Psi) = \emptyset$ and $A(\Delta) \cap A(\Psi) = \emptyset$, then

$$\Gamma^\Theta_{fRI}[\Delta^\Psi_{gSJ}]^I = (\Gamma^\Theta_{fRI} \otimes (\Delta^\Psi_{gSJ} \oplus^S (\{0\}|^\Psi_{SJ} \otimes ([\Delta_g|^{\{0\}}_{SJ}]^N)^{\text{nov}(A(\Delta))})))[\bot]^F.$$

(I) If $A(\Delta \cup \Psi) \subseteq A(\Gamma \cup \Theta)$ and $S = [R]_{\Gamma \cup \Theta}$,

$$\Gamma^\Theta_{fRI}[\Delta^\Psi_{gSJ}]^I = (\Gamma^\Theta_{fI} \otimes^R (\Delta^\Psi_{gSJ} \oplus^R ([\Delta_g]^N|^\Psi_{SJ})))[\bot]^F.$$

Finally, we expand the Query operation to allow us to ask about the probability of something in light of a given view.

Definition 5.19 (Query). We define $\Gamma^\Theta_{fIR}[\Delta^\Psi_{gSJ}]^Q$ as follows, assuming $U_S \subseteq U_R$. Let

$$M'_{IJ} = \{\langle t, e \rangle \in M_{IJ} : e \in E_S \backslash E_R\}.$$

Then

$$\Gamma^\Theta_{fRI}[\Delta^\Psi_{gSJ}]^Q = H + \sum_{\gamma \in \Gamma} \sum_{\delta \in \Delta \text{ s.t. } \Phi(\gamma, \delta)} \{w_{\gamma, \delta} . \delta\}\Big|^\Theta_{R \bowtie \langle U_R, E_S \backslash E_R, D_{S'}\rangle, I \cup J}$$

where

$$H = \begin{cases} \{0\}^\Theta|_{RI} & \text{if } \exists \gamma \in \Gamma. \forall \delta \in \Delta. \neg \Phi(\gamma, \delta) \\ \{\}^\Theta|_{RI} & \text{otherwise,} \end{cases}$$

and where

$$w_{\gamma,\delta} = \begin{cases} g(\delta) & \text{if } g(\delta) \neq \langle\!\langle\rangle\!\rangle \\ f(\gamma) & \text{otherwise,} \end{cases}$$

and where $\Phi(\gamma, \delta)$ is by definition

$$\exists \psi \in \Psi \exists n \geq 0 \exists \langle t_1, e_1 \rangle, \ldots, \langle t_n, e_n \rangle \in M'_{IJ} (\forall i, j. e_i = e_j \rightarrow i = j) \wedge$$
$$(\psi \cup \delta[t_1/e_1, \ldots, t_n/e_n] \subseteq \gamma) \wedge (f(\gamma) = g(\delta)[t_1/e_1, \ldots] \vee g(\delta) = \langle\!\langle\rangle\!\rangle);$$

Finally, $D_{S'}$ is defined in the same way as in the definition of Query in chapter 4.

We will consider a brief example of query with weights. Suppose, we are given conditional probabilities of rain given clouds and the probability of clouds, represented by terms p_C, $p_{\overline{C}}$, $p_{R|C}$, $p_{\overline{R}|C}$, $p_{R|\overline{C}}$, $p_{\overline{R}|\overline{C}}$, which we intend to look up later, by updating with the sequence of views:

$$\{=(p_C, \tfrac{55}{100})\}, \{=(p_{\overline{C}}, \tfrac{45}{100})\}, \ldots$$

So:

$$\{(p_C \overline{\times} p_{R|C}).RC, (p_C \overline{\times} p_{\overline{R}|C}).\overline{R}C, (p_{\overline{C}} \overline{\times} p_{R|\overline{C}}).R\overline{C}, (p_{\overline{C}} \overline{\times} p_{\overline{R}|\overline{C}}).\overline{RC}\}[\{\langle\!\langle\rangle\!\rangle.R\}]^Q$$
$$= \{\langle\!\langle (p_C \overline{\times} p_{R|C}), (p_{\overline{C}} \overline{\times} p_{R|\overline{C}})\rangle\!\rangle.R, 0\}$$

Using the operations we have just defined, we will now define the default procedure for tasks that involve asking about the probability of some outcome. What this procedure does is attempt to find the "probability" of Δ based on EAPs encoded in our integrated premise view. If the premises do not provide an answer, we evenly assign what fraction of P_{max} (the maximum probability on our imputed scale) remains after taking into account alternatives states with determinate EAPs, to those alternatives in our integrated premise view that have an empty weight. It is likely that a better procedure can be devised that fits a broader set of empirical data. However, it will do for the cases we are considering. In the below, we let $\#\{x \in X : \Phi(x)\}$ stand for the number of elements of X that satisfy the condition Φ.

Definition 5.20 (Default procedure for "what is the probability of Δ?" tasks).
For $S = \langle P_1, \ldots, P_n \rangle$ a sequence of Views incrementally given as premises, all satisfying the novelty constraint of $\circlearrowright$ at their initial point of introduction,
(*Basic step*) Let $G' = \top[P_1]^{\circlearrowright}[\top]^D[P_2]^{\circlearrowright}\ldots[P_n]^{\circlearrowright}[\bot]^F$
(*Sub-procedure for "what is the probability of Δ^Ψ?" tasks (0 to 100)*)
(1) Let $G'' = G'[\Delta^\Psi]^Q$. If $G''[\Delta]^{\mathbb{EP}} \in [0, 100]$, report G''. Otherwise go to (2).
(2) Let

$$x = \frac{100 - \sum_{\gamma \in \Gamma} \sum \langle\!\langle \alpha \in f(\gamma) : \alpha \in \mathbb{R} \rangle\!\rangle}{\#\{\gamma \in \Gamma : f(\gamma) = \langle\!\langle \rangle\!\rangle\}}$$

and put $G'' = G'[\{\langle\!\langle x \rangle\!\rangle.0\}^{\{\gamma_1\}}]^I \ldots [\{\langle\!\langle x \rangle\!\rangle.0\}^{\{\gamma_n\}}]^I [\Delta^\Psi]^Q$ where $\gamma_1, \ldots, \gamma_n$ is an arbitrary ordering of $\{\gamma \in \Gamma : f(\gamma) = \langle\!\langle \rangle\!\rangle\}$. Then if $G''[\Delta]^{\mathbb{EP}} \in [0, 100]$, report G'', otherwise report $\emptyset$.

For now, we only know how to update with EAP-free premises, but this will suffice to begin to consider some data points. Let us consider sample derivations for the examples in the opening section that were drawn from Johnson-Laird et al. (1999), in which participants gave probability judgments based on purely propositional information. We will take it that "there is a box in which there is a yellow card, or a brown card, but not both" can be regimented as $\{By, Bb\} \otimes \{\bar{B}y, \bar{B}b\}[\bot]^F = \{By\bar{B}b, \bar{B}yBb\}$. We then get,

Example 79. [Example 71 derivation]

$$\{By\bar{B}b, \bar{B}yBb\}[\{\frac{100}{2}.0\}^{\{By\bar{B}b\}}]^I[\{\frac{100}{2}.0\}^{\{\bar{B}yBb\}}]^I[\{By\bar{B}b\}]^Q$$
$$= \{\frac{100}{2}.By\bar{B}b, \frac{100}{2}.\bar{B}yBb\}[\{By\bar{B}y\}]^Q$$
$$= \{\frac{100}{2}.By\bar{B}y, 0\}$$

Moving on to the next example, we take it that "there is a box in which there is at least a red marble, or else there is a green marble and there is a blue marble, but not all three marbles" can be regimented as $\{Br, Bg, Bb\} \otimes \{\bar{B}r, \bar{B}g, \bar{B}b\}[\bot]^F = \{BgBb\bar{B}r, Br\bar{B}g, Br\bar{B}b\}$. We then get,

Example 80. [Example 72 derivation]

$$\{BgBb\bar{B}r, Br\bar{B}g, Br\bar{B}b\}[\{\frac{100}{3}.0\}^{\{BgBb\bar{B}r\}}]^I [\{\frac{100}{3}.0\}^{\{Br\bar{B}g\}}]^I$$

$$[\{\frac{100}{3}.0\}^{\{Br\bar{B}b\}}]^I [\{BrBb\}]^Q$$

$$= \{\frac{100}{3}.BgBb\bar{B}r, \frac{100}{3}.Br\bar{B}g, \frac{100}{3}.Br\bar{B}b\}[\{BrBb\}]^Q$$

$$= \{\frac{100}{3}.BrBb, 0\}$$

We can also consider responses for additional questions from the same study by Johnson-Laird et al. (1999) that used the same main premise as in example 71.

Example 81.
There is a box in which there is a yellow card, or a brown card, but not both.

Given the preceding assertion, according to you, what is the probability of the following situation?

(At least A) In the box there is at least a yellow card (mean response = 45%).

(A and B) In the box there is a yellow card and a brown card (mean response 6%).

(Neither A nor B) In the box there is neither a yellow card nor a brown card (mean response 16%).

Our default procedure fits this data well, yielding 50 for (At least A), 0 for (A and B), and 0 for (Neither A nor B). The default procedure also works fairly well for problems from the same Johnson-Laird et al. (1999) study involving a conditional premise.

Example 82.
There is a box in which if there is a yellow card then there is a brown card.

Given the preceding assertion, according to you, what is the probability of the following situation?

> (At least A) In the box there is at least a yellow card (mean response 58%).
> (A and B) In the box there is a yellow card and a brown card (mean response 68%).
> (A and not B) In the box there is a yellow card and there is not a brown card (mean response 0%).
> (Neither A nor B) In the box there is neither a yellow card nor a brown card (mean response 38%).

In this case, we have a conditional premise $\{ByBb\}^{\{By\}}$. Applying our default reasoning procedure (recall that the default procedure applies Depose to the first premise), we get 50 for (At least A), 50 for (A and B), 0 for (A and not B). For (Neither A nor B), the default procedure would return 0. If a reasoner were to depart from the default procedure and Inquire on $\{\bar{B}b\}$ to obtain a new G', before applying the step that introduces EAPs, we would get 33.

We will now consider further cases from Johnson-Laird et al. (1999) that yielded biased estimates.

> **Example 83.** (Further illusory probability inferences)
> There is a box in which there is at least a red marble, or else there is a green marble and there is a blue marble, but not all three marbles.
> *What is the probability of the following situation:*
> There is a red marble and a blue marble in the box? (18 of 25 participants were within +5% of the answer 0)
> There is a green marble and there is a blue marble (17 of 25 within +-5% of 50% answer).

If we assumed an unbiased inference that takes all possibilities compatible with the statement to be equally likely, then there is a 25% probability of having a red marble and a blue marble. Taking the first premise to be regimented as $\{Br, BgBb\} \otimes \{\bar{B}r, \bar{B}g, \bar{B}b\}[\bot]^F = \{BgBb\bar{B}r, Br\bar{B}g, Br\bar{B}b\}$, the default procedures gives us the result 0, which fits the observed response pattern better than the unbiased estimate. For the second question, the unbiased estimate would again be 25. The default procedure gives us $\frac{100}{3}$, which is higher than the unbiased estimate but still lower than the observed responses. A reasoner could potentially get 50 by ignoring the but clause in interpreting the premise.

CONDITIONALS AND UNCERTAINTY 215

Johnson-Laird et al. (1999) found that problems of the following kind elicited significantly more unbiased responses than the previous kind.

> **Example 84.**
>
> There is a box in which there is a grey marble and either a white marble or else a mauve marble, but not all three marbles are in the box.
>
> Given the preceding assertion, what is the probability of the following situation?
>
> In the box there is a grey marble and there is a mauve marble (14 of their 25 participants were within 5% of the unbiased response 50%).
>
> There is a box in which there is a grey marble, or else a white marble, or else a mauve marble, but no more than one marble.
>
> Given the preceding assertion, what is the probability of the following situation?
>
> In the box there is a grey marble and there is a mauve marble (24 out of 25 were within 5% of 0).

For the first problem, we will take the premise to regiment as $\{BgBw, BgBm\}$ $\otimes \{\bar{B}g, \bar{B}w, \bar{B}w\}[\bot]^F = \{BgBw\bar{B}m, BgBm\bar{B}w\}$. Applying the default procedure, we get 50. For the second problem, taking the premise as $\{Bg, Bw, Bm\} \otimes \{\bar{B}g\bar{B}w, \bar{B}g\bar{B}m, \bar{B}m\bar{B}w\}[\bot]^F = \{Bg\bar{B}w\bar{B}m, Bw\bar{B}m\bar{B}g, Bm\bar{B}w\bar{B}g\}$, the default procedure yields 0.

In sum, with our newly gained expressive power, our updated default reasoning procedure fits data on probabilistic conclusions from propositional premises well, both in cases in which those conclusions are "biased" or fallacious, and when they are "unbiased" or correct.

5.4 Conditionals and Uncertainty

We want to be able to interpret statements like, "If H, then there is a 90% probability that the Data obtains" and "If H is false, then there is a 1% probability that the data obtains," etc. We already have an analysis of "if... then" statements from Chapter 3. Setting aside the discussion of what it takes for $[\![A]\!]$ to be an acceptable supposition (which will not be relevant to this section), we have $[\![if\,A,C]\!] = T[[\![A]\!]]^S \otimes ([\![C]\!][T]^D)$. We now need an analysis of "there is a...probability that H."

There is important relatively recent work in linguistic semantics on modals and probability talk that a fully systematic account of the interpretation of probability talk would have to take into account (notably, Kratzer (2012); Kratzer (1991), Lassiter (2011); Holliday et al. (2013)). We will have to set these connections aside for future work and press ahead for the simplest avenue to interpretation rule sketches that can help us with the inference patterns we are concerned with. For the purposes of this chapter, we shall not allow probability talk within the scope of probability talk. In addition, for now, we avoid discussion of probability talk about something other than single states (so we will not cover statements like "the probability that *A or B* will happen is 90%"). We will then use the following interpretation rule.

Definition 5.21 (Interpretation rule for probability of a state).
For $[\![H]\!] = \{\langle\rangle.\gamma\}_{RI}^{\{0\}}$, let
$[\![$ There is an x% probability that H $]\!] = \{x.\gamma\}_{RI}^{\{y\}}$

For example, for $[\![$ the coin comes up heads $]\!] = \{Hc\}$, we have $[\![$ There is a 50% probability that the coin comes up heads $]\!] = \{50.Hc\}^{\{Hc\}}$.

Johnson-Laird et al. (1999) suggest that the following should be an easy inference problem. Intuitively, the answer 0.2 is quite obvious.

Example 85. (Easy partial probability inference)
There is a box in which there is one and only one of these marbles: a green marble, a blue marble, or a red marble. The probability that a green marble is in the box is .6, and the probability that a blue marble is in the box is .2. What is the probability that a red marble is in the box?

Our default reasoning procedure proceeds as follows. First we, go through the basic steps.

$\{Bg, Bb, Br\}[\{(0.6).Bg\}^{\{Bg\}}]^{\circlearrowleft}[\{(0.2).Bb\}^{\{Bg\}}]^{\circlearrowleft} = \{(0.6).Bg, (0.2).Bb, Br\}$.

We then apply the part of procedure specific to probability questions, yielding,

$\{(0.6).Bg, (0.2).Bb, Br\}[\{(1-(0.6+0.2)).0\}^{\{Br\}}]^I[\{x.Br\}]^W =$
$\{(0.6).Bg, (0.2).Bb, (0.2).Br\}[\{x.Br\}]^W = \{0.2.Br, 0\}.$

While the foregoing seems easy, the problem below seems to mislead default intuition. It is intuitively tempting to conclude that the answer is 0.2 just like in the previous problem, even though a moment's reflection suggests that that is unlikely to be correct.

> **Example 86.** (Illusory partial probability inference)
> You have a hand of several cards with only limited information about it.
>
> There is an ace and a queen or a king and a jack or a ten.
> The probability that there is an ace and a queen is 0.6
> The probability that there is a king and a jack is 0.2
>
> What is the probability that there is a ten?

Our default reasoning procedure proceeds as follows. First we, go through the basic steps.

$\{AQ, KJ, X\}[\{(0.6).AQ\}^{\{AQ\}}]^\circ[\{(0.2).KJ\}^{\{KJ\}}]^\circ = \{(0.6).AQ, (0.2).KJ, X\}.$

We then apply the part of procedure specific to probability questions, yielding,

$\{(0.6).AQ, (0.2).KJ, X\}[\{(1-(0.6+0.2)).0\}^{\{X\}}]^I[\{x.X\}]^W =$
$\{(0.6).AQ, (0.2).KJ, (0.2).X\}[\{x.X\}]^W = \{0.2.X, 0\}.$

These results suggest that our definitions so far are on a reasonable track for our purposes. In order to make these definitions fully operational, we need to update our definition of Suppose, which in turn requires updating its constituent operations. Before turning to that, we will look at how those definitions will give us an interpretation of conditional probability statements.

> **Example 87.** Where defined,
> $[\![\textit{If H then there is an x probability that D}]\!] = \mathsf{T}[\![\![H]\!]]^S \otimes$
> $([\![\textit{there is an x probability that D}]\!][\mathsf{T}]^D)$

> ⟦*If H, then there is a 90% probability that D*⟧ = $\{90.DH, H\bar{D}\}^{\{H\}}$
> ⟦*If H is false, then there is a 1% probability that D*⟧ = $\{1.\bar{H}D, \bar{H}\bar{D}\}^{\{H\}}$
> ⟦ *If H, then there is a 90% probability that the Data obtains and a 10% that the Data does not obtain*⟧
> = $T[\{H\}]^S \otimes (\{90.D\}^{\{D\}}[T]^D \otimes \{10.\bar{D}\}^{\{\bar{D}\}}) =$
> = $\{90.HD, 10.H\bar{D}\}^{\{H\}}$

We can now consider the evidence fallacy of estimating the probability of guilt of someone with a DNA match to be high, solely based on the information that if the suspect is not guilty, then the probability of such a DNA match is 1 in a million.

(**Example 69 derivation**)
The basic step in the default procedure gives us:
$\{Ms\}[\{10^{-6}.\bar{G}sMs, \bar{G}s\bar{M}s\}^{\{Gs\}}[]^D]^{\circlearrowleft}[\bot]^F = \{10^{-6}.\bar{G}sMs, GsMs\}$.
We then apply the sub-procedure for probability questions, yielding
$\{10^{-6}.\bar{G}sMs, GsMs\}[\{(10^6 - 10^{-6}).0\}^{\{GsMs\}}]^I[\{x.Gs\}]^W =$
$\{10^{-6}.\bar{G}sMs, (10^6 - 10^{-6}).GsMs\}[\{x.Gs\}]^W = \{(999\,999.999\,999).Gs, 0\}$.

In words, even though we only have a conditional probability, the default reasoning procedure provides the spurious conclusion that the probability of the person being guilty gets assigned very high weight, which could explain why the probability of guilt is taken to be very high.

We will ultimately want to show that under the right conditions, we can construct a probability measure out of EAP functions. If our analysis of conditional probability statements is going to work, we will want to make sure that views resulting from conditional probability statements can be regarded as encoding the right probabilities via their EAP functions.

Recall from the definition of conditional probability that $P(A|B) = \frac{P(A \cap B)}{P(B)}$. It would be nice if it turned out that treating $\mathbb{EP}$ as a quasi-probability measure, a view corresponding to a conditional probability statement "If H, then there is a 0.9 probability that D and a 0.1 probability that not-D" would encode that the ratio $\frac{P(H \cap D)}{P(H)}$ equals 0.9. We in fact get this.

$$\frac{\{(0.9).DH, (0.1).D\bar{H}\}^{\{H\}}[T]^D[\{DH\}]^{\mathbb{EP}}}{\{(0.9).DH, (0.1).D\bar{H}\}^{\{H\}}[T]^D[\{H\}]^{\mathbb{EP}}} = \frac{0.9}{0.9 + 0.1} = 0.9.$$

In addition, for a wide range of cases, our default reasoning procedure will have the consequence that we will get the same result for "what's the probability of if P then Q?" and "Suppose P, what's the probability of Q?" Thus, it would appear that the erotetic theory can make sense of the tight connection between judgments of the probability of "if...then" statements, and conditional probability that has often been observed empirically (Oberauer and Wilhelm (2003); Over et al. (2007)), and that is part of the motivation of Bayesian approaches to reasoning with conditionals (Oaksford and Chater (2007)).

This result should give us an inkling that this way of treating conditional probability statements might not conclusively prevent us from modeling forms of reasoning with uncertainty that respect Bayes's Rule. Details will be left for a later sections once we properly consider success in reasoning with uncertainty in detail.

Returning to the problem of making sense of reasoning failures, note that taking $\mathbb{E}P$ as a pseudo-probability measure, we also get that a conditional probability statement alone gives us a view from which we can get a determinate (pseudo-)probability for *D and H*. Of course, a mere conditional probability statement does not encode a particular probability for this conjunction. Such discrepancies between what we can get from a view and what is normatively warranted are welcome, since we want to generate empirically observed judgments about probability that are not warranted.

We now turn to updating our definitions of the operations we just appealed to. Suppose stays essentially the same, though we will only allow "propositional" suppositions, not involving substantive EAPs (i.e. we are restricted to $\langle\!\langle\rangle\!\rangle$).

Definition 5.22 (Suppose).

(O) If $A(\Gamma \cup \Theta) \cap A(\Delta \cup \Psi) = \emptyset$ and $\Delta^\Psi_{gSJ} = \Delta^\Psi_{SJ}$, then

$$\Gamma^\Theta_{fRI}[\Delta^\Psi_{gSJ}]^S = \Gamma^{\Theta'}_{[R\bowtie R'][I \cup I']}[\Delta^\Psi_{gSJ}]^U[\Delta^\Psi_{gSJ}]^E[\Delta^\Psi_{gSJ}]^A[\Delta^\Psi_{gSJ}]^M,$$

where

$$\Theta'^{\{0\}}_{f'R'I'} = \Theta^{\{0\}}_{fRI} \otimes \text{Nov}(\Delta^\Psi_{g[S]NJ}[\ ]^D),$$

where Nov() uniformly replaces all arbitrary objects in its scope by novel ones.

(I) If $A(\Delta) \subseteq A(\Gamma \cup \Theta)$, $[R]_\Delta = S$, and $\Delta^\Psi_{gSJ} = \Delta^\Psi_{SJ}$, then

$$\Gamma^{\Theta}_{fRI}[\Delta^{\{0\}}_{gSJ}]^S = \Gamma^{\Theta\otimes\Delta}_{fRI}[\Delta^{\{0\}}_{gSJ}]^U[\Delta^{\{0\}}_{gSJ}]^E[\Delta^{\{0\}}_{gSJ}]^A[\Delta^{\{0\}}_{gSJ}]^M.$$

Depose similarly stays virtually the same.

Definition 5.23 (Depose).

$$\Gamma^{\Theta}_{fRI}[\top]^D = (\Gamma_f + [\Theta]^N)\Big|^{\{0\}}_{R[I]^N}$$

With suppose in place we will turn to ward invited inferences to conditional probabilities. For example, we easily get from the premise that 94% of CEOs grew up with pets to the conclusion that the conditional probability of being a CEO given that you grow up with pets is 94%.

(Example 67 derivation)
$\{94.CP, \bar{C}\}[\{P\}]^S[\{x.C\}]^W = \{94.C, 0\}$

We will next turn to Merge. To update our definition or Merge, we need to bring up to date our notion of Product over multiple arguments, as in Chapter 4.

Definition 5.24 (Multiproduct). For a finite set $G = \{\Gamma^{\{0\}}_{i f_i, R_i, I_i} : i \in I\}$, we define $\bigotimes G$ by

$$\bigotimes^T \emptyset = \{0\}\Big|^{\{0\}}_{0_{\mathcal{R}}, \emptyset}$$

for $|I| = 0$, and

$$\bigotimes^T \{\Gamma^{\{0\}}_{fRI}\} = \Gamma_f\Big|^{\{0\}}_{\top\bowtie R, I}$$

for $|I| = 1$, and

$$\bigotimes^T \{\Gamma^{\{0\}}_{i f_i, R_i, I_i} : i \in I\} = \left(\bigotimes^T_{i \in I} \Gamma^{\{0\}}_{i R_i I_i}\right)$$

for $|I| \geq 2$.

We also need to update our notion of substitution. As in Chapter 4, we stick with a relatively informal definition.

Definition 5.25 (Substitution (informal) (no change)). For $A(\Gamma) \cap A(\Theta) = \emptyset$,

$$\mathrm{Sub}^T_{\langle t,a \rangle}(\Gamma^\Theta_{fRI}) = \Gamma'^\Theta_{f'T'I'},$$

where

- (Γ') Recall that arbitrary objects in a View can be grouped into "Matryoshka"-levels, as in Figure 4. Then, Γ' is $\Gamma[t/a]$ where additionally all arbitrary objects at the same or lower Matryoshka-level (in T) as a replaced by novel ones that have not yet appeared in the computation of the conclusion of the step.
- (f') f' is a copy of f in which all the same novelization replacements as in Γ' have occurred and in which all occurrences of a are replaced by t.
- (T') T' is T chained (using the $\bowtie$ operation) with a copy of T in which the same novelization replacements as in Γ' have occurred, and that is restricted to only the novelized arbitrary objects.
- (I') I' is a copy of I in which all the all the same novelization replacements as in Γ' have occurred and in which all occurrences of a are replaced by t.

Our updated definition of Merge is then as follows.

Definition 5.26 (Merge). For either $A(R) \cap A(S) = \emptyset$ or $[R]_{\Delta \cup \Psi} = S$, and with $M'_{IJ}(\gamma) = \{\langle t, u \rangle \in M_{IJ} : u \in U_S \wedge \exists \psi \in \Psi(\psi[t/u] \subseteq \gamma \wedge \psi \not\subseteq \gamma)\}$,

$$\Gamma^\Theta_{fRI}[\Delta^\Psi_{gSJ}]^M = \bigoplus_{\gamma \in \Gamma}^{R \bowtie S} \{f(\gamma).\gamma\}|^\Theta_{RI} \otimes^{R \bowtie S} \Delta^\Psi_{gSJ} \otimes^{R \bowtie S} \bigotimes_{\langle t,u \rangle \in M'_{IJ}(\gamma)}^{R \bowtie S} \mathrm{Sub}^{R \bowtie S}_{\langle t,u \rangle}(\Delta^{\{0\}}_{gSJ}).$$

We already defined Answer, so with Merge in place, we also get Update for all cases that do not involve Universal Product or Existential Sum, which we will turn to later.

As Johnson-Laird et al. (1999) point out, we can make inferences similar to the base-rate neglect inferences with non-probabilistic statements. In the case from Johnson-Laird, straightforward updating suffices to get a "disease" conclusion.

(Example 70 derivation)
$\{D,B\}[\{DS\}^{\{D\}}]^\circ[\{S\}]^\circ = \{D\}$

We now want to turn to the "psylicrapitis" base-rate neglect case. However, this will require us to first say something about how to interpret statements like "if someone Φs the probability is 90% that they Ψ." We will also need to update our definition of universal product.

5.5 Universal Product

Even though "someone" is indefinite, what is conveyed by "if someone Φs the probability is 90% that they Ψ" is clearly universal rather than existential. We can set aside for now in virtue of what such statements would be true. Plausible examples would come from taking Φ to be the property of being randomly drawn with replacement from a certain population of people, 90% of whose members have the property Ψ. We will similarly stipulate that a statement like "the probability that one of the Φs Ψs is 90%" is interpreted akin to a universally quantified statement with the universal quantifier taking wide scope over the probability assignment.

Definition 5.27 (Interpretation rules: Universal conditional probability).
⟦If someone Ps the probability is 90% that they Q⟧ = $\{90.PxQx, Px\bar{Q}x\}^{\{Px\}}$
⟦The probability that one of the Ps Qs is 3%⟧ =
⟦For all x, if Px, then the probability that Qx is 3%⟧ =
$\{3.PxQx, Px\bar{Q}x\}^{\{Px\}}$

In addition, we will need to take a view on how reasoners deal with statements like "1% of the population has the disease." In order to be able to make inferences about individual cases from such statements, we need a view on how reasoners take it that such statements relate to the probabilities of individual cases. If we want a view that most directly plugs into our reasoning machinery, we might immediately recast such statements as "For all x, if x is part of the population, then there is a 1% chance that x has the disease," which would correspond to $\{1.PxDx, Px\bar{D}x\}^{\{Px\}}$. This is not a trivial assumption, since it basically requires attributing at least a tacit statistical theory to our reasoners. It is fairly clear that our native reasoning apparatus does not have such a theory hard-wired into it. This is witnessed by the fact that, for example, when frequency data became available in the history of medicine, doctors often tended to dismiss such data as *irrelevant* for the purposes of making decisions about individual patients (Gigerenzer (2002), p. 88). From a logical perspective, such data of course *is* irrelevant without further assumptions about how a given individual in the doctor's office is supposed to relate to the data set. This observation alone could in principle account for the fact that the "base-rate" information is not taken into account by reasoners in the "psylicrapitis" case (example 64). We already know from other examples that make the base-rate information more directly relevant that this approach will not fit all versions of base-rate neglect. However, it will still be useful to proceed with a sample derivation in which we treat the statement "roughly, 1% of the population has the disease" as completely orthogonal, so that it makes no substantive difference to the derivation.

The final step of the calculation will require Universal Product, so we will update that definition now.

Definition 5.28 (Universal product). For $A(\Gamma) \cap A(\Theta) = \emptyset$; $M'_{IJ} = \{\langle u, t \rangle : \langle u, t \rangle \in M_{IJ} \wedge u \in U_R - A(\Theta)\} \neq \emptyset$; and $A(R) \cap A(S) = \emptyset \vee [R]_\Delta = S$, we have

$$\Gamma^\Theta_{fRI}[\Delta^{\{0\}}_{gSJ}]^U = \{0\}|^\Theta_{R,I} \otimes^{R \bowtie S} \bigotimes_{\langle t,u \rangle \in M'_{IJ}}^{R \bowtie S} \mathrm{Sub}^{R \bowtie S}_{\langle t,u \rangle}(\Gamma_f|^{\{0\}}_{RI}).$$

With this approach, the "psylicrapitis" base-rate neglect example proceeds as follows.

(Example 64 derivation)
Derivation where we take population info at face value without adding connective "tissue."

$\{90.SxTx, Sx\bar{T}x\}^{\{Sx\}}[\top]^D[\{1.\bar{S}xTx, \bar{S}x\bar{T}x\}^{\{\bar{S}x\}}]^\circlearrowleft[\{Ts\}]^\circlearrowleft[\bot]^F[\{x.Ss\}]^W$
$= \{90.SxTx, Sx\bar{T}x, 1.\bar{S}xTx, \bar{S}x\bar{T}x\}[\{1.PxSx, Px\bar{S}x\}^{\{Px\}}]^\circlearrowleft[\{Ts\}]^\circlearrowleft[\bot]^F[\{x.Ss\}]^W =$
$\{90.SsTs, 1.\bar{S}sTs\}[\{x.Ss\}]^W = \{90.Ss, 0\}$

Derivation where we take everything to be conditional on membership in the mentioned population.

$\{90.PxSxTx, PxSx\bar{T}x\}^{\{PxSx\}}[\top]^D[\{1.Px\bar{S}xTx, Px\bar{S}x\bar{T}x\}^{\{Px\bar{S}x\}}]^\circlearrowleft$
$[\{1.PxSx, Px\bar{S}x\}^{\{Px\}}]^\circlearrowleft[\{PsTs\}]^\circlearrowleft[\bot]^F[\{x.Ss\}]^W =$
$\{90.PxSxTx, PxSx\bar{T}x, \bar{P}x, \bar{S}x\}[\{1.PxSx, Px\bar{S}x\}^{\{Px\}}]^\circlearrowleft[\{PsTs\}]^\circlearrowleft[\bot]^F[\{x.Ss\}]^W =$
$= \{90.PxSxTx, 90.PxSxTx\bar{S}x, 1.PxSx\bar{T}x, PxSx\bar{T}x\bar{S}x, \bar{P}x, \bar{S}x\}[\{PsTs\}]^\circlearrowleft[\bot]^F[\{x.Ss\}]^W =$
$\{90.PsSsTs, 90.PsSsTs\bar{S}s\}[\bot]^F[\{x.Ss\}]^W = \{90.PsSsTs\}[\{x.Ss\}]^W = \{90.Ss, 0\}$

Derivation where we take everything to be conditional on membership in the mentioned population, but we depose both conditional probability statements to avoid second premise being ignored.

$\{90.PxSxTx, PxSx\bar{T}x, \bar{P}x, \bar{S}x\}[\{1.Px\bar{S}xTx, Px\bar{S}x\bar{T}x, \bar{P}x, Sx\}]^{\circ}$
$[\{1.PxSx, Px\bar{S}x\}^{\{Px\}}]^{\circ}[\{PsTs\}]^{\circ}[\bot]^{F}[\{x.Ss\}]^{W} =$
$\{90.PxSxTx, PxSx\bar{T}x, \bar{S}x\}[\{1.Px\bar{S}xTx, Px\bar{S}x\bar{T}x, \bar{P}x, Sx\}]^{AA,M}[\{1.PxSx, Px\bar{S}x\}^{\{Px\}}]^{\circ}$
$[\{PsTs\}]^{\circ}[\bot]^{F}[\{x.Ss\}]^{W} = \{90.PxSxTx, PxSx\bar{T}x\}[\{1.PxSx, Px\bar{S}x\}^{\{Px\}}]^{\circ}[\{PsTs\}]^{\circ}$
$[\bot]^{F}[\{x.Ss\}]^{W} = \{90.PsSsTs\}[\{x.Ss\}]^{W} = \{90.Ss, 0\}$

(Example 65 derivation)
The probability that one of these people has colorectal cancer is 0.3%.

$\{(0.3).PxCx, Px\bar{C}x\}^{\{Px\}}[T]^{D}[\{50.PxCxTx, PxCx\bar{T}x\}^{\{PxCx\}}]^{\circ}$
$[\{3.Px\bar{C}xTx, Px\bar{C}x\bar{T}x\}^{\{Px\bar{C}x\}}]^{\circ}[\{PaTa\}]^{\circ}[\{x.Ca\}]^{W} =$
$= \{(0.3 \bar{\times} 50).PxCxTx, (0.3).PxCx\bar{T}x, Px\bar{C}x, \bar{P}x\}$
$[\{3.Px\bar{C}xTx, Px\bar{C}x\bar{T}x\}^{\{Px\bar{C}x\}}]^{\circ}[\{PaTa\}]^{\circ}[\{x.Ca\}]^{W} =$
$\{(0.3 \bar{\times} 50).PxCxTx, (0.3).PxCx\bar{T}x, 3.Px\bar{C}xTx, Px\bar{C}x\bar{T}x, \bar{P}x\}[\{PaTa\}]^{\circ}$
$[\{x.Ca\}]^{W} = \{(0.3 \bar{\times} 50).PaCaTa, 3.Pa\bar{C}aTa\}[\{x.Ca\}]^{W} = \{0.3 \bar{\times} 50.Ca, 0\}$

The result here, 15%, is still much higher than the correct estimate (approx. 4.7%). However, the most popular answer was 50%.

Hoffrage and Gigerenzer (2004) provide a very interesting observation about the doctors who participated in their study.

> Six physicians explicitly remarked on their inability to deal with numbers, stating, for instance, "But this is mathematics. I can't do that. I'm too stupid for this." ... Finally, a university professor–an ears, nose, and throat specialist–seemed agitated and affronted by the test and refused to give numerical estimates. "This is not the way to treat patients. I throw all these journals [with statistical information] away immediately. One can't make a diagnosis on such a basis. Statistical information is one big lie."
>
> (Hoffrage and Gigerenzer (2004))

Of course, if we want to use the premises provided in a way that directly provides an answer to the question without requiring multiplication, we can simply proceed as in the evidence fallacy cases considered earlier. We can take the premise that is most directly relevant to the information that is specific to the individual we are being asked about (i.e. discussion about probabilities related to a positive test), and use that for an answer, which yields $\{50.PxCxTx, PxCx\bar{T}x\}^{\{PxCx\}}[T]^D[\{PaTa\}]^\circ[\{x.Ca\}]^W = \{50.Ca, 0\}$

As mentioned at the beginning of the section, Gigerenzer and Hoffrage found that certain ways of presenting these kinds of problems in terms of frequencies dramatically improved the success of participants. In order to give a fully systematic treatment of premises of this kind, we would need numerical quantifiers. For now, we do not want to concern ourselves with this added bit of expressive power. We can nonetheless hint at how our approach can make sense of their results. We will imagine the following paraphrase. Instead of "Think of 100 people. One has the disease psylicrapitis, and he is likely to test positive. Of those 99 who do not have the disease, 1 will also test positive." We will take it that we have "either we are in one of 98 situations of no disease, in one situation of disease and positive test, or in one situation of no disease but positive test." We then take "How many of those who test positive do have the disease? out of?" as asking about the equilibrium answer potential of *disease and positive test* out of the equilibrium answer potential of *positive test*.

(**Example 66 derivation**)
$\{1.DT, 1\bar{D}T, 98\bar{D}\}[\{DP\}]^E P = 1$
$\{1.DT, 1\bar{D}T, 98\bar{D}\}[\{P\}]^E P = 2$, so 1 out of 2, which is the correct answer for this problem.

In sum, for a frequentist presentation of this kind of inference problem there are plausible regimentations on which the default reasoning procedure is tractable and suffices to produce the correct answer.

5.6 Conjunction Fallacy and Memory Search

The main data points we want to make sense of in this section are the conjunction fallacy inferences discussed in the beginning of this chapter. The core reasoning pattern behind the fallacy will be essentially the same as that behind illusory inferences from disjunction discussed through out previous chapters. Besides the probabilistic setting of the problem, the main difference from the sorts of reasoning problems we have discussed so far is that the conjunction fallacy involves inferences that are recruiting background knowledge on the part of the reasoner. Part of what is required is memory search for relevant information, and we have to postulate that participants have appropriate contents in their memory, where previously everything directly needed was supplied in the form of premises.

Our starting point will be a closer look at the following inference in example 76 from Sablé-Meyer and Mascarenhas (2020). More than half of their participants answered "yes" to the following.

(P1) The gun fired and the guitar was out of tune, or else someone was in the attic.

(P2) The trigger (of the gun) was pulled. *Does it follow that the guitar was out of tune?*

For simplicity we will model these premises as follows, with G for 'gun', F for 'fired', U for 'guitar', E for 'out-of-tune', A for 'was in the attic', and Tx for 'the trigger of x was pulled'. Moreover, we will assume that it is understood that the trigger is the trigger of the gun. We then have,

$$\{FiGiUjEj, Aa\}$$
$$\{Ti\}$$

As it stands, the default procedure would not yield the observed conclusion, because there is no overlap at all between the first and the second premise. We need to take a view on how background knowledge is recruited in the inference process to allow reasoners to treat (P2) as an answer to (P1). We will provisionally proceed with the following hypothesis. Roughly, if a view we are about to update with does not have any atoms in common with our current view, we consult background knowledge to try to create a link been the two views.

To make this rough idea workable, there are several issues to consider. Our atoms include predicates, terms, and arbitrary objects, so we cannot usefully take atomic overlap between premises to be an indication of whether premises would be likely to interact to generate new conclusions in default reasoning. We would be missing the relevance of too many views, particularly those involving generalizations. At the same time, since inferences like that in example 76 feel quite immediate, it would not be plausible to require complex background reasoning to determine whether we should attempt to recruit further information from memory. Moreover, our search criteria cannot be so broad as to guarantee combinatorial explosion.

One way to get an estimate of whether premises are likely to interact without further additions is to see whether there is atomic overlap after abstracting away all argument terms. Concretely, this means comparing the sets of predicates $P \in \mathbf{P}$ that occur for overlap between two views. We wish to avoid postulating additional special purpose methods in the erotetic system, thus we formulate linkage potential in terms of *free atoms*. We can formulate this in a way that uses the atomic answer potential operation.

Definition 5.29 (Pipe to free atoms).
Let $\mathcal{A}_? = \{P^k(?, \ldots, ?) : P^k \in \mathbf{P}\}$. For an atom $A = P^k(t_1, \ldots, t_k) \in \mathcal{A}$, let $A|_? = P^k(?, \ldots, ?) \in \mathcal{A}_?$. Extend to states by $\gamma|_? = \{A|_? : A \in \gamma\}$ and to sets of states by $\Gamma|_? = \{\gamma|_? : \gamma \in \Gamma\}$.

The set $\mathcal{A}_?$ of free atoms is closely connected with the set $\mathbf{A}_1$ of open atoms defined before: the differences are that (i) members of the former are not restricted to precisely one occurrence of ?; and (ii) members of the latter can contain terms $t \in \mathbf{T}$ as well as open terms $t' \in \mathbf{T}$ different to "?". As an aside, there is a natural common generalization of these two notions which we might have called *open atoms*, calling $\mathcal{A}_1$ the set of *unitary open atoms*, but we do not need this additional flexibility. We emphasize that the free atoms $\mathcal{A}_?$ are just ordinary atoms of a system where ? is an additional constant symbol, hence all the operations of our theory make sense for views with states containing free atoms.

If we are looking for relevant background information based on free atoms, we are blind to agent-patient relations. For example, the views we might articulate as "cows drink water and produce milk," and "cows drink milk and produce water" will have the same free atoms, which we might awkwardly articulate as "something is a cow, something drinks, something is milk, something produces something, and something is water." There are at least some reasons to think that rapid human memory search has a component that abstracts away from what is predicated of what. A theoretical reason is that we could otherwise not detect the relevance of generalizations in memory without first attempting an instantiation of the relevant arbitrary objects and looking for logically constrained matches. However, this seems like it might slow down the search process too much. A more empirical reason to think that background memory search works in terms of something like free atoms comes from the kinds of recall errors people are likely to commit. For example, it is by now part of psychological lore that people are sometimes tempted to say "milk" when asked to respond to the following without allowing

228 REASONING WITH UNCERTAINTY

any pause between question and answer: "what do cows drink?." We could diagnose such cognitive illusions as a kind of illusory conjunction in memory search, made possible by the fact that background memory search proceeds via bundles of free atoms without the constraint of respecting particular binding relations, similar to the way visual illusory conjunctions have sometimes been hypothesized to be due to features in the visual array being unbound before further attentive processing (Treisman and Schmidt (1982)).

Besides deciding when to recruit background information, we have to consider that we can build linkages between premises in two directions: We can include information in the first premise to make it more likely to interact with the second premise, or we can include information in the second premise to make it more likely to interact with the first. We could also do both at the same time.

What would relevant background knowledge look like? We have already discussed generic views in Chapter 4 and matchbox conditionals in Chapter 3. We might then hypothesize that our background information that might be recruited for the problem in example 76 is along the following lines:

(1) Guns whose triggers are pulled fire. $\{GxTxFx, 0\}^{\{GxTx\}}$
(2) Fired guns have had their triggers pulled. $\{GxFxTx, 0\}^{\{GxFx\}}$

Item (1) would allow us to make a connection between the premises going upward from premise 2 to premise 1. Item (2) would allow us to make a connection from premise 1 to premise 2.

Both (1) and (2) are plausible candidates for inclusion in a normal reasoners' set of background commitments. However, so are many other things like "if a gun fires, someone might get hurt," "if a gun fires, there is danger," "if a gun fires, there is a noise," and so on. We cannot possibly include all of those things. Luckily, we are only interested in those aspects of our background commitments that create a linkage between two views.

One plausible way of defining views with the potential to serves as a link between two other views G and D is as follows. We take those views whose supposition has answer potential with respect to the main set of alternatives of G and whose main set of alternatives has answer potential with respect to the main set of alternatives of D. We regiment this as follows.

Definition 5.30 (Linkage potential views).
$$L(C, \Gamma^{\Theta}_{fRI}, \Delta^{\Psi}_{gSJ}) = \{\Phi^{\chi}_{hSK} \in C : \chi|_?[\Gamma|_?]^{AP} \times \Phi|_?[\Delta|_?]^{AP} \neq 0\}.$$

A tentative procedure would then be that if we reach a $G[D]^{\circlearrowleft}$ step, but G and D do not have overlap in terms of their open atoms (thereby guaranteeing that D will not have a chance to interestingly interact with G, let alone serve as an answer), we first update G with linkage commitments $L(C,G,D)$ to obtain G', and update D with linkage commitments, "in the other direction," $L(C,D,G)$ to obtain D' before obtaining $G'[D']^{\circlearrowleft}$ instead of $G[D]^{\circlearrowleft}$.

For example 76 the inference would then proceed as follows, assuming that (1), (2), but nothing else are among our background commitments.

(Example 76 derivation part 1)
$\{FiGiUjEj, Aa\}[\{GxFxTx, 0\}^{GxFx}]^{\circlearrowleft}[\{Ti\}[\{GxTxFx, 0\}^{GxTx}]^{\circlearrowleft}]^{\circlearrowleft} =$
$= \{FiGiUjEjTi, FiGiUjEj, Aa\}[\{Ti\}]^{\circlearrowleft} = \{FiGiUjEjTi\}$

In this case, only the "downward" linkage ($L(C,G,D)$) makes a difference, since the only upward linkage view does not end up having its supposition satisfied, given the particular background generalizations that we have assumed.

A possible objection to this approach might go as follows: embarrassingly many further facts about almost everything follow from my general world knowledge. The envisaged procedure risks leaving us on the hook for too many links to update with. Particularly if those links have a tendency to introduce multiple alternative states, as in the case considered, we could quickly end up with an explosion of alternative states that would make our inference grind to a halt.

This objection should not worry us too much. An empirical reason not to worry about there being too many linkage commitments is that we are only considering, if you will, "narrow" commitments in our inference state $\langle C, G \rangle$ rather than all commitments that can be inferred from our narrow commitments. We have already seen evidence that not every connection we in principle know how to make is recruited in default inference. For example, as discussed in the previous chapter, people are willing to infer "Quacky lays eggs" from "Quacky is a duck," but they are much less likely to infer "Quacky is female" from "Quacky is a duck," even though Quacky must be female if Quacky lays eggs (Khemlani et al. (2009); Khemlani et al. (2012a)). This pattern makes sense if we take it that "ducks lay eggs" is a commitment people tend to possess, while "females lay eggs" and "ducks are female" are not, witnessed by the fact that the first statement seems true, while the latter two do not.

More generally, we might think that if the views we tend to "save" as distinct commitments have relatively few atoms, the total number of potentially eligible linkage views is constrained by the fact that links have to happen in virtue of those atoms, and fewer atoms mean fewer distinct possibilities for linkages in background commitments. On the other hand, if we have views with many atoms, there are more opportunities for more specific linking commitments to have *greater* overlap than any of the others. A fully articulated theory of memory access for linkages would most likely limit the inclusion of potential linkages to those that are maximally promising. We will leave further exploration of these issues for future work.

We will move ahead with our preliminary notion of linkage views. We could at this stage revise the definition of the default reasoning procedure to include clauses for adding linkage views if a normal update does not succeed in providing a novel conclusion (it should be fairly obvious to the reader by now how such clauses can be designed). Since we are not attempting to give a full theory of how memory gets recruited in reasoning in this book, we omit such extra formal revisions and simply explain how linkages would be included in particular cases.

We can now turn to the classical examples of the conjunction fallacy. These problem can only be tackled by reasoners if they can marshall background beliefs connecting the features in them in a probabilistic way. We would like to model the probabilistically incoherent result in a way that does not assume that the background beliefs of our reasoner are already incoherent. Otherwise, we would not get an *explanation* of the fallacy, but merely a redescription of a reasoning fallacy in terms of fallaciously adopted background commitments.

We will begin with the medical case from example 74. Doctors made estimates of the probability of various symptoms, given the information that they were looking at a "55-year-old woman had pulmonary embolism documented angiographically 10 days after a cholecystectomy." The crucial observation was that "Dyspnea and hemiparesis" was ranked as more probable than "Hemiparesis." We will simplify our exposition a bit by leaving out the other symptom options.

We would treat problem as generating a question about possible additional symptoms to be answered by "embolism" as an answer.

We will have to assume some medical background commitments in order for any inferences to be possible. Dyspnea is a common symptom of pulmonary embolism. Hemiparesis could happen together with pulmonary embolism but a brief google search makes it hard to find a clear statement of the degree of connection between between hemiparesis and pulmonary embolism, so we might assume it is not a frequent cooccurrence. For the sake of concreteness, we will translate that into the following background commitments:

(1) $\{(0.85).ExDx, (0.15).Ex\bar{D}x\}^{\{Ex\}}$
(2) $\{(0.1).ExHx, (0.9).Ex\bar{H}x\}^{\{Ex\}}$

We then get the following, where we use P as a stand-in for some other symptom possibility.

(Example 74 derivation)
$\{DjHj, Hj, Pj\}[\{Ej\}]^{\circlearrowleft}$

Since this update has no hope of producing a novel conclusion, we will add linkages:

$\{DjHj, Hj, Pj\}[\{Ej\}[(1)]^{\circlearrowleft}[(2)]^{\circlearrowleft}]^{\circlearrowleft} =$
$= \{DjHj, Hj, Pj\}[\{(0.85) \times (0.1).EjDjHj, (0.85) \times (0.9).EjDj\bar{H}j, (0.15) \times (0.1).\}Ej\bar{D}jHj, (0.15) \times (0.9).Ej\bar{D}j\bar{H}j]^{\circlearrowleft} =$
$= \{DjHj\}$

Once we include the linkage commitments, we find that we get the conjunction fallacy in a way that parallels illusory inferences from Chapter 2.

Having seen a derivation for a conjunction fallacy problem in one setting, it should be relatively clear how to produce similar derivations for the Linda problem from example 75, and for other examples of the conjunction fallacy from the literature. The details will hinge on how we regiment plausible background knowledge, which requires making some design choices, so we will not produce another derivation here.

For Linda, we might say that we learn from the vignette that she is "smart" and "concerned." We might then say that we have background commitments that if Linda has the "smart" feature, then this is diagnostic in favor of being a banker, and that if Linda has the "concerned" feature, then this is diagnostic in favor of being active in the feminist movement. As in the embolism case, this will result in more EAP support for her being a banker and active in the feminist movement than it will for just being a banker.

In sum, reasonable extensions of the default procedure that yielded illusory inferences in the propositional reasoning case, now extended to allow consideration of background commitments, also seems to yield a conjunction fallacy in probabilistic judgment.

5.7 Remaining Operations

For the sake of completeness, we will lift the remaining ETR reasoning operations to extended views. We will not defend this particular avenue for the remaining operations here, doubtlessly other variants are possible, but merely illustrate one way of proceeding.

Definition 5.31 (Division). If $\forall \delta \in \Delta \exists \psi \in \Psi \exists \gamma \in \Gamma. \delta \subseteq \gamma \wedge \psi \subseteq \gamma)$ then define

$$\Gamma^{\Theta}_{fRI} \oslash \Delta^{\Psi}_{gSJ} = \sum_{\gamma \in \Gamma} \{f(\gamma).(\gamma \oslash_{\Gamma} \Delta^{\Psi})\}\Big|^{\Theta}_{RI}$$

where $\gamma \oslash_\Gamma \Delta^\Psi = \gamma - \iota\delta(\delta \in \Delta \wedge \delta \subseteq \gamma \wedge \exists \psi \in \Psi(\psi \subseteq \gamma))$.

Definition 5.32 (Factor (central case)). For $\Delta^{\Psi} \neq \{\}^{\{0\}}$,

$$\Gamma^{\Theta}_{fRI}[\Delta^{\Psi}_{gSJ}]^F = \sum_{\gamma \in \Gamma} \{f(\gamma).\gamma[\Delta^{\Psi}]^F\}\Big|^{\Theta}_{RI},$$

where $\gamma[\Delta]^F = \ldots$ (as before).

Definition 5.33 (Which?). We define $\Gamma^{\Theta}_{fIR}[\Delta^{\Psi}_{gSJ}]^W$ as follows, assuming $U_S \subseteq U_R$. Let

$$M'_{IJ} = \{\langle t,e \rangle \in M_{IJ} : e \in E_S \backslash E_R\}.$$

Then

$$\Gamma^{\Theta}_{fRI}[\Delta^{\Psi}_{gSJ}]^W = H + \sum_{\gamma \in \Gamma} \langle\!\langle w.\xi : \Xi(\gamma, w.\xi) \rangle\!\rangle\Big|^{\Theta}_{RI}$$

where

$$H = \begin{cases} \{0\}^{\Theta}|_{RI} & \text{if } \exists \gamma \in \Gamma. \forall \delta \in \Delta. \neg \Phi(\gamma, \delta) \\ \{\}^{\Theta}|_{RI} & \text{otherwise,} \end{cases}$$

and where $\Phi(\gamma, \delta)$ is by definition

$$\exists \psi \in \Psi \exists n \geq 0 \exists \langle t_1, e_1 \rangle, \ldots, \langle t_n, e_n \rangle \in M'_{IJ} . (\forall i,j. e_i = e_j \to i = j) \wedge$$
$$(\psi \cup \delta[t_1/e_1, \ldots, t_n/e_n] \subseteq \gamma) \wedge$$
$$(f(\gamma) = g(\delta)[t_1/e_1, \ldots] \vee f(\gamma) = g(\delta)[t_1/e_1, \ldots] \vee g(\delta) = \langle\!\langle\rangle\!\rangle);$$

and $\Xi(\gamma, w.\xi)$ is by definition

$$\exists \psi_{\in\Psi} \exists \delta_{\in\Delta} \exists n_{\geq 0} \exists \langle t_1, e_1\rangle, \ldots, \langle t_n, e_n\rangle_{\in M'_{IJ}} (\forall i, j.(e_i = e_j \to i = j)) \wedge$$
$$(\xi \cup \psi \subseteq \gamma \wedge w.\xi = (g(\delta).\delta)[t_1/e_1, \ldots, t_n/e_n]).$$

Definition 5.34 (Existential sum). For $A(\Gamma) \cap A(\Theta) = \emptyset$ and either $A(R) \cap A(S) = \emptyset$ or $[R]_\Delta = S$; $M'_{IJ} = \{\langle e, t\rangle \in M_{IJ} : e \in E_R - A(\Theta \cup \Delta) \wedge \neg \exists x (\langle e, x\rangle \in D_R)\} \neq \emptyset$; for $e \in E_R$ and $\gamma \in \Gamma$, let $N(\gamma, I, e) = \{x[e/?] \in \gamma : \langle e, x\rangle \in I\}$.

$$\Gamma^\Theta_{fRI}[\Delta^{\{0\}}_{gSJ}]^E = \Gamma^\Theta_{fRI} \oplus^{R\bowtie S}$$

$$\bigoplus_{\langle e,t\rangle \in M'_{IJ}}^{R\bowtie S} \mathrm{Sub}^{R\bowtie S}_{\langle t,e\rangle} \left(\left(\bigcup_{\substack{\gamma \in \Gamma, \\ e \in A(\gamma)}} \{\gamma\} \cup \{x_{\in\gamma} : e \notin A(x)\} \cup \delta : \right. \right.$$

$$\left. \left. \delta \in \bigotimes_{x \in N(\gamma,I,e)} \{\{x\},\{\bar{x}\}\} \wedge \delta \not\subseteq \gamma \right\} \right)\bigg|^\Theta_{S,J}$$

The following operation will be useful for further extensions into arithmetical reasoning (which we leave for future work).

Definition 5.35 (Factor (identity)). For $J = \{\langle It_1?, t_2\rangle\}$ or $J = \{\langle I?t_2, t_1\rangle\}$,

$$\Gamma^\Theta_{fRI}[\{w.It_1t_2\}|^{\{0\}}_{R,J}]^F = \{\gamma \in \Gamma : It_1t_2 \notin \gamma\}|_f +$$
$$\sum_{\gamma \in \Gamma \text{ s.t. } It_1t_2 \in \gamma} \{(f(\gamma)[t_1/t_2]).(\gamma[t_1/t_2])\}\bigg|^\Theta_{R,I}.$$

We should get this inference with identity factor.

Example 88. (Probability via identity)
(P1) There is a 90% chance Superman can fly.
(P2) Clark is Superman.
  Is (C) a warranted conclusion?
(C) There is a 90% chance that Clark can fly.

5.8 Bayesian Updating

We now want to turn to making sense of coherent information gain. So far, existing approaches to fallacious reasoning with uncertainty tend not to treat the possibility of systematic success in Bayesian updating in a way that is continuous with the account of the fallacies. For example, Johnson-Laird et al. (1999) conclude that for some kinds of problems "the only route to the answer appears to be to use Bayes' theorem.... Naive reasoners are neither familiar with the theorem nor easily able to carry out its computations." It seems to me that there is something right about Cosmides and Tooby (1996)'s thought that one could not "elicit Bayesian reasoning unless our minds contained mechanisms that embody at least some aspects of a calculus of probability." They suggested that frequentist representations would somehow trigger a special mental calculus of probability. It seems to me that Johnson-Laird et al. (1999), Howson and Urbarch (1993), and others are right in concluding that this is unlikely. However, we still have to explain why Bayesian updating seems normatively correct from the perspective of the kind of reasoning that we wish to be engaged in when we engage in probabilistic reasoning. Otherwise, we have to treat Bayesian reasoning as a purely formal imposition from without. Johnson-Laird et al. (1999) tend to sound like that is what they have in mind, when they write, that for expertise with probability, "still another component is the explicit acquisition of laws of probability, such as Bayes' theorem." However, they continue "underlying this ability to acquire these technical matters, in our view, are the simple principles of extensional reasoning based on mental models." What has not been shown is how the "explicit acquisition of laws of probability, such as Bayes' theorem" is in fact possible if we are only given "the simple principles of extensional reasoning based on mental models."

One potential for confusion is that discussions in the psychology literature sometimes talk about mathematical theorems as if they were computational procedures. For example, Johnson-Laird et al. (1999) write that "naive reasoners can infer posterior probabilities without having to carry out the computations required by Bayes's theorem." Such talk makes it sound like Bayes's Theorem is a computational procedure rather than an equation that imposes a coherence constraint. Of course, a theorem itself does not require any computations. However, if we have a computational procedure that we interpret in some domain, we would hope that its inputs and outputs are readily interpretable in such a way that they are consistent with the relevant theorems of that domain. We will now show that with the erotetic theory, we in fact can make sense of Bayesian updating as being grounded in our naïve reasoning capacities.

A Bayesian coherent posterior probability must satisfy the following condition:

$$P_{Posterior}(H|D) = \frac{P(E|H) \times P(H)}{P(E|H) \times P(H) + P(E|\neg H) \times P(\neg H)}$$

This is equivalent to :

$$P_{Posterior}(H|D) = \frac{P(E\&H)}{P(E\&H) + P(E\&\neg H)}$$

Now, in many practical cases, we have a set of competing hypotheses that we are considering in light of some data D, but the competing hypotheses, while exclusive, are far from exhaustive. We may have decided that we wish to answer the question "Hypothesis 1 or 2?" given the priors we have for these hypotheses, likelihoods for these hypotheses and D, and given the fact that D obtains. A rational way of going about this would be to pick on the basis of the relative odds, or the ratio of the posterior probabilities of H1 and H2.

$$\frac{P(H1|E)}{P(H2|E)} = \frac{P(E|H1) \times P(H1)}{P(E|H2) \times P(H2)}$$

We now want to show that the erotetic theory allows for a Bayesian-coherent updating strategy. We want to show that if we begin with the question of "is the hypothesis true or false?" (e.g. $\{H, \bar{H}\}$) and have commitments that are the view interpretations of "the (prior) probability of H is d," "the (prior) probability of not H is p," "If H, then the probability of D is T_1," and "If not H, then the probability of D is T_2," then we can obtain a view that encodes the correct posterior probabilities. Moreover, we want to show that if we begin with the question "$H_1, H_2, \ldots$, or H_n" with corresponding further commitments for some *but not all* hypotheses 1 through n, we can obtain a view that encodes the correct likelihood ratios between those hypotheses about which we have information. In what follows we will take it that probabilities are retrieved from a view by taking Answer Potential and then normalizing by the Answherhood potential of truth ({0}). This is slightly simpler than the default procedure described in Definition 5.20 since this latter also uses Query just before Answer Potential, but that makes no difference to the results here.

We first consider the normal Bayesian case. Let G be the following.

$$G = \{H, \bar{H}\}[\{d.H\}^{\{H\}}]^{\circlearrowleft}[\{p.\bar{H}\}^{\{\bar{H}\}}]^{\circlearrowleft}[\{T_1.DH, H\bar{D}\}^{\{H\}}]^{\circlearrowleft}[\{T_2.D\bar{H}, \bar{H}\bar{D}\}^{\{\bar{H}\}}]^{\circlearrowleft}$$
$$= \{d.H, p.\bar{H}\}[\{T_1.DH, H\bar{D}\}^{\{H\}}]^{\circlearrowleft}[\{T_2.D\bar{H}, \bar{H}\bar{D}\}^{\{\bar{H}\}}]^{\circlearrowleft}$$
$$= \{(d\bar{\times}T_1).DH, d.H\bar{D}, (p\bar{\times}T_2).D\bar{H}, p.\bar{H}\bar{D}\}$$

We then find that:

$$P(H|D) = \frac{\dfrac{G[\{H,D\}]^{\text{EP}}}{G[\{0\}]^{\text{EP}}}}{\dfrac{G[\{D\}]^{\text{EP}}}{G[\{0\}]^{\text{EP}}}} = \frac{G[\{H,D\}]^{\text{EP}}}{G[\{D\}]^{\text{EP}}} = \frac{dT_1}{dT_1 + pT_2}$$

Of course, d was our prior probability of H, p was our prior that $\neg H$, T_1 was $P(D|H)$, and T_2 was $P(D|\bar{H})$, so our result correctly corresponds to

$$\frac{P(D|H) \times P(H)}{P(D|H) \times P(H) + P(D|\bar{H}) \times P(\bar{H})}.$$

If we continue our derivation by updating with the data, we get

$$G' = G[\{D\}]^{\circlearrowleft} = \{d\bar{\times}T_1.DH, p\bar{\times}T_2.D\bar{H}\}.$$

and we now get the correct posterior probability of H:

$$\frac{G'[\{H\}]^{\text{EP}}}{G'[\{0\}]^{\text{EP}}} = \frac{dT_1}{dT_1 + pT_2}.$$

In sum, there exists a reasoning strategy on the erotetic theory that yields a probabilistically coherent way to update with data.

We next turn to the case of obtaining posterior likelihood ratios. Let G be the following.

$$G = \{H_1, H_2, H_3\}[\{d.H_1\}^{\{H_1\}}]^{\circlearrowleft}[\{p.H_2\}^{\{H_2\}}]^{\circlearrowleft}[\{r.H_3\}^{\{H_3\}}]^{\circlearrowleft}$$
$$[\{T_1.DH_1, \bar{D}H_1\}^{\{H_1\}}]^{\circlearrowleft}[\{T_2.DH_2, \bar{D}H_2\}^{\{H_2\}}]^{\circlearrowleft}$$
$$= \{d.H_1, p.H_2, r.H_3\}[\{T_1.DH_1, \bar{D}H_1\}^{\{H_1\}}]^{\circlearrowleft}[\{T_2.DH_2, \bar{D}H_2\}^{\{H_2\}}]^{\circlearrowleft}$$
$$= \{d\bar{\times}T_1.DH_1, p\bar{\times}T_2.DH_2, d.H_1\bar{D}, p.H_2.\bar{D}, r.H_3\}$$

We then find that

$$\frac{\frac{G[\{H_1\}]^{EP}}{G[\{0\}]^{EP}}}{\frac{G[\{H_2\}]^{EP}}{G[\{0\}]^{EP}}} = \frac{G[\{H_1\}]^{EP}}{G[\{H_2\}]^{EP}}$$

is the correct posterior probability ratio for hypotheses 1 and 2.

We might sometimes be a in a situation where we just want to treat some input as an independent information source on our hypothesis without bothering with likelihoods and data. You might call this a kind of testimony. Now, recall that the result of our Bayesian update derivation before learning D was $\{d\overline{\times}T.DH, d.H\bar{D}, p\overline{\times}F.D\bar{H}, p.\bar{H}\bar{D}\}$. Suppose now we learn that D is the case. We get $\{d\overline{\times}T.DH, p\overline{\times}F.D\bar{H}\}$. Now suppose we are not interested in remembering that D is the case and factor it out, so we get $\{d\overline{\times}T.H, p\overline{\times}F.\bar{H}\}$. We can also vacuously suppose $\{H, \bar{H}\}$ and Factor out contradictions, to obtain $\{d\overline{\times}T.H, p\overline{\times}F.\bar{H}\}^{\{H,\bar{H}\}}$. All information relevant to H in addition to our prior that is included in our two likelihood conditionals and the statement of the data is compressed into this view, which we might call a "Bayes Factor" view. We can correctly absorb this information by simply updating with this view. One might call this a witness view. One might suspect that this is the format of probabilistic information that is most readily digested by the erotetic reasoner.

5.9 Erotetic Equilibrium and Probabilistic Coherence

We want to show that the answer potential we just defined can explain the possibility of systematic correspondence to the axioms of probability. This will allow us to maintain that there is truth in the notion that probability as described by standard axiomatizations is in an interesting sense grounded in common sense (to be more precise, in our naïve reasoning capacity), in something like the way in which we showed that classical soundness can be seen as ultimately grounded in common sense. The key, as before, lies in erotetic equilibrium.

Discussions of coherence in the context of systems that have the expressive power of first order logic rather than just propositional logic within the scope of probability are quite rare. The erotetic theory obviously does have first-order equivalent expressive power, so a full consideration of when the erotetic theory yields coherence would have to relate to probability axioms like those in Gaifman and Snir (1982), rather than the more familiar Kolmogorov axioms. However, we will limit the discussion of the relationship to probabilistic coherence to the propositional fragment. In other words, we will only consider views from which arbitrary and indefinite tokens, as well as identity features have been eliminated.

We are not concerned with derivations of the axioms of probability from rational norms such as "Dutch book" arguments, and we will take it as given that on a finite set Ω the only coherent notion of probability measure is a function $\mathbb{P} : \mathcal{P}(\Omega) \to [0,1]$ from subsets of Ω to real numbers between 0 and 1 satisfying:

(1) $\mathbb{P}(\Omega) = 1$,
(2) $\mathbb{P}(A \cup B) = \mathbb{P}(A) + \mathbb{P}(B)$ for $A \cap B = \emptyset$.

(Since we are dealing only with finite sample spaces Ω we need not be concerned with issues of measurability or countable additivity). The following triviality is useful to keep in mind.

Lemma 5.1. *There is a one-to-one correspondence between probability measures $\mathbb{P}$ on a finite set Ω and functions $p : \Omega \to [0,1]$ such that $\sum_{\omega \in \Omega} p(\omega) = 1$.*

Proof. Given $\mathbb{P}$, let $p(\omega) = \mathbb{P}(\{\omega\})$. Given p, let $\mathbb{P}(A) = \sum_{\omega \in A} p(\omega)$. □

For a given view $G = \Gamma_f^{\{0\}}$, we now have to define a sample space Ω_G for which the view G supports probability judgments. We take Ω_G to be the set of states δ such that, for every $a \in A(G)$, precisely one of a and $\bar{a}$ is in δ. Provided $G = G[\bot]^F$, then for all $\gamma \in \Gamma$ there is an $\omega \in \Omega_G$ with $\gamma \subseteq \omega$.

There is now a problem of coherence for probability which does not feature in the traditional presentations. Ordinarily, the events of a sample space are supposed to form a *Boolean algebra*, and it is a straightforward mathematical exercise to prove that every finite Boolean algebra has a representation as the powerset of some finite set. Let $\mathcal{F}_G$ be the set of views $\Delta^{\{0\}}$ such that $\forall a \in \delta \in \Delta . a \in A(G) \vee \bar{a} \in A(G)$. Then we might interpret the Boolean connectives as operations on $\mathcal{F}_G$ with the following interpretations.

$$\vee \leftrightarrow \oplus \qquad \wedge \leftrightarrow \otimes \qquad \neg \leftrightarrow [\ ]^N \qquad \bot \leftrightarrow \{\} \qquad \top \leftrightarrow \{0\}$$

However, unless $A(G) = \emptyset$, $\mathcal{F}_G$ is not a Boolean algebra because it does not satisfy all of the necessary equational laws. For example,

$$\{\{a\}\} \oplus [\{\{a\}\}]^N \neq \{0\},$$
$$\{0\} \oplus \{\{a\}\} \neq \{0\}.$$

There is a "realization" operation $[\![\ ]\!]_G : \mathcal{F}_G \to \mathcal{P}(\Omega_G)$ which is defined by

$$[\![\Delta]\!] = \{\omega \in \Omega_G : \exists \delta \in \Delta.\ \delta \subseteq \omega\}.$$

This is a surjective function, since for $\mathcal{P}(\Omega_G) \subseteq \mathcal{F}_G$ and, for $A \in \mathcal{P}(\Omega_G)$, $[\![A]\!] = A$. Moreover it preserves Boolean operations, in the sense that $[\![\Delta_1 \oplus \Delta_2]\!] = [\![\Delta_1]\!] \cup [\![\Delta_2]\!]$, etc. Thus $[\![\ ]\!]$ is not a bijection since, for example, $[\![\{\{a\},\{\bar{a}\}\}]\!] = \Omega_G = [\![\{0\}]\!]$. This is a reflection of the fact that a view is a richer form of content than a mere truth-condition.

The view G encodes probabilities for the views $\Delta \in \mathcal{F}_G$ by taking $G[\Delta]^{EP}$ and normalizing by $G[\{0\}]^{EP}$. We assume that complex terms which can be reduced to real numbers have been so reduced. Thus the question of probabilistic coherence breaks down into two parts. We say that G *affords coherent probabilitistic judgments* if the following hold.

(1) For $\Delta \in \mathcal{F}_G$, the value of $G[\Delta]^{EP}$ is a function only of $[\![\Delta]\!] \in \mathcal{P}(\Omega_G)$. Equivalently, $G[\Delta]^{EP} = G[[\![\Delta]\!]]^{EP}$.
(2) For $A \in \mathcal{P}(\Omega_G)$, the assignment $A \mapsto G[A]^{EP}/G[\{0\}]^{EP}$ is a coherent probability measure.

In particular, (2) means that the Answer Potentials $G[\Delta]^{EP}$ are real numbers. The import of (1) is the reasoner does not report different probabilities for the same event according to the view that describes it.

We now characterize a class of views G which give rise to coherent probability judgments. Recall the definition of erotetic equilibrium from Chapter 2. G is in erotetic equilibrium with respect to a finite set of views Σ if and only if $\forall D(D \in \Sigma \to G[D]^I = G)$.

Definition 5.36 (Equilibrium basis view). $G = \Gamma_f^{\{0\}}$ is an equilibrium basis view if and only if,

(1) G is in erotetic equilibrium with respect to $\{\langle\!\langle\rangle\!\rangle.p, \langle\!\langle\rangle\!\rangle.\bar{p}\} : p \in A(G)\}$, and

(2) for all $\gamma \in \Gamma$, $f(\gamma) = \langle\!\langle c_\gamma \rangle\!\rangle$ for some non-negative real number $c_\gamma \in \mathbb{R}_{\geq 0}$, and $c_\gamma > 0$ for at least one $\gamma \in \Gamma$.

In particular, (2) implies that $G \neq \top$ and $G \neq \bot$. Also, (1) implies that $\Gamma \subseteq \Omega_G$.

We now verify the first part of probabilistic coherence.

Lemma 5.2. For $G = \Gamma_f^{\{0\}}$ and equilibrium basis view and $\Delta, \Delta' \in \mathcal{F}_G$ with $[\![\Delta]\!] = [\![\Delta']\!]$, we have
$$G[\Delta]^{EP} = G[\Delta']^{EP}.$$

Proof. Since G is in erotetic equilibrium, the set $Y = \{\gamma \in \Gamma : \exists \delta \in \Delta.\ \delta \subseteq \gamma\}$ appearing in the definition of $[\ ]^{EP}$ is actually equal to $[\![\Delta]\!]$. $\square$

Theorem 5.3. *If $G = \Gamma_f^{\{0\}}$ is an equilibrium basis view the G affords coherent probabilistic judgments.*

Proof. We have checked condition (1) so it remains to check (2). Write $c_\gamma \in \mathbb{R}_{\geq 0}$ for the real numbers satisfying $f(\gamma) = \langle\!\langle c_\gamma \rangle\!\rangle$ for $\gamma \in \Gamma$, and $c_\omega = 0$ for $\omega \in \Omega_G \setminus \Gamma$. Then the encoded probability measure $\mathbb{P}_G : \mathcal{P}(\Omega_G) \to [0,1]$ satisfies, for $\omega \in \Omega_G$,
$$\mathbb{P}_G(\{\omega\}) = \frac{1}{M} G[\{\omega\}]^{EP} = \frac{1}{M} c_\omega$$

where $M = G[\{0\}]^{EP} = \sum_{\gamma \in \Gamma} c_\gamma = \sum_{\omega' \in \Omega_G} c_{\omega'}$. Here we have used the fact that G is in erotetic equilibrium, and the fact $c_\omega \leq 0$ with $c_\gamma > 0$ for at least one γ means that the normalizing constant M is positive and hence the probability function is well-defined. We have

$$\sum_{\omega \in \Omega} \mathbb{P}_G(\{\omega\}) = \frac{1}{M} \sum_{\omega \in \Omega} c_\omega = \frac{1}{M} M = 1.$$

Thus, by Lemma 5.1, there is a unique probability measure on Ω_G determined by the assignment $\omega \mapsto \mathbb{P}_G(\{\omega\}) = \frac{1}{M} c_\omega$. It now remains to check that $\mathbb{P}_G$ agrees with this probability measure on the non-singleton sets as well, i.e. that

$$\mathbb{P}_G(A) = \sum_{\omega \in A} \mathbb{P}_G(\{\omega\}) = \frac{1}{M} \sum_{\omega \in A} c_\omega.$$

But this is immediate from the definition of [ ]^{EP} and the fact that G is in erotetic equilibrium. □

5.10 Expert Forecasting and Restricted Erotetic Equilibrium

The main conclusions of this section are as follows. Firstly, expert judgment in the academic sense is a kind of judgment that is intrinsically outside of absolute erotetic equilibrium and has to be evaluated with respect to restricted erotetic equilibrium. Secondly, the quality of our judgment can probably be improved by aiming further toward erotetic equilibrium, at least to a degree.

For various areas in which technical expertise is possible given humanity's present state of knowledge, we rely on experts to give us estimates about the probabilities of uncertain events. For example, we might ask a specialist engineer what the risk of accident is for a space vehicle launch. Gigerenzer (2002) reports that, when asked, representatives of the European Space Agency cited a 99.6% probability of a successful launch for a DASA Ariane launch vehicle. He acerbically notes that this does not quite correspond to a history of 8 accidents out of 94 launches, amounting to only a 91.5% success rate at the time he wrote. Small differences matter. For example, according to Wikipedia, NASA Commercial Crew Program (CCP) standards demand that the probability of loss on ascent does not exceed 1 in 500, if humans are aboard (so 99.8% success on ascent). Gigerenzer reports that the engineers take their estimate from failure propensities of individual design parts of the launch vehicle. He further notes that the engineers do not take frequencies as the basis since that would include failures due to human error. The lesson Gigerenzer suggests throughout his book is that it is simply a mistake not to rely on frequency in virtually all domains of risk assessment.

One difficulty with a pure frequency approach is that in many contexts, the system whose behavior we are trying to predict keeps changing in a way that means we are not, in statistical terms, sampling from the same population. For example, the Ariane 5 had its maiden flight in 1996, which resulted in an explosion. After over 100 successful launches since then (among some further failures), it is being phased out in favor of the Ariane 6. It is by no means obvious when in the life-cycle of a rocket model it starts being better to rely on frequency rather than propensity estimations in determining risk. Of course, each new rocket series is refined in part with the intention of achieving a higher success rate. What is clear is that we often require estimates when we simply do not have a large enough sample of "the same type" of rocket launch, and so on for other applications.

Setting aside the frequency issue, it is interesting that the propensity estimate from the engineer that Gigerenzer discusses explicitly does not include an estimate of human errors. In a certain light, we could see this as an independent reason for relying on frequency estimates instead of propensity estimates, since surely an astronaut is just as dead and a satellite just as broken if a rocket explodes due to human error than if it explodes due to some parts malfunctioning. If what we care about are results, it may well make sense to regard the entire designer+engineer+rocket+crew+control-center combination as a biomechanical device with both technical and human components that delivers objects from a loading dock on earth to space. As we know from disasters like Chernobyl, engineering problems and human control problems are intertwined. Companies like Apple that sell complex engineering products are precisely successful because the functioning of their products is quite robust to technical ignorance on the part of their users. As some older readers might remember, with very early computer printing technology, it was still possible to send user commands to a printer that might physically damage it. Nowadays, this is almost ruled out for consumer peripheral devices.

The notion that the human factor should be taken into consideration in evaluating the safety of a complex technology that requires multiple people to operate does not by itself show that we ought to think about frequencies rather than propensities. What we do get is a serious question about what we really have in mind when we are asking about a risk assessment and how it relates to expertise.

Few people have enough expert knowledge of a rocket system to be able to provide an expert estimate of the failure propensities of its critical components. Even fewer people would *additionally* be able to estimate the propensity of a normally trained operator making mistakes of a critical nature, which would presumably have to involve some knowledge of human attention, decision-making under stress, and so on. Notice that studying such "propensities" sounds pretty much like studying the relevant *cognitive capacities* and their properties; in other words, cognitive science. Simply put, it is hard to be both a rocket scientist and a cognitive scientist. A pure frequency-based estimate has the advantage that we do not have to address any of these propensities separately and we need less knowledge of underlying structures that generate outcomes. However, the strategy of relying on a blind frequency estimate requires us to assume that we are still sampling from the same population of rocket launches, which amounts to assuming that there are no changing sources of variance. Of course, everything changes all the time in some degree, so we have to draw a line somewhere (do we draw the line at staff changes or at a new type of engine?). For an extremely complex system operating in a dynamic environment with atmospheric, stellar, and political factors, none of which obey simple statistical distributions, this is by no means a small assumption.

It seems to us that the following picture emerges: properly *expert* judgment unavoidably is a kind of *restricted erotetic equilibrium* judgment. For various questions like "what are the chances of this container successfully getting delivered to space?", there is a very large number of disparate factors that can materially change the outcome. For a rocket launch, this could include any number of things, notably the engineering of rocket parts, the performance of human operators, weather, obstacles in space, perhaps even sabotage or acts of war. Everybody can see how such factors have the power to potentially influence the outcome. However, almost nobody would genuinely want to claim to be an expert on all of those factors, *while knowing full well* that they exist and can make a difference. After all, we have experts in rocket science, meteorology, psychology, space junk, site security, politics, etc., and it is hard enough to become one in any *one* of these areas. As a result, when asked to offer an *expert* judgment, we should have a tendency to give a judgment that is informed only (or primarily) by those dimensions of the overall problem for which we can claim special expertise. We can of course add in our speculations about other factors that we know can have an impact, but that would simply result in an expert-judgment-non-expert-judgment hybrid, not an expert judgment in an academic sense.

Note that expertise in a subject area does not necessarily come with authoritative expertise in determining for what applications one's expertise is primarily relevant for making an estimate. You might also say that expertise does not generally entail meta-expertise.

In sum, expert judgment about complex objects in the real world plausibly almost never is absolute erotetic equilibrium judgment, because it relies on not raising issues on which the expert fails to have expertise, while it normally being clear to the expert that those issues are in fact relevant, just as it would be to their non-expert brothers and sisters with (merely) some general world knowledge.

Note that the foregoing does not suggest that equilibrium in judgments with uncertainty, or at least moving closer toward equilibrium, is not potentially useful or epistemically relevant. Indeed, one of the most exciting bodies of recent work on human probability judgment suggests that certain cognitive habits can markedly improve accuracy of various kinds of forecasts, in some cases beating expert knowledge. In the erotetic framework, we would regard those cognitive habits as tending toward bringing use closer to erotetic equilibrium. This approach might offer the beginings of an explanation of how beating expert knowledge can be possible in certain areas.

Tetlock and collaborators conducted long-term studies over twenty years with nearly 300 participants who professionally make analyses of political and economic events (Tetlock (2005)). Their studies showed that the average "subject experts" did no better than chance on many political and economic forecasting questions. In judging the probability of events three to five years in the future even experts tend to approach dart-throwing chimpanzee in the quality of their predictions. However, they also found that some experts had real, substantially better success than others. Tetlock and collaborators have argued that the main difference between ordinary forecasters and more successful forecasters was driven by the thought process they employed rather than by a difference in subject knowledge (Tetlock and Gardner (2015)).

In a forecasting competition sponsored by IARPA, involving roughly 500 forecasting questions about world affairs with time horizons between a month and a year, Tetlock and Mellers' Good Judgment Project outperformed not only control groups and university-affiliated competitors by as much as 78% but "even outperformed professional intelligence analysts with access to classified data" (Tetlock and Gardner (2015)). The core method of the Good Judgment Project was to identify good forecasters over successive periods and put the best ones together into groups, whose judgments were then aggregated, and "extremized" to reflect that fact that the group judgment should be more confident. Tetlock and Gardner triumphantly conclude that, "Thanks to IARPA, we now know that a few hundred ordinary people and some simple math can not only compete with professionals supported by a multibillion-dollar apparatus but also beat them" (Tetlock and Gardner (2015)).

Some forecasters within the Good Judgment Project teams were consistently better than others. Moreover, they concluded that a tutorial about good forcasting procedure, "improved accuracy by roughly 10% through the entire tournament year" (Tetlock and Gardner (2015), p. 18). To put this improvement into perspective, they cite both hedge fund managers and professional poker players in support of the view that a consistent 10% increase in accuracy in prediction can make the difference between consistent profit and bancruptcy. They argue that the recommendations of the tutorial that produced the increase in accuracy also reflect the kind of thought process that Tetlock and Mellors' earlier twenty-year study had identified in superior expert forecasters.

Tetlock and Gardner (Tetlock and Gardner (2015)) provide ten summary guidelines that, in their words, "distill key themes... in training systems that have been experimentally demonstrated to boost accuracy in real-world forecasting contests" (p. 277). It seems worth separating their "commandments" into three kinds of tools: (1) recommendations for "micro" cognitive policies to adopt in reasoning through forecasting problems; (2) indicators that tend to mark good forecasters; and (3) bird's-eye-view maxims about how to continue to develop one's forecasting performance. We will for now only consider (1). We will use slightly different labels for their recommendations, indicating which of their commandments we take them to correspond to.

Example 89. (Cognitive policies for superforecasters)

(Fermi-izing) Begin the construction of a probability estimate of an event by ("Fermi-izing") decomposing the event into different possible ways in which it might happen, representing the different assumptions underlying those different possible contingencies, keeping in mind that larger time-ranges for the event may increase the number of contingencies in which the event may happen. (Commandment 2)

(Modulated external view) Represent future possibilities as instances of classes of events for which we can estimate how often they have happened in the past. Begin with a broader comparison class but judiciously use information about the causal structure of the future event of interest to narrow the class. For example, if we know a specific academic Bill is particularly efficient, then in assessing how likely it is he will finish a project on time, we might ask how often especially efficient academics finish projects on time instead of how often academics in general finish projects on time, keeping in mind that attributing those special properties with specific causal consequences is itself an assumption that may not hold, requiring further considerations of ways that assumption may hold or fail to hold. (Commandments 2 and 3)

(Proportional update with information) In revising predictions in light of new information, look for empirical indicators "about what would have to happen before X could" where X are particular alternative scenarios on which the overall prediction is based. Say, if a prediction that a particular party will win an election is largely dependent on one's assessment that a win is highly likely when a certain state is won, then learning that that state has been lost should strongly affect one's prediction. On the other hand, if new data merely affects a minor possibility in one's Fermi-ized contingency analysis, then the new data should only have a correspondingly small impact on the prediction. (Commandment 4)

(Explicit negative contingencies) In building your analysis of different contingencies on which you base our estimate of the likelihood of the proposition you are concerned with, be diligent in uncovering different ways in which the event may fail to take place. Ask how likely various scenarios are that would prevent the event from occurring. (Commandment 5)

(Precision) Make nuanced numerical estimates of the likelihood of various contingencies. (Commandment 6)

A larger theme that emerges in these policies is that bringing more alternative possibilities into view, for both positive and negative contingencies relative to the proposition being assessed, in coming up with a probability estimate correlates with better forecasts. On the erotetic picture, we can at least partly make sense of the possibility of beating expert predictions as follows. By its nature, expert judgment is narrow in its question-base, centering on factors on which expertise is to be had. At the same time, various types of events we might be interested in predicting are determined by a wide base of potential factors, meaning that an aggregate of less-informed estimates of different ways in which something may happen ends up being more faithful to reality than an estimate based on much more detailed views of just a few ways in which something may happen.

One might hypothesize that classes of judgment problems usefully divide into those that have high inquisitive load, in the sense that doing well at them will always require asking about a broad range of possible contingencies, while other problems have low inquisitive load, in the sense that fewer issues need to be considered or in the sense that those issues are in a sense very similar from a bird's-eye perspective (e.g. different states of some engine part). In the former case, inquiring about more possible contingencies is more important than knowing a lot about individual possible contingencies. In the latter case, it may be more important to know a lot about the type of contingency that tends to be dominant in most cases of a given type. It seems to us that this latter case is the prime area for successful deference to experts, while the former may be an area where traditional notions of "expert knowledge" are simply a mirage.

On this view, Tetlock and his team succeeded because the judgment problems were ones in the domain of high inquisitive load where expertise is hard to come by. We will return to some of these concepts in the next and final chapter on decision-making. It seems like we are the sorts of creatures that flourish at some optimal range of inquisitive load for the kinds of questions we face as decisions.

In moving on to consider decision-making, it may also become clearer why taking equilibrium answer potential as fundamental, rather than probability, is not an arbitrary choice. Why would a system have equilibrium answerhood potential instead of probability? Because at the end of the day what matters most is settling questions of *what to do*.

Knowing the probability of an outcome independently of its value is often useless, while knowing the value of something in the abstract regardless of the chance of that thing being realized is also often useless. A useful example discussed by Russell and Norvig (2016) is that in early medical expert systems the emphasis was on ranking possible diagnoses in order of likelihood and then reporting the most likely diagnosis. As they point out,

> unfortunately, this can be disastrous! For the majority of patients in general practice, the two most likely diagnoses are usually "There's nothing wrong with you" and "You have a bad cold," but if the third most likely diagnosis for a given patient is lung cancer, that's a serious matter. Obviously, a testing or treatment plan should depend both on probabilities and utilities. (p. 652)

For choice, what matters is a weight that combines probability and value; equilibrium answerhood potential can serve as this weight. However, unlike in the classical concept of expected utility, we, as before, will be able to eschew hyper-rational idealization and make sense of failures of decision-making, while also making sense of the possibility of success by the classical standards of rational choice.

6
Decision and Practical Reasoning

Philipp Koralus, Sean Moss

Much of the human conduct we care most about involves decisions to pursue one option rather than another. For example, we choose what goods to purchase in the marketplace, what political party will receive our vote, and with whom we spend our lives. We also make important choices without much reflection, like jumping out of the way of a speeding car or returning a tennis serve. Like in the case of inferential reasoning, a key feature of the nature of human decision-making is that it poses both a problem of success and a problem of failure. Humans are capable of systematically making decisions that leave them better off in controlled and intended ways, yielding full pantries and complex societies. Attributing this capacity may be fairly central to what it takes to think of someone as an agent. At the same time, there is a less distinguished side to human decision-making. We systematically fail to be in control of many of our decisions. More specifically, there are systematic breakdowns of control in contexts in which we take ourselves to be in control. These are decision contexts in which we do not already have some interfering external factor that is adversely affecting the core process of practical reasoning that yields our decisions. There are many possible interfering external factors, of considerable interest in their own right, such as a lack of information, time, or power; extreme emotion, or fundamental shifts in our priorities. We will largely set those kinds of phenomena aside and focus on systematic breakdowns of control that plausibly flow from the general process of human practical reasoning, in cases when all the basic conditions for a controlled decision appear to be available to the agent. The empirical case for these more fundamental kinds of control failure has been broadly popularized in recent years (Kahneman (2011); Thaler and Sunstein (2008); Ariely (2008)).

One pattern of failure that emerges from the literature is that we often tend to consider too few alternative possibilities in making decisions, leaving us worse off, often by our own lights (Kahneman (2011); Heath and Heath (2013)). Heath and Heath discuss a number of studies that make a strong case for this claim. They recount a study by Nutt (1993) who collected data on business decisions over a period of decades. The data was based on interviews with primary decision-makers like a CEO, and interviews with less-senior managers who saw the decisions unfold, and who were also later asked to evaluate whether the result of the decision was a success. Nutt (1993) found that only 29% of decisions involved whether-or-not decisions with no substantive alternatives. Nutt also found that of the whether-or-not decisions, 52% failed according to later evaluation by informants in the companies concerned, while only 32% of multi-alternative decisions failed. In a similar study focusing on one business rather than a cross section of businesses, Gemünden and Hauschild (1985) examined every major decision made by the executive board of a medium-sized German technology company over a period of eighteen months. They classified decisions by the number of alternatives that were considered in the decision. They found that 40% were whether-or-not decisions, 55% were two-alternative decisions, and no decisions involved more than three alternatives. Several years later, the board of the company assessed the quality of eighty-three of those decisions in a rating procedure. They rated 40% of their multi-alternative decisions as very good, but only 6% of their whether-or-not decisions as very good.

As a particularly striking example of a failed whether-or-not business decision, Heath and Heath (2013) recount the acquisition of Snapple by Quaker in 1994, which resulted in losses in excess of a billion dollars. They quote the responsible CEO, William Smithburg as reflecting that "we should have had a couple of people arguing the 'no' side of the evaluation." Heath and Heath (2013) remark that "that's a pretty staggering confession... unbelievably, there was *no one within Quaker arguing against the acquisition!* Quaker wasn't even making a 'whether or not' choice; it was making a 'yes or yes' choice" (ibid., p. 36).

The idea that simply reminding people that their money could be spent in other ways can change decisions also has support in controlled studies.

Example 90. (Opportunity cost neglect) Frederick et al. (2009) presented study participants with the following vignette.

(1) Imagine that you have been saving some extra money on the side to make some purchases, and on your most recent visit to the video store you come across a special sale of a new video. This video is one with your favorite actor or actress, and your favorite type of movie (such as a comedy, drama, thriller, etc.). This particular video that you are

> considering is one you have been thinking about buying a long time. It is available at a special sale price of $14.99. What would you do in this situation? Please circle one of the options below.
>
> One randomly selected group of participants was asked to decide between "Buy this entertaining video" and "Not buy this entertaining video." Another group was asked to decide between "Buy this entertaining video" and "Keep the $14.99 for other purchases." Of the first group, 75% of participants chose to buy the video, while only 55% of the participants in the second group made the same choice. In a follow-up experiment with a new set of participants, Frederick et al. (2009) also found that asking participants to list things they would like to buy in an ostensibly unrelated prior task, made them less likely to pick a more expensive cell-phone in a choice task.

In the example above, there is no difference in the objective choice situation presented to the two groups. Both are told, "imagine that you have been saving some extra money on the side to make some purchases," so it should be clear to both groups that not buying the video has the result that the "extra money on the side to make some purchases" will remain to "make some purchases." Yet, framing the decision about the video purchase as a whether-or-not question yielded a substantially larger number of decisions to purchase the video among participants than the multi-alternative frame that highlights the possibility of other purchases.

There is an intuition that the decision in the condition in which the alternative to purchasing the video is presented as "keep the money for other purchases" is a better reflection of control on the part of the decision-maker. If I purchased the video, but I would not have decided to purchase the video had somebody asked me if I wanted to keep the money for other purchases, then it should be doubtful by my own lights that the decision was a good one. There is a sense that if my decision is fragile enough to be changed just by somebody drawing my attention to options I already knew I had, without adding new information, then my decision-making process is probably not entirely as it ought to be. As in the case of reasoning, it seems that our thought process is not entirely as it ought to be if it results in a decision or conclusion that is not in a certain kind of erotetic equilibrium.

In the study that Frederick et al. (2009) reported, the participants were randomly assigned to the two conditions, so we can reasonably conclude that some of the participants would not have decided in favor of the purchase had they been asked a different question. Thus, we can plausibly conclude that not all participants were in full control of their decision.

In response to such observations, should we take a simple recommendation from the business literature like "avoid a narrow frame" (Heath and Heath (2013)) in our decisions? We have to proceed with caution. As a rule of thumb, it does seem that adding more alternatives to a decision question can increase the extent to which we are able to arrive at an equilibrium decisions by our priorities. However, as it turns out, adding more alternatives does not always lead to more control over our decisions. For example, Heath and Heath acknowledge that more options can result in *no* substantive alternative being chosen. Iyengar and Lepper (2000) found that offering a limited array of six gourmet jam choices makes a purchase more likely than a larger array of twenty-four or thirty choices. One attractive explanation for this phenomenon is that we tend to make decisions in favor of things in virtue of these things having properties that we prioritize. If we have a growing set of increasingly similar choices, the chances that the priorities we are entertaining can distinguish one of the possibilities shrinks. We then either have to make an additional effort to bring to mind more less salient priorities, investigate properties of the options further, or pick something at random, all of which involve some effort or discomfort.

As it turns out, the picture is more complicated. Even adding one "decoy" option can sometimes change decisions in a way that does not seem to be reflecting an increase of control on the part of the decision-maker. It would appear that sometimes even one additional alternative choice can change decisions in a way that looks like the opposite of an improvement. Huber, Payne, and Puto (1982) found evidence that the introduction of a "decoy" option that is worse than two existing options can reverse preferences between the existing options. This kind of effect is relatively fragile and only seems to occur when participants are close to indifferent between the original non-decoy options, and when the decoy option is easily recognizable as worse than one of the main (Huber et al. (2014)). Ariely (2008) describes a very simple experiment showing this pattern.

Example 91. (Decoy effect) Two randomly selected groups of MIT students were presented with different options for subscriptions to the *Economist* magazine. The first group got three options: a web-only subscription for $59, a print-only subscription for $125, and a web-and-print option for $125. In this group, 84% of students chose the web-and-print option, 16% chose

> the web-only option, and nobody chose the print-only option. The second group got only two options: the web-only subscription for $59, and the web-and-print option for $125. In this second group, 68% of the students chose the web-only option, and 32% chose the web-and-print option. The presence of the dominated option of a print-only subscription for $125 made a large majority chose the expensive print-and-web subscription. Without the presence of this dominated print-only option that nobody chose, a majority of students picked the cheap web-only subscription.

In this case, it would appear that adding another option does not necessarily lead to better decisions. Ariely suggests the following about this case: "I may not have known whether the Internet-only subscription at $59 was a better deal than the print-only option at $125. But I certainly knew that the print-and-Internet option for $125 was better than the print-only option at $125" (Ariely (2008)). The suggestion is that we somehow use the conclusion that the print-and-Internet option for $125 is better than the print-only option for $125 to settle the question which of the three options to choose. The erotetic theory is very much in the spirit of this kind of explanation. We jump to conclusions in treating a partial answer to a question as a full answer. However, Ariely does not seem to offer an explanation of how the notion that the print-and-Internet option for $125 is better than the print-only option for $125 could (fallaciously) lead to the conclusion that the print-and-Internet option is better than the remaining option. This is something we will return to later. In sum, while there clearly is value to the idea that it is good to avoid a "narrow frame" in decision-making, simply adding more alternative choices does not automatically improve decision-making, and can in fact potentially lower decision-quality. We will ultimately argue that the more subtle notion of erotetic equilibrium, as developed in previous chapters, can capture what is right in the intuition behind the "narrow frame" idea.

Logical connections between properties are not automatically grasped in inference, as we saw in previous chapters. We would expect this to be no different in the context of decision-making. A number of studies have shown that decisions can change depending on whether we are asking whether to choose or reject options, in the context of mutually exclusive and exhaustive options that give us equivalent objective choice situations regardless of whether we consider choosing or rejecting. Shafir (1993) used a hypothetical child custody case in an experiment that is particularly evocative.

Example 92. (Choosing versus rejecting) Shafir (1993) presented two groups of subjects with the following vignette:

(2) "Imagine that you serve on the jury of an only-child sole-custody case following a relatively messy divorce. The facts of the case are complicated by ambiguous economic, social, and emotional considerations, and you decide to base your decision entirely on the following few observations."

For half of the participants, this vignette was followed by the question, "To which parent would you award sole custody of the child?" For the other half, it was followed by the question, "Which parent would you deny sole custody of the child?" In both cases, the question was followed by the following information:

(3) Parent A: average income, average health, average working hours, reasonable rapport with the child, relatively social life.

(4) Parent B: above-average income, very close relationship with the child, extremely active social life, lots of work-related travel, minor health problems.

Given the "award" question, Parent B was the majority choice for being awarded custody, and given the "deny" question, Parent B was *also* the majority choice for being denied custody.

Shafir, Simonson, and Tversky (1993) suggest that what explains this pattern is that decision-makers "are likely to focus on reasons for choosing an option when deciding which to choose, and to focus on reasons for rejecting an option when deciding which to reject." Parent B offers both more positive and more negative reasons, so the shift in focus would predict that Parent B is chosen more often in both cases, relative to the "impoverished" Parent A option. Like Shafir, Simonson, and Tversky, we also suggest that what is responsible for this effect is how reasons interact with options. However, the view effectively seems to be that you apply different sets of reasons to the same options, depending how the choice is framed. This potentially obscures the fact that something irrational is going on here. If the reasons that we find motivating change depending on the choice context, we might as well say that we are rational but that our fundamental preferences change in different contexts. But preference change is not obviously irrational, since it is compatible with being a perfectly good utility maximizer for whatever our preferences happen to be. Instead, it would seem more attractive to be able to say that people's core priorities with regard to custody cases are stable and that there is something irrational in how their decision-making process applies priorities to resolving the custody question.

The pattern of asymmetry in judgment between "accept" and "reject" frames seems to generalize quite well. For example, Koralus and Alfano (2017) even found a similar effect in the case of moral judgment about obligatory versus impermissible acts. Koralus and Alfano presented two groups of participants with scenarios like the following.

> Governor Cooper is presented with a plea for pardon concerning an 18-year-old delinquent, Mary. She is about to be sent to prison for a crime that deserves a five-year prison term, but she was sentenced to a thirty-year prison term, and has exhausted all of her rights of appeal. Cooper can either grant a pardon, which means that Mary goes Scot free, or deny the pardon, which means that Mary will go to prison for thirty years. There are various ambiguous social and emotional considerations, but you want to decide which course of action is morally obligatory for Governor Cooper to follow, based on the information you have.

Participants were then presented with the following response prompts, either presented with the term "morally obligatory" or with the term "morally impermissible":

> Please select what it is [morally obligatory/morally impermissible] for Governor Cooper to do:
>
> (1) It is [morally obligatory/morally impermissible] for Cooper to grant the pardon:
>
> Making Mary's family happy
> Being involved in what is happening in his state being lenient
> Making the prison less crowded
>
> (2) It is [morally obligatory/morally impermissible] for Cooper to deny the pardon:
>
> Ensuring that crime does not go unpunished
> Respecting the judgment of the court
> Destroying a young woman's life
> Allowing the justice system to appear unduly harsh

Koralus and Alfano (2017) found 75.4% "morally obligatory" judgments in favor of granting the pardon when the question was about what is morally obligatory but only 56.3% "morally impermissible" judgments against denying the pardon when the question was about what is morally impermissible. Yet, we should think that if granting the pardon is obligatory, denying it is impermissible in this context. The 19.1% discrepancy was statistically significant. The discrepancy was not due to an asymmetry introduced by the difference between the terms "obligatory" and "impermissible" alone, as there was only a 3.5% discrepancy (not statistically significant) when the suggested reasons in favor of the options were omitted.

As in the child custody example, it appears that the availability of reasons in favor of an alternative answer to a decision question can interact with the framing of the decision question in such a way as to yield asymmetries in decision-making in the face of objectively equivalent choice situations.

Classical examples in which framing the same objective choice scenario in different ways yields significantly different judgments can also be found in a context that combines outcomes with uncertainty. Tversky and Kahneman (1981) provided two groups of participants with one each of the following questions (slightly abbreviated below).

Example 93. (The "Asian Disease Problem") The U.S. is preparing for the outbreak of an unusual Asian disease, which is expected to kill 600 people. There are two possible treatments (A) and (B) with the following results.

(Group 1) (A) 400 people die. (B) Nobody dies with 1/3 chance, 600 people die with 2/3 chance. Which treatment would you choose?

(Group 2) (A) 200 people saved. (B) All saved with 1/3 chance, nobody saved with 2/3 chance. Which treatment would you choose?

78% of participants in group 1 selected treatment (B), while only 28% of participants selected treatment (B) in group 2.

Objectively, the facts about treatment B are the same in both cases (the result of 400 people dying and the result of 200 people being saved is the same if 600 are in jeopardy overall), yet, the majority choice here depended on how the consequences were described.

Another example of an apparent breakdown of our decision-making capacity in a controlled setting comes from the well-known endowment effect (Kahneman et al. (1990)). This phenomenon is interesting in part because of what successive studies have shown about when this effect is observed and when it disappears. The endowment effect is also interesting because it has been shown many times with real transactions in a controlled setting, beyond hypothetical decisions in imagined scenarios. We will start by considering the basic effect. Intuitively, it should not matter to our preference over a set of alternative goods whether we happen to have been given one of those goods in a transparently random fashion, rather than another. However, it appears that being randomly "endowed" with a good tends to produce a reluctance to exchange it for a different good.

> **Example 94.** (Endowment effect) Kahneman, Knetsch, and Thaler (1990) gave various items to study participants in a group. Each participant was either given a mug, a pen, or $2. It was made transparent to the participants that the assignment of items was random. Participants were then given the opportunity to trade those items with each other. All participants had to complete a questionnaire about all possible trades they would or would not be willing to accept and were told that feasible trades based on the questionnaires would then be executed by the experimenters. Regardless of which item a participant was initially given, over 80% of them preferred to keep it rather than offer to trade it for a different one.

It seems that we would not intuitively want to be the sort of person who choses an option just because it was randomly assigned to us, even though all other options are still potentially available without additional effort. The setup and questionnaires for determining willingness to trade used in the experiment make it implausible to suppose that transaction costs were in the way of trades, since equal effort was required to respond to the questionnaire no matter what trade preferences participants wished to express. Neither would it be plausible to suppose that the assignment of goods somehow provided information that the good is somehow uniquely suited to the recipient, given that the assignment was explained to be random. Kahneman, Knetsch, and Thaler (1990; 2008) put forward the hypothesis that the endowment effect is due to loss aversion, the idea being that decision-makers attach more value to the loss of something they already have than to the value of what they might gain. On this sort of view, there is something intrinsically irrational in our fundamental priorities, from the perspective of expected utility maximization. Less technically, if what matters is what we end up with when all the trades are done, treating losses and gains asymmetrically does not make sense.

There are several reasons to find an account in terms of loss aversion at a fundamental level of value assignment dissatisfying. Arguably, the endowment effect provides a reason to think that we are prone to making decisions in a way that is not maximizing our control. However, if our fundamental priorities are intrinsically irrational, this threatens to make the question of how to make decisions with control meaningless. This conclusion might be welcomed by some, as it opens the door for paternalistic intervention without taking any meaningfully existing control away from the subjects of this paternalism. We suggest that we should be reluctant to give up the possibility of a self-conception that provides at least the possibility of control over our judgments with the fundamental priorities we have. If control failure in decision-making resides in the basic ingredients to our decisions, then we can at best try to become a different person or change our fundamental priorities. It is one thing to reject the idea that we are always already perfectly rational; it is another thing to adopt the view that we are irrational, so to speak, all the way down. If one were available, an explanation on which we often are irrational but on which we also can be systematically rational is preferable, and accords more with common sense (another alternative of a kind we dismissed as unattractive in Chapter 1 would involve postulating two systems, one with irrational priorities and one with rational ones).

Let us briefly return to the endowment effect. An empirical reason to doubt an account of the endowment effect in terms of fundamental loss-aversion is that we can find an endowment effect even when the decision-maker does not herself stand to "lose" the item offered up for trade. For example, in a similar experimental setup in which "brokers" are deciding on the trade on behalf of a "client," an endowment effect was found if those brokers themselves owned the same kind of item, but not otherwise (Morewedge et al. (2009); Morewedge and Giblin (2015)).

Another empirical reason to doubt an account of the endowment effect in terms of fundamental priorities is that experienced traders do not seem to exhibit the endowment effect with the goods they normally trade. List ((2003); (2004)) studied traders in a sports card market. A random group of participants were given roughly equivalent cards as compensation for completing a questionnaire. The participants were then offered the opportunity to switch cards. Those participants who were traders with below-average experience switched cards 6.7% of time and also requested a significantly larger amount of money to sell the card they were given than they were willing to offer for an equivalent card. In other words, inexperienced traders exhibited the endowment effect. By contrast, experienced traders switched cards 46.8% of the time, which is roughly what would be predicted if the traders experienced no endowment effect. It was also found that the endowment effect essentially disappeared in the novice traders as they gained more experience.

It appears that we are not irretrievably lost to the endowment effect. On a view on which the endowment effect is due to intrinsically irrational priorities, the decrease of the endowment effect through experience is puzzling. Suppose we accept that experience somehow changes our fundamental loss-aversion priority. If that is the case, we would expect that if we "unlearn" the endowment effect in one setting, we should just generally be rid of it, in virtue of having rid ourselves of the offending loss-aversion priority. As far as we can tell, the endowment effect is not generally unlearned in this way. One might reflect on the fact that Kahneman, Knetsch, and Thaler (1991) open their discussion with the anecdotal example of an economist colleague who exhibits an endowment effect, but presumably knows better *as an economist*. Moreover, many of the participants in experiments showing an endowment effect were business school students. It seems somewhat strained to imagine that all of these people simply lack trading experience in all settings, and that if they had had such experience in at least one setting, they would not have exhibited the endowment effect. Of course, there always remains the response that multiple decision-systems are at work, that experience causes us to switch systems, or perhaps even that experience adds new heuristic modules. As discussed in Chapter 1, such views create other fundamental problems. In this particular case, we might simply observe adding modules or systems to account for the additional data points does not seem explanatory.

Instead of postulating special-purpose heuristic modules or fundamentally irrational priorities to account for failures of decision-making, we could try to make sense of both successes and failures as flowing from the same fundamental principles of how we decide. What could those fundamental principles be? In this chapter, we argue for an erotetic theory of decision-making. The theory holds that decision-making involves raising a decision question, considering views of consequences of alternative choices, and then treating our priorities as answers to those questions. We will argue that the kinds of decisions that leave us only partially in control result from jumping to conclusions in attempting to answer our decision question with our views of consequences and our priorities, in much that same way in which we jump to conclusions in reasoning about what is the case. The kinds of illusory inferences in reasoning that we have seen over the previous five chapters are mirrored by what one might call the acceptance of "illusory reasons" in decision-making.

As in the case of inferential reasoning, we suggest that it is just as important to account for our capacity for rational change in view as it is to account for our systematic failures. As noted, we can overcome the problems of decision-making just described in many cases. On the erotetic theory, if we do not jump to conclusions as we attempt to answer our decisions questions, these problems are mitigated and we can in principle make choices in a way that systematically respect the constraints of classical rational choice theory.

In sum, we will argue that the data points concerning decision-making failure discussed above can be made sense of on an erotetic model of decision. As in the case of failures of reason in previous chapters, under a certain kind of erotetic equilibrium, these failures go away. As before, the erotetic theory offers a way to make sense of both systematic failure and systematic success.

The present approach might help bridge what seems like an unhelpful gulf between standard economic theory and behavioral economics. Just as we have suggested in previous chapters that we can understand classical approaches to reasoning and to linguistic meaning as studies of meaning and reasoning under erotetic equilibrium, we could come to understand certain aspects of classical economics as the study of decision-making under erotetic equilibrium. This conception has the advantage that we can fully take on board the data points discussed in this section that mainstream economics used to somewhat dismissively refer to as "anomalies," without in turn dismissing models that build on the assumption of classical rationality. Experienced economic agents plausibly *are* in erotetic equilibrium with respect to a significant range of decision questions, so it may well often be appropriate to model such agents in classical terms. If you will, the erotetic theory of decision could be interpreted as a project in cognitive microfoundations of economics.

6.1 Decision-Making as an Inquiry

On the classical mathematical approach to rational decision-making, a rational agent considers the set of actions available to them, where the alternative actions in this set are mutually exclusive and jointly exhaustive. The agent has a conditional probability distribution for each alternative action, tying down the subjective probabilities of all possible outcomes of the action. The agent further has a function that assigns a unique numerical value to each possible outcome, corresponding to its utility or desirability. The rational agent then decides what to do by picking the action (or set of actions) that maximize the product the probabilities of its possible outcomes and their associated utility values. In other words, the rational agent picks the action whose expected consequences, discounted by their probabilities, have the greatest utility or desirability.

As we saw, human decision-making does not generally follow the constraints of rational agency in this sense, so we will need a different approach as far as descriptive adequacy is concerned. At the same time, we will want to make sense of the intuition that there is something importantly right about the classical notion of rational decision-making, even for humans.

As a first step, we want to observe that implemented agents of any serious complexity cannot directly follow the structure of classically rational decision-making, because considering all available alternative actions (let alone their complete expected consequences) is too demanding. Moreover, the classical notion of rational decision-making, in asking the agent to choose among fully specified actions that jointly make up an exclusive and exhaustive set of all possible actions, has an "all at once" character that leaves no room for steps like committing to a plan and then continuing to deliberate about how to best carry out that plan. In other words, the classical theory of rational decision-making leaves out practical reasoning as humans experience it.

Harman (1986) and Bratman (Bratman et al. (1987)) both argue for a view on which practical reasoning centers on the revision of intentions. This idea, particularly as elaborated by Bratman, fundamentally conceives of practical reasoning as a dynamic process that takes us from a prior intention to a posterior intention. Crucially, this differs from the classical approach in that any prior intention is already more specific and restricted than an exhaustive set of all alternative possible actions available to the agent. Practical reasoning then either applies a kind of filter yielding a posterior intention that further narrows what is considered in the prior intention, or practical reasoning leads us to broaden our prior intention, allowing us to arrive at a posterior intention that amounts to a reconsideration of what the prior intention would have committed us to. For example, given the prior intention of either driving to the store or walking to the store, we might arrive at a narrower posterior intention of walking, in light of the fact that we place more value on saving gas than on comfort. Alternatively, given the same prior intention, practical reasoning might lead us to arrive at a broadened posterior intention of either driving or walking to the store, or not going to the store at all.

This view of practical reasoning, and the account of how decisions are made that it entails, is dynamic in the sense that we can think of practical reasoning as primarily generating potential changes to intentions, rather than generating intentions statically and wholesale from scratch. This makes the approach reminiscent of dynamic approaches to other aspects of cognition, for example, linguistic meaning (Kamp (1981); Heim (1983), among others) and belief (Gärdenfors (1988); Groenendijk and Stokhof (1991), among others). Bratman's (Bratman et al. (1987)) version of a dynamic account of practical reasoning, the belief-desire-intention model, has led to a number of influential formalizations used in AI (Georgeff and Rao (1991); Cohen and Levesque (1991); Wooldridge (2003)). Besides technical applications, the BDI framework seems a better fit than the classical view with how philosophers and ordinary people talk about the business of decision-making.

On a standard way of taking the BDI-model of dynamic practical reasoning, the agent wishes to reason her way to a posterior intention, given a prior intention, a set of beliefs, and a set of desires. Intentions are either primitive or they decompose into sets of alternative intentions. Beliefs yield conclusions about the expected consequences of adopting an alternative intention. Desires are valuations attached to states of the world that could be the outcomes of acting on an intention. The agent then adopts as her posterior intention the subset of the prior intention that maximizes expected desirability. Alternatively, the agent may adopt a broadened posterior intention that introduces new alternatives.

We will take on board the view that a central part of practical reasoning involves a dynamic mapping with three primary inputs. However, we have a slightly different take on the inputs and distinctly erotetic take on the nature of the mapping.

We will first consider the notion of intention. Both Harman (1986) and Bratman (Bratman et al. (1987)) spend a good amount of time trying to make sense of the ordinary notion of intending to do something. Harman seems to fear that "intention" is ambiguous, though he makes clear that he hopes that it is not ambiguous. Harman further suggests that our judgments about whether such-and-such act is done intentionally may be confounded by other considerations, for example whether the act is praise- or blameworthy. Knobe (2003) experimentally demonstrated that people are more likely to treat an action with harmful results as intentional than an action with beneficial results. In light of these complexities, we suspect that instead of building a technical notion of practical reasoning on an ordinary concept that is hard to pin down, it is worth trying to start with a slightly more technical notion and to set aside the connection between the technical notion and the ordinary notion as its own project (cf. the use of formal concepts of "meaning" as applied in the study of formal languages and the project of trying to elucidate ordinary notions of meaning in terms of the formal concept, as we do in natural language semantics).

Since we want to develop an erotetic, or question-based, account of practical reasoning, it is worth considering Castañeda's (1975) notion of intention.

> An intention is a possible first-person answer to the question "shall I do that?" or the question "what shall I do?", *asked* of oneself, provided the answer does constitute a solution to the problem posed by the question.

Setting aside talk of intentions, we will say that practical reasoning takes us from a prior decision question of what to do to a posterior decision question of what to do, and, that decision questions are sets of alternative *doings*, possibly singletons (N.B. it may be that Castañeda would accept our below characterization of doings as an account of what he calls "practitions," but we are not sure and thus use a fresh term). Something like the technical notion of doings is crucial to allow for something that is indeed practical reasoning, rather than just more theoretical reasoning about what one should do or what one believes one will do, and so on (cf. opening remarks on practical reasoning in Harman (1986)).

We will tie down the notion of doings as follows. Taking some inspiration from the Minimalist Program (Chomsky, 1995) view of the language faculty, we will hypothesize that the faculty of reason has interfaces with other systems, but that only some of the outputs of reason can be grasped by those systems. We will take it that *doings* are instructions that various performance systems can carry out. Ordinarily, a singleton set with a doing as its sole element can be carried out by some performance system, while a set with multiple alternative doings cannot. We can then say that practical reasoning normally has the aim of finding an answer to the question of what to do that performance systems can act on and that reflects our views of the value of various actions and their consequences. Some performance systems will be close to motor systems and directly initiate motor actions, while others may simply generate more reasoning problems (doings can be mental doings, in the sense intended). For example, to act on "acquire Snapple" or "go to the airport" most likely involves non-motor performance systems generating a new inquiry deliberating about appropriate plans to "acquire Snapple" or "go to the airport," etc.

The erotetic theory of reason is a content-based theory, as noted in Chapter 1. With our extension to practical reasoning, it will now be necessary to clarify that our notion of representational content is broader than it may have first appeared (and broader than would be necessary if our sole concern was inferential reasoning of the kind considered in the previous four chapters). On more restrictive notions, representational content is the kind of content characteristically associated with declarative sentences or formulas in the predicate calculus. We, however, are happy to include aspects of content that may not be reducible to the sort of content that is normally expressed by declarative sentences. On some usages, this would mean that our notion of content falls under the broader rubric of "intentional" content (see Klein (2007) for a discussion of intentional versus representational content in that sense). For example, we do not just have contents "that things are thus-and-so," but also questions. Now, for the fragments of reasoning we were concerned with in previous chapters, this distinction was not particularly important, since there is close correspondence between, e.g. disjunctive representational contents and questions. Now that we have moved on to reasoning toward action, this distinction becomes more important again. Doings, as we conceive them, are instructions. Thus, we are committed to instructions being in the realm of contents, as are the other ingredients to questions in the erotetic theory. It should not be too difficult to home in on an intuitive sense of instructions as in the realm of contents, rather than in the realm of sentences or expressions. You might consider that "Halt," "Stop," and "Alto" are different expressions for the same instruction. As noted before, we include as many types of objects in our ontology as we feel yields a theoretical and descriptive benefit with little heed for reductivist inclinations (see remarks on arbitrary objects in Chapters 1 and 4 for comparison), so instructions and, more specifically, doings, will be welcome while they earn their keep. We do not need to take a strong stance here on whether instructions must remain their own type of semantic object or whether they are reducible to something else. However, there may be independent reasons to think we need something like doings to make sense of perceptual phenomenology, which we will return to in a later section.

Formally, we will regiment *do* atoms as follows.

Definition 6.1 (Do-atoms $\mathcal{A}^{do}$). We postulate a primitive object *do* and a subset $\mathcal{A}^{do} \subseteq \mathcal{A}$ such that, $\mathcal{A}^{do} = \{do(s), \overline{do}(s) : s \subseteq \mathcal{A}\backslash\mathcal{A}^{do} \text{ finite}\}$. We stipulate that substitution operations defined in Chapter 5 apply arbitrarily deeply inside do-atoms and that issue structures apply regardless of whether states are embedded under *do*. We write $do(A) = do(\{A\})$ when $A \in \mathcal{A}\backslash\mathcal{A}^{do}$ is a single atom.

For example, we might have a decision question $\{do(s), \overline{do}(s)\}$ to stand up or not to stand up, with $do(s)$ being a *do* atom for standing up, and s an atom for standing.

We will take it that doings are as multifaceted as their central goals and that any state can be a goal. If X is the goal state of an action we admit $do(X)$ as a doing. We need a notion of negated do-atoms to allow us to inquire on alternative doings. The negations of *do* atoms then correspond to instructions *not* to carry out the underlying intention.

We will also need our notion of primitive absurdity to cover do-atoms. We will say that $\{do(x), \overline{do(x)}\}$ is primitively absurd. Note that this not mean that $\{do(x), \overline{do(x)}\}$ is a classical contradiction, since $do(x)$ does not stand for a classical proposition. Our notion of absurdity translates into classical contradiction if we are only concerned with views like those in Chapter 4, but this is no longer the case once we include doings. As in Chapter 4, we will take it that a considerable amount of our knowledge of various concepts involves knowledge of further primitive absurdities. So, just as we said in Chapter 4 that, for example, it is primitively absurd to say that New York is south of Toronto and that New York is north of Toronto, we will say that to both go north and go south (at the same time) is primitively absurd, and so on for various relevant doings that may appear in examples we want to model. Since we are not primarily concerned here with modeling inferential relations between doings, we will generally help ourselves to stipulating primitive absurdities rather liberally, without thereby wishing to commit ourselves to our usage reflecting a settled theory of what inferences in particular count as conceptual, in the sense of Chapter 4, and what inferences do not.

While we need negation and absurdity, we will not take a stand here on inferential connections between e.g. x and $do(x)$ in this chapter, since this will not be necessary for the applications we want to consider. To fully specify the relationship between doings and what is being done, we would again have to add considerable expressive power, including tense, to be able to talk about actions having effects *after* they take place (for example, see the system in Wooldridge (2003)). Adding this kind of expressive power in the same spirit that has guided us so far, seeking descriptive adequacy rather than just formal completeness, we would have to take a closer look at the psychology of tense and causal reasoning than we have the space to do here. Instead, we will only sketch partial definitions as far as necessary to show what is distinctive of an erotetic theory of decision.

Using our notion of do-atoms, we will define pure decision questions as follows.

Definition 6.2 (Pure decision questions $\mathbb{DQ}$).
   Let $\mathbb{DQ} = \{G \in \mathbb{V} : \mathcal{A}(G) \subseteq \mathcal{A}^{do}\}$

We can then further distinguish two kinds of decision questions: open decision questions and closed decision questions. An open decision question includes 0 as one of its alternatives. A closed decision question, by contrast, does not. We can use our reasoning operations to convert a closed decision question to an open one. For example, if our decision question already has more than one alternative (which we generally assume, otherwise we take it that the agent would already be acting), we can simply reduce one of these alternatives to 0 via uses of Factor (otherwise more steps are required). It may make sense to think of our cognitive economy as including views of the form $\{do(x), 0\}$, for all things we can primitively do.

We can then provide an erotetic account of the process of broadening a prior decision question in practical reasoning. If we take an open prior decision question and wish to arrive at a broadened posterior decision question, we can do that by simply inquiring on whatever additional doing we wish to consider. For example, suppose we have the decision question $\{do(\text{go north}), 0\}$. By inquiring on $\{do(\text{go south}), 0\}$, keeping in mind from the discussion further above that we treat the combination of $do(\text{go south})$ and $do(\text{go north})$ as absurd, we get $\{do(\text{go north}), do(\text{go south}), 0\}$. We could treat all doings as mutually exclusive of each other, so that having more than one do-atom in a state is automatically absurd, to make these expansions as simple as possible. We will return to this issue once we consider the relationship between erotetic decision-making and classical rational choice.

6.2 Direct Consequence Views

Now, if deciding involves settling a question, we will require something that can serve as an answer. Let us briefly return to ingredient list for a BDI model. The central ingredient was intentions, and we have replaced that with decision questions. What then of beliefs and desires?

We will start with our counterpart to belief. In the context of formal models of decision-making, belief is often understood in terms of fully specified possible outcomes of actions together with their respective probabilities. Of course, in practice, it is unrealistic to expect an agent of even moderate complexity to try to reason out all possible completely specified outcomes of an action, which is at the heart of the so-called frame problem (McCarthy and Hayes (1981); Dennett (1984)). Moreover, as we saw in previous chapters, what we are inclined to infer from our background knowledge varies with context in a way that makes it non-straightforward to say what we should count as our beliefs, from among those potential commitments we would need further inferences to obtain. If we take the view of inference from the previous chapters seriously, belief may itself be best understood as depending on a certain kind of inquiry (for independent arguments for the view that belief is question-sensitive, see Yalcin (2018)).

The primary contribution a notion of belief is supposed to make in practical reasoning is to supply us with a view of the consequences of our actions. We will set aside the issue of belief and directly focus on views of consequences. We will take the following approach. For doings that we are capable of evaluating in terms of their consequences, we have a view of what the *direct consequences* of these doings are. We allow that what views of direct consequences we have depends on the sort of person we are and the sort of experience we have had. However, we would expect there to be quite a bit of commonality in what people take to be direct consequences of ordinary actions. For example, we would take illumination to be a direct consequence of switching on the lights, and possibly also the flowing of electrical current through a circuit connected to the lights. By contrast, we would not normally take a marginal increase of the temperature in the room to be a direct consequence in this sense. Somewhere in this area, it would seem that views of direct consequences come apart from a more comprehensive notion of belief, since it does seem appropriate to say that we believe that turning on the lights increases the temperature.

We suspect that the direct consequence views we have on board dynamically change as we draw inferences. For example, if we have just inferred or been advised that electrical current flowing through light bulbs will heat up a room, we might now well treat heating up the room as a direct consequence of turning on the lights. The main idea behind direct consequence views is that for each doing we can seriously entertain, we have a finite and usually relatively small set of views of the direct consequences of those doings (usually far less than the set of things we would claim to believe are consequences, if asked about them), while a full view of the consequences of those doings would require further inquiry that we may not engage in without a further reason to do so.

We will regiment direct consequence views as follows. Direct consequence views have doings in their supposition, and their main body of alternatives at most contains doings that also occur in the supposition.

Definition 6.3 (Direct consequence views).
$\Delta_{gSJ}^{\{\psi\}}$ is in CV iff $\Delta_{gSJ}^{\{0\}} \in \mathbb{V}$, $\psi \subseteq \mathcal{A}^{do}$ and $\mathcal{A}(\Delta) \cap \mathcal{A}^{do} \subseteq \psi$.

This definition leaves open what kind of EAP weight is attached to alternative consequences (or, indeed, whether there is any non-empty weight at all). In practice, we will often want to model consequence views that assign EAP weights that can be interpreted as probabilities, along the lines discussed in Chapter 5. For example, we might have a direct consequence view with the following structure for tossing a fair coin. $\{(0.5).Heads,(0.5).Tails\}^{\{do(toss\ coin)\}}$. In addition to these kinds of, if you will, "classical" consequence views, we could also explore consequence views that follow the discussion of disequilibrium conditionals in Chapter 3 and the discussion of generics in Chapter 4. For example, we might have $\{match\ lights, 0\}^{\{do(strike\ match)\}}$.

A total picture as to what is at stake in our decision would mean having taken on board all direct consequence views concerning alternative doings under consideration, as well as any further consequences of those consequences determined by the views in our cognitive economy. In practice, we suspect that default decision-making only goes as far as considering direct consequences (or even less—a point we will return to in a later section), unless experience or instruction teaches us to consider additional consequences in the type of case at hand.

6.3 Priorities

Having considered consequences, the remaining missing ingredient for practical reasoning relative to the BDI framework would be desires. Desires in this context are normally modeled as assignments of value to (fully specified) outcomes. For example, I could assign high value to the possible outcome of having a chocolate brownie and ice cream for dessert. Against the background of the way we have been thinking about reason throughout this book, treating this notion of desire as primitive leaves, if you will, something to be desired. For example, treating desires for outcomes as primitive does not give us an obvious way of saying in virtue of what outcomes are desirable.

A related difficulty with treating desire as the relevant input to help answer our decision questions is that desires as we attribute them to people in ordinary talk seem about as dynamic as practical reasoning itself. From someone saying that he wants to die peacefully you notoriously cannot infer that if such a person is given the means to die peacefully, he will take them. It seems that you only get a reasonable prediction to behavior here if you can take it that the person is entertaining a decision question in which you are deciding between dying peacefully and dying non-peacefully. On a reading on which "he wants to die peacefully" sounds likely to be true of a normal person, you are likely really saying "of ways to die, he prefers the peaceful ways" or "*How* does he want to die? Peacefully!" With Phillips-Brown (Phillips-Brown, 2018), we suggest that the notion of desire we often use in ordinary discourse is really a question-relative attitude; it is the outcome of an inquiry. It would appear that this kind of inquiry is closer to an inquiry about what to do than it is to an independent ingredient to an inquiry about what to do.

Finally, if desires for particular outcomes are treated as primitive, we have no reason to regard "punctate" desires as the exception rather than the norm. By punctate desires we mean desires that do not seem accompanied by similar desires for similar objects. It would appear that many everyday desires are systematic rather than punctate. For example, many people like chocolate cake and chocolate ice cream, because, for them, chocolate flavor counts strongly in favor of any dessert. If you show me someone who chooses chocolate cake outcomes when a relevant chance presents itself, and chocolate ice cream outcomes when a relevant chance presents itself, I will normally be fairly confident that they will also choose other chocolate desserts when a relevant chance presents itself. For similar reasons, Dietrich and List (2013) propose a "reasons-based" formal account of rational choice.

Dietrich and List's particular approach involves orderings over bundles of features that some alternative choice might have, leaving maximal flexibility in how various bundles of features are ordered. Rather than take a detour through an order-theoretic account, we will do something in a similar spirit using weighted views. Among other things, this approach will have the benefit of making the connection to classical utility maximization relatively obvious; a connection we will turn to in a later section.

In essence, we will take priority views to be structured in such a way that updating with them allows us to change the EAP weights of those alternatives to which the priorities apply. Since an erotetic decision-maker is supposed to be able to answer the question of what to do even without having reasoned her way through to maximally specific consequences of her actions, we need a notion of priorities that applies to separable features a situation might have. Priorities in our sense structurally correspond to what are often called pro tanto reasons, as the agent sees them, each of which has separable positive or negative bearing on the subjective value of a state. A pro tanto reason here is a reason that can independently speak for (or against) things in virtue of some feature, without guaranteeing that there is no other countervailing reason that is stronger. Here, the independence of a pro tanto reason R_1 lies in the fact that the presence of a stronger countervailing reason R_2 (again, as the agent sees their reasons) does not mean that R_1 is no pro tanto reason at all; it just means that if R_1 and R_2 are all the reasons we have, we do not have most reason in favor of whatever R_1 would recommend. The reader may or may not find the analogy with reasons helpful. For our purposes, we will speak of priorities instead of reasons, to avoid various muddles about what counts as a reason that are orthogonal to our project.

Let us consider an example on how a set of priorities may contribute to a choice ranking. For example, suppose I rank sweet candy over savory candy, and sour candy over sweet candy, but rank candy that is both sweet and sour below savory candy. One way a set of priorities in our sense might lead to this ranking is by contributing low positive weight to states involving savory things, higher weight to states involving sweet things, still higher weight to states involving sour things, but yet contributing negative weight to states involving things that are both sweet and sour. If the weight contributed by the latter priority has sufficiently high negative value, then even in the face of the combined positive contributions of our (independent) priorities for sweet things and for sour things, the sweet and sour candy option may end up getting a combined weight below that of the savory option.

We will now have to consider how to regiment the foregoing. Ultimately, we want to end up with views that have equilibrium answerhood potential (EAP) in favor of actions with features we prioritize. We already used EAP weights to bring uncertainty into the system, which we discussed at length in Chapter 5. We now need to do the same for the contribution of our priority views.

We could rely on the same types of views we used in Chapter 5 to capture priority views, and simply add an index of some sort to mark the distinction between a view that a state is likely to a degree from a view that a state is prioritized to a degree. However, this will not quite suffice. The weights of views in Chapter 5 combine multiplicatively when we update. While this makes sense for views about uncertainty, it does not quite make sense for priority views. If we have a state that satisfies several priorities, we do not want be limited to the total priority weight in favor of the state having to be the product of the priorities that state satisfies. To make this more concrete, observe that one does not measure wealth by multiplying the nominal values of banknotes kept under the mattress. The most plausible way in which the weights of priorities combine is additive.

To bring this into the system, we will extend our definition of weights from Chapter 5 to accommodate both a multiplicative and an additive component.

270 DECISION AND PRACTICAL REASONING

Definition 6.4 (Weights). The set $\mathbb{W}_2$ of *double-weights* consists of all pairs $\langle m, m' \rangle$ where m, m' are finite multisets of terms. We write $m^\times.m'^+$ for the pair $\langle m, m' \rangle$, omitting mention of the empty multiset. We write expressions such at $t^\times.u^+$ for $\langle \!\langle t \rangle\!\rangle, \langle\!\langle u \rangle\!\rangle \rangle$ and so on when unambiguous.

By taking an extended set of states now to mean Γ_f with $\Gamma \subseteq S$ finite and $f : \Gamma \to \mathbb{W}_2$ any function, we can interpret the entire extended erotetic system as applying to this new notion of extended view, with only the following adjustments required. First we need a version of Equilibrium Answer Potential that accounts for both parts of the weights in $\mathbb{W}_2$.

Definition 6.5 ($\mathbb{E}$ Answer potential).

$$\Delta_g[\Gamma]^{EP} = \sigma\Big(\langle\!\langle \sigma(g_\times(\delta)) : \delta \in Y \rangle\!\rangle\Big) \overline{\times} \sigma\Big(\langle\!\langle \sigma(g_+(\delta)) \rangle\!\rangle\Big)$$

where $Y = \{\delta \in \Delta \mid \exists y \in \Gamma . y \subseteq \delta\}$ and $g(\delta) = \langle g_\times(\delta), g_+(\delta) \rangle$.

The Sum of views is defined in terms of a sum of weights. Thus we simply need to define the sum of double-weights, given by

$$v^\times.a^+ + w^\times.b^+ = (v+w)^\times.(a+b)^+$$

where the $v + w$ and $a + b$ are the usual sums of multisets.

The Product of views is defined in terms of a product of weights. This is perhaps the most substantial divergence from the Chapter 5 system. We define the product of double-weights by

$$v^\times.a^+ \times w^\times.b^+ = (v \times w)^\times.(a+b)^+$$

where $a + b$ is the usual sum of multisets, and $v \times w$ is what was called the product of weights in Chapter 5, defined by

$$v \times \langle\!\langle \rangle\!\rangle = v$$
$$\langle\!\langle \rangle\!\rangle \times w = w$$

in the case that either v or w is empty and, when $v = \langle\!\langle s_1, \ldots, s_m \rangle\!\rangle$ and $w = \langle\!\langle t_1, \ldots t_n \rangle\!\rangle$ with $m, n \geq 1$,

$$v \times w = \langle\!\langle (s_i \overline{\times} t_j) : 1 \leq i \leq m, 1 \leq j \leq n \rangle\!\rangle.$$

Finally, it is necessary to adjust the definitions of Query and Which. These make reference to the empty weight $\langle\!\langle\rangle\!\rangle$ in the test conditions "$g(\delta) \neq \langle\!\langle\rangle\!\rangle$" and "$g(\delta) = \langle\!\langle\rangle\!\rangle$". One simply reads $\langle\!\langle\rangle\!\rangle^{\times}.\langle\!\langle\rangle\!\rangle^{+} = \langle\langle\!\langle\rangle\!\rangle, \langle\!\langle\rangle\!\rangle\rangle$ in place of $\langle\!\langle\rangle\!\rangle$.

Note that the Chapter 5 system "embeds" in the new system by the following mapping on weighted states $w.y \mapsto w^{\times}.\langle\!\langle\rangle\!\rangle^{+}.y$ and there is the evident "projection" in the other direction. It is easy to formulate and check similar conservativity principles as described in §B.6, so we omit details.

We remark that other ways of extending the Chapter 5 system to double-weights would be possible. For example, we could consider versions of the definitions of Query and Which one should refine the test "$g(\delta) = \langle\!\langle\rangle\!\rangle$" from two possibilities into the four possibilities given by the cases where either, both, or neither of the two components of $g(\delta)$ are empty. As this makes no difference in the examples of this chapter we stick with the formally simpler option just given.

Definition 6.6 (Priority views *PR*). Let $\mathbb{V}_{PR}$ be a distinguished subset of $\mathbb{V}$, whose elements have the form $\{w.0\}_{RI}^{\{y\}}$. When speaking of views, we will generally assume that we are concerned with views that are not elements of $\mathbb{V}_{PR}$, unless we specifically say that they are.

For our purposes, we will normally take priorities to have weights with an empty multiplicative component and a non-empty additive component (though the system as defined does not rule out priorities with multiplicative weights). For example, we might have the following priorities, concerning vanilla flavor (v), chocolate flavor (c), and dairy content (d).

$$\{1^{+}.0\}^{\{v\}} \qquad \{2^{+}.0\}^{\{c\}} \qquad \{(-1)^{+}.0\}^{\{d\}}$$

If we now take a view involving a state in which we have vanilla and chocolate flavor paired with dairy content and update this view with the above priority views, we get: $\{\langle\!\langle 1, 2, -1\rangle\!\rangle^{+}.vcd\}$. Helping ourselves to automatic arithmetic, as in Chapter 5, this gives us $\{2^{+}.vcd\}$.

With all the necessary ingredients in place, we can now define a default decision procedure for erotetic agents, which plays a similar role to that of "filtering" in a BDI-framework. We can then consider how the erotetic theory extended to decision-making can make sense of the phenomena discussed in the opening section of this chapter.

6.4 Default Decision

The first step for an erotetic decision-maker is to take on board a decision question. Loosely speaking, the default decision procedure could be looked at as first asking, "what are the direct consequences of the alternatives?", "what priority value do those consequences have?", and, finally, "which alternative doings have the most answer weight in favor of it them?"

Definition 6.7 (Default decision).
For a decision question dq, a set of direct consequence views CV, and set of priority views PR, the default decision is defined as,

$$dq\big[dq[CV]^{\circlearrowleft}[\emptyset]^{F}[PR]^{\circlearrowleft}\big]^{A}$$

A couple of technical remarks about this definition are in order. The first remark is that we can unambiguously update a decision question with a *set* of direct consequence views, since the order of update does not matter for the final result. The reason the order does not matter is that the effect of updating with one consequence view does not affect which other direct consequence views apply or what effect is obtained by updating with further direct consequence views. We can then take the result of such an update and unambiguously update it with the set of our priorities, since the order in which the priority views are taken will similarly not matter. The second technical remark concerns a slight idealization that is required. In order for derivations involving arbitrary objects to go through, we will generally need an appropriate issue structure guiding instantiation (see Chapters 4 and 5). In the case of decision-making, we can no longer rely on the information structure of natural language premises to supply issue structures, so the relevant role will need to be played by attention instead. Detailed integration with the material in this chapter will need to be left for future work, but the foundation for a relevant account of attention was proposed in Koralus (2014b) and (2014a). To keep things manageable, we will assume for the purposes of this chapter that we always have an appropriate issue structure present and suppress the relevant notation in the example derivations.

Having given an erotetic account of decision-making through practical reasoning, we turn to exploring how this account can help make sense of the kinds of failures of decision-making we discussed in the opening section of the chapter. We turn to the question concerning the relationship between the erotetic account and classically rational decision-making in a subsequent section. In a later section, we will also consider aspects of rapid decision-making that do not take a route through a consideration of consequences.

For now, the cases of decision-making failure we will turn to involve a genuine attempt to consider consequences of choices but where different conditions produced differences in decisions even though objectively the same choice scenario was presented, in terms of available actions and possible outcomes. We will ultimately trace back these failures to different forms of erotetic disequilibrium.

We begin with the case of opportunity cost neglect.

(Example 90 derivation)

We have to take a stand on the consequence views and priorities we attribute to the average participant in the experiment. We will model this so that we have the same roughly plausible consequence views and priorities giving us a preference for buying in condition A and relative indifference in condition B, which roughly corresponds to the majority responses in Frederick et al.'s study (2009). As noted, the explanatory value comes from the fact that we end up with different decisions across conditions, varying the decision question while keeping consequence views and priorities constant.

We regiment the decisions questions in the two conditions as follows.

To buy video or not to buy video $\quad\quad A = \{do(Bv), \overline{do}(Bv)\}$.
"To buy video or to buy something (else)."
$B = \{do(Bv), do(Ba)\}$.

We then postulate a very simple consequence view and a simple priority. We will assume a direct consequence view that takes "fun" (F) to be a certain consequence of buying something (B). $C = \{F\}^{\{do(Bx)\}}$. Next, we assume that we have a priority in favor of fun. $P = \{1^+.0\}^{\{F\}}$.

We then have the following two derivations according to the default decision procedure: For condition A, we have,

$$\{do(Bv), \overline{do}(Bv)\}[\{do(Bv), \overline{do}(Bv)\}[\{F\}^{\{do(Bx)\}}]\circlearrowleft[\{1^+.0\}^{\{F\}}]\circlearrowleft]^A =$$
$$= \{do(Bv), \overline{do}(Bv)\}[\{1^+.do(Bv)F, \overline{do}(Bv)\}]^A = \{do(Bv)\}$$

For condition B, we have,

$\{do(Bv), do(Ba)\}[\{do(Bv), do(Ba)\}[\{F\}^{\{do(Bx)\}}]^{\cup}[\{1^+.0\}^{\{F\}}]^{\cup}]^A =$
$\{do(Bv), do(Ba)\}[\{1^+.do(Bv)F, 1^+.do(Ba)F\}]^A =$
$= \{do(Bv), do(Ba)\}$

Thus, the present analysis gives us the result we aimed for, namely a decision in favor of purchasing the video in the first condition, and indifference in the second condition. As noted in the opening section of this chapter, there is a clear sense that opportunity cost neglect is rightly considered a kind of fallacy. Intuitively, we are not entirely as we ought to be as decision-makers if we only purchase something because we have not considered the possibility of alternative purchases.

We will now consider how to capture the intuition that the result for condition B is a better reflection of the agent. In Chapter 2, it was proposed that we are not entirely as we ought be if our judgments are not in equilibrium with respect to an appropriate set of questions. In the case at hand, we can plausibly say that we ought be in equilibrium with respect to the question about possibly purchasing something else. Assuming that in the problem at hand $do(Bv)$ and $do(Ba)$ are mutually incompatible so that a state including both is absurd, we can observe that while the decision for B is in equilibrium with respect to this question, the decision in A is not. For A, we get $\{do(Bv), \overline{do(Bv)}\}[\{do(Ba), 0\}]^I = \{do(Bv), \overline{do(Bv)}, do(Ba)\overline{do(Bv)}\}$. Applying the same default decision procedure as before, we no longer get a judgment in favor of purchasing the video. In the case of B, we have $\{do(Bv), do(Ba)\}[\{do(Ba), 0\}]^I = \{do(Bv), do(Ba)\}$ so the judgment is already in equilibrium with respect to this question. We, of course, get the same judgment if we bring our decision question into full erotetic equilibrium with respect to its own atoms (recall discussion in Chapter 2).

We next turn to the case of different decisions emerging from "choosing" versus "rejecting" decision frames. We will focus on Shafir's custody example.

(**Example 92 derivation**)

For simplicity, we regiment the decision questions as follows, with A and D for "award sole custody of the child" and "deny sole custody of the child" and j and m for Parent A and Parent B, respectively. The initial decision questions for the two conditions then are, $G_1 = \{do(Aj), do(Am)\}$ and $G_2 = \{do(Dj), do(Dm)\}$.

The primary consequences of the actions are then as follows (with C for sole custody): $C_1 = \{Cx\}^{\{do(Ax)\}}$, $C_2 = \{\bar{C}x\}^{\{do(Dx)\}}$. We also have information about facts concerning the parents, which hold independently of any particular action. For simplicity, we can treat that information as a pseudo-consequence view that is not dependent on any particular action. Simplifying to the descriptions to medium/high rapport (*MR/HR*) and medium/low time (*MT/LT*), we can capture the flavor of this information about the parents as, $C_3 = \{MRjMTjHRmLTm\}^{\{0\}}$.

There are various ways in which we could model the priorities people are likely to have with regard to the properties under consideration. We will take an approach that assigns degrees of support to combinations of having custody with levels of rapport and available time: $P_1 = \{1^+.0\}^{\{CxMRx\}}$, $P_2 = \{3^+.0\}^{\{CxHRx\}}$, $P_3 = \{1^+.0\}^{\{CxMTx\}}$. Similarly, we might think that (merely) medium rapport and low time would partially support not having custody, so that we have, $P_4 = \{1^+.0\}^{\{\bar{C}xMTx\}}$, $P_5 = \{2^+.0\}^{\{\bar{C}xLTx\}}$.

For the "award" condition, we then have:

$$\{do(Aj), do(Am)\}[\{do(Aj), do(Am)\}[\{C_1, C_2, C_3\}]^{\circlearrowleft}[\{P_1, P_2, P_3, P_4, P_5\}]^{\circlearrowleft}]^A$$
$$= \{do(Am)\}.$$

For the "deny" condition,

$$\{do(Dj), do(Dm)\}[\{do(Dj), do(Dm)\}[\{C_1, C_2, C_3\}]^{\circlearrowleft}[\{P_1, P_2, P_3, P_4, P_5\}]^{\circlearrowleft}]^A$$
$$= \{do(Dm)\}.$$

We can then diagnose the failure of decision-making in this case as follows: the decision is not in equilibrium with respect to the full questions concerning awarding and denying custody. To explore this formally, we will again have to make a working assumption about what combinations of doings are primitively absurd. We will take it that both awarding and denying sole custody to the same person is absurd, as is awarding sole custody to one without denying it to the other. With these absurdities in mind, we could get to equilibrium with respect to questions about whether to award or deny custody as follows. Let us assume our starting point is from the "Award" condition. First we inquire on the possibility of available actions not yet under consideration, just as in the previous example, in this case $\{do(Dj), 0\}$ and $\{do(Dm), 0\}$. Then, we could further bring the result into erotetic equilibrium with respect to its own atoms. This then gives us $\{do(Aj)\overline{do}(Dj)do(Dm)\overline{do}(Am), do(Am)do(Dj)\overline{do}(Dm)\}do(Aj)$. Whatever our priorities favor, a decision based on asking both whom to award and whom to deny sole custody seems like a more respectable one.

We next consider Tversky and Kahneman's disease problem.

(Example 93 derivation)

In this case, the decision question stays the same in both conditions, but the consequence views provided change between conditions. However, given the background information provided, in both conditions, the total consequences we could reason our way to are the same. This should lead us to suspect that the problem here is a lack of erotetic equilibrium not in the decision question itself but in the consequence views. As with the previous examples, we will first show how we get the discrepancy in judgment between the two conditions (choice of treatment B in condition 1 and a choice of treatment A in condition 2) and then turn to making sense of what could rationally eliminate the discrepancy.

For both conditions, we have $D = \{do(A), do(B)\}$. We need to attribute plausible priorities regarding death and survival to the participants. There are any number of ways we might model such priorities. All we need to show is that there are some reasonably plausible ways we might model the relevant priorities so that we get the observed choice patterns. We might prioritize a group of people dying in inverse proportion to their number, with zero people dying being best and corresponding to the unit, and such that the difference between two groups of people dying becomes progressively less as the size of those groups increases.

$$P_1 = \{\langle\!\langle (1+\log(x+1))^{-1}\rangle\!\rangle^+.0\}^{\{Dx\}}$$

Similarly, we might prioritize a group of people being saved in proportion to their number, where the difference in priority between two groups of people being saved becomes progressively less as the number of people saved goes up, with zero saves having the least weight.

$$P_2 = \{\langle\!\langle 1+\log(x+1)\rangle\!\rangle^+.0\}^{\{Sx\}}$$

We obtain consequence views roughly following the analysis of conditional probability statements from Chapter 5. We then have the following for condition 1.

$$C_1 = \{D400\}^{\{do(A)\}}$$
$$C_2 = \{\langle\!\langle 0.33\rangle\!\rangle^\times.D0, \bar{D}0\}^{\{do(B)\}}$$
$$C_3 = \{\langle\!\langle 0.67\rangle\!\rangle^\times.D600, \bar{D}600\}^{\{do(B)\}}$$

This then gives us

$$\{do(A), do(B)\}[[\{do(A), do(B)\}[\{C_1, C_2, C_3\}]^\circlearrowleft[\emptyset]^F[P_1, P_2]^\circlearrowleft]^A.$$

By inspection, we can tell that updating with P_2 will have no effect, we can set that aside. Taking the derivation in parts, we first evaluate:

$$\{do(A), do(B)\}[\{C_1, C_2, C_3\}]^\circlearrowleft[\emptyset]^F$$
$$= \{do(A)D400, \langle\!\langle 0.33, 0.67\rangle\!\rangle^\times.D0do(B)D600, \langle\!\langle 0.67\rangle\!\rangle^\times.D600\bar{D}0do(B),$$
$$\langle\!\langle 0.33\rangle\!\rangle^\times.D0do(B)\bar{D}600, do(B)\bar{D}0\bar{D}600\}[\emptyset]^F$$

We assume that $\{D0D600\}$ is a primitive absurdity ("zero people die and 600 die" sounds absurd enough). Plugging the result back into the main derivation, we get

$$\{do(A), do(B)\}[\{do(A)D400, \langle\!\langle 0.67\rangle\!\rangle^\times.D600\bar{D}0do(B),$$
$$\langle\!\langle 0.33\rangle\!\rangle^\times.D0do(B)\bar{D}600, do(B)\bar{D}0\bar{D}600\}$$
$$[\{\langle\!\langle (1 + \log(x+1))^{-1}\rangle\!\rangle^+.0\}^{\{Dx\}}]^\circlearrowleft]^A.$$

Assuming, as before, that we can take arithmetic for granted, we get

$$\{do(A), do(B)\}[$$
$$\{\langle\!\langle 0.28\rangle\!\rangle^+.do(A)D400, \langle\!\langle 0.67\rangle\!\rangle^\times.\langle\!\langle 0.26\rangle\!\rangle^+.D600\bar{D}0do(B),$$
$$\langle\!\langle 0.33\rangle\!\rangle^\times.\langle\!\langle 1\rangle\!\rangle^+.D0do(B)\bar{D}600, do(B)\bar{D}0\bar{D}600\}]^A.$$

Here, the equilibrium answerhood potential in favor of $do(A)$ is 0.28, compared to $(0.67 \times 0.26) + (1 \times 0.33) = 0.5$ for $do(B)$, thus our result is $\{do(B)\}$.

Moving on, for Condition 2, we have

$$C_4 = \{S200\}^{\{do(A)\}}$$
$$C_5 = \{\langle\!\langle 0.33\rangle\!\rangle^\times.S600, \bar{S}600\}^{\{do(B)\}}$$
$$C_6 = \{\langle\!\langle 0.67\rangle\!\rangle^\times.S0, \bar{S}0\}^{\{do(B)\}}$$

We then get,

$$\{do(A), do(B)\}[[\{do(A), do(B)\}[\{C_4, C_5, C_6\}]^\circlearrowleft[\emptyset]^F[P_1, P_2]^\circlearrowleft]^A$$

By inspection, we can tell that this time P_1 will not make a difference so we set it aside. We first evaluate

$$\{do(A), do(B)\}[\{do(A), do(B)\}[\{C_4, C_5, C_6\}]^{\circlearrowright}[\varnothing]^F$$
$$= \{do(A)S200, \langle\!\langle 0.33, 0.67\rangle\!\rangle^{\times}.S600S0do(B), \langle\!\langle 0.67\rangle\!\rangle^{\times}.\bar{S}600S0do(B),$$
$$\langle\!\langle 0.33\rangle\!\rangle^{\times}.S600\bar{S}0do(B), \bar{S}600\bar{S}0do(B)\}[\varnothing]^F$$

We assume $\{S600S0\}$ is a primitive absurdity ("save 600 and save 0"), thus we get

$$= \{do(A)S200, \ \langle\!\langle 0.67\rangle\!\rangle^{\times}.\bar{S}600S0do(B), \ \langle\!\langle 0.33\rangle\!\rangle^{\times}.S600\bar{S}0do(B), \ \bar{S}600\bar{S}0do(B)\}.$$

Plugging the result into the main derivation, we get

$$\{do(A), do(B)\}[\{do(A)S200, \ \langle\!\langle 0.67\rangle\!\rangle^{\times}.\bar{S}600S0do(B),$$
$$\langle\!\langle 0.33\rangle\!\rangle^{\times}.S600\bar{S}0do(B), \ \bar{S}600\bar{S}0do(B)\}[\{\langle\!\langle 1+\log(x+1)\rangle\!\rangle^{+}.0\}^{\{Sx\}}]^{\circlearrowright}]^A$$
$$= \{do(A), do(B)\}[\{\langle\!\langle 3.3\rangle\!\rangle^{+}.do(A)S200, \ \langle\!\langle 0.67\rangle\!\rangle^{\times}.\langle\!\langle 1\rangle\!\rangle^{+}.\bar{S}600S0do(B),$$
$$\langle\!\langle 0.33\rangle\!\rangle^{\times}.\langle\!\langle 3.8\rangle\!\rangle^{+}.S600\bar{S}0do(B), \ \bar{S}600\bar{S}0do(B)\}]^A$$

We have an EAP of 3.3 in favor of $do(A)$, and an EAP of $0.67 + (0.33 \times 3.8) = 1.9$ in favor of $do(B)$, thus our result is $\{do(A)\}$.

In this case, the problem giving rise to the framing effect is not that our decision question fails to be in equilibrium but that our consequence views are not in equilibrium with respect to issues that our priorities are concerned with, which we would have to address by performing some inferential reasoning on the relationship between numbers of people dying in the scenario and numbers of people being saved and updating with the result as an additional consequence view. If we are going to consider death as a consequence in a scenario where the number of deaths ties down the number of survivors, we also must consider survival as a consequence, given that we will be updating with priority views that care about both survival and death. In light of our discussion of judgments about probability in Chapter 5, what we would expect to need here for a rational judgment is an equilibrium basis view concerning the uncertain consequences of the two options.

Moving on, we next consider the case in which the addition of a dominated decoy option can sometimes change which of two other options is chosen. When we encounter the three-option selection with difficult tradeoffs, it is plausible that our priorities will tend not to directly produce a unique solution.

There are tradeoffs between different features and prices to be considered, and our priorities may not be sufficient to suggest a clear winner, certainly not without further calculation. However, we may at least have *picking the best deal* as a priority. Again, as Ariely plausibly notes, "I may not have known whether the Internet-only subscription at $59 was a better deal than the print-only option at $125. But I certainly knew that the print-and-Internet option for $125 was better than the print-only option at $125" (Ariely (2009)). In order for this line of thought to get us all the way to a decision, we need to somehow explain how the observation that A is better than C could enable a decision-maker to jump to the conclusion that A is best among A,B, and C. This kind of "over-concluding" is of the sort of thing that the erotetic theory provides a natural mechanism for.

(**Example 91 derivation**)

Firstly, we treat this case as essentially centering on the problem of inferring what the best deal is, where we hypothesize that the decision-making aspect of the problem will just be driven by the result of that inference to settle the question of what to pick.

One way we could regiment this problem in a way that yields the decoy effect is via the question of which of the three options is best, where we can further analyze "best among A,B,C" via a "better than" relation. We let "$x > y$" stand for "x is a better deal than y," and we use W, PW, and P, respectively, for web-only, print-and-web, and print-only. If we then ask which option is best, this would amount to

$$\{\{W > P, W > PW\}, \{P > W, P > PW\}, \{PW > P, PW > W\}\}.$$

It may still be hard to find an answer to this complicated question. Luckily, it seems very obvious that print-and-web is better than print-only, since they cost the same but the former has an additional feature. Now, if we update with $\{\{PW > P\}\}$, we in fact get all the way to $\{\{PW > P, PW > W\}\}$, since this update involves treating $PW > P$ as a maximally strong answer to the question. After all, the only envisaged alternative, in the minimal question as to *what is best*, that satisfies $PW > P$ is the alternative in which print-and-web is best.

By contrast, if we only have the web-only and the print-and-web options to choose from, we are forced to actually consider the trade-offs and it turns out that the cheaper option prevails more often. There is no obvious shortcut for the decision-making process. This supports the intuition that our choices in the presence of a decoy option are less reflective of us as agents in control of our decisions. Indeed, as Ariely (2009) reported, the *Economist* magazine withdrew this particular subscription menu after Ariely asked them about their use of a decoy option. We cannot directly conclude that the *Economist* magazine was trying to be manipulative. Jenny Zhao has suggested to us that from a practical marketing perspective, it is possible that pricing the print-and-web option the same as the print-only option might have come about through mechanisms having nothing to do with attempts at recruiting a decoy effect. It may reflect the fact that increasing web-traffic has a marginal benefit to the magazine, but passing that on to the consumer by making print-and-web cheaper than print-only may be seen as offensive by older subscribers who do not read the magazine on the web.

Finally, we now move on to consider how one might make sense of the endowment effect on the erotetic theory. As noted in the opening section of this chapter, there is evidence to suggest that the endowment effect is generated by the effects of ownership rather than by loss-aversion (Morewedge et al. (2009); Morewedge and Giblin (2015)). Moreover, the endowment effect is fragile to trading experience at least within the domain of the type of objects involved in the trading experience (List (2004); List (2003)).

We take as a starting point Morewedge and Giblin (2015) view that effects of ownership are behind the endowment effect. We now need an account of how ownership can yield this effect. As noted before, it is preferable to seek an account that does not involve postulating intrinsically irrational fundamental preferences. A familiar idea in social psychology is that being able to use or manipulate something is a core psychological feature of ownership (Pierce et al. (2001); Pierce et al. (2003)). Fully entertaining one's ownership of a cup plausibly involves entertaining some of the many alternative ways in which one could use the cup. Your cup is yours to drink out of, to give away, to put on display, etc. It seems plausible in this light that owning a type of item would normally make various alternative things someone could do with this type of item more salient. We suggest that some of these alternatives enter into the set of alternatives that are considered when someone who has been endowed with a cup, or who owns a similar cup, is offered a chance to trade the cup for another item (regardless of whether this is on behalf of himself or a client). This means that the cup is considered in various alternative courses of action, involving different properties that each have a chance of matching the priorities that the individual may have (or that are speculatively attributed to a client). By contrast, the alternative of trading the cup for some other particular object may not as readily involve considering the trade as itself branching into performing the trade followed by various uses of the new object.

In this way, the owner of a cup (or the agent who owns a similar cup) may be asking himself a decision question that simply gives much more traction to reasons favoring scenarios that do not involve trading, because ownership more readily calls up alternative ways one may dispose of the item that positively interact with our priorities. The mechanism generating the endowment discrepancy then parallels that for the opportunity cost neglect case we modeled at the start of this section. The basic form of the kind of derivation we would propose remains essentially the same, so we will omit a formalization. Even if ownership of a cup only calls up the alternative "do something else fun with the cup," this already creates an asymmetry that could potentially generate an endowment effect.

Now, of course, an endowment effect is irrational, just as neglecting alternatives is irrational. The decision-maker should be asking herself what she (or a client) can do with, say, the pen to the same extent that she is asking herself what she (or a client) can do with the cup. Of course, if the items in question do not invoke any substantially different actions at all, there should be no endowment effect. In line with that observation, another study showed that there is no endowment effect for simple tokens of directly assigned monetary value (Kahneman et al. (1990)).

Experienced traders do not show the endowment effect for items they routinely trade, as noted above (List (2004); List (2003)). We can make sense of this without invoking any notion of a distinct rational system taking over from a fallacy-prone system. We would say that experienced traders simply entertain more symmetrical decision questions for the items they have experience with. I believe that this is a fairly intuitive explanation of the endowment effect sketched above. The more we come to think of a particular kind of good as primarily a repository of exchange value in the marketplace rather than as an object for various uses, the less our decision questions will treat what we already own differently from the things we consider acquiring in exchange. The idea is that with increased experience of a particular kind of decision, our decision questions will tend to evolve in a way that makes it more likely that our priorities will yield equilibrium answers.

6.5 Utility Maximization under Erotetic Equilibrium

We now turn to the connection between erotetic agents and classically rational choice. The picture of classically rational choice that is a standard point of reference in both AI (e.g. see Russell and Norvig (2016); Wooldridge (2003)) and a number of other disciplines can be given as follows.

An agent is classically rational if and only if the action she chooses from the set of all possible actions maximizes the utility of the possible outcomes of this action, discounted by the subjective probability of these outcomes. In other words, a classically rational agent chooses her actions to maximize her expected utility. Formally, we define expected utility maximization as follows, more or less following the exposition in Wooldridge (2003).

Definition 6.8. Let $A = \{\alpha_1, \alpha_2, \ldots\}$ be the set of all possible actions for the agent. Let $\Omega = \{\omega_1, \omega_2, \ldots\}$ be the set of possible worlds corresponding to all possible outcomes. Let $P(\omega|\alpha)$ be the subjective probability of ω given that the agent performs α. Let $U : \Omega \to \mathbb{R}$ be the agent's utility function, where $U(\omega) > U(\omega')$ if and only if the agent strictly prefers the outcome ω over the outcome ω'. We then define the expected utility of an action α as follows.

$$EU(\alpha) = \sum_{\omega \in \Omega} U(\omega)P(\omega|\alpha)$$

We define utility maximization as

$$MEU = \arg\max_{\alpha \in A} EU(\alpha)$$

It cannot be stressed enough how influential this view of rationality has been. In the 2010 edition of their standard textbook on artificial intelligence, Russell and Norvig go as far as defining "the goal of AI as creating systems that try to maximize expected utility" (2010), which is only slightly weakened in their 2020 edition to include learning a utility function, as well as maximizing it. In a sense, we're suggesting to "weaken" this further by taking the appropriate goal to be to find the best answers to the most appropriate questions.

We now want to show how default decision-making of an erotetic agent relates to expected utility maximization. The rest of this section is given to a sketch of a proof of the following.

Theorem 6.1 (Utility maximization under erotetic equilibrium). *Let dq be a decision question in erotetic equilibrium with respect to all questions about action possibilities $\{do(s), 0\}$, and that is further in erotetic equilibrium with respect to its own atoms. Let CV be a set of direct consequence views for each alternative in dq, such that elements of CV are equilibrium basis views of the total consequences of these actions. Then,*

UTILITY MAXIMIZATION UNDER EROTETIC EQUILIBRIUM

(1) *for a given utility function over the outcomes of each action in dq, there exists a set of priority views PR so that the default decision procedure is equivalent to maximizing expected utility; and*

(2) *for any set of priority views, there exists a utility function such that the default decision procedure is equivalent to maximizing expected utility.*

An erotetic agent exists in a framework with infinitely many possible worlds and only ever takes views on a finite set of states. Thus we must instead consider rationality with respect to finitary decisions and their outcomes regarding a finite set of atoms considered to be at issue.

Let $dq = \{\alpha_1, \alpha_2, \ldots, \alpha_n\}$, in erotetic equilibrium with respect to all possible actions $\{do(s), 0\}$ and with respect to its own atoms, be given. Let $\mathbb{O} \subseteq \mathcal{A} \backslash \mathcal{A}^{do}$ be a finite set of closed atoms all of the form $P^k(t_1, \ldots, t_k)$ for some positive predicate $P^k \in \mathbf{P}^\top$. Suppose that for each $\alpha_i \in dq$ we have an equilibrium basis view $\Gamma_{i f_i}^{\{0\}}$ corresponding to a probability distribution over the 2^N states formed from the atoms and negations of atoms in $\mathbb{O}$, where $|\mathbb{O}| = N$. We refer to these 2^N states as $\mathbb{O}$-*worlds*. We suppose that the set CV consists of precisely the views

$$\{f_i^\times(\gamma).\langle\!\langle\rangle\!\rangle^+.(\gamma \cup \{\alpha_i\}) : \gamma \in \Gamma_i\}^{\{\alpha_i\}}$$

for $i = 1, \ldots, n$. Thus the agent is faced with a choice between n alternatives, and for each of these an equilibrium basis view of the probabilities of the $\mathbb{O}$-worlds.

Now recall that, as we defined it, the default decision procedure for an erotetic agent is as follows.

$$dq\left[dq[CV]^\circlearrowright[\varnothing]^F[PR]^\circlearrowright\right]^A.$$

In this situation, the result of $dq[CV]^\circlearrowright[\varnothing]^F$ is simply

$$\{\{f_i^\times(\gamma).\langle\!\langle\rangle\!\rangle^+.(\gamma \cup \{\alpha_i\}) : \gamma \in \Gamma_i\} : i = 1, \ldots, n\}^{\{0\}}$$

where in particular each γ is an $\mathbb{O}$-world.

Suppose that a "payout" $U(\gamma) \in \mathbb{R}$ is associated to each $\mathbb{O}$-world γ. We can choose the priority views PR such that the agent will end up making the decision that maximizes the expected payout. We simply take, for each $\mathbb{O}$-world γ, the priority view

$$\{\langle\!\langle\rangle\!\rangle^\times.U(\gamma)^+.0\}^{\{\gamma\}}.$$

It then follows that the answer potential associated to the possible action α_i is given by

$$\sigma\big(\langle\!\langle \sigma(\langle\!\langle f_i^\times(\gamma)\rangle\!\rangle)\,\overline{\times}\,\sigma(\langle\!\langle U(\gamma)\rangle\!\rangle)\,\big|\,\gamma\in\Gamma_i\rangle\!\rangle\big) \approx \sum_{\gamma\text{ an }\mathbb{O}\text{-world}} \mathbb{P}(\gamma\,|\,\alpha_i)\times U(\gamma)$$

where $\mathbb{P}(\gamma\,|\,\alpha_i)=0$ if $\gamma\notin\Gamma_i$ and $\mathbb{P}(\gamma\,|\,\alpha_i)=f_i^\times(\gamma)$ otherwise, and $\approx$ indicates equality modulo "side-reasoning," to reduce the arithmetic of weights. Thus, in maximizing on this answer potential, the Answer operation can be represented as maximizing expected utility.

It remains to consider the more general situation where we rely on an agent's arbitrary set of priority views. We again assume a set of direct consequence views CV that consists of equilibrium basis views over $\mathbb{O}$-worlds for each alternative in dq. However, we do not need to constrain the priority views for them to induce a utility function.

First we note the role that arbitrary objects play here: they allow us to work with continuous variables in our priorities (consider the disease problem from the previous section). When priority views contain arbitrary objects, updating with them is directed by issue structures. Thus the observation we now make is that any set PR of priority views induces an implied utility function on the set of $\mathbb{O}$-worlds *for a given fixed $\mathbb{O}$-issue structure*, where by the latter we mean a set of pairs $\langle t,x\rangle$ with $x\in\mathcal{A}_1$ and $x[t/?]\in\mathbb{O}\vee\bar{x}[t/?]\in\mathbb{O}$. In the default procedure, the relevant $\mathbb{O}$-issue structure comes from the intermediate view $dq[CV]^\circ[\varnothing]^F$.

For the $\mathbb{O}$-issue structure I and set PR of priority views, the induced utility function on $\mathbb{O}$-worlds is given by

$$U(\gamma) = \sum \langle\!\langle w : \{\langle\!\langle\rangle\!\rangle^\times.w^+.0\}_J^{\{n\}} \in PR \wedge \pi \subseteq \gamma\rangle\!\rangle +$$
$$\sum \langle\!\langle w[t/a] : \{\langle\!\langle\rangle\!\rangle^\times.w^+.0\}_{a,J}^{\{n\}} \in PR \wedge$$
$$\exists t\in\mathbb{T}, \exists x\in\mathcal{A}_1.\pi[t/a]\subseteq\gamma\wedge\langle t,x\rangle\in I\wedge\langle a,x\rangle\in J\rangle\!\rangle.$$

Adapting the discussion above, it is straightforward to see that an erotetic agent, faced with the decision question dq as above and having consequence views CV also as above, may be represented as maximizing expected utility according to the formula for utility given above.

The case with arbitrary objects may be reduced to the case with none for particular questions: one simply replaces the priority views of the form $\{\langle\!\langle\rangle\!\rangle.w^+.0\}_{a,J}^{\{n\}}$ with every relevant instance $\{\langle\!\langle\rangle\!\rangle.w[t/a]^+.0\}^{\{n[t/a]\}}$ for closed terms t. In the resulting case, there is an intuitive interpretation of $U(\gamma)$ for an

O-world γ. Each π with $\{\langle\!\langle\rangle\!\rangle.w^+.0\}^{\{\bar{\pi}\}} \in PR$ can be seen as a graded pro tanto reason, of magnitude w, in favor of an O-world γ with $\pi \subseteq \gamma$, and the default judgment of the utility of γ is simply the sum of the magnitudes of all pro tanto reasons in its favor.

Finally, we make a remark about the constraints on dq. There are reasonable decision questions where the alternatives are conjunctions of several do-atoms and perhaps also of negated do-atoms. This makes no difference to our analysis of rationality provided each alternative action is associated with precisely one consequence view. When the alternatives in the decision question are nested, as in $\{do(s)\} \subseteq \{do(s)\overline{do}(s')\}$, it is not possible to have separate consequence views for each alternative, since $\{do(s)\overline{do}(s')\}$ will accumulate the consequences that were intended for $\{do(s)\}$.

6.6 Affordances and Action-Centered Priorities

In response to an early presentation of the erotetic theory in inferential reasoning, David Chalmers once asked, "but where do questions come from?". The answer Koralus gave was, "in the beginning was the question!". On one way of looking at Chalmers's question, the answer should be obvious now after almost 300 pages of erotetic theory: for given problems, premise statements or memory supply questions. Alternatively, we can start from a "null" issue {0} and use the Inquire operation.

Yet, there remains an interesting question in the area: Do substantive questions arise from outside of reason at all, or do they only emerge by using reason or by listening to someone give voice to their faculty of reason through language? This section will provide some considerations in favor of the view that questions do arise outside of the faculty of reason. In the process, we will find independent motivation for the idea that *do* atoms have an important part to play in an account of the content of our mental states outside of reason narrowly conceived.

Our starting point will be the following claim: perceptual experience has aspects that are fairly directly action-oriented in a way that can bypass full-blown practical reasoning. One of the most influential versions of this claim, due to Gibson (1979), is that that we perceive what he called "affordances." In Gibson's words:

> The affordances of the environment are what it offers the animal, what it provides or furnishes, either for good or ill. The verb to afford is found in

the dictionary, but the noun affordance is not. I have made it up. I mean by it something that refers to both the environment and the animal in a way that no existing term does.... Terrestrial surfaces, of course, are also climb-on-able or fall-off-able or get-underneath-able or bump-into-able relative to the animal. Different layouts afford different behaviors for different animals, and different mechanical encounters.... if a surface is horizontal, flat, extended, rigid, and knee-high relative to a perceiver, it can in fact be sat upon. If it can be discriminated as having just these properties, it should look sit-on-able. If it does, the affordance is perceived visually.

Had Gibson consulted the *Oxford English Dictionary* rather than Webster's, he may have found that "affordance" is not in fact a new word (a rare piece of regional nineteenth-century Cumberland dialect for the amount a person can pay), but the new meaning he introduced has justly caught on among psychologists, philosophers, and architects. The idea that perception has a tight connection with the detection of opportunities for action has empirical support. For example, when objects are perceived, it appears that we automatically prime motor codes for actions associated with them (Tucker and Ellis, 1998; Anderson et al., 2002).

Gibson's notion of affordances has parallels with the earlier notion of *Aufforderungscharacter* proposed by the Gestalt psychologists, whose descriptions, to use a technical term, have a slightly creepy Alice-in-Wonderland character.

> Each thing says what it is—a fruit says "eat me"; water says "drink me"; thunder says "fear me"; and woman says "love me." (Koffka, 1935)

While the Gestaltists saw theselves as characterizing something purely phenomenological, Gibson took his affordances to be objective aspects of the environment and its relationship to the organism.

Many psychologists and philosophers have taken it that there is something importantly right in the ball-park of what Gibson says about affordances. However, there are various conflicting views about how exactly affordances relate to action and to the contents of experience. Some have concluded that, properly understood, the theory of affordances should radically lead us away from classical mainstream notions of cognitive science, in favor of an "ecological" or "embodied" view of cognition as a kind of dynamics of a brain-body-environment system. This was the line that Gibson (1979) himself took, and others have followed in his footsteps (e.g. Noë et al. (2004); Chemero (2011); see Aizawa (2015); Fodor and Pylyshyn (1981) for some criticism).

Other authors have argued that we can make sense of affordances in representational terms (Prosser, 2011; Nanay, 2011; Siegel, 2014). One important type of proposal takes the representational content of affordances to be a one-place predicate of objects, where what is predicated is the possibility of acting on them in various ways and where we allow that what grounds the correct application of this predicate is a relational property between the agent and what the agent is perceiving (Prosser, 2011). Nanay takes affordances or, "action oriented" perceptual states to involve perceiving objects as what he calls "Q-able," an action type Q (Nanay, 2011). So, for example, we see objects as edible, climbable, and so on. Siegel (Siegel, 2014) similarly talks about affordances as "Phi-ability."

Now, the foregoing appears to leave out an important aspect of affordances that has been chiefly stressed by those who are not representationalists, namely that affordances "solicit a certain kind of activity" (Dreyfus and Kelly, 2007). This take on affordances is perhaps closer to the Gestaltist's notion of *Aufforderungscharacter*, in that a central aspect of the action-involving character of experience is that it is a kind of urgent invitation, demand, or imperative. The intuition here is that perception can very directly lead to action.

> To say that the world solicits a certain activity is to say that the agent feels immediately drawn to act a certain way. This is different from deciding to perform the activity, since in feeling immediately drawn to do something the subject experiences no act of the will. Rather, he experiences the environment calling for a certain way of acting, and finds himself responding to the solicitation. (Dreyfus and Kelly, 2007)

> When the Grandmaster is playing lightning chess, as far as he can tell, he is simply responding to the patterns on the board. At this speed he must depend entirely on perception and not at all on analysis and comparison of alternatives. Dreyfus (2005, cited in Siegel (2014))

Siegel takes on board the idea that affordances can be "soliciting" and sometimes even amount to "experienced mandates" (Siegel, 2014). For example, "With the ball coming toward you in a tennis game, the felt solicitation to swing your racket and hit it might be so strong that no other option enters your mind" (Siegel, 2014). It is this aspect of affordances that presents a potential challenge to representationalist accounts of cognition, since it could make representation seem dispensable. After all, if perception can directly yield action, "there is no need for the current experience to represent the possibility of acting in the way the situation mandates, and more generally, no need for experiential representations to guide the subject in planning and executing the mandated action.... There might then seem to be no explanatory role for contents of experience to play" (Siegel, 2014).

Siegel, unlike Dreyfus and Kelly, maintains that we can give a representationalist account not only of "phi-ability" affordances, but also of soliciting affordances. Siegel's proposal for the content of the experience is "It is answered that: X is to-be-phi'd." The idea is that "X is to-be-phi'd" leaves open a parameter for a type of norm, such as epistemic or social norms, which, once fixed, would give us accuracy conditions.

Though the conclusion that we can make sense of affordances in terms of content seems right, there are a few outstanding concerns. The first concern is about the route from affordances to action. To handle the experience of affordances in cases like expert lightning chess or returning a tennis serve, the connection to action might still be too indirect. As Harman (1986) points out, reasoning "about what one *ought* to do or what one has reasons to do," "is really a particular kind of theoretical reasoning." The same observation plausibly applies to *judgments* about what X it has been answered that "X is to-be-phi'd." However, it would appear that what is distinctive about our affordance experiences in the relevant cases like tennis and speed chess is not that they issue in beliefs or judgments about what we *ought* to do (with or without a free variable for a type of norm) but that they can somewhat directly lead us to forming an intention to act (it is not entirely clear whether this is a problem for Siegel on her own terms, since the overall picture here will depend on more general views on action and practical reason).

A second concern has to do with the relationship between affordance experiences that bring us close to action and those that do not. As I look around the room, I perceive various affordances, notably two chairs and a sofa that afford sitting. However, these affordances are not experienced as involving a mandate, strong invitation, and so on. Yet, if I now spend an hour doing an intense training session, that will change. Suppose we want to locate affordance contents of the kind considered specifically in the contribution of vision (without ruling out affordances in other modalities), which seems attractive in light of the above scenarios. Then, on an approach that distinguishes mere "Phi-able" affordance content from "mandate"-type "it is answered that: X is to-be-phi'd" content, it might look like visual perception has to treat the sofa stimulus as something like an ambiguous figure with respect to affordances presented. One might compare Jastrow's duck-rabbit, made famous in philosophy by

Wittgenstein. There we have a constant visual stimulus that we can perceive alternately as depicting a duck or a rabbit, partly depending on our background expectations. In semantics, it is often taken that an ambiguity analysis should be a last resort. Moreover, unlike in the case of duck-rabbit the two "readings" are clearly very closely, perhaps even constitutively, related.

A different worry more directly attaches to the idea that the contribution of affordance-perception itself includes a mandate at all (even if we grant a link to action that can bypass full practical deliberation). Examples like speed chess and tennis seem to have a common feature that sets them apart, namely that relevant affordances such as moving the queen or returning a ball across the net are only present in a very restricted set of circumstances. For various other affordances that are ubiquitous for those with a certain set of skills, it seems both implausible and uncomfortable to take them as (possibly ambiguously) mandating action directly from the perceptual level. We will try to motivate this intuition with a scenario. We happen to know someone who is both a philosophy professor (Professor X) at an Ivy League university and a black belt in Brazilian Jiu-Jitsu. Suppose we are standing in front of a blackboard with Professor X and raise an arm to write Bayes's Rule. In raising an arm to write Bayes's Rule, we are both creating an affordance for bringing to mind something relevant to epistemology, but also an affordance for a duck-under to arm triangle and any number of ways of being folded into a pretzel (for this example, we are indebted to Dr. Rosemary Sexton, formerly of the UFC and, like one of the authors of this chapter, an old member of Trinity College, Cambridge). We strongly suspect that in this case, we are not ambiguously triggering a mandate for being folded into a pretzel in Professor X's perceptual system (N.B. this claim does not rule out that since we wrote something boring on the blackboard, X may think about Jiu-Jitsu in the back of his mind until we move on to something more interesting). *Pace* Gestaltists like Koffka, whom we quoted further above, it just does not seem quite right that *in perception*, "woman says 'love me' " (Koffka, 1935), or that our arm says "fold me into a pretzel!" somewhere in Professor X's visual system (cf. on standard views, all disambiguations of lexical items are primed by their occurrence, even if they do not enter into the current interpretation of a sentence). At any rate, even from a safe distance in Oxford isolated by travel bans, we hope we are right about this.

In sum, it might be worth exploring an account that can get us more directly to action, but that is also continuous with "neutral" cases like the sofa, and that does not entail that Professor X's perceptual system ambiguously encodes a mandate to fold us into a pretzel.

On a first look, the foregoing considerations seem to pull us in opposing directions that are hard to reconcile. However, we suggest that the erotetic theory can provide an account that reconciles these intuitions, and that seems to maintain some of the spirit of Siegel's proposal. We can model the contents in experience of affordances with views of the following form: $\{do(x), 0\}$. Following the preliminary approach to possibility talk discussed in Chapter 3, we might (very very) imperfectly paraphrase that in English as "possibly do x?" (or simply "do x?"), though natural language paraphrases will not work in the final analysis, since "do x" here corresponds to a kind of primitive intention (see discussion of do-atoms earlier in this chapter).

The accuracy conditions are trivial, since no substantive commitments are made. However, we will additionally say that when our affordance detectors in our visual system fire (e.g. the visual counterpart of interpreting an utterance) thereby contributing $\{do(x), 0\}$ to the contents of our experience, they further *presuppose* that $do(x)$ can be executed by our performance systems. If we do not have the corresponding motor skill or if the situation does not allow for its application, then the presupposition fails. Learning more motor skills then allows us to "see" more.

What then of affordances that seem tightly coupled to action? If you see a very fast tennis serve coming over the net, you will ideally hit it as soon as it becomes hittable (with proper form), without consideration of consequences (unless you're very significantly better than the person serving). The erotetic theory allows for this in potentially two ways that are more or less directly generated by just feeding less into the default decision procedure we defined earlier in this chapter (we could consider different procedures as well—the erotetic theory is not committed to one single procedure being followed in all cases). We can simply "degrade" the default decision procedure by leaving out the update with consequence views. At the extreme, we can even leave out the update with priority views. If we skip these updates, the default decision procedure would have an erotetic agent treating an affordance as an answer to the very question it raises, directly resulting in an intention: $\{do(x), 0\}[\{do(x), 0\}]^A = \{do(x)\}$. This formally just is the default decision procedure if we omit updates with consequences and priorities! While there may be extreme cases of this sort (deciding like a trained headless chicken, in a manner of speaking), this seems like it may not be ideal even for the tennis case. After all, we may be perceiving a number of different (and not jointly executable) affordances at the same time, in which case we cannot let the affordances settle their own questions. Yet, by degrading our default decision procedure slightly less we can find a more plausible middle ground between "I-see-I-do" and time-intensive rational deliberation. The key is that in addition to the consequentialist priorities we used to model the decision phenomena earlier in this chapter, we can plausibly postulate priorities that are centered on "doings" (deontological priorities, if you will). For example, we might have a priority in favor of hitting a ball coming over the net in a tennis game. We might now have a view on board that we are in a tennis game, and then perceive affordances for hitting a ball or ducking it. Our hyper-practical reasoning may then take the form $\{do(hit\ ball), do(duck), 0\}[\{do(hit\ ball)Tennisgame, do(duck)Tennisgame, Tennisgame\}[\{1^+.0\}^{\{do(hit\ ball)Tennisgame\}}]\circlearrowright]^A = \{do(hit\ ball)\}$. In this case, we are still not considering consequences or deliberating in a meaningful way, but merely including a view of the gist of the circumstances we are in to trigger an action-oriented priority that is just minimally sensitive to whether we are in a tennis game. This allows for different results if we do not take ourselves to be playing tennis, and, via different priorities, it would allow us to react differently depending on whether we are playing tennis or dodge ball, but again without full rational deliberation. We know that perception of the gist of a scene is extremely rapid (Li et al., 2002). This may be some reason to think that our "hyper"-practical reasoning based on affordances, gist, and deontological priorities could plausibly be executed extremely rapidly by humans in a way that matches the intuitive time-scale of speed chess or tennis.

On this view, we have given content to affordance experiences and we have provided a direct link from affordances to action. Note that we have not provided an account of the content of the experience of affordances in terms of a restricted notion of representational content that might correspond to the content of a declarative sentence. As noted earlier in the chapter, our notion of representational content corresponds to a broader notion that is sometimes called "intentional content" (see Klein (2007)).

Though we do not have the space to do justice to these issues here, we might consider that it plausibly is a virtue for an erotetic agent to possess action-centered priorities against action types with potentially catastrophic consequences, such as killing, which are normally unlikely to be chosen under erotetic equilibrium. After all, as we have seen, we are often not particularly reliable in reasoning out the consequences of our actions, so we may be more reliably in erotetic equilibrium with certain acts if we have priorities against them in advance of having considered consequences. In other words, there may be a case to be made that deontological priorities are contingently rationally required for erotetic agents. Note that on this view there is no necessary connection between emotional responses and deontological priorities, as has sometimes been supposed, while we may still expect a tendency for scenarios in which decisions are strongly driven by such priorities to also trigger emotional responses (see next section for some reflections on emotion).

6.7 The Erotetic Agent with a Human Face

As defined in Chapter 1, an erotetic agent is an agent whose behavior is controlled by their capacity to reason, as described by the erotetic theory. In this chapter, we have finally shown how this picture gets us all the way to action. In the final two sections, we will informally sketch a few additional perspectives that, if you will, put a human face on erotetic agents and that suggest avenues for future investigation.

As we saw over the course of several chapters, a wide variety of failures of human reason can be accounted for as resulting from erotetic disequilibrium. At the same time, we found that sufficiently strong erotetic equilibrium can secure valid inference, probabilistic coherence, and classically rational choice. Various considerations suggested that it would be impossible for humans, and indeed any resource bounded creature based on erotetic reason, to generally restrict their thinking in such a way that strong erotetic equilibrium is always guaranteed. At the same time, we have to at least weakly aim for erotetic equilibrium, because our judgments are otherwise driven neither by the facts nor by our priorities but by the vagaries of how we happen to have framed our questions. The erotetic agent seeks to answer their questions as directly as possible, but has to be on the lookout for signs that her judgments are not in erotetic equilibrium, which would threaten to undermine her judgments by her own lights. If we are making choices that are not in erotetic equilibrium, then we are under threat of failing to be in control as agents. After all, it means that without changing our priorities and without changing our overall view of how the facts stand, we are liable to get different actions.

If we cannot always aim for absolute erotetic equilibrium in advance, regulating how we raise questions becomes key to being an agent. A well-designed agent with an erotetic capacity to reason at its core will need some ways of regulating how many and what kinds of further questions are raised in a way that is not just another reasoning problem. Emotion or affective processing might partly be understood as serving this regulatory role in humans. We could see emotions as macro-cognitive states that help regulate questioning in our cognitive economy. This could sometimes substantively change our judgments in a way that makes them more rational, given the machinery we have described. In other words, the erotetic theory creates an opening for a non-evidentiary epistemic role for emotions (for recent arguments in favor of a non-evidentiary epistemic role for emotions, see Dietz (2020)).

With respect to practical rationality, various hypotheses about the role of emotions with respect to question regulation could be explored. We will just very briefly sketch a few. For example, fear might make us generate fewer further questions, and thereby make us more disposed to draw conclusions at face value, which would decrease our chances of false negatives in a high stakes threat inquiry. In other words, fear might encourage the kind of reasoning discussed at the end of Chapter 2. Similarly, joy might make it less likely for us to spend time on raising questions about alternative possibilities and actions, which might be beneficial if we already have the benefit of a highly rewarding resource that would make it unlikely that considering alternatives changes what we do (i.e. joy could be a signal that we plausibly already are in equilibrium). We could then perhaps see anxiety as a trigger for increasing our consideration of alternative possibilities, to avoid being blindsided or to avoid noticing potentially life-saving hidden opportunities. This would then come at the cost of tending to inhibit action or highly directed chains of reasoning because it increases our inquisitive load at every step, but it will perhaps tend toward lessening the chance of narrow questions in the face of high stakes decisions. We could perhaps see anger as making us less likely to take on board somebody else's issues. This would make it less likely for our naturally cooperative nature to help our enemies in their designs against us. For someone skilled in conflict, anger might be counterproductive because it also narrows our view in ways that might make us miss important details about what is in front of us. This does not make a disposition to anger an automatic defect. For someone not used to conflict, avoiding the basic instinct to cooperatively take on board someone else's issues might well be worth the price of a slightly worse understanding of the situation. Anger might turn out to be, on balance, rational for those unskilled in conflict but mostly irrational for those skilled in conflict. This view might get support from the intuition that anger can often seem immature or primitive. We do not need to commit ourselves to any of these particular analyses of emotions here, sketchy as they are, but the foregoing observations suggest that with an erotetic theory of reason, there are prospects for understanding even some of the strangest aspects of human nature as in some sense a "spandrel" (in the sense of Gould and Lewontin (1979)) of the cathedral of reason.

Moving on, another aspect of human experience that seems fairly pervasive is what Herbert Simon (1956) called "satisficing." Setting aside a review of the empirical evidence for this phenomenon for now, we might simply observe that there is a strong intuition that in many decisions we make, ranging from things like selecting fruit in the supermarket, deciding on a business venture, a career, or new research topics to investigate, we are not making a real effort to find the optimal choice from all alternatives we could possibly find, but instead are content with finding something of a sufficiently high standard (of course, this standard can be high enough that the outcome is very similar to that achieved by genuine optimization). Moreover, it seems like this way of living our lives is rationally permissible. At the same time, there seems something amiss if we said, "sure, I can see that apple #1 is not as good as apple #2, but I nonetheless am at best indifferent between them, because I'm a satisficer." Moreover, there is clear evidence that people respond to evidence that their lot is much less good than it could be. To an extent, people do seem to aim higher if they see themselves as markedly falling behind their peers. Interestingly, in simulation, aggregates of satisficing agents whose thresholds of satisfaction are weakly coupled along those lines seem to behave very much like aggregates of utility maximizers (Madsen et al., 2020).

With the erotetic framework, we can reconcile these two countervailing intuitions: satisficing is rationally acceptable, but being indifferent when a new option is brought to consideration is better is not rational. An erotetic agent will only tend to be in restricted erotetic equilibrium, rather than in erotetic equilibrium with respect to questions about all possible actions. As was suggested in Chapter 2, being in restricted erotetic equilibrium is sometimes sufficient to be rationally as we ought to be. However, if we do raise further questions, then reason cannot ignore them. Yet, as observed in Chapter 2, it is far from clear that raising more questions would always make us more rational.

We might plausibly take the view that raising more questions is not always rational. For example, suppose we are lucky enough to be having dinner in the garden of a Tuscan villa in late spring, surrounded by friends and enjoying fresh pasta and local wine. It does not seem rational to stop for no special reason to inquire whether, say, by walking across the hill, we could be having an even better dinner in the garden of an even better villa, with a few extra entertaining special guests (though we might still suggest we move over if you show us this option). In sum, we can regard satisficing as an effect of restricted erotetic equilibrium and we can see it as rational to the extent to which restricted erotetic equilibrium is rational.

Moving on, since (1) no default procedure can easily yield equilibrium answers in all cases, (2) non-default decision-making is effortful, and (3) we nonetheless hope for equilibrium as agents, it seems reasonable to think that we would tend to regularize our environment to support easy equilibrium. We might consider a potentially useful notion of "erotetic home" as an environment where your default way of making decisions as applied to normal views of your situation will tend to produce equilibrium decisions. Home in this technical sense is where erotetic equilibrium is effortless for you. We could then consider a notion of inquisitive load of a set of circumstances for an agent. A low-inquisitive load circumstance for an agent would allow that agent to reach equilibrium judgments by following essentially a default reasoning procedure. An erotetic home would have minimal inquisitive load. By contrast, a high inquisitive load circumstance would be one in which an agent would have to generate many additional questions to ensure an equilibrium judgment, or in which the circumstances force questions upon us that have many alternatives that will turn out to be useless (one might explore these ideas together with what we said about affordances as a cognitive basis for Marie Kondo's (2014) recommendations on home organization). Of course, any actual home will only allow low inquisitive load at the price of constraining the set of options to consider. Nobody with substantive projects or a growing family can stay at home indefinitely, even if well supplied, and even if a pandemic is raging outside. The erotetic agent must venture onwards and bear the inquisitive load.

6.8 The Sphinx and the Kingdom of Erotetic Agents

In this final section, we will consider a particular kind of threat to their agency that erotetic agents may face and we will then end with some remarks about what might be distinctive about how groups of erotetic agents might govern themselves. Some concerns here echo concerns about freedom and domination familiar in the literature on civic republicanism (Pettit, 1997; Skinner, 2008).

We begin by considering the threat. We might say that the archetypical nemesis of the erotetic agent is a sphinx-like creature that weighs you down with inquisitive load without yet worsening the objectively available outcomes. Even if we are guaranteed to have a path through the system for realizing our goals, we could still be dominated by a sphinx, if that path requires superhuman inquisitiveness and corresponding processing capacity. We may find our agency undermined if we can no longer reasonably hope for equilibrium.

It is hard to quantify processing cost for humans in individual cases. However, we can ask whether a new arrangement, while keeping objectively available options constant, in fact increases my inquisitive load relative to the original arrangement, in the sense of requiring me to raise more questions to be able to get to an equilibrium judgment. To the extent that inquisitive load has increased, achieving meaningful agency becomes more difficult.

In many ways, it would seem that our inquisitive load in ordinary life tends to increase. Even people who do not work in finance now often have to consider questions about markets in the context of pensions. People who communicate with their friends through social media increasingly have to ask questions previously reserved for those who work in public relations. We may well get better outcomes on average relative to our priorities with those innovations, particularly if we are the sorts of people who read or write books like the one before you. However, making *equilibrium* judgments arguably gets harder. One of the authors of this chapter noticed one day that in order to properly answer the question of whether to take a stack of t-shirts out of the drawer, it first needed to be asked whether the airline he expected to travel with that day was insured by a certain insurance giant suddenly on the brink of collapse due to the sub-prime mortgage crisis (airlines cannot fly without insurance), and, in turn, whether a government on the other side of the Atlantic would likely prevent such a collapse from happening (all questions that themselves raise many further questions relative to what a normal person knows). If the so-called "butterfly effect" is an illustration of chaos-theory, then perhaps this t-shirt case is an illustration of something we might call inquisitive chaos. The point here is not about uncertainty or lack of knowledge, but about the fact that, all of a sudden, a question about t-shirts can only reasonably be answered *in equilibrium* if we first raise a large number of other questions. This does not seem much less striking than the idea that the weather might turn on whether a butterfly flaps its wings on the other side of the planet. Of course, insofar as our judgments are not in erotetic equilibrium, our decisions are more easily controlled from outside the agent or significantly the result of chance. At the limit, if our the inquisitive load is too high, the Sphinx can, as it were, devour our agency.

There are many areas in which it might be useful to consider inquisitive load independently of expected value (or risk) calculated in terms of frequencies of adversarial events. For example, we might have areas with comparable frequencies of crimes but large differences in the inquisitive load produced by crime (say, how often we have to ask ourselves which streets to avoid, etc.). Similar observations can be made about management of terrorism. The expected lives lost from terrorism are sometimes compared to those lost to lightning strikes in terms of total numbers affected. However, the inquisitive load terrorism produces for a society is incomparably greater than that produced by lightning strikes. For example, if an architect is considering how to keep an area clean and attractive for people with take-away lunches in disposable wrappers, they may also have to ask what a person who wishes to indiscriminately murder the greatest possible number of people might consider doing. The range and scope of these sorts of questions is unlimited in principle because terrorism is adaptive to reactions against it while lightning strikes are not. The point is that similarities in expected frequency of outcomes can mask vast differences in inquisitive load produced by the overall circumstances that generate those outcomes. Similar observations can be made about human relationships, ranging from terms of employment to marriage. Easy relationships allow people to largely interact in their not-so-inquisitive default mode. Tyrants do not just force us to do things we do not want to do, they also force us to keep wondering what they will consider demanding of us next (or to keep wondering how to secure our interests against them), increasing our inquisitive load.

Sphinx-worthy inquisitive load can emerge as a by-product of innovations that are intended to generally improve outcomes. One systematic way in which excessive inquisitive load may emerge is in the context a phenomenon Adam Elga (Jowett Society lecture 2013) has called "risk pollution," which can emerge as systems become more highly interconnected. Suppose I have a set of individual banks. Each bank has a slight chance of going bankrupt. If all banks are legally bound to lend each other money in case a bank experiences a cash shortfall, then the chances of any individual bank defaulting goes down dramatically. However, the chances of the entire set of banks collapsing will increase, since the fortunes of all banks are now linked. These linkages create tail risks that often emerge as a kind of externality (similar to how air pollution is an externality to factory production) of certain kinds of risk management. Whether, on balance, the added tail-risk of additional linkages buys us an overall improvement *on average* depends on the details (and there is a further question whether better averages adequately compensate for new possibilities of total failure). Elga has suggested that these tail risk externalities of risk management focused on improving average outcomes can be considered "risk pollution." Just like other externalities like toxic waste, the costs of risk pollution can sometimes outweigh the benefits of the process that gives rise to it. Now, there is evidence to suggest that even if we have a highly linked system that would be on average better overall, it may still end up performing dramatically worse if we are not dealing with ideal managers that can fully appreciate the added complexity that linkages entail. Elga and

Oppenheimer (2021) conducted three experiments in which participants had to manage fictional power-grid systems both with and without the kind of mutual-support linkages just discussed in the case of banks. The aim was to produce profit. Power outages commanded a financial penalty, unsold energy units generated loss, and power demand exceeding supply would produce outages. The possible profit in the case in which power stations were linked to each other was theoretically greater, but the actual profit generated was lower, since the participants were not sufficiently good at managing the risk of cascading failures in a highly connected system. In other words, the managers performed worse with a theoretically more efficient system.

From the point of view of the erotetic theory, a natural observation is that the more efficient but highly linked system creates higher inquisitive load. Because the fortune of each power plant is linked to the fortunes of all the others, the question of what the appropriate setting is for each individual plant cannot be properly answered without in some way raising questions about the other plants. The experimental results seem to suggest that this inquisitive load may easily become too hard.

Elga and Oppenheimer offer various suggestions for how to use behavioral nudges improve human management of such linked systems that are subject to cascading failures. One might think that if a particular system of this nature is going to function well enough, the solution probably is to use formal tools to settle on acceptably safe parameters, without giving significant leeway to human managers. It would seem like being confident in particular nudges would in fact depend on having a normative model in the background so that we know in which direction the nudges should push. However, the phenomenon of risk pollution in highly linked systems clearly is not limited to systems that are simple enough so that we can easily settle on a normative model that could be automated. Yet, even in the absence of a full normative model, we can tell that added linkages will increase inquisitive load. If the amount of inquisitive load that humans can bear is intrinsically limited, we can be virtually sure that the result will not be reliable equilibrium judgments. The post-modern world seems to be increasing inquisitive load in many contexts. Even if this world is superior in terms of objective choices available to people, the hidden costs of this increasing inquisitive load at the individual level and at the level of economies may well be underestimated if our standard model of decision-making is the classical kind that always treats all possible issues as already considered.

Finally, we might consider how problems of shared control and agency may play out for erotetic agents. In a democracy, citizens have to be in control of the government in some sense. However, since our judgments about what ought to be done by the government may differ, citizens cannot all be in complete control. One traditional response to this problem addresses this problem through preference aggregation. For example, we might register individual people's preferences over whether to implement a certain proposition or hand power to a particular political party, and then carry out whatever corresponds to the preferences of the majority.

In light of the picture of human reason presented in this book, certain weaknesses of the aggregative conception of democracy become more salient. The more complex the issues we might vote on, the greater the chance that the judgments of individual voters are not in erotetic equilibrium. Judgments that are not in erotetic equilibrium are potentially deficient as reflections of agency and control. Aggregating many judgments that are not themselves reflections of *individual* agential control may not obviously seem like reflections of *collective* agency or control. From the perspective of the individual, we might ask if we have a legitimate demand on others to partially let their affairs be determined by judgments that may not even be correct judgments by our own lights if we were to consider an appropriate set of questions. What questions I happen to consider in making my decision could have an essentially random component. At the limit, we might ask whether I have a legitimate claim on others to let their affairs be partly determined by my coin toss. Note that this concern is almost entirely separable from concerns we might have about demanding special subject knowledge or special logical prowess: erotetic equilibrium judgment, as we have developed the notion in this book, requires neither of these things in general.

For an erotetic citizen, a form of deliberative democracy might be better at implementing an idea of shared control than a purely aggregative notion of democracy. Many contemporary political theorists have argued for forms of deliberative democracy (Bessette (1994); Fishkin (2011); Cohen (1997); Dryzek (2012); Gutmann and Thompson (2009), among many others). Setting aside details of implementation and scope, we might contrast deliberative conceptions of democracy with aggregative conceptions as follows. On the aggregative conception, the political process primarily has legitimacy and reflects control of the citizens in virtue of being guided by a suitable aggregation of individual preferences. On the deliberative conception, the political process primarily has legitimacy and reflects control of the citizens in virtue of being guided by the outcome of a suitable form of collective deliberation. For example, we might ask a representative sample of the population to engage in group deliberation before voting on an issue, as in Fishkin's deliberative opinion polls (2011).

On a pure classical rational choice model of individual agents, the scope for benefits we may attribute to deliberative models of democracy may be quite limited. On this model, every agent has a fixed utility function and the only way to change someone's choices through the conduit of reason is by providing new information to change their view of the relative likelihoods of various outcomes. Insisting on the benefit of deliberation for collective agency might then amount to no more than insisting on sufficiently well-informed voters. While the importance of information should certainly not be neglected, the history of democracy in practice has generally moved away from the idea that participation in the electorate can be legitimately limited to those with a certain level knowledge or cognitive ability. While these issues are complex, if the only benefit of deliberative democracy is to be found in information gain, its contribution to legitimacy is on potentially fragile ground. If by contrast, the benefit of deliberation is to be found in non-rational change in judgment, we might similarly wonder to what extent this can ground a gain in legitimacy for the project of shared agency.

For erotetic agents, there is a third route to change in judgment besides information gain or non-rational influence. Entertaining further issues that I have not yet considered can show me that my initial judgment was not in erotetic equilibrium. Whether these issues are prompted by the contributions of an interlocutor that I substantively disagree with or who is ignorant is irrelevant. Regardless of how these further issues were prompted, taking them on board may change my judgment, and, moreover, change my judgment in a way that leaves me with a stronger sense of having a judgment that is a proper reflection of me as an agent in control. The secondary aim of our capacity to reason to weakly pursue erotetic equilibrium more or less directly requires minimal respect for the suggestion that we are not in reasonable equilibrium. Moreover, we might plausibly take it that, even completely ignorant fellow citizens might have a claim to have their questions heard.

We almost unavoidably see our hope for equilibrium as answerable to other people's questions because our language faculty more or less forces us to understand what they say, which means that there is in a sense a minimal form of cognitive respect for others that is built into our minds. This means that others unavoidably have a claim on us by our own lights to have a say in what we can regard as an equilibrium judgment. If we are not in equilibrium with respect to an appropriate set of questions, we are not fully in control and thus lack a certain kind of autonomy. Discussion with others can bring such lack of equilibrium to light. However, rather than undermine our autonomy (we were already in disequilibrium even if we did not realize this), this strengthens our control, as we now may be closer to equilibrium (with some caveats considered earlier in this chapter). This could ground a plausible gain in legitimacy for deliberative democracy relative to purely aggregative democracy: in the kingdom of erotetic agents, collective judgment at the end of a suitable deliberative process is a better reflection of group agency because it tends to be a better reflection of individual agency.

APPENDIX A

Formulas and Definitions

A.1 Formula Sheet for Chapter 2

Definition A.1 (Atoms $\mathcal{A}$). Let $\mathcal{A}$ be the set of atomic verifiers p and their corresponding atomic falsifiers $\bar{p}$.

Definition A.2 (States $\mathbb{S}$).
Let $\mathbb{S}$ be the set of finite subsets of $\mathbb{A}$. Write "0" for "{ }" in $\mathbb{S}$.

Definition A.3 (Primitive absurd states $\mathbb{K}$).
Let $\mathbb{K}_{\subseteq \mathbb{S}}$ contain, $\forall p_{\in \mathcal{A}}$, at least: $\{p, \bar{p}\}$

Definition A.4 (Views $\mathbb{V}$).
For Γ, Θ finite subsets of $\mathbb{S}$, $\langle \Gamma, \Theta \rangle \in \mathbb{V}$ (abbreviated $\Gamma^\Theta \in \mathbb{V}$). Write $\top$ for $\{0\}^{\{0\}}$ and $\bot$ for $\varnothing^{\{0\}}$.

Definition A.5 (Commitments $\mathbb{C}$).
For $C \subseteq \mathbb{V}, G \in \mathbb{V}, \langle C, G \rangle \in \mathbb{C}$.

Definition A.6 (Product of sets of states).
Let $\Gamma, \Delta \subseteq \mathbb{S}$ be finite sets of states. We define the product or conjunction of Γ and Δ to be

$$\Gamma \otimes \Delta = \{\gamma \cup \delta : \gamma \in \Gamma, \delta \in \Delta\}.$$

Definition A.7 (Negation on sets of states).
For a finite set of states $\Gamma = \{\gamma_1, \ldots, \gamma_n\}$, we define the *negation* by

$$\hat{\Gamma} = \{\{\bar{p}\} : p \in \gamma_1\} \otimes \ldots \otimes \{\{\bar{p}\} : p \in \gamma_n\},$$

Definition A.8 (Product).
$\Gamma^\Theta \otimes \Delta^\Psi = \left(\{\gamma_{\in \Gamma} \cup \delta_{\in \Delta} : \exists \psi_{\in \Psi}(\psi \subseteq \gamma)\} \cup \{\gamma_{\in \Gamma} : \neg \exists \psi_{\in \Psi}(\psi \subseteq \gamma)\}\right)^\Theta$
$\bigotimes_{i \in P} \Delta_i^{\Psi_i} = \{0\}^{\{0\}} \otimes \Delta_1^{\Psi_1} \otimes \ldots \otimes \Delta_n^{\Psi_n}$, given $\Delta_1^{\Psi_1} \ldots \Delta_n^{\Psi_n}$

Definition A.9 (Sum).
$\Gamma^\Theta \oplus \Delta^\Theta = (\Gamma \cup \Delta)^\Theta$
$\bigoplus_{i \in P} \Delta_i^\Psi = \varnothing^\Psi \oplus \Delta_1^\Psi \oplus \ldots \oplus \Delta_n^\Psi$

Definition A.10 (Atomic answer potential). $\Gamma[\Delta]^{AP} = |\mathcal{A}(\Gamma) \cap \mathcal{A}(\Delta)|$

Definition A.11 (Answer).
$\Gamma^\Theta[\Delta^{\{0\}}]^A = (\arg\max_{\gamma \in \Gamma} \Delta[\{\{p\} : p \in \gamma\}]^{AP})^\Theta$

Definition A.12 (Merge).
$$\Gamma^\Theta[\Delta^\Psi]^M = \bigoplus_{\gamma \in \Gamma} \left(\{\gamma\}^\Theta \otimes \Delta^\Psi\right).$$

Definition A.13 (Update).
$$\Gamma^\Theta[\Delta^\Psi]^U = \Gamma^\Theta[\Delta^\Psi]^A[\Delta^\Psi]^M$$

Definition A.14 (Negation).
$$[\Gamma^\Theta]^N = (\Theta^{\{0\}} \otimes (\hat{\Gamma})^{\{0\}})$$

Definition A.15 (Division).
If $\forall \delta_{\in \Delta} \exists \psi_{\in \Psi} \exists \gamma_{\in \Gamma} (\delta \subseteq \gamma \wedge \psi \subseteq \gamma)$, then
$\Gamma^\Theta \oslash \Delta^\Psi = \{\gamma \oslash_\Gamma \Delta^\Psi : \gamma \in \Gamma\}^\Theta$, where
$\gamma \oslash_\Gamma \Delta^\Psi = \gamma - \iota\delta(\delta \in \Delta \wedge \delta \subseteq \gamma \wedge \exists \psi_{\in \Psi} (\psi \subseteq \gamma))$

Definition A.16 (Factor).
For $\Delta^\Psi = \bot$,
$\Gamma^\Theta[\bot]^F = \{\gamma \in \Gamma : \neg \exists \delta_{\in \mathbb{K}} (\delta \subseteq \gamma)\}^\Theta$
For $\Delta^\Psi \neq \bot$,
$\Gamma^\Theta[\Delta^\Psi]^F = \{(\gamma \oslash_\Gamma \Delta^\Psi) : \gamma \in \Gamma\}^\Theta$

Definition A.17 (Suppose).
$$\Gamma^\Theta[\Delta^\Psi]^S = \Gamma^{(\Theta \otimes (\Delta \cup \Psi))}[\Delta^\Psi]^A[\Delta^\Psi]^M$$

Definition A.18 (Depose).
$$\Gamma^\Theta[\top]^D = \Gamma^{\{0\}} \oplus \hat{\Theta}^{\{0\}}$$

Definition A.19 (Inquire).
$$\Gamma^\Theta[\Delta^\Psi]^I = \Gamma_{RI}^\Theta \otimes (\Delta \oplus \hat{\Delta})^\Psi)[\bot]^F.$$

Definition A.20 (Query).
$\Gamma^\Theta[\Delta^\Psi]^Q = (\{0 : \neg \exists \delta_{\in \Delta} \exists \gamma_{\in \Gamma}. \Phi(\gamma, \delta)\} \cup \{\delta \in \Delta : \exists \gamma_{\in \Gamma}. \Phi(\gamma, \delta)\})^\Theta$,
where $\Phi(\gamma, \delta) \leftrightarrow \exists \psi_{\in \Psi}(\psi \cup \delta \subseteq \gamma)$

Definition A.21 (Commit).
$$\langle C, \Gamma^\Theta \rangle[\top]^C = \langle C \cup \{\Gamma^\Theta\}, \Gamma^\Theta \rangle$$

Definition A.22 (Reorient).
For $\Delta^\Psi \in (C \cup \{\Gamma^\Theta\}), \langle C, \Gamma^\Theta \rangle[\Delta^\Psi]^R = \langle C, \Delta^\Psi \rangle$

A.2 Formula Sheet for Chapter 4

Definition A.23 (Basic objects).
Let $A, F, \{?\}, P^\top, P^\bot$ be pairwise disjoint countable sets.
(F arity) $\alpha : F \to \mathbb{N}$. Write $f \in F$ as f^k when $\alpha(f) = k$.
(Constants) $\exists w_{\in F}\, \alpha(w) = 0$.
(P polarity) Let $N : P^\top \to P^\bot$ be a bijection. Write $\bar{P}$ for $N(P_{\in P^\top})$.
    Let $P = P^\top \cup P^\bot$.
(P arity) $\alpha' : P \to \mathbb{N}$. Write P as P^k for $\alpha'(P) = k$. $\alpha'(P) = \alpha'(\bar{P})$.
(Identity) $=^2 \in P$.

Definition A.24 (Terms T).
$A \subseteq T$. If $f^0 \in F$, then $\langle f^0 \rangle \in T$. If $f^k \in F \wedge \{t_1 \ldots t_k\} \subseteq T$, then $\langle f^k, \langle t_1 \ldots t_k \rangle \rangle \in T$.

Definition A.25 (Atoms $\mathcal{A}$).
If $P^k \in P$ and $\vec{t} = \langle t_1 \ldots t_k \rangle$ for $t_i \in T$, then $\langle P^k, \vec{t} \rangle \in \mathcal{A}$ (abbrv. $P\vec{t}$). $|\vec{t}| = \{t_1 \ldots t_k\}$.

Definition A.26 (States $\mathbb{S}$).
$\mathbb{S} = \mathcal{P}(\mathcal{A})$. Abbreviate '$\{\}$' as '0'.

Definition A.27 (Dependency relations $\mathcal{R}$).
Let $\Gamma \in \mathcal{P}(\mathbb{S})$. Let $U, E \subseteq A(\Gamma)$ and $D \subseteq E \times U = \{\langle e, u \rangle : e \in E \wedge u \in U\}$. Define $\langle U, E, D \rangle \in \mathcal{R}_\Gamma$ iff
  (Bipartite) $U \cap E = \emptyset \wedge D \subseteq E \times U$, and
  (Matryoshka) For all $u, u' \in U$ $\{e \in E : \langle e, u \rangle \in D\} \subseteq \{e \in E : \langle e, u' \rangle \in D\}$
    or $\{e \in E : \langle e, u' \rangle \in D\} \subseteq \{e \in E : \langle e, u \rangle \in D\}$.
For $R \in \mathcal{R}$ write $R = \langle U_R, E_R, D_R \rangle$. For $\langle \emptyset, \emptyset, \emptyset \rangle$ write $0_\mathcal{R}$.

Definition A.28 (Open terms T_1 and atoms $\mathcal{A}_1$).
$? \in T_1$ and $\langle f^k, \langle t_1, \ldots, t_k \rangle \rangle \in T_1$ whenever $f^k \in F$ and for some $1 \leq i \leq k$, $t_i \in T_1$ and $t_j \in T$ for $j \neq i$. $\langle P^k, \langle t_1, \ldots, t_k \rangle \rangle \in \mathcal{A}_1$, whenever $P^k \in P$ and for some $1 \leq i \leq k$, $t_j \in T$ for all $j \neq i$ and $t_i \in T_1$.

Definition A.29 (Issue structures $\mathbb{I}$).
$I \in \mathbb{I}_\Gamma$ iff I consists of pairs $\langle t, x \rangle$, s.t. $x \in \mathcal{A}_1$ and $x[t/?] \in \mathcal{A}(\Gamma)$.

Definition A.30 (Issue matches M_{IJ}).
For $I, J \in \mathbb{I}_\Gamma$, define,
$$M_{IJ} = \{\langle t_1, t_2 \rangle : \exists x (\langle t_1, x \rangle \in I \wedge (\langle t_2, x \rangle \in J \vee \langle t_2, \bar{x} \rangle \in J))\}$$
where, for $x = \langle P^k, \langle t_1, \ldots, t_k \rangle \rangle$, $\bar{x} = \langle \bar{P}^k, \langle t_1, \ldots, t_k \rangle \rangle$.

Definition A.31 (Views $\mathbb{V}$).
For Γ, Θ finite subsets of $\mathbb{S}$, $R \in \mathcal{R}_{\Gamma \cup \Theta}, I \in \mathbb{I}_{\Gamma \cup \Theta}$, $\langle \Gamma, \Theta, R, I \rangle \in \mathbb{V}$ (abbreviated $\Gamma_{RI}^\Theta \in \mathbb{V}$).
Write $\top$ for $\{0\}_{0_\mathcal{R}\emptyset}^{\{0\}}$ and $\bot$ for $\emptyset_{0_\mathcal{R}\emptyset}^{\{0\}}$.

Definition A.32 (Commitments $\mathbb{C}$).
For $C \subseteq \mathbb{V}, G \in \mathbb{V}, \langle C, G \rangle \in \mathbb{C}$.

Definition A.33 (Primitive absurd states $\mathbb{K}$).
Let $\mathbb{K}_{\subseteq \mathbb{S}}$ contain, $\forall t, t'_{\in T} \forall p_{\in \mathcal{A}} \forall x_{\in \mathcal{A}_1}$, at least:
  (LNC) $\{p, \bar{p}\}$,
  (Aristotle) $\{\neq tt\}$,
  (Leibniz) $\{=tt', x[t/?], \bar{x}[t'/?]\}$.

FORMULA SHEET FOR CHAPTER 4

Definition A.34 ($\mathcal{R}$ Restriction).
$[R]_X = \langle U_R \cap X, E_R \cap X, D_R \cap ((E_R \cap X) \times (U_R \cap X)) \rangle$.
$[R]_\Gamma = [R]_{A(\Gamma)}$.
Given $\langle \Gamma, \Theta, R, I \rangle$, we allow ourselves to write $\langle \Gamma, \Theta, [R], I \rangle$ for $\langle \Gamma, \Theta, [R]_{\Gamma \cup \Theta}, I \rangle$.

Definition A.35 ($\mathbb{I}$ Restriction).
Within a quadruple $\langle \Gamma, \Theta, R, [I] \rangle$, let

$$[I] = \{\langle t, x \rangle : \langle t, x \rangle \in I \wedge x[t/?] \in \mathcal{A}(\Gamma \cup \Theta)\}$$

Definition A.36 ($\mathcal{R}$ Algebra).
Let $R \bowtie S = \langle U_R \cup U_S, E_R \cup E_S, D_R \cup D_S \cup E_S \times U_R \rangle$ and let $0_\mathcal{R} \bowtie 0_\mathcal{R} = 0_\mathcal{R}$.
Let
$$R \bowtie S = \langle U_0, E_0, \emptyset \rangle \bowtie ([R]_{A(R)-(E_0 \cup U_0)} \bowtie [S]_{A(S)-(E_0 \cup U_0)})$$

where $E_0 = \{e_{\in E_R \cup E_S} : \forall u. \langle e, u \rangle \notin D_R \cup D_S\}$ and
$U_0 = \{u_{\in U_R \cup U_S} : \forall e \notin E_0. \langle e, u \rangle \notin (E_R \times U_R - D_R) \cup (E_S \times U_S - D_S)\}$.

Definition A.37 (Product).
$\Gamma^\Theta \otimes \Delta^\Psi = (\{\gamma_{\in \Gamma} \cup \delta_{\in \Delta} : \exists \psi_{\in \Psi}(\psi \subseteq \gamma)\} \cup \{\gamma_{\in \Gamma} : \neg \exists \psi_{\in \Psi}(\psi \subseteq \gamma)\})^\Theta$
$(\Gamma \otimes \Delta)^{\{0\}} = \Gamma^{\{0\}} \otimes \Delta^{\{0\}}$
$\bigotimes_{i \in P} \Delta_i^{\Psi_i} = \{0\}^{\{0\}} \otimes \Delta_1^{\Psi_1} \otimes \ldots \otimes \Delta_n^{\Psi_n}$
$\Gamma_{RI}^\Theta \otimes^T \Delta_{SJ}^\Psi = (\Gamma^\Theta \otimes \Delta^\Psi)_{[(T \bowtie R) \bowtie (T \bowtie S)][I \cup J]}$
$\Gamma_{RI}^\Theta \otimes \Delta_{SJ}^\Psi = \Gamma_{RI}^\Theta \otimes^{0_\mathcal{R}} \Delta_{SJ}^\Psi$
$\bigotimes_{i \in P}^T \Delta_{i S_i J_i}^{\Psi_i} = \top \otimes^T \Delta_{1 S_1 J_1}^{\Psi_1} \otimes^T \ldots \otimes^T \Delta_{n S_n J_n}^{\Psi_n}$

Definition A.38 (Sum).
$\Gamma_{RI}^\Theta \oplus^T \Delta_{SJ}^\Theta = (\Gamma \cup \Delta)_{[(T \bowtie R) \bowtie (T \bowtie S)][I \cup J]}^\Theta$
$\Gamma_{RI}^\Theta \oplus \Delta_{SJ}^\Theta = \Gamma_{RI}^\Theta \oplus^{0_\mathcal{R}} \Delta_{SJ}^\Theta$
$\bigoplus_{i \in P}^T \Delta_{S_i J_i}^{\Psi_i} = \emptyset_{0_\mathcal{R} \emptyset}^\Psi \oplus^T \Delta_{1 S_1 J_1}^\Psi \oplus^T \ldots \oplus^T \Delta_{n S_n J_n}^\Psi$

Definition A.39 ($\mathcal{A}$ Answer potential).
$\Gamma[\Delta]^{AP} = |\mathcal{A}(\Gamma) \cap \mathcal{A}(\Delta)|$

Definition A.40 (Answer).
$$\Gamma_{RI}^\Theta[\Delta_{SJ}^{\{0\}}]^A = (\underset{\gamma \in \Gamma}{\arg\max}\ \Delta[\{\{p\} : p \in \gamma\}]^{AP})_{[R][I]}^\Theta$$

Definition A.41 (Negation).
$[\Gamma_{RI}^\Theta]^N = (\Theta^{\{0\}} \otimes ([\Gamma]^N)^{\{0\}})_{[R]^N [I]^N}$
$[\Gamma]^N = \bigotimes_{\gamma \in \Gamma} \hat{\gamma}^{\{0\}}$
$\hat{\gamma} = \{\{\bar{p}\} : p_{\in \gamma}\}$
$\bar{p} = \vec{F\tau}$ if $p = F\vec{\tau}$; $\bar{p} = F\vec{\tau}$ if $p = \vec{F\tau}$
$[R]^N = \langle E_R, U_R, \{\langle a, b \rangle \in U_R \times E_R : \langle b, a \rangle \notin D_R\} \rangle$
$[I]^N = I \cup \{\langle t, \bar{x} \rangle : \langle t, x \rangle \in I\}$

306 FORMULAS AND DEFINITIONS

Definition A.42 (Novelty). $a \in A$ is *novel* during an inference step $\langle C, G \rangle [D]^O$ if $a \notin A(G) \cup A(D)$ and a has not yet appeared in the computation of the conclusion of the step. A function $v : X \to A$, where $X \subseteq A$ is finite, is novel during an inference step if each $v(x)$ is novel and v is injective, and then $[v]_X$ denotes the simultaneous substitution $[v(a_1)/a_1, \ldots, v(a_k)/a_k]$, where $X = \{a_1, \ldots, a_k\}$. Let $(-)^{\text{nov}(X)}$ stand for $(-)[v]_X$ where $v : X \to A$ is novel.

Definition A.43 (Substitution). Let $Z(T, a) = \{u \in U_T : u \triangleleft_T a\} \cup \{e \in E_T : e \lesssim_T a\} - \{a\} = \{a_1, \ldots, a_k\}$. For $A(\Gamma) \cap A(\Theta) = \emptyset$,

$$\text{Sub}^T_{\langle t,a \rangle}(\Gamma^\Theta_I) = \langle \Gamma[v_1]_{Z(T,a)}[t/a], \Theta, [T \bowtie ([T]_{Z(T,a)}[v_1]_{Z(T,a)})], I[v_1]_{Z(T,a)}[t/a] \rangle,$$

where $v_1 : Z(T, a) \to A$ is novel.

Definition A.44 (Merge).

For either $A(R) \cap A(S) = \emptyset$ or $[R]_{\Delta \cup \Psi} = S$,

$$\Gamma^\Theta_{RI}[\Delta^\Psi_{SJ}]^M = \bigoplus_{y \in \Gamma}^{R \bowtie S} \left(\{y\}^\Theta_{RI} \otimes^{R \bowtie S} \Delta^\Psi_{SJ} \otimes^{R \bowtie S} \bigotimes_{\langle t,u \rangle \in M'_{IJ}(y)}^{R \bowtie S} \text{Sub}^{R \bowtie S}_{\langle t,u \rangle}(\Delta^{\{0\}}_J) \right),$$

where $M'_{IJ}(y) = \{\langle t, u \rangle \in M_{IJ} : u \in U_S \wedge \exists \psi \in \Psi(\psi[t/u] \subseteq y \wedge \psi \not\subseteq y)\}$

Definition A.45 (Update).

For $D \in C$, but with all arbitrary objects novelized,

$$\langle C, \Gamma^\Theta_{RI} \rangle [D]^\circlearrowright = \langle C, \Gamma^\Theta_{RI}[D]^U[D]^E[D]^A[D]^M \rangle$$

Definition A.46 (Universal product).

For $A(\Gamma) \cap A(\Theta) = \emptyset$ and either $A(R) \cap A(S) = \emptyset$ or $[R]_\Delta = S$,

$$\Gamma^\Theta_{RI}[\Delta^{\{0\}}_{SJ}]^U = \{0\}^\Theta_{RI} \otimes^{R \bowtie S} \bigotimes_{\langle u,t \rangle \in M'_{IJ}}^{R \bowtie S} \text{Sub}^{R \bowtie S}_{\langle t,u \rangle}(\Gamma^{\{0\}}_I), \text{ where }$$

$M'_{IJ} = \{\langle u, t \rangle : \langle u, t \rangle \in M_{IJ} \wedge u \in U_R - A(\Theta)\} \neq \emptyset$

Definition A.47 (Reorient).

For $\Delta^\Psi_{SJ} \in (C \cup \{\Gamma^\Theta_{RI}\})$ and $J' \in \mathbb{I}_{\Delta \cup \Psi}$,

$$\langle C, \Gamma^\Theta_{RI} \rangle [\Delta^\Psi_{SJ'}]^R = \langle C, \Delta^\Psi_{SJ'} \rangle$$

Definition A.48 (Existential sum).

Let the following conditions be met:

(1) $A(\Gamma) \cap A(\Theta) = \emptyset$ and either $A(R) \cap A(S) = \emptyset$ or $[R]_\Delta = S$.
(2) $M'_{IJ} = \{\langle e, t \rangle : \langle e, t \rangle \in M_{IJ} \wedge e \in E_R - A(\Theta \cup \Delta) \wedge \neg \exists x (\langle e, x \rangle \in D_R)\} \neq \emptyset$.

Then,

$$\Gamma^\Theta_{RI}[\Delta^{\{0\}}_{SJ}]^E = \Gamma^\Theta_{RI} \oplus^{R \bowtie S} \bigoplus_{\langle e,t \rangle \in M'_{IJ}}^{R \bowtie S}$$

$$\text{Sub}^{R \bowtie S}_{\langle t,e \rangle}((\bigcup_{y \in \{y \in \Gamma : e \in A(y)\}} (\{y\} \cup \{\{x_{\in y} : e \notin A(x)\} \cup \delta :$$

$$\delta \in \bigotimes_{x \in B(y,I,e)} \{\{x\}, \{\bar{x}\} \wedge \delta \not\subseteq y\})\}^\Theta_I),$$

where for $e \in E_R$ and $y \in \Gamma$, let $B(y, I, e) = \{x[e/?] \in y : \langle e, x \rangle \in I\}$.

FORMULA SHEET FOR CHAPTER 4

Definition A.49 (Division).

If $\forall \delta_{\in \Delta} \exists \psi_{\in \Psi} \exists \gamma_{\in \Gamma} (\delta \subseteq \gamma \wedge \psi \subseteq \gamma)$, then
$$\Gamma_{RI}^{\Theta} \oslash \Delta_{SJ}^{\Psi} = \{\gamma \oslash_\Gamma \Delta^\Psi : \gamma \in \Gamma\}_{[R][I]}^{\Theta}$$
$$\gamma \oslash_\Gamma \Delta^\Psi = \gamma - \iota\delta(\delta \in \Delta \wedge \delta \subseteq \gamma \wedge \exists \psi_{\in \Psi}(\psi \subseteq \gamma))$$

Definition A.50 (Factor).

For $\Delta_{SJ}^{\Psi} \neq \bot$,
$$\Gamma_{RI}^{\Theta}[\Delta_{SJ}^{\Psi}]^F = \{\gamma[\Delta^\Psi]^F : \gamma \in \Gamma\}_{[R][I]}^{\Theta} \text{ where}$$
$\gamma[\Delta^\Psi]^F = (\gamma \oslash_\Gamma \Delta^\Psi) \cap \bigcap \{\gamma \oslash_\Gamma (\Delta^\Psi[t/a]) : \langle t, a \rangle \in M_{IJ} \wedge a \in U_S\}$, and where we let $\gamma' \cap \bigcap \varnothing = \gamma'$.

For $\Delta_{SJ}^{\Psi} = \bot$,
$$\Gamma_{RI}^{\Theta}[\bot]^F = \{\gamma \in \Gamma : \neg \exists \delta \in \mathbb{K}. \delta \subseteq \gamma\}_{[R][I]}^{\Theta}.$$

Definition A.51 (Matryoshka level ordering).

For existentials, we have $e \lesssim_R e'$ iff $\forall \langle e', u \rangle \in D_R(\langle e, u \rangle \in D_R)$. For both existentials and universals, let the relation $\triangleleft_R$ be the transitive closure of the relation made up by the ordered pairs in $D_R \cup (E_R \times U_R - D_R)^{op}$, where op reverses the order of pairs in a set of pairs.

Definition A.52 (Query).

For $U_S \subseteq U_R$ and $M'_{IJ} = \{\langle t, e \rangle \in M_{IJ} : e \in E_S \backslash E_R\}$, we define
$$\Gamma_{RI}^{\Theta}[\Delta_{SJ}^{\Psi}]^Q =$$

$$(\{0 : \neg \exists \delta_{\in \Delta} \exists \gamma. \Phi(\gamma, \delta)\} \cup \{\delta \in \Delta : \exists \gamma_{\in \Gamma}. \Phi(\gamma, \delta)\})_{[R \bowtie \langle U_R, E_S \backslash E_R, D_{S'} \rangle][I \cup J]}^{\Theta}$$

where

$$\Phi(\gamma, \delta) \leftrightarrow \exists \psi_{\in \Psi} \exists n_{\geq 0} \exists \langle t_1, e_1 \rangle, \ldots, \langle t_n, e_n \rangle_{\in M'_{IJ}} \forall i, j$$
$$(\psi \cup \delta[t_1/e_1, \ldots, t_n/e_n] \subseteq \gamma \wedge e_i = e_j \rightarrow i = j);$$

and $D_{S'} = D_1 \cup D_2 \cup D_3 \cup D_4 \cup D_5 \cup D_6$ is constructed by taking: original dependencies from the internal argument
$$D_1 = [D_S]_{A/E_R},$$

extra dependencies for multiple terms substituted with same e

$$D_2 = \{\langle e_m, u \rangle : \exists m \exists m' \in M'_{IJ}(e_m = e_{m'} \wedge t_m \neq t_{m'}) \wedge u \in U_R\},$$

dependencies resulting from complex terms being substituted

$$D_3 = \{\langle e_m, u \rangle : \langle t_m, e_m \rangle \in M'_{IJ} \wedge u \in U_R(t_m)\},$$
$$D_4 = \{\langle e_m, u \rangle : \langle t_m, e_m \rangle \in M'_{IJ} \wedge e \in E_R(t_m) \wedge \langle e, u \rangle \in R\},$$
$$D_5 = \{\langle e_m, u \rangle : \langle t_m, e_m \rangle \in M'_{IJ} \wedge u \in U_R \wedge \forall u'_{\in U_R(D_3 \cup D_4)}(u' \triangleleft_R u)\},$$

additional dependencies necessary to preserve the dependency order of existentials in S

$$D_6 = \{\langle e, u \rangle : e, e' \in E_S - E_R \wedge e \lesssim_S e' \wedge$$
$$(\forall m, m' \in M'_{IJ}(e_m = e' \wedge e_{m'} = e') \rightarrow t_m = t_{m'}) \wedge$$
$$\langle e', u \rangle \in D_1 \cup D_2 \cup D_3 \cup D_4 \cup D_5\}.$$

Definition A.53 (Wh-Query). Provided that $U_S \subseteq U_R$,
$$\Gamma_{RI}^{\Theta}[\Delta_{SJ}^{\Psi}]^W = \Big(\{0 : \exists \gamma \in \Gamma. \neg \exists \delta_{\in \Delta}.\Phi(\gamma,\delta)\} \cup \{\delta \in \Delta : \exists \gamma_{\in \Gamma}.\Psi(\gamma,\xi)\}\Big)_{[R][I]}^{\Theta},$$
where $\Psi(\gamma,\xi)$ iff

$$\exists \psi_{\in \Psi} \exists n_{\geq 0} \exists \langle t_1,e_1 \rangle, \ldots, \langle t_n,e_n \rangle_{\in M'_{IJ}} \exists \delta_{\in \Delta}.$$
$$(\xi \cup \psi \subseteq \gamma \wedge \xi = \delta[t_1/e_1, \ldots, t_n/e_n]$$
$$\wedge \forall i,j.(e_i = e_j \rightarrow i = j)).$$

Definition A.54 (Inquire).

(O) If $A(\Gamma \cup \Theta) \cap A(\Delta \cup \Psi) = \emptyset \wedge A(\Delta) \cap A(\Psi) = \emptyset$, then
$$\Gamma_{RI}^{\Theta}[\Delta_{SJ}^{\Psi}]^I = \Gamma_{RI}^{\Theta} \otimes \Big(\Delta_{SJ}^{\Psi} \oplus (\{0\}_{[S][J]}^{\Psi} \otimes \mathcal{N}ov([\Delta^{\{0\}}]_{[[S]^N][J]^N}^{N}))\Big)[\bot]^F,$$
where $\mathcal{N}ov()$ uniformly replaces all arbitrary objects in its scope by novel ones.
(I) If $A(\Delta \cup \Psi) \subseteq A(\Gamma \cup \Theta)$, then
$$\Gamma_{RI}^{\Theta}[\Delta_{SJ}^{\Psi}]^I = \Gamma_{RI}^{\Theta} \otimes (\Delta_{0_{\mathcal{R}}J}^{\Psi} \oplus ([\Delta]_{0_{\mathcal{R}}[J]^N}^{N})^{\Psi})[\bot]^F.$$

Definition A.55 (Suppose).

(O) If $A(\Gamma \cup \Theta) \cap A(\Delta \cup \Psi) = \emptyset$, then
$$\Gamma_{RI}^{\Theta}[\Delta_{SJ}^{\Psi}]^S = \Gamma_{[R \bowtie R'][I \cup I']}^{\Theta'}[\Delta_{SJ}^{\Psi}]^U[\Delta_{SJ}^{\Psi}]^E[\Delta_{SJ}^{\Psi}]^A[\Delta_{SJ}^{\Psi}]^M, \text{ where}$$
$$\Theta'^{\{0\}}_{R'I'} = \Theta^{\{0\}}_{RI} \otimes \mathcal{N}ov(\Delta_{[S]^NJ}^{\Psi}[\ ]^D),$$
where $\mathcal{N}ov()$ uniformly replaces all arbitrary objects in its scope by novel ones.
(I) If $A(\Delta) \subseteq A(\Gamma \cup \Theta)$ and $[R]_\Delta = S$,
then $\Gamma_{RI}^{\Theta}[\Delta_{SJ}^{\{0\}}]^S = \Gamma_{RI}^{\Theta \otimes \Delta}[\Delta_{SJ}^{\{0\}}]^U[\Delta_{SJ}^{\{0\}}]^E[\Delta_{SJ}^{\{0\}}]^A[\Delta_{SJ}^{\{0\}}]^M$

Definition A.56 (Depose).
$$\Gamma_{RI}^{\Theta}[T]^D = \langle \Gamma^{\{0\}} \oplus ([\Theta]^N)^{\{0\}}, R, [[I]^N \cup I] \rangle.$$

Definition A.57 (Commit).
$$\langle C, \Gamma_{RI}^{\Theta} \rangle [T]^C = \langle C \cup \{\Gamma_{RI}^{\Theta}\}, \Gamma_{RI}^{\Theta} \rangle$$

Definition A.58 (Inference). An inference $\mathcal{J}$ is a finite sequence of inference steps defined as follows, relative to an inference state consisting of a commitment $\langle C, G \rangle \in \mathbb{C}$. If $E \in \mathbb{V}$ and $O \in \{[D]^\circ, [D]^S, [D]^Q, [D]^F, [D]^R, [D]^I, [D]^D, [D]^E, [D]^U, [D]^C\}$, then O is an inference step applicable to $\langle C, G \rangle$, whose result is an inference state in $\mathbb{C}$. We write $C \models_{\text{ETR}} E$ if and only if there is an erotetic theory inference $\mathcal{J}$ s.t. $\langle C, \mathsf{T} \rangle \mathcal{J} = \langle C', E' \rangle$, where E' is identical to E up to uniform replacement of $\mathbf{A}$ objects.

A.3 Formula Sheet for Chapter 5

Definition A.59 (Weights).

(Weights) The set $\mathbb{W}$ of weights consists of all finite multisets of terms. Given a finite sequence of terms $t_1, \ldots, t_n$, we denote the underlying multiset of that sequence (the set of members in the sequence weighted by their number of occurrences) by $\langle\!\langle t_1,\ldots,t_n\rangle\!\rangle$.

Definition A.60 (Additional terms).

(Real numbers) Every real number $\alpha \in \mathbb{R}$ is a constant term.
(Multiplication) $\overline{\times}$ is a function symbol of arity 2.
(Summation) σ is function symbol, but rather than taking as an argument a list of terms of fixed size, it takes an arbitrary finite multiset of terms. Thus, whenever $t_1,\ldots,t_n$ is a sequence of terms, $\sigma\langle\!\langle t_1,\ldots,t_n\rangle\!\rangle$ is a term.

Definition A.61 (Extended set of states). Γ_f is an *extended set of states* if and only if Γ is a finite set $\Gamma \subseteq \mathbb{S}$ of states and f is an assignment $f : \Gamma \to \mathbb{W}$.

Definition A.62 (Extended views $\overline{\mathbb{V}}$). An *extended view* Γ^Θ_{fRI} is a view Γ^Θ_{RI} such that Γ_f is an extended set of states and such that $\forall y \in \Gamma . A(f(y)) \subseteq A(R)$.
We use the convention that $f(y) = \langle\!\langle\rangle\!\rangle$ for $y \notin \Gamma$ (but we do not rule out $f(y) = \langle\!\langle\rangle\!\rangle$ for some $y \in \Gamma$).

Definition A.63 (Extended commitments $\overline{\mathbb{C}}$). For $C \subseteq \overline{\mathbb{V}}, G \in \overline{\mathbb{V}}, \langle C, G\rangle \in \overline{\mathbb{C}}$.

Definition A.64 ($\mathbb{E}$ Answer potential).

$$\Delta_g[\Gamma]^{\mathbb{E}P} = \sigma\big(\langle\!\langle \sigma(g(\delta)) \mid \delta \in Y\rangle\!\rangle\big),$$

where $Y = \{\delta \in \Delta \mid \exists y \in \Gamma. y \subseteq \delta\}$.

Definition A.65 (Pipe to extended view). Given an extended set of states Γ_f, and given Θ, R, I, such that $A(\Gamma \cup \Theta) \subseteq A(R)$ we define $\Gamma_f|^\Theta_{RI}$ to be the extended View $\langle \Gamma, g, \Theta, S, J\rangle$ where:

(1) $S = [R]_{\Gamma \cup \Theta}$,
(2) For $y \in \Gamma$, $g(y) = \langle\!\langle t \in f(y) : A(t) \subseteq A(S)\rangle\!\rangle$.
(3) $J = [I]_{\Gamma \cup \Theta}$.

Definition A.66 ($\mathbb{E}$ Answer).

$$\Gamma^\Theta_{fRI}[\Delta^{\{0\}}_{gSJ}]^{\mathbb{E}A} = \left(\operatorname*{arg\,max}_{y \in \Gamma} \Delta_g[\{\{p\} : p \in y\}]^{\mathbb{E}P}\right)_f \bigg|^\Theta_{RI}$$

Definition A.67 (Atomic answer potential).

$$\Delta[\Gamma]^{AP} = |\mathcal{A}(\Gamma) \cap \mathcal{A}(\Delta)|$$

Definition A.68 ($\mathcal{A}$ Answer).

$$\Gamma^\Theta_{fRI}[\Delta^{\{0\}}_{gSJ}]^{\mathcal{A}A} = (\operatorname*{arg\,max}_{y \in \Gamma} \Delta[\{\{p\} : p \in y\}]^{AP})_f \bigg|^\Theta_{RI}$$

Definition A.69 (Answer). $\Gamma^\Theta_{fRI}[\Delta^{\{0\}}_{gSJ}]^A = \Gamma^\Theta_{fRI}[\Delta^{\{0\}}_{gSJ}]^{EA}[\Delta^{\{0\}}_{gSJ}]^{AA}$.

Definition A.70 (Sum). For Γ_f, Δ_g weighted sets of states,
$\Gamma_f + \Delta_g = (\Gamma \cup \Delta)_h$, where $h(\gamma) = f(\gamma) + g(\gamma)$.
We then have,
$$\Gamma^\Theta_{fRI} \oplus^T \Delta^\Theta_{gSJ} = (\Gamma_f + \Delta_g)|^\Theta_{(T\bowtie R)\bowtie(T\bowtie S), I\cup J}.$$

Definition A.71 (Product).
$$\Gamma_f \otimes \Delta^\Psi_g = P + \sum_{\gamma\in\Gamma\setminus P}\sum_{\delta\in\Delta}\{(f(\gamma)\times g(\delta)).(\gamma\cup\delta)\}$$

where $P = \{f(\gamma).\gamma \in \Gamma \mid \neg\exists\psi \in \Psi.\psi \subseteq \gamma\}$ and $\times$ is the product of weights. As a special case, $\Gamma_f \otimes \Delta_g = \Gamma_f \otimes \Delta^{\{0\}}_g$. $\Gamma^\Theta_{fRI} \otimes^T \Delta^\Psi_{gSJ} =$
$(\Gamma_f \otimes \Delta^\Psi_g)|^\Theta_{[(T\bowtie R)\bowtie(T\bowtie S)][I\cup J]}$.

This definition relies on products of weights, which are characterized as follows. Given weights $w, v \in \mathbb{W}$, the *product* $w \times v$ is given by

$$w \times \langle\!\langle\rangle\!\rangle = w$$
$$\langle\!\langle\rangle\!\rangle \times v = v$$

in the case that either w or v is empty, and when $w = \langle\!\langle s_1, \ldots, s_m\rangle\!\rangle$ and $v = \langle\!\langle t_1, \ldots, t_n\rangle\!\rangle$ with $m, n \geq 1$ we have
$$w \times v = \langle\!\langle (s_i \overline{\times} t_j) : 1 \leq i \leq m, 1 \leq j \leq n\rangle\!\rangle.$$

Definition A.72 (Negation). $[\Gamma^\Theta_{fRI}]^N = (\Theta \otimes [\Gamma]^N)\Big|^{\{0\}}_{[R]^N[I]^N}$ (N.B. f is not used on the RHS).

Definition A.73 (Factor (contradictions)). For $\Delta^\Psi = \{\}^{\{0\}}$,
$$\Gamma^\Theta_{fRI}[\bot]^F = \{\gamma \in \Gamma : \neg\exists\kappa \in \mathbb{K}.\kappa \subseteq \gamma\}_f\Big|^\Theta_{RI}.$$

Definition A.74 (Inquire).

(O) If $A(\gamma\cup\Theta)\cap A(\Delta\cup\Psi) = \emptyset$ and $A(\Delta)\cap A(\Psi) = \emptyset$, then
$$\Gamma^\Theta_{fRI}[\Delta^\Psi_{gSJ}]^I = (\Gamma^\Theta_{fRI} \otimes (\Delta^\Psi_{gSJ} \oplus^S (\{0\}|^\Psi_{SJ} \otimes ([\Delta_g|^{\{0\}}_{SJ}]^N)^{\text{nov}(A(\Delta))})))[\bot]^F.$$

(I) If $A(\Delta\cup\Psi) \subseteq A(\Gamma\cup\Theta)$ and $S = [R]_{\Gamma\cup\Theta}$,
$$\Gamma^\Theta_{fRI}[\Delta^\Psi_{gSJ}]^I = (\Gamma^\Theta_{fI} \otimes^R (\Delta^\Psi_{gSJ} \oplus^R ([\Delta_g]^N|^\Psi_{SJ})))[\bot]^F.$$

Definition A.75 (Query). We define $\Gamma^\Theta_{fIR}[\Delta^\Psi_{gSJ}]^Q$ as follows, assuming $U_S \subseteq U_R$. Let
$$M'_{IJ} = \{\langle t, e\rangle \in M_{IJ} : e \in E_S\setminus E_R\}.$$

Then

$$\Gamma^{\Theta}_{fRI}[\Delta^{\Psi}_{gSJ}]^Q = H + \sum_{\gamma \in \Gamma} \sum_{\delta \in \Delta \text{ s.t. } \Phi(\gamma,\delta)} \{w_{\gamma,\delta} \cdot \delta\}\Big|^{\Theta}_{R \bowtie \langle U_R, E_S \setminus E_R, D_{S'} \rangle, I \cup J}$$

where

$$H = \begin{cases} \{0\}^{\Theta}|_{RI} & \text{if } \exists \gamma \in \Gamma. \forall \delta \in \Delta. \neg \Phi(\gamma,\delta) \\ \{\}^{\Theta}|_{RI} & \text{otherwise,} \end{cases}$$

and where

$$w_{\gamma,\delta} = \begin{cases} g(\delta) & \text{if } g(\delta) \neq \langle\!\langle\rangle\!\rangle \\ f(\gamma) & \text{otherwise,} \end{cases}$$

and where $\Phi(\gamma,\delta)$ is by definition

$$\exists \psi \in \Psi \exists n \geq 0 \exists \langle t_1, e_1 \rangle, \ldots, \langle t_n, e_n \rangle \in M'_{IJ} (\forall i,j. e_i = e_j \to i = j) \wedge$$
$$(\psi \cup \delta[t_1/e_1, \ldots, t_n/e_n] \subseteq \gamma) \wedge (f(\gamma) = g(\delta)[t_1/e_1, \ldots] \vee g(\delta) = \langle\!\langle\rangle\!\rangle);$$

Finally, $D_{S'}$ is defined in the same way as in the definition of Query in chapter 4.

Definition A.76 (Suppose).

(O) If $A(\Gamma \cup \Theta) \cap A(\Delta \cup \Psi) = \emptyset$ and $\Delta^{\Psi}_{gSJ} = \Delta^{\Psi}_{SJ}$, then

$$\Gamma^{\Theta}_{fRI}[\Delta^{\Psi}_{gSJ}]^S = \Gamma^{\Theta'}_{[R\bowtie R'][I\cup I']}[\Delta^{\Psi}_{gSJ}]^U[\Delta^{\Psi}_{gSJ}]^E[\Delta^{\Psi}_{gSJ}]^A[\Delta^{\Psi}_{gSJ}]^M,$$

where

$$\Theta'^{\{0\}}_{f'R'I'} = \Theta^{\{0\}}_{fRI} \otimes \text{Nov}(\Delta^{\Psi}_{g[S]^NJ}[\ ]^D),$$

where Nov() uniformly replaces all arbitrary objects in its scope by novel ones.

(I) If $A(\Delta) \subseteq A(\Gamma \cup \Theta)$, $[R]_{\Delta} = S$, and $\Delta^{\Psi}_{gSJ} = \Delta^{\Psi}_{SJ}$, then

$$\Gamma^{\Theta}_{fRI}[\Delta^{\{0\}}_{gSJ}]^S = \Gamma^{\Theta \otimes \Delta}_{fRI}[\Delta^{\{0\}}_{gSJ}]^U[\Delta^{\{0\}}_{gSJ}]^E[\Delta^{\{0\}}_{gSJ}]^A[\Delta^{\{0\}}_{gSJ}]^M.$$

Definition A.77 (Depose).

$$\Gamma^{\Theta}_{fRI}[T]^D = (\Gamma_f + [\Theta]^N)\Big|^{\{0\}}_{R[I]^N}$$

Definition A.78 (Multiproduct). For a finite set $G = \{\Gamma^{\{0\}}_{if_i,R_i,I_i} : i \in I\}$, we define $\bigotimes G$ by

$$\bigotimes{}^T \emptyset = \{0\}\Big|^{\{0\}}_{0_{\mathcal{R}},\emptyset}$$

for $|I| = 0$, and

$$\bigotimes^T \{\Gamma_{fRI}^{\{0\}}\} = \Gamma_f\big|_{T\bowtie R, I}^{\{0\}}$$

for $|I| = 1$, and

$$\bigotimes^T \{\Gamma_{if_i, R_i, I_i}^{\{0\}} : i \in I\} = \left(\bigotimes^T_{i \in I} \Gamma_{iR_iI_i}^{\{0\}}\right)$$

for $|I| \geq 2$.

Definition A.79 (Merge). For either $A(R) \cap A(S) = \emptyset$ or $[R]_{\Delta \cup \Psi} = S$, and with $M'_{IJ}(\gamma) = \{\langle t,u \rangle \in M_{IJ} : u \in U_S \wedge \exists \psi \in \Psi(\psi[t/u] \subseteq \gamma \wedge \psi \not\subseteq \gamma)\}$,

$$\Gamma_{fRI}^{\Theta}[\Delta_{gSJ}^{\Psi}]^M = \bigoplus_{\gamma \in \Gamma}^{R\bowtie S} \{f(\gamma).\gamma\}\big|_{RI}^{\Theta} \otimes^{R\bowtie S} \Delta_{gSJ}^{\Psi} \otimes^{R\bowtie S} \bigotimes_{\langle t,u \rangle \in M'_{IJ}(\gamma)}^{R\bowtie S} \mathrm{Sub}_{\langle t,u \rangle}^{R\bowtie S}(\Delta_{gSJ}^{\{0\}}).$$

Definition A.80 (Universal product). For $A(\Gamma) \cap A(\Theta) = \emptyset$; $M'_{IJ} = \{\langle u,t \rangle : \langle u,t \rangle \in M_{IJ} \wedge u \in U_R - A(\Theta)\} \neq \emptyset$; and $A(R) \cap A(S) = \emptyset \vee [R]_{\Delta} = S$, we have

$$\Gamma_{fRI}^{\Theta}[\Delta_{gSJ}^{\{0\}}]^U = \{0\}\big|_{R,I}^{\Theta} \otimes^{R\bowtie S} \bigotimes_{\langle t,u \rangle \in M'_{IJ}}^{R\bowtie S} \mathrm{Sub}_{\langle t,u \rangle}^{R\bowtie S}(\Gamma_f|_{RI}^{\{0\}}).$$

Definition A.81 (Pipe to free atoms).
Let $\mathcal{A}_? = \{P^k(?, \ldots, ?) : P^k \in \mathbf{P}\}$. For an atom $A = P^k(t_1, \ldots, t_k) \in \mathcal{A}$, let $A|_? = P^k(?, \ldots, ?) \in \mathcal{A}_?$. Extend to states by $\gamma|_? = \{A|_? : A \in \gamma\}$ and to sets of states by $\Gamma|_? = \{\gamma|_? : \gamma \in \Gamma\}$.

Definition A.82 (Linkage potential views).
$L(C, \Gamma_{fRI}^{\Theta}, \Delta_{gSJ}^{\Psi}) = \{\Phi_{hSK}^{\chi} \in C : \chi|_?[\Gamma|_?]^{AP} \times \Phi|_?[\Delta|_?]^{AP} \neq 0\}.$

Definition A.83 (Division). If $\forall \delta \in \Delta \exists \psi \in \Psi \exists \gamma \in \Gamma. \delta \subseteq \gamma \wedge \psi \subseteq \gamma)$ then define

$$\Gamma_{fRI}^{\Theta} \oslash \Delta_{gSJ}^{\Psi} = \sum_{\gamma \in \Gamma} \{f(\gamma).(\gamma \oslash_\Gamma \Delta^{\Psi})\}\bigg|_{RI}^{\Theta}$$

where $\gamma \oslash_\Gamma \Delta^{\Psi} = \gamma - \iota\delta(\delta \in \Delta \wedge \delta \subseteq \gamma \wedge \exists \psi \in \Psi(\psi \subseteq \gamma)).$

Definition A.84 (Factor (central case)). For $\Delta^{\Psi} \neq \{\}^{\{0\}}$,

$$\Gamma_{fRI}^{\Theta}[\Delta_{gSJ}^{\Psi}]^F = \sum_{\gamma \in \Gamma} \{f(\gamma).\gamma[\Delta^{\Psi}]^F\}\bigg|_{RI}^{\Theta},$$

where $\gamma[\Delta]^F = \ldots$ (as before).

FORMULA SHEET FOR CHAPTER 5   313

Definition A.85 (Which?). We define $\Gamma^\Theta_{fIR}[\Delta^\Psi_{gSJ}]^W$ as follows, assuming $U_S \subseteq U_R$. Let

$$M'_{IJ} = \{\langle t, e \rangle \in M_{IJ} : e \in E_S \setminus E_R\}.$$

Then

$$\Gamma^\Theta_{fRI}[\Delta^\Psi_{gSJ}]^W = H + \sum_{\gamma \in \Gamma} \langle\!\langle w.\xi : \Xi(\gamma, w.\xi) \rangle\!\rangle \Big|^\Theta_{RI}$$

where

$$H = \begin{cases} \{0\}^\Theta|_{RI} & \text{if } \exists \gamma \in \Gamma. \forall \delta \in \Delta. \neg\Phi(\gamma, \delta) \\ \{\}^\Theta|_{RI} & \text{otherwise,} \end{cases}$$

and where $\Phi(\gamma, \delta)$ is by definition

$$\exists \psi \in \Psi \exists n_{\geq 0} \exists \langle t_1, e_1 \rangle, \ldots, \langle t_n, e_n \rangle \in M'_{IJ} (\forall i, j. e_i = e_j \to i = j) \wedge$$
$$(\psi \cup \delta[t_1/e_1, \ldots, t_n/e_n] \subseteq \gamma) \wedge$$
$$(f(\gamma) = g(\delta)[t_1/e_1, \ldots] \vee f(\gamma) = g(\delta)[t_1/e_1, \ldots] \vee g(\delta) = \langle\!\langle \rangle\!\rangle);$$

and $\Xi(\gamma, w.\xi)$ is by definition

$$\exists \psi \in \Psi \exists \delta \in \Delta \exists n_{\geq 0} \exists \langle t_1, e_1 \rangle, \ldots, \langle t_n, e_n \rangle \in M'_{IJ} (\forall i, j. (e_i = e_j \to i = j)) \wedge$$
$$(\xi \cup \psi \subseteq \gamma \wedge w.\xi = (g(\delta).\delta)[t_1/e_1, \ldots, t_n/e_n]).$$

Definition A.86 (Existential sum). For $A(\Gamma) \cap A(\Theta) = \emptyset$ and either $A(R) \cap A(S) = \emptyset$ or $[R]_\Delta = S$; $M'_{IJ} = \{\langle e, t \rangle \in M_{IJ} : e \in E_R - A(\Theta \cup \Delta) \wedge \neg\exists x(\langle e, x \rangle \in D_R)\} \neq \emptyset$; for $e \in E_R$ and $\gamma \in \Gamma$, let $N(\gamma, I, e) = \{x[e/?] \in \gamma : \langle e, x \rangle \in I\}$.

$$\Gamma^\Theta_{fRI}[\Delta^{\{0\}}_{gSJ}]^E = \Gamma^\Theta_{fRI} \oplus^{R\bowtie S}$$

$$\bigoplus_{\langle e,t \rangle \in M'_{IJ}}^{R \bowtie S} \text{Sub}^{R \bowtie S}_{\langle t, e \rangle} \Bigg(\Bigg(\bigcup_{\substack{\gamma \in \Gamma, \\ e \in A(\gamma)}} \{\gamma\} \cup \{\{x_{\in \gamma} : e \notin A(x)\} \cup \delta : \delta$$

$$\in \bigotimes_{x \in N(\gamma, I, e)} \{\{x\}, \{\bar{x}\} \wedge \delta \not\subseteq \gamma\} \Bigg) \Bigg|^\Theta_{S, J} \Bigg)$$

Definition A.87 (Factor (identity)). For $J = \{\langle It_1?, t_2 \rangle\}$ or $J = \{\langle I?t_2, t_1 \rangle\}$,

$$\Gamma^\Theta_{fRI}[\{w.It_1t_2\}|^{\{0\}}_{R,J}]^F = \{\gamma \in \Gamma : It_1t_2 \notin \gamma\}|_f +$$

$$\sum_{\gamma \in \Gamma \text{ s.t. } It_1t_2 \in \gamma} \{(f(\gamma)[t_1/t_2]).(\gamma[t_1/t_2])\} \Bigg|^\Theta_{R,I}.$$

APPENDIX B
Meta-theory for Chapters 4 and 5

B.1 A Theory of Dependency Relations

Here we gather some facts about dependency relations, either useful for calculation or important for subsequent meta-theoretic properties of the system.

B.1.1 An Alternative Characterization of Dependency Relations

Definition B.1. A *δ-map* is a function $\delta : \mathbb{A} \to \mathbb{N}$ such that
- $\delta(a) = 0$ for all but finitely many $a \in \mathbb{A}$,
- $\{\delta(a) : a \in \mathbb{A}\} \cup \{1\}$ is a downwards-closed subset of $\mathbb{N}$.

Thus, a δ-map represents a shift of finitely many $\mathbb{A}$-objects away from 0 to the right on the number line, skipping no integers except possibly the integer 1. Given a δ-map δ, write $E_\delta = \delta^{-1}(\{1, 3, 5, \ldots\})$ for the set of $\mathbb{A}$-objects sent to odd numbers, and $U_\delta = \delta^{-1}(\{2, 4, 6, \ldots\})$ for the set of $\mathbb{A}$-objects sent to postive even numbers. Write $D_\delta \subseteq E_\delta \times U_\delta$ for the set of pairs $\langle e, u \rangle$ with $e \in E_\delta$, $u \in U_\delta$, and $\delta(e) \leq \delta(u)$.

Proposition B.1. $\langle U_\delta, E_\delta, D_\delta \rangle$ is a dependency relation.

Proof. Clearly U_δ and E_δ are finite and disjoint, and $D_\delta \subseteq E_\delta \times U_\delta$. Let $u, u' \in U_\delta$. Without loss of generality, $\delta(u) \leq \delta(u')$, and hence

$$\{e \in E_\delta : \langle e, u \rangle \in D_\delta\} \subseteq \{e \in E_\delta : \langle e, u' \rangle \in D_\delta\}$$

as required. $\square$

Conversely, every dependency relation R gives rise to a δ-map δ_R defined by the following recursive clauses:

- $\delta_R(a) = 0$ for $a \in \mathbb{A} \setminus A(R)$,
- $\delta_R(e) = 1 + \max\{\delta_R(u) : \langle e, u \rangle \in D_R\}$ for $e \in E_R$,
- $\delta_R(u) = 2 + \max\{\delta_R(e) - 1 : \langle e, u \rangle \in (E_R \times U_R) \setminus D_R\}$ for $u \in U_R$,

where the maximum of an empty set is considered to be 0.

Proposition B.2. δ_R is a δ-map.

Proof. We must in particular check that δ_R is a well-defined function. Consider the following sequence $E_1, U_1, E_2, U_2, \ldots$ of subsets of $\mathbb{A}$ defined recursively as follows.

$$E_n = \{e \in E_R \setminus \bigcup_{i<n} E_i : \forall u. \langle e,u \rangle \in D_R \implies u \in \bigcup_{i<n} U_i\}$$
$$U_n = \{u \in U_R \setminus \bigcup_{i<n} U_i : \forall e. \langle e,u \rangle \in (E_R \times U_R) \setminus D_R \implies e \in \bigcup_{i \leq n} E_i\}$$

The recursion is well-defined since each step only refers to earlier sets in the sequence. It is clear from the definition that the sets in the sequence are mutually disjoint. To see that $U_R = \bigcup U_i$ observe that, if not, then there is a $u \in U_R \setminus \bigcup U_i$ with $\{e \in E_R : \langle e,u \rangle \in D_R\}$ minimum amongst all others. Since $u \notin \bigcup U_i$ there is an $e \in E_R$ with $\langle e,u \rangle \in (E_R \times U_R) \setminus D_R$ and $e \notin \bigcup E_i$, but since u was chosen to be minimal the fact that $\langle e,u \rangle \notin D_R$ means that $e \in \bigcup E_i$, a contradiction. From $U_R = \bigcup U_i$ it follows that $E_R = \bigcup E_i$. Now, writing

$$X_0 = A \setminus A(R) \qquad X_{2i-1} = E_i \qquad X_{2i} = U_i$$

for $i \geq 1$, it is a straightforward induction to check that $a \in X_k$ implies that the recursion for $\delta_R(a)$ terminates with $\delta_R(a) \leq k$. Moreover, it is easy to see that one cannot have $X_n \neq \emptyset, X_{n+1} = \emptyset, X_{n+2} \neq \emptyset$ for any $n \geq 1$, and that if $e \in E_{n+1}$ for $n \geq 1$ then $\langle e,u \rangle \in D_R$ for some $u \in U_n$, and that if $u \in U_{n+1}$ for $n \geq q$ then $\langle e,u \rangle \in (E_R \times U_E) \setminus D_R$ for some $e \in E_{n+1}$. Hence one can show by induction on k that, indeed, $a \in X_k$ if and only if $\delta_R(a) = k$ and moreover that δ_R is a δ-map. □

Definition B.2. Let R be a dependency relation. Then δ-map $\delta_R : A \to \mathbb{N}$ described above is called the *depth-map* of R, with $\delta_R(a)$ being the *depth of a in R*.

Theorem B.3. *The assignments $R \mapsto \delta_R$ and $\delta \mapsto \langle U_\delta, E_\delta, D_\delta \rangle$ establish a bijection between dependency relations and δ-maps.*

Proof. Straightforward given the above and left to the reader. □

B.1.2 The Induced Ordering on A(R)

Recall from Definition A.51 that a dependency relation induces relations $\lesssim_R$ and $\lhd_R$ on subsets of **A**. The following definition extends and supersedes that one.

Definition B.3. Let R be a dependency relation. The relations $\lesssim_R$ and $\lhd_R$, both on $A(R)$, are given by $x \lesssim_R y \iff \delta_R(x) \geq \delta_R(y)$ and $x \lhd_R y \iff \delta_R(x) > \delta_R(y)$. (N.B. reversal of inequalities).

The next three lemmas are trivial.

Lemma B.4. *Let R be a dependency relation. The relation $\lesssim_R$ is reflexive, transitive and satisfies $\forall a,b \in A(R)$. $a \lesssim_R b \lor b \lesssim_R a$. The relation $a \lhd_R b$ is irreflexive, transitive, equivalent to $a \lesssim_R b \land \neg(b \lesssim_R a)$, and satisfies $\forall e \in E_R, u \in U_R$. $e \lhd_R u \lor u \lhd_R e$.*

Lemma B.5. *Let $u, u' \in U_R$. Then $u \lesssim_R u'$ iff $\{e \in E_R : \langle e,u \rangle \in D_R\} \subseteq \{e \in E_R : \langle e,u' \rangle \in D_R\}$.*

Lemma B.6. *Let $e \in E_R, u \in U_R$. Then $e \lesssim_R u$ iff $e \lhd_R u$ iff $\langle e,u \rangle \in D_R$.*

From the above the following is an easy exercise. It provides a more direct characterization of $\lesssim_R$ and $\vartriangleleft_R$ (not using δ-maps) and shows that the new definitions agree with Definition A.51.

Lemma B.7 (Intrinsic characterization of $\lesssim_R$ and $\vartriangleleft_R$). *Let R be a dependency relation.*
  (i) *If $e \in E_R$, $u \in U_R$, then $e \lesssim_R u$ iff $e \vartriangleleft_R u$ iff $\langle e, u \rangle \in D_R$ iff $\neg(u \lesssim_R e)$ iff $\neg(u \vartriangleleft_R e)$.*
  (ii) *If $u, u' \in U_R$, then*
    (a) $u \lesssim_R u'$ *iff* $\forall e \in E_R.\langle e, u \rangle \in D_R \implies \langle e, u' \rangle \in D_R$,
    (b) $u \vartriangleleft_R u'$ *iff* $\exists e \in E_R.\langle e, u \rangle \notin D_R \wedge \langle e, u' \rangle \in D_R$.
  (iii) *If $e, e' \in E_R$, then*
    (a) $e \lesssim_R e'$ *iff* $\forall u \in U_R.\langle e', u \rangle \in D_R \implies \langle e, u \rangle \in D_R$,
    (b) $e \vartriangleleft_R e'$ *iff* $\exists u \in U_R.\langle e', u \rangle \notin D_R \wedge \langle e, u \rangle \in D_R$.
  (iv) $\vartriangleleft_R$ *is the transitive closure of* $D_R \cup (E_R \times U_R \setminus D_R)^{op}$.

B.1.3 Sequential Composition: Chain

Intuitively, $R \bowtie S$ is constructed by simply placing S below R in the hierarchy of quantifiers, i.e. every existential in S depends on every universal in R.

Proposition B.8. *Let R, S be dependency relations with $A(R) \cap A(S) = \emptyset$. Then $R \bowtie S$ is a well-defined dependency relation.*

Proof. This is straightforward given the observations that, for $u \in U_S$,

$$\{e \in E_{R \bowtie S} : \langle e, u \rangle \in D_{R \bowtie S}\} = \{e \in E_S : \langle e, u \rangle \in D_S\}$$

and, for $u' \in U_R$,

$$\{e \in E_{R \bowtie S} : \langle e, u \rangle \in D_{R \bowtie S}\} = \{e \in E_R : \langle e, u \rangle \in D_R\} \cup E_S. \qquad \square$$

Proposition B.9. $0_\mathcal{R}$ *is an identity element for $\bowtie$. Additionally, $\bowtie$ is associative where defined, in the sense that $R \bowtie S$ and $(R \bowtie S) \bowtie T$ are both defined iff $S \bowtie T$ and $R \bowtie (S \bowtie T)$ are both defined, and in this case $(R \bowtie S) \bowtie T = R \bowtie (S \bowtie T)$.*

Proof. Trivial. $\qquad \square$

We can use $\bowtie$ to generate all dependency relations from very simple ones in the following sense. Suppose that $\max\{\delta_R(a) : a \in A\} = K > 0$. Then

$$R = [R]_{X_1} \bowtie [R]_{X_2} \bowtie \ldots \bowtie [R]_{X_K}$$

where $X_i = \delta_R^{-1}(\{i\})$. Each component $[R]_{X_i}$ is 'simple' in the sense that $[R]_{X_i} = \langle X_i, \emptyset, \emptyset \rangle$ for i even and $[R]_{X_i} = \langle \emptyset, X_i, \emptyset \rangle$ for i odd.

B.1.4 Parallel Composition: Fuse

Recall the definition of Fuse from Definition 4.26. Firstly, note that the definition implicitly depends on $U_R \cap E_S = \emptyset = E_R \cap U_S$.

Definition B.4. Dependency relations R, S are *compatible* if $U_R \cap E_S = \emptyset = E_R \cap U_S$.

Secondly, note that the definition is recursive, and actually the recursion need not terminate in general, even when R, S are compatible. Although we will not need it, it seems worth mentioning an alternative recursive definition of Fuse which does terminate for all compatible pairs, and which agrees with Definition 4.26.

Definition B.5 (Extended Fuse). Let R and S be compatible dependency relations. Then $R \bowtie' S$ is defined recursively by $0_\mathcal{R} \bowtie' 0_\mathcal{R} = 0_\mathcal{R}$ and

$$R \bowtie' S = \langle U_0, E_0, \emptyset \rangle \rtimes ([R]_{A(R) \setminus (E_0 \cup U_0)} \bowtie' [S]_{A(S) \setminus (E_0 \cup U_0)}),$$

where

$$E_0 = \{e \in E_R \cup E_S : \forall u \in U_R \cup U_S.\ \neg(e \triangleleft u)\},$$
$$U_0 = \{u \in U_R \cup U_S : \forall e \in E_R \cup E_S \setminus E_0.\ (u \triangleleft e) \to (e \triangleleft u)\},$$

and $\triangleleft$ is the transitive closure of $\triangleleft_R \cup \triangleleft_S$.

Proposition B.10. *Let R, S be compatible dependency relations. Then the recursion defining $R \bowtie' S$ always terminates.*

Proof. It suffices to check that $E_0 \cup U_0 \neq \emptyset$ assuming $A(R) \cup A(S) \neq \emptyset$. Define an equivalence relation on $A(R) \cup A(S)$ by $x \sim y$ iff $x \triangleleft y \wedge y \triangleleft x$. Then $\triangleleft$ induces a partial order on the set of equivalence classes $(A(R) \cup A(S))/\sim$. Since this is a finite set, one can find a minimal element X (not necessarily unique). If $u \in X$ with $u \in U_R \cup U_S$ then $u \in U_0$, but if $X \cap (U_R \cup U_S) = \emptyset$ then $\exists e \in X$ with $e \in E_R \cup E_S$ and $e \in E_0$. □

As the proof above shows, there are cases where $\triangleleft$ is not antisymmetric or even irreflexive, even though $\triangleleft_R$ and $\triangleleft_S$ always are individually. It is essentially this that causes the failure of termination in Definition 4.26, and so we make it a definition.

Definition B.6 (Mutually acyclic). Compatible dependency relations R and S are *mutually acyclic* if $\forall a, b \in A(R) \cap A(S). \neg(a \triangleleft_R b \wedge b \triangleleft_S a)$.

Proposition B.11. *R, S are mutually acyclic iff the transitive closure of $\triangleleft_R \cup \triangleleft_S$ is irreflexive.*

Proof. The "if" direction is trivial. For the "only if," suppose we are given a sequence $x_0, x_1, x_2, \ldots, x_k$ with $x_0 = x_k$, $k > 0$, and, for each $0 \le i < k$, either $x_i \triangleleft_R x_{i+1}$ or $x_i \triangleleft_S x_{i+1}$. By transitivity of $\triangleleft_R$ and $\triangleleft_S$ we can combine consecutive appearances of the same relation and thus assume that their appearances alternate as in

$$x_0 \triangleleft_R x_1 \triangleleft_S x_2 \triangleleft_R x_3 \ldots \triangleleft_S x_k$$

also guaranteeing that each $x_i \in A(R) \cap A(S)$ (and that k is even). Now, consider the sequence

$$(\delta_R(x_0), \delta_S(x_0)), (\delta_R(x_1), \delta_S(x_1)), \ldots, (\delta_R(x_k), \delta_S(x_k)).$$

Since one of $\triangleleft_R$ or $\triangleleft_S$ obtains between each consecutive pair of X_i's, each step in the sequence of $(\delta_R(x_i), \delta_S(x_i))$'s makes a strict increase in one of its two components and, since R and S are mutually acyclic, does not decrease in the other component. But $x_0 = x_k$ so the sequence returns to its starting value, a contradiction. □

One can check readily that the sets E_0 and U_0 in Definition B.5 agree with those of Definition 4.26 in the case that R and S are mutually acyclic. It might be helpful to note that the sets can also be described as follows.

$$E_0 = \{e \in E_R \cup E_S : \neg \exists u.\, e \triangleleft_R u \vee e \triangleleft_S u\}$$
$$U_0 = \{u \in U_R \cup U_S : \forall e.\, (u \triangleleft_R e \vee u \triangleleft_S e) \implies e \in E_0\}$$

We will make no further mention of Definition B.5 henceforth.

Proposition B.12. *Let R, S be mutually acyclic. Then the recursive definition of $\bowtie$ in Definition 4.26 terminates.*

Proof. Supposing $E_0 = \emptyset = U_0$ it suffices to show that $R = 0_{\mathcal{R}} = S$. If $R \neq 0_{\mathcal{R}}$ then there is $a \in A(R)$ with $\delta_R(a)$ minimal, and hence there is $b \in A(S)$ with $a \triangleleft_S b$. We may choose this b to have $\delta_S(b)$ minimal. But then since $E_0 \cup U_0 = \emptyset$, there must be $c \in A(R)$ with $b \triangleleft_R c$. But $c \lesssim_R a$ by our choice of a, hence $b \triangleleft_R a$, a contradiction. □

Conversely, R, S being mutually acyclic is also a necessary condition for the recursion in Definition 4.26 to terminate. If there are $a, b \in A(R) \cap A(S)$ with $a \triangleleft_R b$ and $b \triangleleft_S a$ then it is easy to see that $a, b \notin E_0 \cup U_0$.

Lemma B.13. *If R, S are mutually acyclic then, for all $x, y \in A(R)$, $x \triangleleft_{R \bowtie S} y \implies x \lesssim_R y$. Moreover, $[R \bowtie S]_{A(R)} = R$.*

Proof. The first claim is by an easy inspect of the recurrence relation, and equivalently says that $y \triangleleft_R x \implies y \lesssim_{R \bowtie S} x$. For the second claim, note that if $e \in E_R$ and $u \in U_R$, then $e \triangleleft_R u$ iff $e \lesssim_R u$, whence $\langle e, u \rangle \in D_R \implies e \lesssim_{R \bowtie S} u \implies \langle e, u \rangle \in D_{R \bowtie S}$ and conversely. □

Proposition B.14. *Let R, S be mutually acyclic, and E_0, U_0 as in Definition 4.26. Then $E_0 = \{a : \delta_{R \bowtie S}(a) = 1\}$ and $U_0 = \{a : \delta_{R \bowtie S}(a) = 2\}$.*

Proof. For the first claim, it suffices to check that if $U_0 = \emptyset$ then $E_0 = A(R) \cup A(S)$. But it $e \in (E_R \cup E_S) \setminus E_0$, then there exists u with $e \triangleleft_R u \vee e \triangleleft_S u$, and moreover u can be chosen with $(\delta_R(u), \delta_S(u))$ minimal. But then we would have to have $u \in U_0$.

For the second claim, we note that if $u \in (U_R \cup U_S) \setminus U_0$ then there is an $e \in (E_R \cup E_S) \setminus E_0$ with $u \triangleleft_R e \vee u \triangleleft_S e$, whence $\delta_{R \bowtie S}(u) \geq 4$. □

We include here some basic properties of Fuse that are trivial to prove.

Proposition B.15. *Let R and S mutually acyclic. Then*
  (i) $R \bowtie S = S \bowtie R$,
  (ii) $R = R \bowtie R = 0_{\mathcal{R}} \bowtie R = R \bowtie 0_{\mathcal{R}}$,
  (iii) $D_R, D_S \subseteq D_{R \bowtie S}$.

B.1.5 Coherence

We now introduce the notion of coherence with respect to some fixed dependency relation T. In the case where $T = 0_\mathcal{R}$, the condition of T-coherence will be vacuous.

Definition B.7 (T-coherent). Let T, R be compatible dependency relations. Then R is T-coherent if $\forall a, b \in A(T) \cap A(R)$

- $\delta_R(a) \leq \delta_T(a)$; and
- $\max\{0, \delta_R(a) - \delta_R(b)\} \leq \max\{0, \delta_T(a) - \delta_T(b)\}$.

Lemma B.16. *If R is T-coherent then R and T are mutually acyclic.*

Proof. For any $a, b \in A(T) \cap A(R)$, if $a \triangleleft_R b$ then

$$0 < \delta_R(a) - \delta_R(b) \leq \max\{0, \delta_T(a) - \delta_T(b)\}$$

whence $\delta_T(a) > \delta_T(b)$ and $a \triangleleft_T b$. □

Definition B.8 (Relative depth). Let T, R be compatible. For $a \in A$, the *relative depth of a in R with respect to T*, or the *T-depth of a in R*, is

$$\delta_R^T(a) = \max\{\delta_T(a), \delta_R(a), \delta_T(t) + \delta_R(a) - \delta_R(t) : t \in A(T) \cap A(R) \wedge a \triangleleft_R t\}.$$

Lemma B.17. *Let T, R be compatible. Then R is T-coherent iff for all $a \in A(T)$,*

$$\delta_T(a) = \delta_R^T(a).$$

Proof. For the "if" direction, let $a, b \in A(T) \cap A(R)$, then $\delta_R(a) \leq \delta_R^T(a) = \delta_T(a)$; and if $\delta_R(a) \leq \delta_R(b)$, then $\delta_T(b) = \delta_R^T(b) \geq \delta_T(a) + \delta_R(b) = \delta_R(a)$, whence $\delta_T(b) - \delta_T(a) \geq \delta_R(b) - \delta_R(a)$, as required.

For the "only if" direction, let $a \in A(T) \cap A(R)$—since the result is trivial if $a \notin A(R)$. For any $t \in A(R) \cap A(T)$, if $a \triangleleft_R t$ then by the second part of T-coherence we have $\delta_R(a) - \delta_R(t) \leq \delta_T(a) - \delta_T(t)$, whence $\delta_T(a) \geq \delta_T(t) + \delta_R(a) - \delta_R(t)$. By the first part of T-coherence we get $\delta_T(a) \geq \delta_R(a)$, whence $\delta_R^T(a) \leq \delta_T(a) \leq \delta_R^T(a)$, as required. □

Lemma B.18. *Let R be T-coherent. Then, for all $a \in A$,*

$$\delta_{T \bowtie R}(a) = \delta_R^T(a).$$

Proof. Consider E_0 and U_0 in the definition of $T \bowtie R$. It is straightforward from inspection that $E_0 = \{a \in \mathbb{A} : \delta_R^T(a) = 1\}$ and $U_0 = \{a \in \mathbb{A} : \delta_R^T(a) = 2\}$. Then one can check that, for $a \in (A(T) \cup A(R)) \setminus (E_0 \cup U_0)$, $\delta_{[R]_{A \setminus (E_0 \cup U_0)}}^{[T]_{A \setminus (E_0 \cup U_0)}}(a) = \delta_R^T(a) - 2$, whence the result follows by induction. □

The following useful lemmas are now straightforward.

Lemma B.19. *Let T,R be dependency relations with $A(T) \cap A(R) = \emptyset$. Then:*
  (i) *R is T-coherent,*
  (ii) *$T \bowtie R$ is T-coherent,*
  (iii) *$T \bowtie R$ is T-coherent.*

Lemma B.20. *Let R be a T-coherent dependency relation. Then:*
  (i) *$[T \bowtie R]_{A(T)} = T$,*
  (ii) *$[T \bowtie R]_{A(R)} = R$,*
  (iii) *$[R]_X$ is T-coherent for any $X \subseteq A$.*

We now introduce the concept of coherence for a finite set of dependency relations, relative to some fixed dependency relation T. Taking $T = 0_{\mathcal{R}}$, a set will be T-coherent iff its members have disjoint A-objects.

Definition B.9 (T-coherent set). Let T be a dependency relation and let $\mathcal{S}$ be a set of mutually compatible dependency relations. Then the set $\mathcal{S}$ is T-coherent if each $R \in \mathcal{S}$ is T-coherent and moreover for distinct $R, S \in \mathcal{S}$ we have $(A(R) \cap A(S)) \setminus A(T) = \emptyset$.

Definition B.10 (Relative fuse). Let $\mathcal{S}$ be a T-coherent set. For $R, S \in \mathcal{S}$, define $R \stackrel{T}{\bowtie} S = [(T \bowtie R) \bowtie (T \bowtie S)]_{A(R) \cup A(S)}$.

Lemma B.21. *Let $\mathcal{S}$ be a T-coherent set. For $R, S \in \mathcal{S}$, $(T \bowtie R)$ and $(T \bowtie S)$ are indeed mutually acyclic, $(\mathcal{S} \setminus \{R, S\}) \cup \{R \stackrel{T}{\bowtie} S\}$ is T-coherent and moreover, for all $a \in A$,*

$$\delta^T_{\left(R \stackrel{T}{\bowtie} S\right)}(a) = \max\{\delta^T_R(a), \delta^T_S(a)\}.$$

Proof. For $a \in A(T \bowtie R) \cap A(T \bowtie S) = A(T)$, $\delta_T(a) = \delta_{T \bowtie R}(a) = \delta_{T \bowtie S}(a)$, thus $T \bowtie R$ and $T \bowtie S$ are coherent with respect to each other. The result follows by applications of the previous results. □

We can now deduce the following crucial result.

Theorem B.22. *Let $\mathcal{S}$ be a finite T-coherent set. Then $\bowtie^T \mathcal{S}$, defined to be $(\ldots(R_1 \stackrel{T}{\bowtie} R_2)\ldots) \bowtie R_n$ for any enumeration $R_1, \ldots, R_n$ of $\mathcal{S}$, is independent of the ordering chosen. Moreover, $\delta^T_{\bowtie^T \mathcal{S}}(a) = \max\{\delta^T_R(a) : R \in \mathcal{S}\}$.*

We can use this result to give a means of calculating iterated $\stackrel{T}{\bowtie}$ in one step from the original T-depth functions.

Corollary B.23 (One-step T-fusion). *Let $\mathcal{S}$ be a finite T-coherent set. Then $\bowtie^T \mathcal{S} = \langle U, E, D \rangle$ where $U = \bigcup_{R \in \mathcal{S}} U_R$, $E = \bigcup_{R \in \mathcal{S}} E_R$, and*

$$D = \bigcup_{R, S \in \mathcal{S}} \{\langle e, u \rangle \in E_R \times U_S : \delta^T_S(u) < \delta^T_R(e)\}.$$

B.2 The Predicate System Is Well Defined

In this section we prove that the inference operations of the predicate system are well-defined, the main technical detail of which is an application of our results on T-coherent dependency relations.

We take for granted the existence of a meta-theory in which all of our set-theoretic constructions can be performed. It remains to show that for each operation of the system, when invoked with appropriate arguments within the context of a valid erotetic inference, the computational procedure specified for that operation:

(i) precisely and deterministically identifies a unique output;
(ii) the output is a well-formed v-model.

Let us clarify the way in which the computational procedure might be non-deterministic. There are two types of free choice that occur in the erotetic operations:

(i) The ordering of summands in a $\bigoplus$ or factors in a $\bigotimes$;
(ii) the choice of a fresh assignment $v : A \to \mathbf{A}$ for a finite subset $A \subseteq \mathbf{A}$.

For the former case we will show that the ordering used to evaluate a $\bigoplus$ or $\bigotimes$ never matters in the environment of a valid erotetic inference. For the latter, we note that the choice of fresh assignment can only affect final outcome up to an injective substitution of the new $\mathbf{A}$-objects, which for us is an inconsequential distinction.

There are only four operations for which these concerns require some theory to address, the rest are obvious. We can handle three of them simultaneously.

Merge, Universal Product, Existential Sum

We outline only the situation for Merge, the other two being simpler. Computing Merge involves calculating

$$\bigoplus_{\gamma \in \Gamma}^{R \bowtie S} \left(\{\gamma\}_{RI}^{\Theta} \otimes^{R \bowtie S} \Delta_{SJ}^{\Psi} \otimes^{R \bowtie S} \bigotimes_{\langle t, u \rangle \in M'_{IJ}(\gamma)}^{R \bowtie S} \mathrm{Sub}_{\langle t, u \rangle}^{R \bowtie S}(\Delta_J^{\{0\}}) \right)$$

where either $A(R) \cap A(S) = \emptyset$ or $[R]_{\Delta \cup \Psi} = S$. Since the hypotheses on R and S imply that $R = [R \bowtie S]_{A(R)}$ and $S = [R \bowtie S]_{A(S)}$, and since the dependency relation of $\mathrm{Sub}(\Delta_J^{\{0\}}, R \bowtie S, t, u)$ is of the form $[(R \bowtie S) \bowtie [R \bowtie S]_{Z(R \bowtie S, u)}[v]]_{\Delta[v]}$, which is clearly $R \bowtie S$-coherent, it is easily seen that the set of all dependency relations to be combined with $\bowtie^{R \bowtie S}$ is $R \bowtie S$-coherent. Order-independence now follows from Theorem B.22.

Query

For Query the issue is whether the dependency relation is well-formed. Observe that for all of $D_1, D_2, D_3, D_4, D_5, D_6$, the only dependencies are of existentials in $E_S \setminus E_R$, and dependencies of existentials in $E_S \cap E_R$ are ignored. It suffices to show that $\langle U_R, E_S \setminus E_R, D_{S'} \rangle$ is well-formed and thus a valid subject for $\bowtie$. This means verifying the Matryoshka condition. We do so in dual form: showing that the existentials are totally pre-ordered (or 'quasi-ordered') by the subset inclusions of the sets of universals they depend on. First note the effect of D_2: all $e \in E_S \setminus E_R$ which admit multiple matches are made dependent upon every universal in U_R. Now observe that the effect of D_6 is to add more dependencies of each

$e \in E_S \backslash E_R$ so that, whenever $e' \in E_S \backslash E_R$ is not one of the existentials which had multiple matches, then we add enough dependencies to preserve the order relation $e \lesssim_S e'$. We now use the fact that $\lesssim_S$ is a total pre-order on $E_S \backslash E_R$, and that this is still the case if certain elements are deleted and the added back in one mass at the end.

B.3 Tarskian Realization

In this section we further develop the link between views and classical logic by showing how to *realize* a view as a predicate on a class of possible worlds. As is commonly known, first-order logic is a sound and complete reasoning system with respect to the Tarskian interpretation of first-order formulae (for details, consult Johnstone (1987)). The main focus of this section is to define a common setting for the Tarskian realization of view models and for first-order logic and to show that these realizations are preserved by the articulation and interpretation procedures.

Definition B.11 (Pre-worlds). A *pre-world* $\mathfrak{M}$ consists of a (non-empty) set $M = M^{\mathfrak{M}}$ together with

- for each $f \in F$, a function $f^{\mathfrak{M}} : M^{\alpha(f)} \to M$;
- for each $P \in P^T$, a relation $P^{\mathfrak{M}} \subseteq M^{\alpha(P)}$.

In a pre-world we can interpret terms and propositional formulas. For each term $t \in T$, the interpretation $[\![t]\!]_{\mathfrak{M}} = [\![t]\!]$ is the function $[\![t]\!] : M^A \to M$ defined as follows:

- $[\![a]\!](\rho) = \rho(a)$ for $a \in A$;
- $[\![f]\!](t_1, \ldots, t_{\alpha(f)})(\rho) = f^{\mathfrak{M}}([\![t_1]\!](\rho), \ldots, [\![t_{\alpha(f)}]\!](\rho))$.

For each atom $A \in \mathcal{A}$, the interpretation $[\![A]\!]_{\mathfrak{M}} = [\![A]\!]$ is the relation $[\![A]\!] \subseteq M^A$ defined by:

- $[\![P(t_1, \ldots, t_{\alpha(P)})]\!] = \{\rho \in M^A : ([\![t_1]\!](\rho), \ldots, [\![t_{\alpha(P)}]\!](\rho)) \in P^{\mathfrak{M}}\}$ for $P \in P^T$;
- $[\![\bar{A}]\!] = M^A \backslash [\![A]\!]$.

Hence we can define the interpretation of a propositional formula φ, and of a state γ and set of states Γ.

- $[\![\varphi \wedge \psi]\!] = [\![\varphi]\!] \cap [\![\psi]\!]$;
- $[\![\varphi \vee \psi]\!] = [\![\varphi]\!] \cup [\![\psi]\!]$;
- $[\![\neg \varphi]\!] = M^A \backslash [\![\varphi]\!]$;
- $[\![\top]\!] = M^A$;
- $[\![\bot]\!] = \emptyset$;
- $[\![\gamma]\!] = \bigcap_{A \in \gamma} [\![A]\!]$;
- $[\![\Gamma]\!] = \bigcup_{\gamma \in \Gamma} [\![A]\!]$.

Note, there is some ambiguity in the meaning of "$[\![\emptyset]\!]$," where $\emptyset$ might refer either to the empty state or the empty set of states, but in practice no confusion will arise.

Definition B.12 (Worlds). A *world* is a pre-world $\mathfrak{M}$ such that $[\![\kappa]\!] = \emptyset$ for every primitive absurd state $\kappa \in \mathbb{K}$.

We extend to an interpretation of full first-order logic by interpreting the quantifiers as follows:

- $[\![\forall x.\varphi]\!] = \{\rho \in M^{\mathbb{A}} : \forall m \in M. \rho[m/x] \in [\![\varphi]\!]\}$;
- $[\![\exists x.\varphi]\!] = \{\rho \in M^{\mathbb{A}} : \exists m \in M. \rho[m/x] \in [\![\varphi]\!]\}$.

Note that a closed formula clearly interprets either the empty set or all of $M^{\mathbb{A}}$, thus it is convenient to write $[\![\varphi]\!] \in \{0,1\}$ or $[\![\varphi]\!] \in \{\bot, \top\}$ when φ is closed. More generally, if the free variables of φ are contained within the set X, then $[\![\varphi]\!]$ is determined by its intersection with M^X: $[\![\varphi]\!] \cong ([\![\varphi]\!] \cap M^X) \times M^{\mathbb{A}\setminus X}$. Where convenient, in such cases we will silently swap between consider $[\![\varphi]\!]$ as a subset of $M^{\mathbb{A}}$ and M^X. The same conventions will apply to views.

For views, we can think of a dependency relation as a set of restrictions on allowable strategies in a certain game (see Hintikka and Sandu (1997)). Given two sets of states Γ^Θ we define $[\![\Gamma^\Theta]\!] = [\![\Gamma \cup [\Theta]^N]\!] = [\![\Gamma]\!] \cup (M^{\mathbb{A}}\setminus[\![\Theta]\!])$, so for now we can work with views of the form Γ_{RI}. Moreover we can ignore I, since it makes no difference to the realization. Now, for Γ_R, we will describe a two-player game played between *Player* and *Opponent*.

At the end of the game, Player will have picked an assignment $\rho_E : E_R \to M$ and Opponent will have picked $\rho_U : U_R \to M$; Player wins if the combined assignment $\rho = \rho_E \cup \rho_U$ is in $[\![\Gamma]\!] \subseteq M^{A(\Gamma)}$. The $\mathbb{A}$-objects are assigned in the order determined by R: in the first turn Player assigns all $e \in E_R$ with $\delta_R(e) = 1$, in the second Opponent assigns all $u \in U_R$ with $\delta_R(u) = 2$, and so on.

For Γ_R, we define $[\![\Gamma_R]\!]$ to be 1 if Player can force a win in this game, and 0 otherwise. The following is straightforward with standard proof techniques.

Theorem B.24. *For any view G, $[\![G]\!] = [\![G^*]\!]$. For any sentence φ of $\mathcal{L}_{PC}$ in prenex form, $[\![\varphi]\!] = [\![\varphi^\circ]\!]$.*

Definition B.13 (Tarskian entailment for views). *For a set $\mathbb{G} \subseteq \mathbb{V}$ of views and view $D \in \mathbb{V}$, we write $\mathbb{G} \vDash D$ to mean that in every world $\mathfrak{M}$ such that $[\![G]\!]_{\mathfrak{M}} = \top$ for all $G \in \mathbb{G}$ it is the case that $[\![D]\!]_{\mathfrak{M}} = \top$.*

It is convenient to slightly rephrase the above definition of $[\![G]\!]$ in terms of the existence of winning *strategies*. In this formulation, Player states in advance how they will react to possible moves by Opponent. Then $[\![G]\!]$ is true if there exists a strategy for Player which beats any sequence of plays by Opponent. The key restriction on strategies is that the declared intention for instantiating e may only depend on how Opponent chooses to instantiate each $u \in U_R$ with $\langle e, u \rangle \in D_R$.

Definition B.14 (Strategies). *Write $R(e) = \{u \in U_R : \langle e, u \rangle \in D_R\}$. A strategy (for Player) for a view Γ_R is an assignment to each $e \in E_R$ of a function $S_e : M^{R(e)} \to M$.*

It is sometimes useful to relax the notion of strategy a bit. A *weak R-strategy* for a view Γ_R is an assignment to each $e \in E_R$ of a subset $X_e \subseteq \mathbb{A}$ with $X_e \cap A(R) \subseteq R(e)$ and a function $S_e : M^{X_e} \to M$. We view the game as one where Opponent gets to instantiate all of $\mathbb{A}\setminus E_R$. The point of this is to be able to redeploy a strategy realizing one view to another related view, which may have a slightly different set of $\mathbb{A}$-objects.

Proposition B.25 (Irrelevance). *Γ_R has a winning strategy iff it has a winning weak R-strategy.*

Proof. A strategy is in particular a weak R-strategy by taking $X_e = R(e)$. Conversely, given a weak R-strategy pick *any* $\varphi : \mathbb{A}\setminus E_R \to M$ and let $S'_e : M^{R(e)} \to M$ be given by instantiating the arguments of $S_e : M^{X_e} \to M$ indexed by $X_e \setminus U_R$ with φ. $\square$

Proposition B.26 (Matricial reduct). *Let Γ_R, Δ_S be views with $S = [R]_{A(\Delta)}$ and such that $\forall \gamma \in \Gamma. \exists \delta \in \Delta. \delta \subseteq \gamma$. Then $[\![\Gamma_R]\!] \leq [\![\Delta_S]\!]$.*

Proof. We have $[\![\Gamma]\!] = \bigcup_{\gamma \in \Gamma}[\![\gamma]\!] \subseteq \bigcup_{\delta \in \Delta}[\![\delta]\!] = [\![\Delta]\!]$. Suppose S is a winning strategy for Γ_R. Then S is a weak strategy for Δ_S. □

B.4 Soundness under Erotetic Equilibrium

Our goal in this section is to establish the soundness of erotetic equilibrium inferences with respect to the articulation procedure into classical first-order logic.

Theorem B.27 (Soundness of CETR inferences). *Let $\mathbb{G} \subseteq \mathcal{M}$ and $D \in \mathcal{M}$. Suppose that $\mathbb{G} \vdash_{\overline{CETR}} D$. Then $\mathbb{G} \models D$.*

To show this, we keep fixed a world $\mathfrak{M}$ and show that if there exists a winner Player-strategy for every $G \in \mathbb{G}$ then there exists a winning Player-strategy for D. We do this by induction on erotetic inferences, assuming that every step computes in erotetic equilibrium.

Lemma B.28 (Soundness of Factor). *Let G, D be views. Then $[\![G]\!] \leq [\![G[D]^F]\!]$.*

Proof. In the case $D \neq \bot$, this is immediate from Proposition B.26. In the case $D = \bot$, this is just the fact that $[\![\gamma]\!] = \emptyset$ whenever $\gamma \supseteq \kappa$ for some $\kappa \in \mathbb{K}$. □

Lemma B.29 (Soundness of Existential Sum). *Let G, D be v-models. Then every winning strategy for G extends to a winning strategy for $G[D]^E$.*

Proof. Write $G = \Gamma_{RI}^{\Theta}$ and $G[D]^E = \Gamma_{R'I'}^{'\Theta}$. Then $[\![\Gamma^{\Theta}]\!] \subseteq [\![\Gamma'^{\Theta'}]\!]$ by definition of $[\ ]^E$. Moreover $[R']_{A(R)} = R$, since R' is the fusion of an R-coherent family of dependency relations. Thus, in fact, every extension of a winning strategy for G to a strategy for $G[D]^E$ is winning. □

Lemma B.30 (Soundness of Universal Product). *Let G, D be v-models. Then every winning strategy for G extends to a winning strategy for $G[D]^U$.*

Proof. Write $G = \Gamma_{RI}^{\Theta}, D = \Delta_{SJ}^{\Psi}$. We can assume all preconditions are met, including $M'_{IJ} \neq \emptyset$. For notational convenience we'll assume there is only one match, $M'_{IJ} = \{\langle t, u \rangle\}$, but the general case is straightforward. We need to give a winning strategy for $\{0\}_R^{\Theta} \otimes^{R \bowtie S} \text{Sub}_{\langle t,u\rangle}^{R \bowtie S}(\Gamma_I^{\{0\}})$. Consulting the definition of Substitution, one has to extend the strategy to include assignments for $v_1(e)$ whenever $e \in Z(t,u) \cap E_R$ (as well as some other existentials coming from S in the case $A(R) \cap A(S) = \emptyset$, but these can be set arbitrarily). The idea is to use the strategy's assignment for e as though u were instantiated with $[\![t]\!](\rho)$, where ρ is the assignment representing the instantiations of $\mathbb{A}(t)$ during the game. Thus it is necessary that the final dependency relation allows $v_1(e)$ to depend on all of $(\mathbb{A}(t) \cap U_S)[v_1]$, as well as $R(e)[v_1]$. One will see that the dependency relation in Substitution does indeed allow this. □

Lemma B.31 (Soundness of Inquire). *Let G, D be views. Then $[\![G]\!] \leq [\![G[D]^I]\!]$.*

Proof. For the case (I), it is straightforward to check that $[\![\Delta]^N]\!] = M^A \setminus [\![\Delta]\!]$, whence the result follows. For the case (O), one can reduce the problem to showing that $[\![\Delta]_{RN}^N]\!] \vee [\![\Delta_R]\!] = \mathsf{T}$. But if every Player-strategy for Δ_R can be defeated by Opponent, then Player in fact has a winning strategy for $[\Delta]_{RN}^N$. □

Lemma B.32 (Soundness of Query). *Let G, D be views. Then $[\![G]\!] \leq [\![G[D]^Q]\!]$.*

Proof. Write $G = \Gamma_{RI}^{\Theta}$, $D = \Delta_{SJ}^{\Psi}$. We extend a winning strategy for G to one to $G[D]^Q$. For $e \in E_S \setminus E_R$, if e does not participate in any matches, we assign it arbitrary. If it participates in a single match $\langle t, e \rangle \in M_{IJ}'$, then if ρ is the assignment built so far, Player should instantiate e with $[\![t]\!](\rho)$. This requires that e be dependent on every universal u which t contains or for which t contains an existential depending u; this is provided by D_3 and D_4 in the definition of Query.

Finally, e receives multiple matches, then denote that D_2 ensures that e will depend on every universal in U_R. Now, for any assignment $\rho : U_R \to M$, the winning strategy for G extends this to an assignment $\rho' : A(R) \to M$ such that $[\![\Gamma \cup [\Theta]^N]\!](\rho') = \bigcup_{\gamma \in \Gamma} [\![\gamma]\!](\rho') \cup [\![[\Theta]^N]\!](\rho') = \mathsf{T}$. If $[\![[\Theta]^N]\!](\rho') = \mathsf{T}$, then every such e can be assigned arbitrarily. Otherwise, pick any $\gamma \in \Gamma$ such that $[\![\gamma]\!](\rho') = \mathsf{T}$. If there is no $\delta \in \Delta$ such that $\Phi(\gamma, \delta)$ then the result is trivial, so pick such a δ. Thus there is a sequence of matches $\langle t_1, e_1 \rangle, \ldots, \langle t_n, e_n \rangle$, with the e_i all distinct, such that $\delta[t_1/e_1, \ldots, t_n/e_n] = \gamma$. Now, for all $e \in E_S \setminus E_R$ participating in multiple matches, the strategy should instantiate e as $[\![t]\!](\rho')$ if $\langle t, e \rangle$ is on the matches in this sequence, and arbitrarily otherwise. □

The soundness of Wh-Query follows by similar (though simpler) methods. The case of Merge is sufficiently similar to the case of Lemma B.30 that there is no need to spell out details.

Lemma B.33 (Soundness of Wh-Query). *Let G, D be views. Then $[\![G]\!] \leq [\![G[D]^W]\!]$.*

Lemma B.34 (Soundness of Merge). *Let G, D be views with $A(G) \cap A(D) = \emptyset$. Then any pair of winning strategies, one for G and one for D, can be amalgamated and extended to a winning strategy for $G[D]^M$.*

Lemma B.35 (Answer under erotetic equilibrium). *Let $G = \Gamma_{RI}^{\Theta}$ and $D = \Delta_{SJ}^{\Psi}$ be views such that either*

 (i) $A(\Gamma) \cap A(\Delta) = \emptyset$; or
 (ii) G and D are both in erotetic equilibrium with respect to $\mathsf{M}_A(\Gamma) \cap \mathsf{M}_A(\Delta)$.

Writing $G[D]^P = \Xi_{TK}^{\Theta}$ and $G[D]^A[D]^P = \Xi_{T'K'}'^{\Theta}$, we have the following.

 (i) $\Xi' \subseteq \Xi$.
 (ii) $\forall \xi \in \Xi \setminus \Xi'. \exists p \in \xi. \bar{p} \in \xi$.
 (iii) $T = T'$.

Proof. The case $\Psi \neq \{0\}$ is trivial, so we may assume $\Psi = \{0\}$. Case (a) is also trivial, since then $G[D]^A = G$. It remains to consider case (b).

The statement (i) is trivial. For (ii), we first show that for every molecule $\gamma \in \Gamma$ either:

 (i) γ is in the body of $\Gamma_{RI}^{\Theta}[\Delta_{SJ}^{\{0\}}]^A$; or
 (ii) there exists an $x \in \gamma$ such that for all $\delta \in \Delta, \bar{x} \in \delta$.

For any $x \in \mathcal{A}(\Gamma) \cap \mathcal{A}(\Delta)$ and every $\alpha \in \Gamma \cup \Delta$ we must have $x \in \alpha$ or $\bar{x} \in \alpha$, by erotetic equilibrium. Moreover, for any atom $x \in \mathcal{A}$ we cannot have both $x, \bar{x} \in \alpha$ for any atom x, since Γ_{RI}^{Θ} and $\Delta_{SJ}^{\{0\}}$ are fixed points of $[\{0\}_{0\mathcal{R}\varnothing}^{\{0\}}]^I$, which is equivalent to the operation $[\bot]^F$. Now if $\xi \in \Xi \backslash \Xi'$, then $xi = \gamma \cup \delta$ where $\delta \in \Delta$ and $\gamma \in \Gamma$ is not in the body of $G[D]^A$. It follows that there is some $x \in \gamma$ such that $\bar{x} \in \delta$, hence $\{x, \bar{x}\} \subseteq \xi$, so that $MC(\xi)$ holds. Now we to show that $T = T'$, it suffices to show that $\mathrm{A}(\Gamma[\Delta]^A) = \mathrm{A}(\Gamma)$ and that $\mathrm{A}(\Gamma[\Delta]^A \otimes \Delta) = \mathrm{A}(\Gamma) \cup \mathrm{A}(\Delta) = \mathrm{A}(\Gamma \otimes \Delta)$. The second follows easily from the first, and in the first equation the inclusion $\subseteq$ is trivial. Let $A = \{x = P^k t_1 \ldots t_k \in \mathcal{A} : x \in \bigcup \Gamma \vee \bar{x} \in \bigcup \Gamma \wedge P^k \in \mathbf{P}^T\}$. By (b), we have that for each $\gamma \in \Gamma$ and $x \in A$, γ contains precisely one of x and $\bar{x}$. It follows that $\mathrm{A}(\gamma) = \mathrm{A}(\Gamma)$ for all $\gamma \in \Gamma$. Since $\Gamma[\Delta]^A$ is empty iff Γ is empty, we see that $\mathrm{A}(\Gamma[\Delta]^A) = \mathrm{A}(\Gamma)$, as required. □

From the preceding development one can easily deduce the following.

Lemma B.36 (Soundness of Update). *Let G, D be views with $\mathrm{A}(G) \cap \mathrm{A}(D) = \varnothing$. Suppose that $G[D]^\circ$ computes in complete erotetic equilibrium. Then any pair of winning strategies, one for G and one for D, can be amalgamated and extended to a winning strategy for $G[D]^\circ$.*

Lemma B.37 (Soundness of Suppose). *Let G, D be views. Suppose that $G[D]^S$ computes in complete erotetic equilibrium. Then $[\![G]\!] \leq [\![G[D]^S]\!]$.*

Proof. For the (O) case, if D has no winning strategy then there is a winning strategy for $[\Theta']^N$ (see definition of Suppose) and therefore $[\![G[D]^S]\!] = \top$. Otherwise, apply Lemma B.36.

For the (I) case, we almost apply the same argument, except that in the final Merge we are not free to choose a winning strategy for D. However, note that for $D = \Delta_{SJ}^{\{0\}}$ Merge does not invoke any substitutions, and hence only involves a simple product. If $G = \Gamma_{RI}^\Theta$ has a winning strategy then the same one is winning for $\Gamma_{RI}^{\Theta \otimes \Delta}$. This extends to a winning strategy for $\Gamma_{RI}^{\Theta \otimes \Delta}[\Delta_{SJ}^{\{0\}}]^U[\Delta_{SJ}^{\{0\}}]^E$; and this strategy is also winning for $\Gamma^{\Theta \otimes \Delta}[\Delta_{SJ}^{\{0\}}]^U[\Delta_{SJ}^{\{0\}}]^E[\Delta_{SJ}^{\{0\}}]^A[\Delta_{SJ}^{\{0\}}]^M$ since by Lemma B.35 it is equivalent to $\Gamma^{\Theta \otimes \Delta}[\Delta_{SJ}^{\{0\}}]^U[\Delta_{SJ}^{\{0\}}]^E[\Delta_{SJ}^{\{0\}}]^M$ and thus to $(\Gamma^{\Theta \otimes \Delta}[\Delta_{SJ}^{\{0\}}]^U \otimes \Delta_{SJ}^{\{0\}}) \oplus [\Delta^{\{0\}}]_{\varnothing J}^N$. □

Proof. Let $\langle C, G \rangle$ and $\langle C', G' \rangle$ be inference states and let $\mathcal{J}$ be a manifest erotetic equilibrium inference such that $\langle C, G \rangle \mathcal{J} = \langle C', G' \rangle$. Supposing that $C \vDash G$, we show $C' \vDash G'$. Since, for any set of views G, we have $\mathsf{G} \vDash \top$ the statement of the theorem follows.

The proof is by induction on the inference $\mathcal{J}$. The base case (empty inference) is trivial. The soundness of each step has been dealt with in the development above, with the exceptions of Reorient, Depose, and Commit, for each of which soundness is trivial. □

B.5 Completeness

Having established that erotetic equilibrium inference is sound with respect to classical reasoning, we now show that the equilibrium fragment is *complete*. It is not interesting to observe completeness without the restriction to equilibrium inferences, since general erotetic inference is unsound by this standard and can prove absurdity.

There are two qualifications to make regarding this completeness. The first is that we do not attempt to show that arbitrary *suppositional* views which are classical consequences of some hypotheses are derivable, but note that every view G is classically equivalent to $G[T]^D$ which is supposition-free. The second is a technical constraint on the set of primitive absurdities $\mathbb{K}$. The base system already satisfies this condition, but in general we must insist that $\mathbb{K}$ is closed under substitution of *arbitrary terms* for $\mathbb{A}$-objects.

Theorem B.38 (Completeness of CETR inferences). *Suppose that $\forall \kappa \in \mathbb{K}.\forall t \in T.\forall a \in A.\kappa[t/a] \in \mathbb{K}$. Let $C \subseteq \mathbb{M}$, let Δ be a finite set of states, and let S be a dependency relation with $A(\Delta) = A(S)$. If $C \vDash_K \Delta_{S\varnothing}^{\{0\}}$, then $C \mid\!\!\frac{}{\text{CETR}}\; \Delta_{S\varnothing}^{\{0\}}$.*

Throughout this section we will tend to omit mention of the issue structure except where it is explicitly used, observing that the Reorient operation allows us to change it on the current view arbitrarily. We will also write Γ_R to mean the view $\Gamma_R^{\{0\}} = \Gamma_{R\varnothing}^{\{0\}}$ where there is no supposition. We can indeed assume that everything in the set C of hypotheses is supposition-free, since Depose preserves classical equivalence.

B.5.1 Herbrand's Theorem for ETR

The proof strategy for the Completeness theorem resembles the resolution method used by automated theorem provers, based on Herbrand's Theorem (see Buss (1994)). The most substantial step is the following: to derive absurdity from a known contradiction. Actually in this step there is no use of Update or Suppose operations, so there is no need to be concerned with erotetic equilibrium.

Theorem B.39 (Herbrand's Theorem for CETR). *Let Γ_R, Θ_T be views with $A(\Gamma) \cap A(\Theta) = \varnothing$. If $\Gamma_R \vDash \bot$, then*

$$\Gamma_{R\bowtie T}^{\Theta} \mid\!\!\frac{}{\text{CETR}}\; \varnothing_T^{\Theta}.$$

The strategy is to prove the contrapositive. That is, if it is not possible to CETR-derive $\varnothing_T^{\Theta}$ from $\Gamma_{R\bowtie T}^{\Theta} = \{0\}_T^{\Theta} \otimes \Gamma_R$, then we will construct a world $\mathfrak{M}$ in which $[\![\Gamma_R]\!] = \top$. The core idea of Herbrand's theorem is that a refutation of a first-order absurdity can be reduced to a finite number of instantiations at ground (closed) terms followed by a refutation of the resulting propositional statement—otherwise the non-termination of a sequence of deductions could be used to build a model of the original formula. The reason for our needing to carry around the supposition Θ_T will become clear later.

The carrier set $M^{\mathfrak{M}}$ consists of 'names' $\ulcorner t \urcorner$ for all terms $t \in T(\mathbb{A} \setminus A(\Theta))$ with $\mathbb{A}$-objects disjoint from $A(\Theta)$. The interpretation of function symbols is given by $f^{\mathfrak{M}}(\ulcorner t_1 \urcorner, \ldots, \ulcorner t_{\alpha(f)} \urcorner) = \ulcorner f(t_1, \ldots, t_{\alpha(f)}) \urcorner$. Our task is to give an interpretation of the predicate symbols such that $\mathfrak{M}$ is a valid world (and not just a pre-world) and to give a winning strategy for Γ_R. To do this we maintain a finite collection of possibilities for a *partially given* interpretation and strategy. The partial interpretations will form the set of states of a view Δ_S where $\Gamma_R \mid\!\!\frac{}{\text{CETR}}\; \Delta_S$, and the strategy will respect the dependency relation S. Subsequent CETR inference steps on Δ_S amount to branching and discarding the possibilities. If before an infinite number of steps a dead-end is reach this will correspond to a CETR inference of $\varnothing_T^{\Theta}$ form $\Gamma_{R\bowtie T}^{\Theta}$.

The basic strategy is to start from Γ_R and then alternate between (i) using Universal Product to accumulate novel existential A-objects e whose names $\ulcorner e \urcorner$ are the witnesses chosen by the strategy, and (ii) using Inquire to saturate the states with either p of $\bar{p}$ for each atom p involving the new existentials.

The follow notion will simplify the argument, since it will mean that all A-objects persist between the steps just describe.

Definition B.15 (Normal views). A view Δ_S is *normal* if (i) for every $a \in A(S)$ and $\delta \in \Delta$ we have $(a = a) \in \delta$; and (ii) $\Delta_S[\bot]^F = \Delta_S$.

Clearly, Δ_S is normal if and only if $\Delta_S = \Delta_S[\{a = a\}_{[S]}]^I$, and this suggests a procedure by which any view can be replaced by a logically equivalent normal view. Hence we can assume without loss of generality that Γ_R is normal. The significance of this is that it will be clear by construction that $A(R) \subseteq A(S)$ for each of our intermediate views Δ_S.

Definition B.16 (Reduct). Let $\Delta_S, \Delta'_{S'}$ be normal views with $A(S) \subseteq A(S')$. We say that Δ_S is a *reduct* of $\Delta'_{S'}$ if $\forall \delta' \in \Delta'. \exists \delta \in \Delta. \delta \subseteq \delta'$ and $[S']_{A(S)} = S$.

The reduct relation is clearly transitive, and the following is straightforward.

Proposition B.40. *In any world, if Δ_S is a reduct of $\Delta'_{S'}$, then $[\![\Delta'_{S'}]\!] \leq [\![\Delta_S]\!]$.*

Let $M \subseteq U_R \times T(A \backslash A(\Theta))$ be a finite set of pairs $\langle u, t \rangle$ of universals in R together with a term t at which we wish to instantiate, where $A(t) \cap A(\Theta) = \emptyset$.

Lemma B.41. *In the situation above, given Δ_S where Γ_R is a reduct of Δ_S, there exists a normal view $\Delta'_{S'}$ such that*

$$\Delta^\Theta_{S \bowtie T} \vdash_{\text{CETR}} \Delta'^\Theta_{S' \bowtie T}$$

and Δ_S, Γ_R, and $\text{Sub}^R_{\langle u,t \rangle}(\Gamma)$ for $\langle u, t \rangle \in M$ are all reducts of $\Delta'_{S'}$.

Proof. Since Γ_R is a reduct of Δ_S we can try to construct

$$\left(\Delta^\Theta_{S \bowtie T} \otimes \bigotimes_{\langle u,t \rangle \in M}^{S} \text{Sub}^S_{\langle u,t \rangle}(\Delta) \right) [\bot]^F$$

(and then normalize), which almost looks like Universal Product. We will treat the case where $M = \{\langle u, t \rangle\}$ is a singleton, the general case follows by iteration.

Let $v : A(S) \to A$ be an injective function whose image is disjoint from $A(S) \cup A(T)$, and let $u \in A \backslash (A(S) \cup A(T) \cup v(A(S)))$. Let $\hat{\Delta}_{\hat{S}}$ be

$$\Delta_S[\{\{v(a) = v(a) : a \in A(S)\} \cup \{u = u\}\}_{S[v] \bowtie \langle \{u\}, \emptyset, \emptyset \rangle}]^I$$

which is a normal model with $\hat{S} = (S \bowtie S[v]) \bowtie \langle \{u\}, \emptyset, \emptyset \rangle$. Writing $J = \{\langle u, ? = u \rangle, \langle x, ? = x \rangle\}$ and $K = \{\langle u, ? = u \rangle, \langle t, ? = x \rangle\}$, take $\Delta'_{S'}$ to be (the normalization of)

$$\hat{\Delta}_{\hat{S}, J}[\{\{u = u, t = x\}\}_{[\hat{S}]K}]^U.$$

Since u sits below all of S in the order induced by $\hat{S}$, the substitution operation for the issue match (u,u) results in a factor with Δ_S as a reduct. □

Proof (Theorem B.39). Given Γ_R, (without loss of generality normal), we construct a sequence of normal views Δ_{nS_n} as outlined above together with a strategy for realizing Γ_R, where at each stage Δ_n already contains as a reduct a sentence asserting that the Γ_R is realized by the strategy at each place where the strategy is defined.

Let us make that more precise. An *R-domain* is a set of the form $V_i = \{u \in U_R : \delta_R(u) \leq 2i+1\}$ for $i \in \mathbb{N}$. For an R-domain V and an assignment $\rho : V \to T(A\backslash A(\Theta))$, a *hyperstrategy* is an extension of ρ to $\sigma : A(R) \to T(A\backslash A(\Theta))$ such that $\sigma(x) \in A$ for $x \notin V$. The empty set V_0 is an R-domain, and the unique assignment for it has a hyperstrategy $\sigma_0 : A(R) \to M^{\mathfrak{M}}$ where $\sigma_0(x) = x$.

If σ is a hyperstrategy for $\rho : V_i \to T(A\backslash A(\Theta))$ and S is a dependency relation with $[S]_{A(R)} = R$ and $A(S) \supseteq A(\sigma)$, then we define $\Gamma_R[\sigma, S]$ to be the view with states given by the substitution $\Gamma[\sigma]$ and dependency relation $[S]_{A(\{\rho(x):x\in V_i\})} \bowtie ([R]_{A(R)\backslash V_i}[\sigma \upharpoonright_{A(R)\backslash V_i}])$. We say that Δ_S realizes a hyperstrategy σ for $\rho : V_i \to T(A\backslash A(\Theta))$ if $\Gamma_R[\sigma, S]$ is a reduct of Δ_S.

We begin with Γ_R and the single hyperstrategy σ_0 for the empty assignment. Suppose we have reached Δ_S and a partial function $\mathbb{S}$ which assigns to an assignment on an R-domain a hyperstrategy for it realized by Δ_S. If some assignment $\rho : V_i \to T(A\backslash A(\Theta))$ with $i > 0$ does not have a hyperstrategy yet, but $A(\{\rho(x) : x \in V_i\}) \subseteq A(S)$ and $\rho \upharpoonright_{V_{i-1}}$ has a hyperstrategy, then we can use the lemma above to expand Δ_S. Given $\sigma = \mathbb{S}(\rho \upharpoonright_{V_{i-1}})$, applying the lemma to the set of substitutions $\{\langle \rho(u), u\rangle : u \in V_i \backslash V_{i-1}\}$, since $\Gamma_R[\sigma, S]$ was a reduct of Δ_S we get that $\Gamma_R[\sigma', S']$ is a reduct of $\Delta'_{S'}$ for hyperstrategy σ' for ρ.

There are countably many assignments on R-domains to find hyperstrategies for, so we can arrange for them to be performed sequentially, interleaving with the countably many steps of the form $\Delta_{n+1 S_{n+1} \bowtie T}^{\Theta} = \Delta_{n S_n \bowtie T}^{\Theta} [\{P\}_{[S_n]}]^I$ for atoms P with $A(P) \subseteq A(S)$. If within finitely many steps we get $\Delta_n = \emptyset$, then we have constructed a CETR inference of $\emptyset_T^{\Theta}$ from $\Gamma_{R \bowtie T}^{\Theta}$, as required. If not, then since at each stage Δ_n is finite and Δ_n is a reduct of Δ_{n+1}, there is an infinite chain $\delta_0 \subseteq \delta_1 \subseteq \delta_2 \ldots$ with $\delta_0 \in \Gamma = \Delta_0$, $\delta_n \in \Delta_n$, $A(\delta_n) = A(S_n)$, each contradiction-free. Then $\delta_\infty = \bigcup_i \delta_i$ is used to define $P^{\mathfrak{M}}$ by $(\ulcorner t_1 \urcorner, \ldots, \ulcorner t_{\alpha(P)} \urcorner) \in P^{\mathfrak{M}}$ if and only if $P(t_1, \ldots, t_{\alpha(P)}) \in \delta_\infty$. It is straightforward to show that this is a valid world and that $[\![\Gamma_R]\!]_{\mathfrak{M}} = \top$, using the hyperstrategies to define a winning strategy for Γ_R. □

B.5.2 Deduction and Completeness

It is now relatively straightforward to deduce the Completeness Theorem. Note that we did not have to use the restriction to CETR in the proof of Theorem B.39. The next lemma shows how use of Update in complete equilibrium allows us to combine multiple commitments into a single v-model representing their conjunction.

Lemma B.42 (Conjunctions). *Let $G, D \in \mathbb{M}$. Then there exists a v-model H such that $G, D \vdash_{\text{CETR}} H$ and $H \vDash G$ and $H \vDash D$.*

Proof. We may assume that $D = D[\top]^D$. By using $[\;]^I$, $[\;]^R$, and $[\;]^C$ only, we may obtain v-models G' and D', semantically equivalent to G and D, respectively, such that the bodies of G' and D' are in complete erotetic equilibrium with respect to each other, and both have empty issue structure. It then follows that $G'[D']^\circlearrowleft[\bot]^F = G'[D']^P[\bot]^F$ computes in complete erotetic equilibrium, and is clearly the desired H. □

The following essentially amounts to a CETR proof of the Law of the Excluded Middle, or the fact that negating twice can be undone.

Lemma B.43 (Double negation elimination). *Let Δ be a finite set of states with $\forall \delta \in \Delta. |\delta| \geq 1$. Then $[[\Delta]^N]^N \leq \Delta$ and $\forall \delta \in \Delta. \exists \xi \in [[\Delta]^N]^N. \delta \subseteq \xi$.*

Proof. Observe that
$$[\Delta]^N = \left\{\{\overline{f(\delta)} : \delta \in \Delta\} : f \in \prod_{\delta \in \Delta} \delta\right\},$$

and that one can write
$$[[\Delta]^N]^N = \left\{\left\{f(d(f)) : f \in \prod_{\delta \in \Delta} \delta\right\} \middle| d : \prod_{\delta \in \Delta} \delta \to \Delta\right\}.$$

Let d be any function $\prod_{\delta \in \Delta} \delta \to \Delta$, $\{f(d(f)) : f \in \prod_{\delta \in \Delta} \delta\}$. Then suppose that there is no $\delta \in \Delta$ such that $\delta \subseteq \{f(d(f)) : f \in \prod_{\delta \in \Delta} \delta\}$. Then for each $\delta \in \Delta$, there is $g(\delta) \in \delta$ such that $g(\delta) \neq f(d(f))$ for any $f \in \prod_{\delta \in \Delta} \delta$. But now g defines an element of $\prod_{\delta \in \Delta} \delta$, hence $g(\delta) \neq g(d(g))$ for any $\delta \in \Delta$, but $d(g) \in \Delta$, so $g(d(g)) \neq g(d(g))$, a contradiction. This proves the first claim.

For the second claim, let $\delta_0 \in \Delta$, and define $d_0 : \prod_{\delta \in \Delta} \delta \to \Delta$ by $d_0(f) = \delta_0$. Then $f(d_0(f)) = f(\delta_0)$ for all $f \in \prod_{\delta \in \Delta} \delta$, from which it follows easily that $\delta_0 \subseteq \{f(d_0(f)) : f \in \prod_{\delta \in \Delta} \delta\}$. □

We are now ready to deduce the Completeness Theorem.

Proof (Theorem B.38). First observe that the hypotheses of the theorem still hold if we replace Δ by Δ_1, where $\Delta_1 = \{\delta \cup \{c = c\} : \delta \in \Delta\}$ for c any function symbol of arity 0. Note also that $\Delta_{1S\varnothing}^{\{0\}} \vdash_{\overline{\text{CETR}}} \Delta_{S\varnothing}^{\{0\}}$, since

$$\Delta_{1S\varnothing}^{\{0\}}[\Delta_{S\varnothing}^{\{0\}}]^Q = \Delta_{S\varnothing}^{\{0\}}.$$

Hence we assume henceforth that $\forall \delta \in \Delta. |\delta| \geq 1$. Secondly, if $\Delta = \varnothing$, then the hypotheses of the theorem still hold if we replace Δ with $\Delta_0 = \{\{c \neq c\}\}$. Since $\{\Delta_0\}_{0_{\mathcal{R}\varnothing}}^{\{0\}}[\bot]^F = \Delta_{0_{\mathcal{R}\varnothing}}^{\{0\}}$, we have $\{\Delta_0\}_{0_{\mathcal{R}\varnothing}}^{\{0\}} \vdash_{\overline{\text{CETR}}} \Delta_{0_{\mathcal{R}\varnothing}}^{\{0\}}$. Hence we also assume henceforth that $|\Delta| \geq 1$.

Letting $v : A(\Delta) \to A$ be novel, and letting $\Theta = [\Delta]^N[v]$, $T = [S]^N[v]$, we have $\varnothing \vdash_{\overline{\text{CETR}}} ([\Delta]^N)_{S \bowtie T}^{\Theta}$. To see this, observe that

$$\{0\}_{0_{\mathcal{R}\varnothing}}^{\{0\}}[[\Delta_{S\varnothing}^{\{0\}}]^N]^S = ([\Delta]^N)_{S \bowtie T}^{\Theta},$$

and that this computes in absolute erotetic equilibrium, since $A(\{0\}) \cap A(\Delta) = \varnothing$.

Now observe that we may assume that C is finite, since v-models are equivalent in expressive power to first-order formulae, so the Compactness Theorem for ordinary first-order logic applies to our Tarskian semantics. Using the construction of Lemma B.42 for each $D \in C$, we may obtain a Δ' and S' with $\Delta_{S' \bowtie T, \varnothing}^{\prime \Theta}$ semantically equivalent to the conjunction of $([\Delta]^N)^\Theta_{S\bowtie T,\varnothing}$ and each $D \in C$ (note the persistence of Θ and T are evident in that construction). Since $C \vDash \Delta_R$, we have $C, [\Delta_R]^N \vDash \bot$, and $C, ([\Delta]^N)^\Theta_{S\bowtie T} \vDash \varnothing^\Theta_{T,\varnothing}$, and hence $\Delta'^\Theta_{S'\bowtie T\varnothing} \vDash \varnothing^\Theta_{T\varnothing}$. Applying Theorem B.39, we see that $\Delta'^\Theta_{S'\bowtie T,\varnothing} \vdash_{\text{CETR}} \varnothing^\Theta_{T\varnothing}$. It follows that $C \vdash_{\text{CETR}} \varnothing^\Theta_{T\varnothing}$.

It remains to show that $\varnothing^\Theta_{T\varnothing} \vdash_{\text{CETR}} \Delta^{\{0\}}_{S\varnothing}$. To see this, observe that

$$\varnothing^\Theta_{T\varnothing}[T]^D = ([[\Delta]^N]^N)^{\{0\}}_{R\varnothing}[v].$$

But by Lemma B.43 we can deduce $\Delta^{\{0\}}_{R\varnothing}[v]$ by applying $[\Delta^{\{0\}}_{R\varnothing}[v]]^Q$. □

B.6 Conservativity of Extended Reasoning over Classical

We refer to the system defined in Chapter 4 as the *classical* ETR and the system defined in Chapter 5 as the *extended* ETR. Our aim in this section is to clarify the connection between the two systems and show that most reasoning in extended ETR conservatively extends reasoning in classical ETR.

Definition B.17 (Inclusion). The *inclusion* $\iota[-] : \mathbb{V} \to \tilde{\mathbb{V}}$ is given as follows. For Γ^Θ_{RI} a classical view, $\iota[\Gamma^\Theta_{RI}]$ is the extended view Γ^Θ_{fRI} where $f(y) = \langle\!\langle\rangle\!\rangle$ for all $y \in \Gamma$. By our convention on suppressing empty weights, we could already write Γ^Θ_{RI}, but $\iota[\Gamma^\Theta_{RI}]$ makes explicit that we are considering an extended view.

Definition B.18 (Projection). The *projection* $\pi[-] : \tilde{\mathbb{V}} \to \mathbb{V}$ is given as follows. For Γ^Θ_{fRI} an extended view, $\pi[\Gamma^\Theta_{fRI}]$ is the classical view Γ^Θ_{RI}. This is indeed well-defined, since the conditions on an extended view require that $f(y) \subseteq A(R)$, and thus $A(\Gamma^\Theta) = A(R)$.

The mappings $\iota[-]$ and $\pi[-]$ extend to commitment sets and states of inference. Each gives us a notion of compatibility between the classical and extended reasoning systems. An operation O which has both classical and extended versions is said to *commute with the inclusion* if for every classical state of inference $\langle C, G \rangle$ and every classical view D we have

$$\iota[\langle C, G\rangle[D]^O] = \iota[\langle C, G\rangle][\iota[D]]^O.$$

Similarly, such an operation O is said to *commute with the projection* if for every extended state of inference $\langle C, G \rangle$ and every extended view D we have

$$\pi[\langle C, G\rangle[D]^O] = \pi[\langle C, G\rangle][\pi[D]]^O.$$

N.B. these equations are only required to hold up to renaming of the A-objects that do not appear in G or D. The same idea applies to service operations as well as reasoning operations.

Theorem B.44. *Every reasoning operation of classical ETR commutes with the inclusion $\iota[-]$.*

Theorem B.45. *Except for uses of Answer (via Update or Suppose), Query, and Which, every reasoning operation of extended ETR commutes with the projection $\pi[-]$.*

Barring the exceptions listed in Theorem B.45 it is straightforward by inspection to see that all extended reasoning operations are given in a computational form that makes no use of the weights of inputs except when determining weights for the output. For Theorem B.44 there are two subtleties.

The first concerns those exceptions Answer, Query, and Which. These have definitions which do inspect input weights to determine the classical content of their output. For Answer, we technically have to be precise about the calculation of Extended Answer Potential $[-]^{EP}$; however, in the case where all weights are $\langle\rangle$, the intended outcome is 0 in every case. Thus Answer will be equivalent to the classical Answer using Atomic Answer Potential $[-]^{AP}$. Extended Query and Which search for matches between a weighted state and a substituted weighted state, but inspection of the definition will show that, when all weights are $\langle\rangle$, the conditions become exactly the same as the classical case.

The second subtlety concerns the arithmetic of weights. This is handled by the fact that $\langle\rangle$ is a neutral element for both addition and multiplication of weights. To demonstrate both the issue that might have arisen and its circumvention, we include the following illustrative case.

Lemma B.46. *Products commute with the inclusion $\iota[-]$.*

Proof. Let Γ_{RI}^{Θ} and Δ_{SJ}^{Ψ} be classical views and T a dependency relation. Then

$$\iota[\Gamma_{RI}^{\Theta}] \otimes^T \iota[\Delta_{SJ}^{\Psi}] = (\Gamma_f \otimes \Delta_g^{\Psi})|_{[(T \bowtie R) \bowtie (T \bowtie S)][I \cup J]}^{\Theta}$$

where $f(\gamma) = \langle\rangle$ for all $\gamma \in \Gamma$ and $g(\delta) = \langle\rangle$ for all $\delta \in \Delta$. It is easily seen that $\pi[-]$ applied to this agrees with $\Gamma_{RI}^{\Theta} \otimes^T \Delta_{SJ}^{\Psi}$, and it remains to check that every state is given weight $\langle\rangle$.

For every state ξ in the outcome, ξ is weighted with the sum of the following collection of weights. If $\xi \in \Gamma$ and $\neg \exists \psi \in \Psi.\psi \subseteq \gamma$ then there is a summand $\langle\rangle$. In addition, whenever $\xi = \gamma \cup \delta$ for some $\gamma \in \Gamma$ with $\exists \psi \in \Psi.\psi \subseteq \gamma$ and $\delta \in \Delta$ then there is a summand of $\langle\rangle \times \langle\rangle$.

Now, since $\langle\rangle$ is a neutral element for multiplication of weights, $\langle\rangle \times \langle\rangle = \langle\rangle$ by definition of $\times$. Moreover, the sum of weights is defined such that $\langle\rangle + \langle\rangle = \langle\rangle$, so indeed every state ξ in the outcome is given weight $\langle\rangle$. □

References

Abelson, Robert P. (1966). *Cognitive Consistency: Motivational Antecedents and Behavioral Consequents*. New York: Academic Press.

Adams, Ernest W. (1975). *Logic of Conditionals*. Dordrecht: Reidel.

Aizawa, Ken (2015). "What is this cognition that is supposed to be embodied?" *Philosophical Psychology*, 28(6):755–75.

Anderson, Alan Ross and Nuel D. Belnap (1962). "Tautological entailments." *Philosophical Studies*, 13(1–2):9–24.

Anderson, Craig A. (1982). "Inoculation and counterexplanation: debiasing techniques in the perseverance of social theories." *Social Cognition*, 1(2):126–39.

Anderson, Stephen J., Noriko Yamagishi, and Vivian Karavia (2002). "Attentional processes link perception and action." *Proceedings of the Royal Society of London. Series B: Biological Sciences*, 269(1497):1225–32.

Ariely, Dan. (2008). *Predictably Irrational: The Hidden Forces That Shape our Decisions*. New York: Harper, 1st edn.

Ariely, Dan (2009). "The end of rational economics." *Harvard Business Review*. July-August.

Arkes, Hal R., David Faust, Thomas J. Guilmette, and Kathleen Hart (1988). "Eliminating the hindsight bias." *Journal of Applied Psychology*, 73(2):305–7.

Atlas, Jay David and Stephen C. Levinson (1981). "It-clefts, informativeness and logical form: radical pragmatics (revised standard version)." In *Radical Pragmatics*, ed. P. Cole, 1–62. New York: Academic Press.

Bach, Kent (1993). "Getting down to cases." *Behavioral and Brain Sciences*, 16(2):334–6.

Barden, Phil P. (2013). *Decoded: The Science Behind Why We Buy*. New York: John Wiley & Sons.

Baron, Jonathan (1993). "Deduction as an example of thinking." *Behavioral and Brain Sciences*, 16(2):336–7.

Barrouillet, Pierre, Caroline Gauffroy, and Jean-François Lecas (2008). "Mental models and the suppositional account of conditionals." *Psychological Review*, 115(3):760–71.

Barrouillet, Pierre, Nelly Grosset, and Jean-François Lecas (2000). "Conditional reasoning by mental models: chronometric and developmental evidence." *Cognition*, 75(3):237–66.

Barwise, Jon and John Etchemendy (1990). *The Language of First-Order Logic Including the Program Tarski's World* CSLI lecture notes, no. 23. Center for the Study of Language and Information, Stanford.

Barwise, Jon and John Perry (1983). *Situations and Attitudes*. Cambridge, MA: MIT Press.

Bellos, Alex (2016). Did you solve it? The logic question almost everyone gets wrong. The Guardian, March 28, 2016.

Bessette, Joseph M. (1994). *The Mild Voice of Reason: Deliberative Democracy and American National Government*. Chicago: Chicago University Press.

Bialek, William (2012). *Biophysics: Searching for Principles*. Princeton, NJ: Princeton University Press, annotated edn.

Block, Ned (1981). "Psychologism and behaviorism." *The Philosophical Review*, 90:5–43.

Block, Ned (2002). "Searle's arguments against cognitive science." In *Views into the Chinese Room: New Essays on Searle and Artificial Intelligence*, ed. John Preston and Mark Bishop, 70–9. Oxford University Press.

Boghossian, Paul (2014). "What is inference?" *Philosophical Studies*, 169(1):1–18.

Boghossian, Paul (2018). "Delimiting the boundaries of inference." *Philosophical Issues*, 28(1):55–69.

Braine, Martin D. and David P. O'Brien (1991). "A theory of if: a lexical entry, reasoning program, and pragmatic principles." *Psychological Review*, 98(2):182–203.

Braine, Martin D. S., Brian J. Reiser, and Barbara Rumain (1984). "Some empirical justification for a theory of natural propositional logic." In *The Psychology of Learning and Motivation*, ed. Gordon H. Bower, 317–71. New York: Academic Press.

Braine, Martin D. S. and Barbara Rumain (1983). "Logical reasoning." In *Handbook of Child Psychology*, Vol. 3: *Cognitive Development*, ed. J. H. Flavell and E. M. Markman, 263–339. New York: Wiley.

Bratman, Michael et al. (1987). *Intention, Plans, and Practical Reason*, vol. 10. Cambridge, MA: Harvard University Press.

Broome, John (2013). *Rationality through Reasoning*. New York: John Wiley & Sons.

Buss, Samuel R. (1994). "On Herbrand's theorem." In *Logical and Computational Complexity. Selected Papers. Logic and Computational Complexity, International Workshop LCC '94, Indianapolis, Indiana, USA, 13–16 October 1994*, vol. 960 of *Lecture Notes in Computer Science*, ed. Daniel Leivant, 195–209. Berlin: Springer.

Byrne, Ruth M. J. (2005). *The Rational Imagination: How People Create Alternatives to Reality*. Cambridge, MA: MIT Press.

Carter, S. (2021). "A suppositional theory of conditionals." *Mind*, 130(530):1059–86.

Castañeda, H. N. (1975). *Thinking and Doing: The Philosophical Foundations of Institutions*. Dordrecht: Reidel.

Chalmers, David (1995). "Facing up to the problem of consciousness." *Journal of Consciousness Studies*, 2(3):200–19. Publisher: Imprint Academic.

Chalmers, David John (1996). *The Conscious Mind: In Search of a Fundamental Theory*. New York: Oxford University Press.

Chapman, L. J. and J. P. Chapman (1959). "Atmosphere effect re-examined." *Journal of Experimental Psychology*, 58(3):220–6.

Chater, Nicholas and Michael Oaksford (1999). "The probability heuristics model of syllogistic reasoning." *Cognitive Psychology*, 38:191–258.

Chater, Nick, Joshua B. Tenenbaum, and Alan Yuille (2006). "Probabilistic models of cognition: conceptual foundations." *Trends in Cognitive Sciences*, 10(7):287–91.

Chemero, Anthony (2011). *Radical Embodied Cognitive Science*. Cambridge, MA: MIT press.

Cheng, Patricia W, and Keith J. Holyoak (1985). "Pragmatic reasoning schemas." *Cognitive Psychology*, 17(4):391–416.

Cherniak, Christopher (1986). *Minimal Rationality*. Cambridge, MA: MIT Press.

Chierchia, Gennaro, Danny Fox, and Benjamin Spector (2012). The grammatical view of scalar implicatures and the relationship between semantics and pragmatics. In *Semantics: An International Handbook of Natural Language Meaning*, ed. Paul Portner, Claudia Maienborn, and Klaus von Heusinger. Berlin: Mouton de Gruyter.

Chomsky, Noam (1967). "A review of B. F. Skinner's verbal behavior." In *Readings in the Psychology of Language*, ed. Leon A. Jakobovits and Murray S. Miron, 142–3. Hoboken, NJ: Prentice-Hall, 1st edn.

Chomsky, Noam (1972). *Language and Mind*. New York: Harcourt Brace Jovanovich.

Chomsky, Noam (1995). *The Minimalist Program*. Cambridge, MA: MIT Press.

Chomsky, Noam (2000a). "Minimalist inquiries: the framework." In *Step by Step: Essays on Minimalist Syntax in the Honor of Howard Lasnik*, ed. R. Martin, D. Michaels, and J. Uriagereka, 89–156. Cambridge, MA: MIT Press.
Chomsky, Noam (2000b). *New Horizons in the Study of Language and Mind*. New York: Cambridge University Press.
Ciardelli, Ivano, Jeroen Groenendijk, and Floris Roelofsen (2018). *Inquisitive Semantics*. Oxford, New York: Oxford University Press.
Ciardelli, Ivano A. (2009). *Inquisitive Semantics and Intermediate Logics*. Master's thesis, University of Amsterdam.
Cimpian, Andrei, Amanda C. Brandone, and Susan A. Gelman (2010). "Generic statements require little evidence for acceptance but have powerful implications." *Cognitive Science*, 34(8):1452–82.
Clark, Andy (2015). *Embodied Prediction*. Frankfurt am Main: MIND Group.
Cohen, Joshua (1997). "Procedure and substance in deliberative democracy." In *Deliberative Democracy: Essays on Reason and Politics*, ed. James Bohman and William Rehg, 407. Cambridge, MA: MIT Press.
Cohen, Philip R. and Hector J. Levesque (1991). "Teamwork." *Nous*, 25(4):487–512.
Cole, David (2004). "The Chinese Room argument." In *The Stanford Encyclopedia of Philosophy*, ed. Edward N. Zalta. Stanford: Metaphysics Research Lab, Stanford University, winter 2020 edn.
Cole, David (2014). "Alan Turing & the Chinese Room argument." http://www.thecritique.com/articles/alan-turing-the-chinese-room-argument/
Cosmides, Leda (1989). "The logic of social exchange: has natural selection shaped how humans reason? Studies with the wason selection task." *Cognition*, 31(3):187–276.
Cosmides, Leda and John Tooby (1996). "Are humans good intuitive statisticians after all? Rethinking some conclusions from the literature on judgment under uncertainty." *Cognition*, 58(1):1–73.
Craik, K. J. W. (1943). *The Nature of Explanation*. Oxford: Oxford University Press.
Dattner, Ben, Tomas Chamorro-Premuzic, Richard Buchband, and Lucinda Schettler (2019). "The legal and ethical implications of using AI in hiring." *Harvard Business Review*. May 20.
Deng, J., W. Dong, R. Socher, L. Li, Kai Li, and Li Fei-Fei (2009). "ImageNet: a large-scale hierarchical image database." In *2009 IEEE Conference on Computer Vision and Pattern Recognition*, 248–55. DOI: 10.1109/CVPR.2009.5206848.
Dennett, D. (1984). "Cognitive wheels: the frame problem of AI, the philosophy of artificial intelligence," in *Minds, Machines and Evolution*, ed. C. Hookway ed., Cambridge University Press, 1984, pp. 129–150.
Dietrich, Franz and Christian List (2013). "Where do preferences come from?" *International Journal of Game Theory*, 42(3):613–37.
Dietz, Christina H. (2020). "Emotions, evidence, and safety." *Synthese* 199(1–2):2027–50.
Dreyfus, Hubert and Sean D. Kelly (2007). "Heterophenomenology: heavy-handed sleight-of-hand." *Phenomenology and the Cognitive Sciences*, 6(1–2):45–55.
Dreyfus, Hubert L. (2005). "Overcoming the myth of the mental: how philosophers can profit from the phenomenology of everyday expertise." *Proceedings and Addresses of the American Philosophical Association*, 79(2):47–65.
Dryzek, John S. (2012). *Foundations and Frontiers of Deliberative Governance*. New York: Oxford University Press.
Eddy, David M. (1982). "Probabilistic reasoning in clinical medicine: problems and opportunities." In *Judgment under Uncertainty: Heuristics and Biases*, ed. Daniel Kahneman, Paul Slovic, and Amos Tversky, 249–67. New York: Cambridge University Press.

Elga, Adam and Daniel M. Oppenheimer (2021). "The policy consequences of cascade blindness." *Behavioural Public Policy*, 5(2):180–201.

Evans, J. St B. T. (1972). "Interpretation and matching bias in a reasoning task." *Quarterly Journal of Experimental Psychology*, 24(2):193–9.

Evans, J. St B. T. and S. E. Newstead (1977). "Language and reasoning: a study of temporal factors." *Cognition*, 5(3):265–83.

Evans, Jonathan St B. T. (2002). "Logic and human reasoning: an assessment of the deduction paradigm." *Psychological Bulletin*, 128(6):978.

Evans, Jonathan St B. T., Simon J. Handley, and David E. Over (2003). "Conditionals and conditional probability." *Journal of Experimental Psychology: Learning, Memory, and Cognition*, 29(2):321.

Evans, Jonathan St B. T., Stephen E. Newstead and Ruth M. J. Byrne (1993). *Human Reasoning: The Psychology of Deduction*. London: Psychology Press.

Fine, Kit (1985a). *Reasoning with Arbitrary Objects*. Oxford: Blackwell.

Fine, Kit (1985b). Natural deduction and arbitrary objects. *Journal of Philosophical Logic*, 14(1):57–107.

Fine, Kit (2012). "A difficulty for the possible world analysis of counterfactuals." *Synthese* 189:29–57.

Fine, Kit (2020). "Yablo on subject-matter." *Philosophical Studies*, 177(1):129–71.

von Fintel, Kai (1999). "The presupposition of subjunctive conditionals." In *The Interpretive Tract. MIT Working Papers in Linguistics*, vol. 25, ed. Uli Sauerland and Orin Percus, 29–44. Cambridge, MA: MITWPL.

Firestone, Chaz and Brian J. Scholl (2016). "Cognition does not affect perception: evaluating the evidence for 'top-down' effects." *The Behavioral and Brain Sciences*, 39:e229.

Fishkin, James S. (2011). *When the People Speak: Deliberative Democracy and Public Consultation*. New York: Oxford University Press.

Fodor, Jerry A. (1979). "Methodological Solipsism Considered as a Research Strategy in Cognitive Psychology." *Behavioral and Brain Sciences*, 3(1):63–73.

Fodor, Jerry A. (1983). *The Modularity of Mind*. Cambridge, MA: A Bradford Book.

Fodor, Jerry A. (1998). *Concepts: Where Cognitive Science Went Wrong*. New York: Oxford University Press.

Fodor, Jerry A. and Zenon W. Pylyshyn (1981). "How direct is visual perception? Some reflections on Gibson's 'ecological approach.'" *Cognition* 9(2):139–96.

Foley, Richard (1991). "Rationality, belief and commitment." *Synthese*, 89(3):365–92.

van Fraassen, Bas (1969). "Facts and tautological entailments." *The Journal of Philosophy*, 66(15):477–87.

Frederick, Shane, Nathan Novemsky, Jing Wang, Ravi Dhar, and Stephen Nowlis (2009). "Opportunity cost neglect." *Journal of Consumer Research*, 36(4):553–61.

Gaifman, Haim and Marc Snir (1982). "Probabilities over rich languages, testing and randomness." *The Journal of Symbolic Logic*, 47(3):495–548.

Gärdenfors, Peter (1988). *Knowledge in Flux: Modeling the Dynamics of Epistemic States*. Cambridge, MA: MIT press.

Gemünden, Hans Georg and Jürgen Hauschildt (1985). "Number of alternatives and efficiency in different types of top-management decisions." *European Journal of Operational Research*, 22(2):178–90.

Georgeff, M. and A. Rao (1991). "Modeling rational agents within a BDI-architecture." In *Proc. 2nd Int. Conf. on Knowledge Representation and Reasoning (KR'91)*, ed. J. F. Allen, R. Fikes, and E. Sandewall 473–84. San Francisco: Morgan Kaufmann.

Gibson, James J. (1979). *The Theory of Affordances: The Ecological Approach to Visual Perception*. Boston: Houghton Mifflin.

Gierasimczuk, Nina and Jakub Szymanik (2009). Branching quantification v. two-way quantification. *Journal of Semantics*, 26(4):367–92.

Gigerenzer, Gerd (2002). *Reckoning with Risk*. London: Penguin.

Gigerenzer, Gerd and Ulrich Hoffrage (1995). "How to improve Bayesian reasoning without instruction: frequency formats." *Psychological Review*, 102(4):684–704.

Gillies, Anthony S. (2009). "On truth-conditions for if (but not quite only if)." *Philosophical Review*, 118(3):325–49.

Girotto, Vittorio, Alberto Mazzocco, and Alessandra Tasso (1997). "The effect of premise order in conditional reasoning: a test of the mental model theory." *Cognition*, 63:1–28.

Gould, Stephen Jay and Richard C. Lewontin (1979). "The spandrels of San Marco and the panglossian paradigm: a critique of the adaptationist programme." *Proceedings of the Royal Society of London. Series B. Biological Sciences*, 205(1161):581–98.

Grice, Paul (1975). "Logic and conversation." In *Syntax and Semantics: Speech Acts*, vol. 3, ed. P. Cole and J. Morgan, 41–58. New York: Academic Press.

Grice, Paul (1989). *Studies in the Way of Words*. Cambridge, MA: Harvard University Press.

Griffiths, Thomas L., Charles Kemp, and Joshua B. Tenenbaum (2008). "Bayesian models of cognition." In *The Cambridge Handbook of Computational Psychology*, ed. Ron Sun, 59–100. New York: Cambridge University Press.

Griggs, Richard A. and James R. Cox (1982). "The elusive thematic-materials effect in Wason's selection task." *British Journal of Psychology*, 73(3):407–20.

Groenendijk, Jeroen (2009). "Inquisitive semantics: two possibilities for disjunction." In *Logic, Language, and Computation*, ed. P. Bosch, D. Gabelaia, J. Lang, 80–94. 7th International Tbilisi Symposium on Logic, Language, and Computation, TbiLLC 2007.

Groenendijk, Jeroen and Martin Stokhof (1991). "Dynamic predicate logic." *Linguistics and Philosophy*, 14(1):39–100.

Gutmann, Amy and Dennis F. Thompson (2009). *Why Deliberative Democracy?* Princeton, NJ: Princeton University Press.

Gärdenfors, Peter (2004). *Conceptual Spaces: The Geometry of Thought*. Cambridge, MA: MIT Press.

Hacking, Ian (1975). *The Emergence of Probability: A Philosophical Study of Early Ideas about Probability, Induction and Statistical Inference*. New York: Cambridge University Press.

Hackl, Martin (2009). "On the grammar and processing of proportional quantifiers: most versus more than half." *Natural Language Semantics*, 17(1):63–98.

Haiman, John (1978). "Conditionals are topics." *Language*, 54(3):564–89.

Hájek, Alan (2005). "Scotching Dutch books?" *Philosophical Perspectives*, 19(1):139–51.

Hamblin, Charles L. (1958). "Questions." *Australasian Journal of Philosophy*, 36(3):159–68.

Hamblin, Charles L. (1973). "Questions in Montague English." *Foundations of Language* 10(1):41–53.

Hammerton, M. (1973). "Processing of numbers and of physical magnitude." *Perceptual and Motor Skills*, 37(1):155–8.

Hao, Karen (2019). "AI is sending people to jail—and getting it wrong." *MIT Technology Review*, Jan. 21.

Harman, Gilbert (1979). "If and modus ponens." *Theory and Decision*, 11(1):41–53.

Harman, Gilbert (1986). *Change in View: Principles of Reasoning*. Cambridge, MA: MIT Press.

Hastie, Reid and Robyn Dawes (2010). *Rational Choice in an Uncertain World: The Psychology of Judgment and Decision Making*. Los Angeles: Sage Publications, Inc.

Haugeland, John (2002). "Syntax, semantics, physics." In *Views into the Chinese Room: New Essays on Searle and Artificial Intelligence*, ed. John M. Preston and Michael A. Bishop, 159-69. New York: Oxford University Press.

Heath, Chip and Dan Heath (2013). *Decisive: How to Make Better Choices in Life and Work*. Toronto: Random House.

Heim, Irene (1983). "On the projection problem for presuppositions." In *Formal Semantics—The Essential Readings*, ed. P. Portner and B. H. Partee, 249-60. Oxford: Blackwell.

Heim, Irene and Angelika Kratzer (1998). *Semantics in Generative Grammar*. New York: Wiley.

Hempel, Carl G. (1949). "Theory of experimental inference." *Journal of Philosophy*, 46(17):557-61.

Hintikka, Jaakko and Gabriel Sandu (1997). "Game-theoretical semantics." In *Handbook of Logic and Language*, ed. Johan van Benthem and Alice ter Meulen, 361-410. Amsterdam: North-Holland.

Hoch, Stephen J. (1985). "Counterfactual reasoning and accuracy in predicting personal events." *Journal of Experimenta Psychology: Learning, Memory, and Cognition*, 11(4):719-31.

Hodges, Wilfrid (1993). "The logical content of theories of deduction." *Behavioral and Brain Sciences*, 16(2):353-54.

Hodges, Wilfrid et al. (1997). *A Shorter Model Theory*. New York: Cambridge University Press.

Hoffrage, U. and G. Gigerenzer (1998). "Using natural frequencies to improve diagnostic inferences." *Academic Medicine*, 73(5):538-40.

Hoffrage, Ulrich and Gerd Gigerenzer (2004). "How to improve the diagnostic inferences of medical experts." In *Experts in Science and Society*, ed. E. Kurz-Milcke and G. Gigerenzer, 249-68. New York: Plenum Publishers.

Holliday, Wesley H., Thomas F. Icard III, et al. (2013). "Measure semantics and qualitative semantics for epistemic modals." *Semantics and Linguistic Theory*, 23:514-34.

Horvitz, E. (1988). "Reasoning about beliefs and actions under computational resource constraints." *International Journal of Approximate Reason*, 2(3):337-8.

Huber, Joel, John W. Payne, and Christopher Puto (1982). "Adding asymmetrically dominated alternatives: violations of regularity and the similarity hypothesis." *Journal of Consumer Research*, 9(1):90-8.

Hume, David (1739). *A Treatise of Human Nature*. London.

Inhelder, Bärbel and Jean Piaget (1958). *The Growth of Logical Thinking from Childhood to Adolescence: An Essay on the Construction of Formal Operational Structures*. London: Psychology Press.

Iyengar, Sheena S. and Mark R. Lepper (2000). "When choice is demotivating: can one desire too much of a good thing?" *Journal of Personality and Social Psychology*, 79(6):995.

Jackendoff, Ray (1988). "Exploring the form of information in the dynamic unconscious." In *Psychodynamics and Cognition*, ed. Mardi J Horowitz, 3-10. Chicago: University of Chicago Press.

James, William (1890). *The Principles of Psychology*. New York: Dover Publications.

Johnson-Laird, P. (1993). "The interaction between reasoning and decision making: an introduction." *Cognition*, 49(1-2):1-9.

Johnson-Laird, Philip, Paolo Legrenzi, Vittorio Girotto, and Maria Legrenzi (1999). "Naive probability: a mental model theory of extensional reasoning." *Psychological Review*, 106(1):62-88.

Johnson-Laird, Philip N. (1983). *Mental Models: Towards a Cognitive Science of Language, Inference, and Consciousness*. Cambridge: Cambridge University Press.

Johnson-Laird, Philip N. (2008). "Mental models and deductive reasoning." In *Reasoning: Studies in Human Inference and its Foundations*, ed. L. Rips and J. Adler, 206–22. Cambridge: Cambridge University Press.

Johnson-Laird, Philip N., Ruth M. Byrne, and Walter Schaeken (1992). "Propositional reasoning by model." *Psychological Review*, 99(3):418.

Johnson-Laird, Philip N., Geoffrey P. Goodwin, and Sangeet S. Khemlani (2018). Mental models and reasoning. In *The Routledge International Handbook of Thinking and Reasoning*, ed. Linden J. Ball and Valerie A. Thompson, 346–65. New York: Routledge/Taylor & Francis Group.

Johnson-Laird, Philip N. and Fabien Savary (1999). "Illusory inferences: a novel class of erroneous deductions." *Cognition*, 71(3):191–229.

Johnson-Laird, Philip Nicholas and Ruth M. J. Byrne (1991). *Deduction*. Hillsdale, NJ: Erlbaum.

Johnson-Laird, P. N., Paolo Legrenzi, and Vittorio Girotto (2004). "How we detect logical inconsistencies." *Current Directions in Psychological Science*, 13(2):41–5.

Johnson-Laird, P. N. and Fabien Savary (1996). "Illusory inferences about probabilities." *Acta Psychologica*, 93(1):69–90.

Johnstone, P. T. (1987). *Notes on logic and set theory*. Cambridge: Cambridge University Press.

Kahneman, Daniel (2011). *Thinking, Fast and Slow*. New York: Farrar, Straus and Giroux.

Kahneman, Daniel, Jack L. Knetsch, and Richard H. Thaler (1990). "Experimental tests of the endowment effect and the coase theorem." *Journal of Political Economy*, 98(6):1325–48.

Kahneman, Daniel, Jack L. Knetsch, and Richard H. Thaler (1991). "Anomalies: the endowment effect, loss aversion, and status quo bias." *Journal of Economic Perspectives*, 5(1):193–206.

Kahneman, Daniel, Jack L. Knetsch, and Richard H. Thaler (2008). "The endowment effect: evidence of losses valued more than gains." *Handbook of Experimental Economics Results*, 1:939–48.

Kahneman, Daniel and Amos Tversky (1979). "Prospect theory: an analysis of decision under risk." *Econometrica*, 47(2):263–91.

Kamp, Hans (1981). "A theory of truth and semantic interpretation". In *Formal Semantics*, ed. P. Portner and B. H. Partee, 189–222. Oxford: Blackwell.

Kant, Immanuel (1781). *Critique of Pure Reason*. London.

Khemlani, Sangeet and Philip N. Johnson-Laird (2012). "Theories of the syllogism: a meta-analysis." *Psychological Bulletin*, 138(3):427.

Khemlani, Sangeet, Sarah-Jane Leslie, and Sam Glucksberg (2009). "Generics, prevalence, and default inferences." *Proceedings of the Cognitive Science Society*, 31: 443–8.

Khemlani, Sangeet, Sarah-Jane Leslie, and Sam Glucksberg (2012a). "Inferences about members of kinds: the generics hypothesis." *Language and Cognitive Processes*, 27(6):887–900.

Khemlani, Sangeet, M. Lotstein, J. G. Trafton, and P. N. Johnson-Laird (2015). "Immediate inferences from quantified assertions." *The Quarterly Journal of Experimental Psychology*, 68(10):2073–96.

Khemlani, Sangeet, Isabel Orenes, and Philip N. Johnson-Laird (2012b). "Negation: a theory of its meaning, representation, and use." *Journal of Cognitive Psychology*, 24(5): 541–59.

Khemlani, S. and P. Johnson-Laird (2022). "Reasoning about properties: A computational theory." *Psychological Review*, 129(2):289–312.

Kiss, Katalin É. (1998). "Identificational focus versus information focus." *Language*, 74(2):245–73.

Klein, Colin (2007). "An imperative theory of pain." *The Journal of Philosophy*, 104(10):517–32.

Knobe, Joshua (2003). "Intentional action and side effects in ordinary language." *Analysis*, 63(3):190–4.

Koffka, K. (1935). *Principles of Gestalt Psychology*. London: Lund Humphries.

Kondo, Marie (2014). *The Life-Changing Magic of Tidying: A Simple, Effective Way to Banish Clutter Forever*. New York: Random House.

Koralus, Philipp (2014a). "Attention, consciousness, and the semantics of questions." *Synthese*, 191(2):187–211.

Koralus, Philipp (2014b). "The erotetic theory of attention: questions, focus and distraction." *Mind & Language*, 29(1):26–50.

Koralus, Philipp and Mark Alfano (2017). "Reasons-based moral judgment and the erotetic theory." In *Moral Inferences*, ed. J.-F. Bonnefon and B. Trémolière, 77–106. New York: Routledge/Taylor & Francis Group.

Koralus, Philipp and Salvador Mascarenhas (2013). "The erotetic theory of reasoning: bridges between formal semantics and the psychology of deductive inference." *Philosophical Perspectives*, 27:312–65.

Koralus, Philipp and Salvador Mascarenhas (2016). "Illusory inferences and the erotetic theory of reasoning." In *An Atlas of Meaning*, ed. Ken Turner and Laurence Horn, 300–322. Leiden: Brill.

Koriat, Asher, Sarah Lichtenstein, and Baruch Fischhoff (1980). "Reasons for confidence." *Journal of Experimental Psychology: Human Learning and Memory*, 6(2):107–18.

Kratzer, Angelika (1991). "Modality." In *Semantics: An International Handbook of Contemporary Research*, ed. A. von Stechow and D. Wunderlich, 639–650.

Kratzer, Angelika (2012). *Modals and Conditionals: New and Revised Perspectives*, vol. 36. New York: Oxford University Press.

Kratzer, Angelika and Junko Shimoyama (2002). "Indeterminate pronouns: the view from Japanese." In *Paper presented at the 3rd Tokyo Conference on Psycholinguistics* March 2002.

Kratzer, Angelika and Junko Shimoyama (2017). "Indeterminate pronouns: the view from Japanese." In *Contrastiveness in Information Structure, Alternatives and Scalar Implicatures*, pages 123–43. New York: Springer.

Kripke, Saul (1980). *Naming and Necessity*. Cambridge, MA: Harvard University Press.

Krugman, P. (2012). "The 'yes, minister' theory of the medicare age." *New York Times*, Dec. 12.

de Laplace, P. S. (1902). *A Philosophical Essay on Probabilities*. New York: Wiley.

Lassiter, Daniel (2011). *Measurement and Modality: The Scalar Basis of Modal Semantics*. Ph.D. thesis, New York University.

Leslie, Sarah-Jane (2007). "Generics and the structure of the mind." *Philosophical Perspectives*, 21:375–403.

Leslie, Sarah-Jane (2008). "Generics: cognition and acquisition." *Philosophical Review*, 117(1):1–47.

Leslie, Sarah-Jane (2017). "The original sin of cognition: fear, prejudice, and generalization." *The Journal of Philosophy*, 114(8):393–421.

Leslie, Sarah-Jane, Sangeet Khemlani, and Sam Glucksberg (2011). "Do all ducks lay eggs? The generic overgeneralization effect." *Journal of Memory and Language*, 65(1):15–31.

Levesque, Hector J. (1988). "Logic and the complexity of reasoning." *Journal of Philosophical Logic*, 17(4):355–89.

Levesque, Hector J. (2014). "On our best behaviour." *Artificial Intelligence*, 212:27–35.

Levesque, Hector J. (2017). *Common Sense, the Turing Test, and the Quest for Real AI: Reflections on Natural and Artificial Intelligence.* Cambridge, MA: MIT Press, 1st edn.

Levinson, Stephen C. (2000). *Presumptive Meanings: The Theory of Generalized Conversational Implicature.* Cambridge, MA MIT press.

Li, Fei Fei, Rufin VanRullen, Christof Koch, and Pietro Perona (2002). "Rapid natural scene categorization in the near absence of attention." *Proceedings of the National Academy of Sciences*, 99(14):9596–601.

List, John A. (2003). "Does market experience eliminate market anomalies?" *The Quarterly Journal of Economics*, 118(1):41–71.

List, John A. (2004). "Neoclassical theory versus prospect theory: evidence from the marketplace." *Econometrica*, 72(2):615–25.

Lorenz, Hendrik (2006). *The Brute Within: Appetitive Desire in Plato and Aristotle.* New York: Oxford University Press.

MacFarlane, John (2004). "In what sense (if any) is logic normative for thought." Draft of April 21, 2004 For presentation at the Central Division APA 2004.

Mackie, John Leslie (1973). *Truth, Probability and Paradox: Studies in Philosophical Logic.* New York: Oxford University Press.

Madsen, Jens Koed, Richard Bailey, Ernesto Carrella and Philipp Koralus (2021). From reactive towards anticipatory fishing agents. *Journal of Simulation*, 15(1–2):23–37.

Mandelbaum, E. (2019). "Troubles with Bayesianism: An introduction to the psychological immune system." *Mind and Language*, 34(2):141–57.

Marr, D. (1977). "Artificial intelligence—a personal view." *Artificial Intelligence*, 9(1):37–48.

Marr, D., T. Poggio, and Sydney Brenner (1979). "A computational theory of human stereo vision." *Proceedings of the Royal Society of London. Series B. Biological Sciences*, 204(1156):301–28. Publisher: Royal Society.

Marr, David (1982). *Vision: A Computational Investigation into the Human Representation and Processing of visual information.* W.H. Freeman and Company.

Mas-Colell, Andreu, Michael D. Whinston, and Jerry R. Green (1995). *Microeconomic Theory.* New York: Oxford University Press.

Mascarenhas, Salvador (2009). "Referential indefinites and choice functions revisited." Unpublished manuscript, NYU.

Mascarenhas, Salvador and Philipp Koralus (2017). Illusory inferences with quantifiers. *Thinking and Reasoning*, 23(1):33–48.

McCarthy, John (1958). "Programs with common sense." Proceedings of the Teddington Conference on the Mechanization of Thought Processes in December 1958: 15.

McCarthy, John and Patrick J Hayes (1981). Some philosophical problems from the standpoint of artificial intelligence. In Bonnie Lynn Webber and Nils J. Nilsson, editors. *Readings in artificial intelligence*, pages 431–450. Elsevier. Publisher: Morgan Kaufmann.

Mendelovici, Angela (2013). "Intentionalism about moods." *Thought: A Journal of Philosophy*, 2(2):126–36.

Mercier, Hugo and Dan Sperber (2017). *The Enigma of Reason.* Cambridge, MA: Harvard University Press.

Minsky. (1986). *The Society of Mind.* New York: Pocket Books, illustrated edition.

Morewedge, Carey K. and Colleen E. Giblin (2015). "Explanations of the endowment effect: an integrative review." *Trends in Cognitive Sciences*, 19(6):339–48.

Morewedge, Carey K., Lisa L. Shu, Daniel T. Gilbert, and Timothy D. Wilson (2009). "Bad riddance or good rubbish? Ownership and not loss aversion causes the endowment effect." *Journal of Experimental Social Psychology*, 45(4):947–51.

Morris, Bradley J. and Uri Hasson (2010). "Multiple sources of competence underlying the comprehension of inconsistencies: a developmental investigation." *Journal of Experimental Psychology: Learning, Memory, and Cognition*, 36(2):277–87.

Mullainathan, Sendhil and Eldar Shafir (2013). *Scarcity: Why Having Too Little Means So Much*. New York: Times Books/Henry Holt and Co.

Muscettola, N, Nayak, P., Pell, B., Williams, B. (1998). "Remote Agent: to boldly go where no AI system has gone before." Artificial intelligence 103, 5–47.

Nanay, Bence (2011). "Do we see apples as edible?" *Pacific Philosophical Quarterly*, 92(3):305–22.

Nematzadeh, Nasim, David M. W. Powers, and Trent Lewis (2020). "Vis-CRF, a classical receptive field model for VISION." arXiv:2011.08363.

Newstead, Stephen E. and Richard A. Griggs (1983). "Drawing inferences from quantified statements: a study of the square of opposition." *Journal of Verbal Learning and Verbal Behavior*, 22(5):535–46.

Noë, Alva, Alva Noë, et al. (2004). *Action in Perception*. Cambridge, MA: MIT press.

Nutt, Paul C. (1993). "The identification of solution ideas during organizational decision making." *Management Science*, 39(9):1071–85.

Oaksford, Michael and Nicholas Chater (2007). *Bayesian Rationality: The Probabilistic Approach to Human Reasoning*. New York: Oxford University Press.

Oaksford, Mike and Nick Chater (2009). "Precis of Bayesian rationality: the probabilistic approach to human reasoning." *Behavioral and Brain Sciences*, 32(1):69–84.

Oberauer, Klaus and Oliver Wilhelm (2003). "The meaning(s) of conditionals: conditional probabilities, mental models, and personal utilities." *Journal of Experimental Psychology: Learning, Memory, and Cognition*, 29(4):680.

Over, David E., Constantinos Hadjichristidis, Jonathan St B. T. Evans, Simon J. Handley, and Steven A. Sloman (2007). The probability of causal conditionals. *Cognitive Psychology*, 54(1):62–97.

Paradis, Carita and Caroline Willners (2006). Antonymy and negation—the boundedness hypothesis. *Journal of Pragmatics*, 38(7):1051–80.

Pettit, Philip (1997). *Republicanism: A Theory of Freedom and Government*. New York: Oxford University Press.

Phillips-Brown, Milo (2018). "I want to, but..." *Sinn Und Bedeutung*, 21:951–68.

Pierce, Jon L, Tatiana Kostova, and Kurt T. Dirks (2001). "Toward a theory of psychological ownership in organizations." *Academy of Management Review*, 26(2):298–310.

Pierce, Jon L., Tatiana Kostova, and Kurt T. Dirks (2003). "The state of psychological ownership: integrating and extending a century of research." *Review of General Psychology*, 7(1):84–107.

Pinker, S. (2021). *Rationality: What It Is, Why It Seems Scarce, Why It Matters*. New York: Penguin.

Pinker, Steven (2002). *The Blank Slate: The Modern Denial of Human Nature*. New York: Viking.

Popper, Karl (1959). *The Logic of Scientific Discovery*. New York: Routledge.

Prosser, Simon (2011). "Affordances and phenomenal character in spatial perception." *Philosophical Review*, 120(4):475–513.

Putnam, Hillary (1975). "The meaning of 'meaning'." *Minnesota Studies in the Philosophy of Science*, 7:131–93.

Quilty-Dunn, Jake (2020). "Attention and encapsulation." *Mind & Language*, 35(3): 335–49.

Quine, W. and O. Van (1960). *Word and Object: An Inquiry into the Linguistic Mechanisms of Objective Reference*. Oxford: John Wiley.

Ragni, Marco and Phil Johnson-Laird (2018). Reasoning about possibilities: human reasoning violates all normal modal logics. In Chuck Kalish, Martina Rau, Jerry Zhu, and Timothy Rogers, editors, *CogSci 2018*, pp. 2309–2314.

Ramsey, Frank P. (1926). "Truth and probability." In *The Foundations of Mathematics and Other Logical Essays*, ed. R. B. Braithwaite, 156–98. McMaster University Archive for the History of Economic Thought Toronto.

Ramsey, Frank P. (1929). "General propositions and causality, repr." In *Foundations: Essays in Philosophy, Logic, Mathematics and Economics*. In Edited by R. B. Braithwaite. The Foundations of Mathematics and other Logical Essays. London: Kegan Paul, Trench, Trübner. pp. 237–255 (1929).

Richard, Michael D. and Richard P. Lippmann (1991). "Neural network classifiers estimate Bayesian a posteriori probabilities." *Neural Computation*, 3(4):461–83.

Rips, Lance (1994). *The Psychology of Proof*. Cambridge, MA: MIT Press.

Russell, Stuart and Peter Norvig (2010). *Artificial Intelligence: A Modern Approach*. Boston: Pearson.

Russell, Stuart and Peter Norvig (2016). *Artificial Intelligence: A Modern Approach, Global Edition*. Boston: Pearson, 3rd edn.

Russell, Stuart J. (1997). "Rationality and intelligence." *Artificial Intelligence*, 94(1–2):57–77.

Sablé-Meyer, M., Mascarenhas, S. Indirect illusory inferences from disjunction: a new bridge between deductive inference and representativeness. *Rev.Phil.Psych.* (2021). https://doi.org/10.1007/s13164-021-00543-8

Searle, John R. (1980). "Minds, brains, and programs." *Behavioral and Brain Sciences*, 3(3):417–24.

Searle, John R. (1999). "The Chinese Room." In *The MIT Encyclopedia of the Cognitive Sciences*, et. Robert Andrew Wilson and Frank C. Keil, 000–000. Cambridge, MA: MIT Press.

Sellars, Wilfrid (1953). "Inference and meaning." *Mind*, 62(247):313–38.

Shafir, Eldar (1993). "Choosing versus rejecting: why some options are both better and worse than others." *Memory & Cognition*, 21(4):546–56.

Shafir, Eldar, Itamar Simonson, and Amos Tversky (1993). "Reason-based choice." *Cognition*, 49(1):11–36.

Shimojo, Shinsuke and Shin'Ichi Ichikawa (1989). "Intuitive reasoning about probability: theoretical and experimental analyses of the 'problem of three prisoners.'" *Cognition*, 32(1):1–24.

Siegel, Susanna (2014). Affordances and the contents of perception. In Berit Brogaard, editor, *Does Perception Have Content?*, pages 39–76. Oxford University Press.

Simon, Herbert A. (1955). "A behavioral model of rational choice." *The Quarterly Journal of Economics*, 69(1):99–118.

Simon, Herbert A. (1956). "Rational choice and the structure of the environment." *Psychological Review*, 63(2):129.

Skinner, B. F. (1974). *About Behaviorism*. Oxford: Alfred A. Knopf.

Skinner, Quentin (2008). *Hobbes and Republican Liberty*. Cambridge: Cambridge University Press.

Sloman, Steven A. (1996). The empirical case for two systems of reasoning. *Psychological Bulletin*, 119:3–22.

Soames, Scott (2002). *Beyond Rigidity: The Unfinished Semantic Agenda of Naming and Necessity*. New York: Oxford University Press, 1st edn.
Sperber, Dan, Francesco Cara, and Vittorio Girotto (1995). "Relevance theory explains the selection task." *Cognition*, 57(1):31–95.
Sperber, Dan and Deirdre Wilson (1986). *Relevance: Communication and Cognition*. Cambridge, MA: Harvard University Press.
St. B. T. Evans, Jonathan, John Clibbens, and Benjamin Rood (1995). "Bias in conditional inference: implications for mental models and mental logic." *The Quarterly Journal of Experimental Psychology*, 48(3):644–70.
Stalnaker, Robert (1975). "Indicative conditionals." *Philosophia*, 5:269–86.
Stanovich, Keith E. (2015). "Rational and irrational thought: the thinking that IQ tests miss." *Scientific American*, 23:12–17.
Stanovich, Keith E., Richard F. West, and Maggie E. Toplak (2016). *The Rationality Quotient: Toward a Test of Rational Thinking*. Cambridge, MA: MIT Press.
Starr, William B. (2014). What 'if'? *Philosophers' Imprint*, 14.
Stevens, Jon Scott (2017). "Pragmatics of focus." In *Oxford Research Encyclopedia of Linguistics*. Oxford: Oxford University Press.
Tenenbaum, Josua B., Thomas L. Griffiths, and Charles Kemp (2006). "Theory-based Bayesian models of inductive learning and reasoning." *Trends in Cognitive Sciences*, 10(7):309–18.
Tetlock, Philip E. (2005). *Expert Political Judgment: How Good Is It? How Can We Know?* Princeton, NJ: Princeton University Press, student edn.
Tetlock, Philip E. and Dan Gardner (2015). *Superforecasting: The Art and Science of Prediction*. New York: Crown Publishing Group.
Thaler, Richard H. and Cass R. Sunstein (2008). *Nudge: Improving Decisions about Health, Wealth, and Happiness*. New Haven, CT: Yale University Press.
Toplak, Maggie E., Richard F. West, and Keith E. Stanovich (2011). "The Cognitive Reflection Test as a predictor of performance on heuristics-and-biases tasks." *Memory & Cognition*, 39(7):1275.
Treisman, Anne and Hilary Schmidt (1982). "Illusory conjunctions in the perception of objects." *Cognitive Psychology*, 14(1):107–41.
Tucker, Mike and Rob Ellis (1998). "On the relations between seen objects and components of potential actions." *Journal of Experimental Psychology: Human Perception and Performance*, 24(3):830.
Turing, A. M. (1950). "Computing machinery and intelligence." *Mind*, LIX(236):433–60.
Tversky, A. and D. Kahneman (1981). "The framing of decisions and the psychology of choice." *Science*, 211(4481):453–8.
Tversky, Amos and Daniel Kahneman (1973). "Availability: a heuristic for judging frequency and probability." *Cognitive Psychology*, 5(2):207–32.
Tversky, Amos and Daniel Kahneman (1983). "Extensional versus intuitive reasoning: the conjunction fallacy in probability judgment." *Psychological Review*, 90:293–315.
Tversky, Amos and Daniel Kahneman (1992). "Advances in prospect theory: cumulative representation of uncertainty." *Journal of Risk and Uncertainty*, 5(4):297–323.
Tylecote, R. (2019). "Why is there more intellectual freedom in Bucharest than Cambridge?" *The Spectator*. 26 November 2019.
Urbach, Peter and Colin Howson (1993). *Scientific Reasoning: The Bayesian Approach*. Chicago Open Court.
Valaris, Markos (2017). "What reasoning might be." *Synthese*, vol. 194, pp. 2007–2024 (2017).

Valiant, Leslie (2013). *Probably Approximately Correct: Nature's Algorithms for Learning and Prospering in a Complex World*. New York: Basic Books, Inc.

Veltman, Frank (1996). "Defaults in update semantics." *Journal of Philosophical Logic*, 25:221-61.

Von Fintel, Kai (2011). "Conditionals." In *Semantics: An International Handbook of Meaning*, vol. 2, ed. Klaus von Heusinger, Claudia Maienborn and Paul Portner, 1515-38. Berlin: de Gruyter Mouton.

Walsh, Clare and Philip N. Johnson-Laird (2004). "Coreference and reasoning." *Memory and Cognition*, 32:96-106.

Wason, P. C. and J. St. B. T. Evans (1974). "Dual processes in reasoning?" *Cognition*, 3(2):141-54.

Wason, Peter C. (1966). Reasoning Peter C. Wason In B. Foss (ed.), New Horizons in Psychology. Harmondsworth: Penguin Books. pp. 135-151 (1966).

Winograd, Terry (1972). "Understanding natural language." *Cognitive Psychology*, 3(1):1-191.

Wisniewski, Andrzej (1995). *The Posing of Questions: Logical Foundations of Erotetic Inferences*. Dordrecht and Boston: Kluwer Academic Publishers.

Wooldridge, Michael (2003). *Reasoning about Rational Agents*. Cambridge, MA MIT press.

Yablo, Stephen (2014). *Aboutness*. Princeton, NJ: Princeton University Press.

Yalcin, Seth (2018). "Belief as question-sensitive." *Philosophy and Phenomenological Research*, 97(1):23-47.

Index

Note: Figures are indicated by "f", following the page number.

aboutness, and predicate views 142–7
absolute erotetic equilibrium 100, 179–81
  inferences 93, 180–1
absurdity 101, 147–50
  absurd states 79, 147–8
  clauses 147–8, 149
  primitive absurd states 67–8, 147–50
action-centred priorities 285–92
Adams, Ernest W. 105
affirming the consequent 107, 108
affordances
  and action-centered priorities 285–92
  defining 285–6
  intentional content 291
  representational content 291
agent-based model (ABM) simulation 58
AI *see* artificial intelligence
Albers, Joseph 5, 6
Alfano, Mark 14, 254, 255
algebra 58, 66, 156–8
  Boolean 238, 239
  dependency relations 154
  $\mathcal{R}$ Algebra 156, 305
alternative states 48–9, 55, 68
  core reasoning and erotetic equilibrium 63–4, 66
analyticity 147–50
anaphora resolution 42
answers 71–8, 205–6
  answerhood 49, 52, 53, 131, 159
  Atomic Answer 206
  equilibrium answer potential (EAP) 203–6, 247, 269, 277
  see also questions
arbitrary objects 45, 46, 137, 140
  sets of dependencies between 139–41
Ariely, Dan 251–2, 279, 280
Aristotle, De Anima 27

articulation 136
  duality 154
  function 70
  inherently ordered systems 71
  $\mathbb{M} \to \text{Sent}(\mathcal{L}_{PC})$ 154
  procedures 70, 71, 93–4, 153–5, 181, 322, 324
  of $\mathcal{R}$ into quantifier strings 153–4
artificial intelligence 1–2, 4, 7, 15, 20, 25, 28, 31, 41, 42
atomic states 66, 67
axioms 133, 140
  first-order 147, 148
  for identity 177
  Kolmogorov 238
  of probability 237, 238

Barrouillet, Pierre 105
base-rate neglect 13
  doctors and realistic disease example 190
  invented disease example 189–90
  inviting inferences in absence of base rate 191
  non-probabilistic statements 221
  "psylicrapitis" case 222
basic objects and dependency relations 137–42
Bayesianism 196, 207, 234–7
  and aims of reason 29–33
  characterization of reasoning 49
  heuristics 31
  posterior probability 189
  probability theory 32
  uncertainty, reasoning with 189, 195
Bayes' Rule 188, 189, 219, 289
behaviorism 33
Belief-Desire-Intention (BDI) model 60, 261, 265

biconditional facilitation 122
Block, Ned 34
bounded optimality 21, 23, 32
bounded optimization 28
bounded satisficing 21
Braine, D. S. 43, 86
Brandone, Amanda C. 182
Bratman, Michael 260, 261
Brenner, Sydney 5
Broome, John 101

calculative rationality 19, 20
Cardinality Problem 135, 136–7
Carter, Sam 106
Castañeda, H. N. 262
categorical diagnosis inference 194
Chalmers, David 35, 285
Chater, Nicholas 105
Cheng, Patricia W. 104
Chernobyl, nuclear meltdown 11
Chinese room (CR) 34–7
Chomsky, Noam 15–16, 26
    Minimalist Program 40
Cicero 105, 106
Cimpian, Andrei 182
cognitive slack, problem of 21, 23
competence
    competence-based approaches 41
    and mental models 33–42
        objections 39–42
completeness 94, 326–7
complexity
    erotetic complexity principle 54, 55
    states 66
    view-change complexity
        principle 54, 56
computational theory of reason 15–18, 29, 31, 44
computing machines, Turing on 40
conditional probability 13, 189
conditionals 103–27, 220
    interpreting 105
    and uncertainty 215–22
conjunction fallacy 225–31
conjunction rule, apparent violations 198
consequence 164, 219
    classical 267
    direct 266–7
    logical 20

plausible 273
strict 101–2
content-based theories of reason 42–9, 64, 262–3
    arbitrary objects 137
    aspects of 56–9
    intentional content 291
    representational content 263, 291
    theory of dynamics of reason 56, 57
    theory of views 56
    view calculus 56
content-representation correspondence
    principle 45
conversion fallacy 132
core propositions 2
core reasoning
    defining views 66–71
    and erotetic equilibrium 61–102
    inquire and query 86–90
    updating questions with answers 71–8
correct control inference disjunctive
    syllogism 63
Cosmides, Leda 234
counterfactuals 35–7, 39
Cox, James R. 104, 116
Craik, K. J. W. 36, 38, 44
creative inquiry, core reasoning
    performance 54

Dawes, Robyn 191, 192, 193
de Morgan's laws 69, 148
decision theory 10, 205
decision-making 14, 250, 252, 255, 259–65, 298
    choosing versus rejecting 253
    decoy effect 251–2
    default decision 272–81
    expert forecasting 247
    failure 275
    and practical reasoning 248–301
    priorities 267–71
    pure decision questions 264–5
default strategy, core reasoning
    performance 54, 55
demands, excessive 101
denying the antecedent (DA) 124
dependency relations 137–42, 155, 156
    meta-theory 314–20
Dietrich, Franz 268

INDEX 349

disequilibrium
  implication 112–14
disjunction, illusory inferences from 61,
  74, 76, 77, 129
disjunctive syllogism 63, 80
  triple 83
Division 168
do-atoms 263, 264
domain-general reason 6, 8, 10, 18, 32, 118
Dreyfus, Hubert L. 287, 288

EAP *see* equilibrium answer potential
  (EAP)
Elga, Adam 297–8
endowment effect 255–8, 280, 281
equilibrium answer potential
  (EAP) 200–6, 219, 247, 259, 267,
  269, 277
equilibrium guarantee hypothesis
  185
erotetic agents
  defining 50
  kingdom of 295–301
erotetic complexity principle 54, 55
erotetic disequilibrium 50, 53, 292
erotetic equilibrium 8, 48, 50
  absolute 100, 179–81
  of an inference 93
  classical soundness and completeness
    under 181
  "if . . . then," erotetic suppositional 105,
    106–9, 111
  and probabilistic coherence 237–41
  restricted 94–9, 182–7, 241–7
  soundness under 94, 324–6
  utility maximization under 281–5
  of views 92–3, 180
Evans, Jonathan St B. T. 115, 116, 121
ex falso quodlibet 85, 86, 102
Existential sum 162–8, 233
expert forecasting 241–7
explosion 101
extended reasoning, conservativity of, over
  classical 331–4
extended views 200–3
externalist revolution, philosophy 41

Fine, Kit 45, 47, 64, 137, 139–40, 142
first-order axioms 147, 148

first-order equivalent 133
first-order logic 322, 324
Fishkin, James S. 300
Fodor, Jerry A. 17
framing effects 14
Frederick, Shane 249–51, 273
Frege, Gottlob 134
function 9, 16, 17, 33, 146, 201, 210, 218,
  238, 239, 298

Gaifman, Haim 238
Gärdenfors, Peter 41
Gardner, Dan 194, 245
Gelan, Susan A. 182
Gemünden, Hans Georg 249
gene transcription 16
generalized quantifiers 148
generics
  bare-plural 184
  generic inference to particulars
    133
  generic statements 132, 133, 184
  and restricted erotetic
    equilibrium 182–7
  striking-property 183
Giblin, Colleen E. 280
Gibson, James J. 285–7
Gigerenzer, Gerd 190, 191, 224, 225,
  241, 242
Girotto, Vittorio 119, 121–2
Glucksberg, Sam 132, 184
Gödel, Kurt 134
Good Judgment Project 244
Gould, Stephen Jay 293
graded uncertainty, generating 206–15
Grice, Paul 61
Griffiths, Thomas L. 29
Griggs, Richard A. 104, 116, 132
Groenendijk, Jeroen 46

Hamblin, Charles L. 46, 63
Hammerton, M. 12–13, 189, 190
Harman, Gilbert 19, 20, 26, 32, 260,
  261, 288
Hastie, Reid 191, 192, 193
Hauschildt, Jürgen 249
Heath, Chip 248, 249, 251
Heath, Dan 248, 249, 251
Heim, Irene 18

heuristics
  Bayesianism 31
  conditionals 104
  heuristic systems, special-purpose 23–4
Hoffrage, Ulrich 190, 224, 225
Holyoak, Keith J. 104
Horvitz, E. 20
Howson, Colin 234
Huber, Joel 251
Hume, David 18

Ichikawa, Shin'Ichi 195
ideal rationality
  mathematical notions 18, 19
  and reason 18–25
"if...then" statements 105, 111, 114, 126, 127
  erotetic suppositional 106–9
illusory consistency judgments 123
illusory inferences 38, 63, 78, 88, 197, 258
  conditional 109
  from disjunction 61, 74, 76, 77, 129
  indefinite 129
impossibility fallacy 126
inferences, direct conceptual 133
informal interpretation rules *see under* interpretation
information source selection 103–27
innovative machine learning models 17
Inquire 87–9, 92, 170–8, 207
inquisitive semantics tradition 46
intelligence 142–7
intention 260, 290, 291
  Belief-Desire-Intention (BDI) model 60, 261, 265
interpretation
  conditionals 105
  function $\circ \mathcal{L}_S \mapsto \mathbb{V}$ 70
  informal focus rule 146–7
  informal rule for "and" 72–3
  informal rule for bare-plural generics 184
  informal rule for "if only if" 122
  informal rule for indicative "if A, then C" 106–9
  informal rule for indicative "P only if Q" 121–2
  informal rule for "not" 78–9
  informal rule for "or" 73–4
  informal rule for possibility talk 125
  linguistic 54, 106
  of $\mathcal{L}_{PC}$ 150–4
    ∘-interpretation
      Sent($\mathcal{L}_{PC} \to \mathbb{M}$) 152–3
  * of views as sentences in $\mathcal{L}$ 70
  procedures 71
  of quantifier-free formulas 151
  revised informal rule for "and" 122
  rule for probability of a state 216–18
Iyengar, Sheena S. 251

James, William 95
Johnson-Laird, Philip 7, 26, 38, 43, 44, 61, 63, 83, 88, 103, 122, 125, 134, 191, 194, 195–6, 212–16, 221, 234

Kahneman, Daniel 43, 193, 197, 198, 199, 255, 258, 275–6
Kant, Immanuel 4, 18
Kelly, Sean D. 287, 288
Khemlani, Sangeet 79, 132, 134, 184
Knetsch, Jack L. 255, 258
Knobe, Joshua 261
knowledge-based agent 35, 36
Koffka, K. 286
Kondo, Marie 295
Koralus, Philipp 14, 42, 51, 61, 62, 65, 73, 76, 82, 90, 94, 106, 109, 129, 130, 143, 153, 254, 255, 272, 285
Kratzer, Angelika 18
Krugman, Paul 129

Laplace, P. S. 194
Leibniz, Gottfried Wilhelm 13
Lepper, Mark R. 251
Leslie, Sarah-Jane 132, 133, 184
Levesque, Hector 7, 20, 131
Lewontin, Richard C. 293
List, Christian 268
List, John A. 257
logical consequence, notion of 20
logical obtuseness 101
logical validity 94
Lorenz, Hendrik 27

McCarthy, John 20
MacFarlane, John 101
Mackie, John Leslie 106
Madsen, Jens Koed 58–9
Marr, David 5, 15–16, 29
married people puzzle 131
Mascarenhas, Salvador 42, 46, 51, 61, 62, 65, 73, 76, 82, 90, 94, 106, 109, 129, 130, 153, 199, 226
Matryoshka condition 140, 141f, 142, 153, 221
Matryoshka level ordering 172
memory search 225–31
mental logic theories 25–8
  and content-based theories 47
mental models
  barriers to an account of the contents 43–4
  characteristics 37–8
  Chinese room (CR) 34–7
  and competence 33–42
    objections 39–42
  conjunctive thought 39
  content-based theories of reason 42–3
  counterfactuals 37–8, 39
  criticisms of theory 43
  defining 38
  erotetic theory as a theory of reasoning based on 42
  "mental model footnotes" 136
  representational vehicles and algorithms 44
  similar relation-structure 36
  Turing test 34, 36, 42
  uncertainty, reasoning with 195
merely associational thinking, and inferences 50–1
meta-reasoning 19–20
meta-theory 314–34
  completeness 326–7
  conservativity of extended reasoning over classical 331–4
  dependency relations theory 314–20
  soundness under erotetic equilibrium 324–6
  Tarskian realization 322–4
microeconomic theory, classical 19, 48
Minimalist Program 262
Minsky 18

modus ponens inference 119, 120
  quantified modus ponens 131
modus tollens inference 119, 120
Morewedge, Carey K. 280
mReasoner program 43

Nanay, Bence 287
neglect *see* base-rate neglect; opportunity cost neglect
Newstead, Stephen E. 121, 132
Newton, Isaac 13
  Newtonian mechanics 48
norms 99–102
  equilibrium requirement for rational judgment 99–102
Norvig, Peter 7, 43, 128, 247, 282
Nutt, Paul C. 248–9

Oaksford, Michael 105
objects
  arbitrary 45, 46, 135–7
  basic 137–42
O'Brien, David P. 43
"only" with "if" conditional 121–5
Oppenheimer, Daniel M. 297–8
opportunity cost neglect 249, 274
optimality, bounded *see* bounded optimality
order effects 119–20

Paradis, Carita 123
Payne, John W. 251
phenomenal glow concept 35
Phillips-Brown, Milo 268
Pinker, Steven 3–4
Plato, Republic 27
Plato's Problem 26–8
Poggio, T. 5
"Politician's syllogism" 129
possibility, asking what is possible and what follows 125–7
possible-worlds semantics 48, 64
posterior probability 29, 189, 235–7
practical judgment 3
practical reasoning
  and decision-making 248–301
  and failures of reason 13
predicate reasoning 128–87
  arbitrary objects, views of 135–7

predicate reasoning (*cont.*)
  axioms, absurdity and analyticity
    147–50
predictive processing 32
presupposition 109–11
primitive absurd states 67–8, 147–8
  duality for primitive absurdity 148–50
  see also absurdity
priorities 101, 267–71
  action-centred 285–92
probabilistic coherence 2, 32
  and erotetic equilibrium 237–41
probability
  axioms 237
  conditional 13, 189
  default procedure 212
  inferences involving 12
  partial 197
  posterior 29, 189, 235–7
  of a state, interpretation rule 216–18
  subjective 191
  theory of probabilities 194
  see also probabilistic coherence; probability theory
problem of cognitive slack 21, 23
problem of shallow success 21–2
product
  sets of states 69
  universal 162–8, 222–5
prospect theory 29
Puto, Christopher 251

quantifier operations 152
quantified premise statements 156
quantifier-free formulas 151
Query 108, 126, 271
  graded uncertainty, generating 210–11
  and Inquire 86–90, 170–8
questions 71–8
  characterization of reasoning as question-answering 49
  content of interrogative sentences as 46
  pure decision 264–5
  semantics of 107
Quine, W. 39

Ragni, Marco 125
Ramsey, Frank P. 105, 108, 109
rational choice 2, 48, 52, 60
  classical 100, 247, 259, 265, 281, 292, 300

rationality
  calculative 19, 20
  ideal 18–25
  inferences 18
  limits to 7
  perfect 7
  practical 293
  rational agency 260
rationality quotient 55
reason
  aims 29–33
  capacity to reason 32
  computational theory of 15–18
  content-based theories 42–9
  core 17
  defining 19
  domain-general 6, 8, 10, 18, 32
  erotetic theory *see* erotetic theory
  failures of 4, 5, 10–15
  and ideal rationality 18–25
  and intelligence 6
  mathematical theory of 10, 61
  nature of 18
  neo-Humean view of 18
  question-answer system 16
  reasonableness standards 18, 97
  single or multi-systems theory 27
  Type 1 theory of 58
reasonableness standards 18, 97
reasoning
  core reasoning 61–102
  default 86, 180
  extended 331–4
  first-order equivalent 133
  human reasoning capacity 51f
  inferential 32
  meta-reasoning 19–20
  practical 13, 248–301
  predicate 128–87
  principles of core reasoning performance 54–5
  propositional *see* propositional reasoning
  restricted erotetic equilibrium
    and expert forecasting 241–7
    generics 182–7
    and generics 182–7
    of an inference 97–9, 185–6
    judgment 243
    predicate reasoning 133
Rips, Lance 25–6

risk pollution 297
Russell, Bertrand 134
Russell, Stuart 7, 19, 20, 21, 23, 43, 128, 247, 282

Sablé-Meyer, Mathias 199, 226
satisficing 293
Searle, John R. 34–5
selection tasks 114–18
    modified Griggs & Cox 117f
    novel card cases 118
    "Underage Drinking" 117
    see also Wason's card selection task
Sellars, Wilfrid 133, 149
semantics
    and erotetic equilibrium 48
    formal 48
    linguistic 54, 106, 216
    possible-worlds 48, 64
    of questions 107
    truth-maker 66
Sexton, Rosemary 289
Shafir, Eldar 13, 15, 252, 253
Shimojo, Shinsuke 195
Siegel, Susanna 287, 288, 290
Simon, Herbert A. 21, 293
Simonson, Itamar 253
simulations, building 58, 59
situation-semantics 47
Skolemized form 148
Smithburg, William 249
Snir, Marc 238
Socrates 28
soundness
    classical 181
    under erotetic equilibrium 94, 324–6
Sperber, Dan 104, 116, 118
sphinx analogy, and erotetic agents 295–301
Stanovich, Keith E. 131
Starr, Will 84
states
    absurd 79, 147–8
    alternative 48–9, 55, 63–4, 66, 68
    articulation as formulas 153
    atomic 66, 67
    extended set of 202
    inconsistent 47
    of inference 68
    negative 66
    primitive absurd 67–8, 147–50
    rule for probability of 216–18

strict consequence 101
substitution, formal 160–1
Sum operation 73
superforecasters, cognitive policies for 245–6
superpower, reason as 1–10
suppositions 68, 109–11
    and commitment 178–9
    reasoning with 83–6
    simplifying reasoning with 84
    Suppose 84, 85, 110

Tarskian realization 322–4
Tenenbaum, Josua B. 29
Tetlock, Philip E. 194, 244, 245, 247
Thaler, Richard H. 255, 258
Tooby, John 234
triple disjunctive syllogism 83
Turing, Alan M. 33, 40
    Turing test 34, 36, 42
Tversky, Amos 43, 193, 197, 198, 199, 253, 255, 275–6
Tylecote, R. 129

uncertainty
    and conditionals 215–22
    graded, generating 206–15
    guns and guitars 199
    Linda Problem 198–9
    reasoning with 188–247
    reduction 49
Universal product 222–5
    derivation 164, 165, 167
    and Existential sum 162–8
    reorient 165–6
Universal Product
    uncertainty 222–5
    Update 163–4
Urbarch, Peter 234
utility maximization, under erotetic equilibrium 281–5

Valiant, Leslie 28
validity 26
    classical 61, 94, 100
    logical 94
    repugnant 86
view-change complexity principle 54, 56
visual illusions 5, 10–11
Von Fintel, Kai 105

Walsh, Clare 61, 63, 88
Wason, Peter C. 103, 116
Wason's card selection task 103, 104f, 114, 115
weak epistemically possible supposition principle 110, 111
weights
 double-weights 270

equilibrium answer potential (EAP) 202, 267
Whitehead, Alfred North 134
Willners, Caroline 123
Winograd Schemas 42
Wittgenstein, Ludwig 289
Wooldridge, Michael 282